Instructor's M

MICROECONOMICS

Instructor's Manual • Nora Underwood

University of California - Davis

MICROECONOMICS

FIFTH EDITION

Robert S. Pindyck
Daniel L. Rubinfeld

Prentice
Hall

Upper Saddle River, New Jersey 07458

Acquisitions editor: Rod Banister
Assistant editor: Holly Brown
Production editor: Theresa Festa
Manufacturer: Victor Graphics, Inc.

ISBN 0-13-019504-9

10   9   8   7

Table of Contents

Preface

OVERVIEW

This *Instructor's Manual* accompanies Pindyck and Rubinfeld's *Microeconomics* Fifth Edition (Prentice Hall, 2001). It offers teaching notes for each chapter and provides detailed answers to all of the end-of-chapter Review Questions and Exercises contained in the text. The answers have been written with the students in mind, making it easy for the instructor to simply hand out the answers if he or she chooses to do so.

ACKNOWLEDGEMENTS

This *Manual* was written with the help of a number of dedicated individuals. Robert S. Pindyck and Daniel Rubinfeld made many helpful comments. Peter Zaleski of Villanova University provided invaluable help with editing and proofing the additions to the fifth edition.

Special thanks go to the talented individuals who authored the previous editions of this *Instructor's Manual*: Geoffrey S. Rothwell of Stanford University, who authored the first and second editions of this *Instructor's Manual*; the late Gilbert B. Davis, formerly University of Michigan who co-authored the third edition; and Valerie Y. Suslow, University of Michigan, who co-authored the third edition and authored the fourth edition.

PART I

INTRODUCTION
MICROECONOMICS AND MARKETS

CHAPTER 1
PRELIMINARIES

TEACHING NOTES

The first two chapters reacquaint students with the microeconomics that they learned in their introductory course: Chapter 1 focuses on the general subject of economics, while Chapter 2 develops supply and demand analysis. The use of examples in Chapter 1 facilitates students' complete understanding of abstract economic concepts. Examples in this chapter discuss markets for prescription drugs (Section 1.2), introduction of a new automobile (Section 1.4), design of automobile emission standards (Section 1.4), the minimum wage (Section 1.3), and real and nominal prices of eggs and education (Section 1.3). Discussing some of these, or another, example is a useful way to review some important economic concepts such as scarcity, making tradeoffs, building economic models to explain how consumers and firms make decisions, and the distinction between competitive and non-competitive markets. Parts I and II of the text assume competitive markets, market power is discussed in Part III, and some consequences of market power are discussed in Part IV of the text.

Review Question (2) illustrates the difference between positive and normative economics and provides for a productive class discussion. Other examples for discussion are available in Kearl, Pope, Whiting, and Wimmer, "A Confusion of Economists," *American Economic Review* (May 1979).

The chapter concludes with a discussion of real and nominal prices. Given our reliance on dollar prices in the chapters that follow, students should understand that we are concerned with prices relative to a standard, which in this case is dollars for a particular year.

REVIEW QUESTIONS

1. It is often said that a good theory is one that can in principle be refuted by an empirical, data-oriented study. Explain why a theory that cannot be evaluated empirically is not a good theory.

There are two steps in evaluating a theory: first, you should examine the reasonability of the theory's assumptions; second, you should test the theory's predictions by comparing them with facts. If a theory cannot be tested, it cannot be accepted or rejected. Therefore, it contributes little to our understanding of reality.

2. Which of the following two statements involves positive economic analysis and which normative? How do the two kinds of analysis differ?

a.   Gasoline rationing (allocating each year to each individual an annual maximum amount of gasoline that can be purchased) is a poor social policy because it interferes with the workings of the competitive market system.

b.   Gasoline rationing is a policy under which more people are made worse off than are made better off.

Positive economic analysis describes *what is*. Normative economic analysis describes *what ought to be*. We know from economic analysis that a constraint placed on supply will change the market equilibrium. Statement (a) merges both types of analysis. First, statement (a) makes a positive statement that gasoline rationing "interferes with the workings of the competitive market system." Second, by making the normative statement (i.e., a value judgment) that gasoline rationing is a "poor social policy," statement (a) confines itself to a conclusion derived from positive economic analysis of the policy.

Statement (b) is positive because it states what the effect of gasoline rationing is without making a value judgment about the desirability of the rationing policy.

3. Suppose the price of unleaded regular octane gasoline were 20 cents per gallon higher in New Jersey than in Oklahoma. Do you think there would be an opportunity for arbitrage (i.e., that firms could buy gas in Oklahoma and then sell it at a profit in New Jersey)? Why or why not?

Oklahoma and New Jersey represent separate geographic markets for gasoline because of high transportation costs. If transportation costs were zero, a price increase in New Jersey would prompt arbitrageurs to buy gasoline in Oklahoma and sell it in New Jersey. It is unlikely in this case that the 20 cents per gallon difference in costs would be high enough to create a profitable opportunity for arbitrage, given both transactions costs and transportation costs.

4. In Example 1.2, what economic forces explain why the real price of eggs has fallen while the real price of a college education has increased? How have these changes affected consumer choices?

The price and quantity of goods (e.g., eggs) and services (e.g., a college education) are determined by the interaction of supply and demand. The real price of eggs fell from 1970 to 1985 because of either a reduction in demand (consumers switched to lower-cholesterol food), a reduction in production costs (improvements in egg production technology), or both. In response, the price of eggs relative to other foods decreased. The real price of a college education rose because of either an increase in demand (e.g., more people recognized the value of an education), an increase in the cost of education (e.g., increase in staff salaries), or both.

5. Suppose that the Japanese yen rises against the U.S. dollar; that is, it will take more dollars to buy any given amount of Japanese yen. Explain why this increase simultaneously increases the real price of Japanese cars for U.S. consumers and lowers the real price of U.S. automobiles for Japanese consumers.

As the value of the yen grows relative to the dollar (and if the costs of production for both Japanese and U.S. automobiles remain unchanged), more dollars exchange for fewer yen. In response to the change in the exchange rate, the purchase of a Japanese automobile priced in yen requires more dollars. Similarly, the purchase of a U.S. automobile priced in dollars requires fewer yen.

EXERCISES

1. Decide whether each of the following statements is true or false and explain why.

a. Fast food chains like McDonald's, Burger King, and Wendy's operate all over the United States. Therefore the market for fast food is a national market.

This statement is false. People generally buy fast food within their current location and do not travel large distances across the United States just to buy a cheaper fast food meal. Given there is little potential for arbitrage between fast food restaurants that are located some distance from each other, there are likely to be multiple fast food markets across the country.

b. People generally buy clothing in the city in which they live. Therefore there is a clothing market in, say, Atlanta that is distinct from the clothing market in Los Angeles.

This statement is true. Given people do generally buy clothing in the city where they live, they will only interact with sellers who are located in the city where they live, and will not be influenced by the price of clothing at stores in different cities. In this case, there is limited potential for arbitrage. Occasionally, there may be a market for a specific clothing item in a faraway market that results in a great opportunity for arbitrage, such as the market for blue jeans in the old Soviet Union.

c. Some consumers strongly prefer Pepsi and some strongly prefer Coke. Therefore there is no single market for colas.

This statement is false. Although some people have strong preferences for a particular brand of cola, the different brands are similar enough that they constitute one market. There are consumers who do not have strong preferences for one type of cola, and there are consumers who may have a preference, but who will also be influenced by price. Given these possibilities, the price of cola drinks will not tend to differ by very much, particularly for Coke and Pepsi.

2. Table E.1 shows the average retail price of milk and the Consumer Price Index from 1980 to 1998.

	1980	1985	1990	1995	1998
CPI	100	130.58	158.62	184.95	197.82
Retail Price of Milk (fresh, whole, 1//2 gal.)	$1.05	$1.13	$1.39	$1.48	$1.61

a. Calculate the real price of milk in 1980 dollars. Has the real price increased/decreased/stayed the same since 1980?

Real price of milk in year X = $\dfrac{CPI_{1980}}{CPI_{year\,X}} * no\min al\ price\ in\ year\ X$.

1980 $1.05   1985 $0.86   1990 $0.88   1995 $0.80   1998 $0.81

Since 1980 the real price of milk has decreased.

b. What is the percentage change in the real price (1980 dollars) from 1990 to 1995?

Percentage change in real price from 1990 to 1995 = $\dfrac{0.80 - 0.88}{0.88} = -0.09 = -9\%$.

c. Convert the CPI into 1990 = 100 and determine the real price of milk in 1990 dollars.

To convert the CPI into 1990=100, divide the CPI for each year by the CPI for 1990. Use the formula from part a and the new CPI numbers below to find the real price of milk.

New CPI			Real price of milk		
	1980	63		1980	$1.67
	1985	82		1985	$1.38
	1990	100		1990	$1.39
	1995	117		1995	$1.26
	1998	125		1998	$1.29

d. What is the percentage change in the real price (1990 dollars) from 1990 to 1995? Compare this with your answer in (b). What do you notice? Explain.

Percentage change in real price from 1990 to 1995 = $\dfrac{1.26 - 1.39}{1.39} = -0.093 = -9.3\%$.

This answer is almost identical (except for rounding error) to the answer received for part b. It does not matter which year is chosen as the base year.

3. At the time this book went to print, the minimum wage was $5.15. To find the current minimum wage, go to   http://www.bls.gov/top20.html

> **Click on: Consumer Price Index- All Urban Consumers (Current Series)**

> **Select: U.S. All items**

This will give you the CPI from 1913 to the present.

a. With these values, calculate the current real minimum wage in 1990 dollars.

$$\text{real minimum wage 1998} = \frac{CPI_{1990}}{CPI_{1998}} * 5.15 = \frac{130.7}{163} * 5.15 = \$4.13.$$

b. What is the percentage change in the real minimum wage from 1985 to the present, stated in real 1990 dollars?

Assume the minimum wage in 1985 was $3.35. Then,

$$\text{real minimum wage 1985} = \frac{CPI_{1990}}{CPI_{1985}} * 3.35 = \frac{130.7}{107.6} * 3.35 = \$4.07.$$

The percentage change in the real minimum wage is therefore

$$\frac{4.13 - 4.07}{4.07} = 0.0147, \text{ or about } 1.5\%.$$

CHAPTER 2
THE BASICS OF SUPPLY AND DEMAND

TEACHING NOTES

This chapter reviews the basics of supply and demand that students should be familiar with from their introductory economics class. The instructor can choose to spend more or less time on this chapter depending on how much of a review the students require. This chapter departs from the standard treatment of supply and demand basics found in most other intermediate microeconomics textbooks by discussing some of the world's most important markets (wheat, gasoline, and automobiles) and teaching students how to analyze these markets with the tools of supply and demand. The real-world applications of this theory can be enlightening for students.

Some problems plague the understanding of supply and demand analysis. One of the most common sources of confusion is between *movements along the demand curve* and *shifts in demand*. Through a discussion of the *ceteris paribus* assumption, stress that when representing a demand function (either with a graph or an equation), all other variables are held constant. Movements along the demand curve occur *only with changes in price*. As the omitted factors change, the entire demand function shifts. It may also be helpful to present an example of a demand function which depends not only on the price of the good, but also on income and the price of other goods directly. This helps students understand that these other variables are actually in the demand function, and are merely lumped into the intercept term of the simple linear demand function. Example 2.9 includes an example of a demand and supply function which each depend on the price of a substitute good. Students may also find a review of how to solve two equations with two unknowns helpful. In general, it is a good idea at this point to decide on the level of math that you will use in the class. If you plan to use a lot of algebra and calculus it is a good idea to introduce and review it early on.

To stress the quantitative aspects of the demand curve to students, make the distinction between quantity demanded as a function of price, $Q = D(P)$, and the inverse demand function, where price is a function of the quantity demanded, $P = D^{-1}(Q)$. This may clarify the positioning of price on the Y-axis and quantity on the X-axis.

Students may also question how the market adjusts to a new equilibrium. One simple mechanism is the partial-adjustment cobweb model. A discussion of the cobweb model (based on traditional corn-hog cycle or any other example) adds a certain realism to the discussion and is much appreciated by students. If you decide to write down the demand function so that income and other prices are visible variables in the demand function, you can also do some interesting examples which explore the linkages between markets and how changes in one market affect price and quantity in other markets.

Although this chapter introduces demand, income, and cross-price elasticities, you may find it more appropriate to return to income and cross-price elasticity after demand elasticity is reintroduced in Chapter 4. Students invariably have a difficult time with the concept of elasticity. It is helpful to explain clearly why a firm may be interested in estimating elasticity. Use concrete examples. For example, a Wall Street Journal article back in the spring of 1998 discussed how elasticity could be used by the movie industry so that different movies could have different ticket prices. This example tends to go over well as college students watch a lot of movies. This type of discussion can also be postponed until revenue is discussed.

REVIEW QUESTIONS

1. Suppose that unusually hot weather causes the demand curve for ice cream to shift to the right. Why will the price of ice cream rise to a new market-clearing level?

Assume the supply curve is fixed. The unusually hot weather will cause a rightward shift in the demand curve, creating short-run excess demand at the current price. Consumers will begin to bid against each other for the ice cream, putting upward pressure on the price. The price of ice cream will rise until the quantity demanded and the quantity supplied are equal.

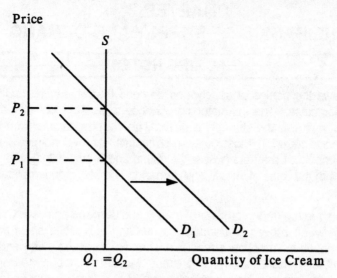

Figure 2.1

2. Use supply and demand curves to illustrate how each of the following events would affect the price of butter and the quantity of butter bought and sold:

a.   An increase in the price of margarine.

Most people consider butter and margarine to be substitute goods. An increase in the price of margarine will cause people to increase their consumption of butter, thereby shifting the demand curve for butter out from D_1 to D_2 in Figure 2.2.a. This shift in demand will cause the equilibrium price to rise from P_1 to P_2 and the equilibrium quantity to increase from Q_1 to Q_2.

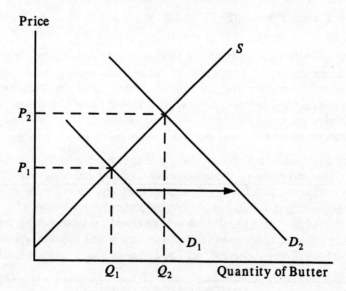

Figure 2.2.a

b.   An increase in the price of milk.

Milk is the main ingredient in butter. An increase in the price of milk will increase the cost of producing butter. The supply curve for butter will shift from S_1 to S_2 in Figure 2.2.b, resulting in a higher equilibrium price, P_2, covering the higher production costs, and a lower equilibrium quantity, Q_2.

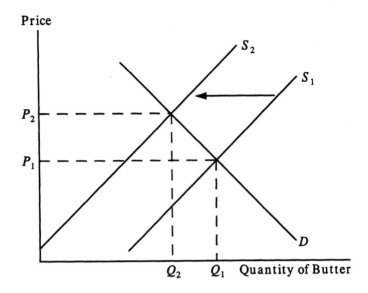

Figure 2.2.b

Note: Given that butter is in fact made from the fat that is slimmed off of the milk, butter and milk are joint products. If you are aware of this relationship, then your answer will change. In this case, as the price of milk increases. so does the quantity supplied. As the quantity supplied of milk increases, there is a larger supply of fat available to make butter. This will shift the supply of butter curve to the right and the price of butter will fall.

c.   **A decrease in average income levels.**

Assume that butter is a normal good. A decrease in the average income level will cause the demand curve for butter to shift from D_1 to D_2. This will result in a decline in the equilibrium price from P_1 to P_2, and a decline in the equilibrium quantity from Q_1 to Q_2. See Figure 2.2.c.

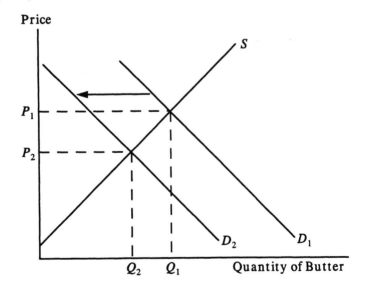

Figure 2.2.c

3. Suppose a 3 percent increase in the price of corn flakes causes a 6 percent decline in the quantity demanded. What is the elasticity of demand for corn flakes?

The elasticity of demand is the percentage change in the quantity demanded divided by the percentage change in the price. The elasticity of demand for corn flakes is $\frac{-6}{+3} = -2$. This is in the elastic region of the demand curve, where the elasticity of demand exceeds -1.0.

4. Why do long-run elasticities of demand differ from short-run elasticities? Consider two goods: paper towels and televisions. Which is a durable good? Would you expect the price elasticity of demand for paper towels to be larger in the short-run or in the long-run? Why? What about the price elasticity of demand for televisions?

Long-run and short-run elasticities differ based on how rapidly consumers respond to price changes and how many substitutes are available. If the price of paper towels, a non-durable good, were to increase, consumers might react only minimally in the short run. In the long run, however, demand for paper towels would be more elastic as new substitutes entered the market (such as sponges or kitchen towels). In contrast, the quantity demanded of durable goods, such as televisions, might change dramatically in the short run following a price change. For example, the initial influence of a price increase for televisions would cause consumers to delay purchases because durable goods are built to last longer. Eventually consumers must replace their televisions as they wear out or become obsolete; therefore, we expect the demand for durables to be more elastic in the long run.

5. Explain why, for many goods, the long-run price elasticity of supply is larger than the short-run elasticity.

The elasticity of supply is the percentage change in the quantity supplied divided by the percentage change in price. An increase in price induces an increase in the quantity supplied by firms. Some firms in some markets may respond quickly and cheaply to price changes. However, other firms may be constrained by their production capacity in the short run. The firms with short-run capacity constraints will have a short-run supply elasticity that is less elastic. However, in the long run all firms can increase their scale of production and thus have a larger long-run price elasticity.

6. Suppose the government regulates the prices of beef and chicken and sets them below their market-clearing levels. Explain why shortages of these goods will develop and what factors will determine the sizes of the shortages. What will happen to the price of pork? Explain briefly.

If the price of a commodity is set below its market-clearing level, the quantity that firms are willing to supply is less than the quantity that consumers wish to purchase. The extent of the excess demand implied by this response will depend on the relative elasticities of demand and supply. For instance, if both supply and demand are elastic, the shortage is larger than if both are inelastic. Factors such as the willingness of consumers to eat less meat and the ability of farmers to change the size of their herds and produce less determine these elasticities and influence the size of excess demand.

Rationing will result in situations of excess demand when some consumers are unable to purchase the quantities desired. Customers whose demands are not met will attempt to purchase substitutes, thus increasing the demand for substitutes and raising their prices. If the prices of beef and chicken are set below market-clearing levels, the price of pork will rise.

7. In a discussion of tuition rates, a university official argues that the demand for admission is completely price inelastic. As evidence she notes that while the university has doubled its tuition (in real terms) over the past 15 years, neither the number nor quality of students applying has decreased. Would you accept this argument? Explain briefly. (Hint: The official makes an assertion about the demand for admission, but does she actually observe a demand curve? What else could be going on?)

If demand is fixed, the individual firm (a university) may determine the shape of the demand curve it faces by raising the price and observing the change in quantity sold. The university official is not observing the entire demand curve, but rather only the equilibrium price and quantity over the last 15 years. If demand is shifting upward, as supply shifts upward, demand could have any elasticity. (See Figure 2.7, for example.) Demand could be shifting upward because the value of a college education has increased and students are willing to pay a high price for each opening. More market research would be required to support the conclusion that demand is completely price inelastic.

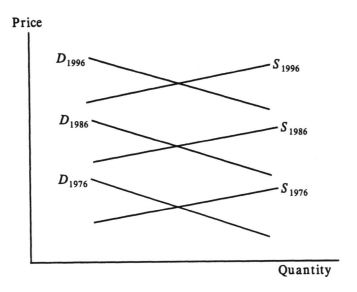

Figure 2.7

8. Use supply and demand curve shifts to illustrate the effect of the following events on the market for apples. Make clear the direction of the change in both price and quantity sold.

a.   **Scientists find that an apple a day does indeed keep the doctor away.**

People will demand more apples, resulting in a rightward shift of the demand curve. The equilibrium price of apples will rise, and the equilibrium quantity will increase.

b.   **The price of oranges triples.**

Since oranges are probably a substitute for apples, the demand curve for apples will shift to the right. The equilibrium price of apples will rise, and the equilibrium quantity will increase.

c.   **A drought shrinks the apple crop to one-third its normal size.**

The supply curve for apples will shift to the left, causing the equilibrium price to rise and the equilibrium quantity to fall.

d.   **Thousands of college students abandon the academic life to become apple pickers.**

The increase in the supply of apple pickers will lead to a decrease in the cost of bringing apples to market. The lower cost of bringing apples to market results in a rightward shift of the supply curve of apples and causes the equilibrium price to fall and the equilibrium quantity to increase.

e.   **Thousands of college students abandon the academic life to become apple growers.**

This would result in a rightward shift of the supply curve for apples, causing the equilibrium price to fall and the equilibrium quantity to increase.

9. Suppose the demand curve for a product is given by Q=10-2P+P$_s$, where P is the price of the product and P$_s$ is the price of a substitute good. The price of the substitute good is $2.00.

(a) Suppose P=$1.00. What is the price elasticity of demand? What is the cross-price elasticity of demand?

First you need to find the quantity demanded at the price of $1.00. Q=10-2(1)+2=10. Price elasticity of demand = $\dfrac{P}{Q}\dfrac{\Delta Q}{\Delta P} = \dfrac{1}{10}(-2) = -\dfrac{2}{10} = -0.2$.

Cross-price elasticity of demand = $\dfrac{P_s}{Q}\dfrac{\Delta Q}{\Delta P_s} = \dfrac{2}{10}(1) = 0.2$.

(b) Suppose the price of the good, P, increases to $2.00. Now what is the price elasticity of demand, and what is the cross-price elasticity of demand?

First you need to find the quantity demanded at the price of $2.00. Q=10-2(2)+2=8.

Price elasticity of demand = $\dfrac{P}{Q}\dfrac{\Delta Q}{\Delta P} = \dfrac{2}{8}(-2) = -\dfrac{4}{8} = -0.5$.

Cross-price elasticity of demand = $\dfrac{P_s}{Q}\dfrac{\Delta Q}{\Delta P_s} = \dfrac{2}{8}(1) = 0.25$.

10. Suppose that rather than the declining demand assumed in Example 2.7, an increase in the cost of copper production causes the supply curve to shift to the left by 40 percent. How will the price of copper change?

If the supply curve shifts to the left by 40% then the new quantity supplied will be 60 percent of the old quantity supplied at every price. The new supply curve is therefore

Q' = 0.6(-4.5+16P) = -2.7+9.6P. To find the new equilibrium price of copper, set the new supply equal to demand so that -2.7+9.6P=13.5-8P. Solving for price results in P=92.0 cents per pound for the new equilibrium price.

11. Suppose the demand for natural gas is perfectly inelastic. What would be the effect, if any, of natural gas price controls?

If the demand for natural gas is perfectly inelastic, then the demand curve is vertical. Consumers will demand a certain quantity and will pay any price for this quantity. In this case, a price control will have no effect on the quantity demanded.

EXERCISES

---

1. Consider a competitive market for which the quantities demanded and supplied (per year) at various prices are given as follows:

Price ($)	Demand (millions)	Supply (millions)
60	22	14
80	20	16
100	18	18
120	16	20

a. **Calculate the price elasticity of demand when the price is $80. When the price is $100.**

We know that the price elasticity of demand may be calculated using equation 2.1 from the text:

$$E_D = \frac{\dfrac{\Delta Q_D}{Q_D}}{\dfrac{\Delta P}{P}} = \frac{P}{Q_D}\frac{\Delta Q_D}{\Delta P}.$$

With each price increase of $20, the quantity demanded decreases by 2. Therefore,

$$\left(\frac{\Delta Q_D}{\Delta P}\right) = \frac{-2}{20} = -0.1.$$

At $P = 80$, quantity demanded equals 20 and

$$E_D = \left(\frac{80}{20}\right)(-0.1) = -0.40.$$

Similarly, at $P = 100$, quantity demanded equals 18 and

$$E_D = \left(\frac{100}{18}\right)(-0.1) = -0.56.$$

b. **Calculate the price elasticity of supply when the price is $80. When the price is $100.**

The elasticity of supply is given by:

$$E_S = \frac{\dfrac{\Delta Q_S}{Q_S}}{\dfrac{\Delta P}{P}} = \frac{P}{Q_S}\frac{\Delta Q_S}{\Delta P}.$$

With each price increase of $20, quantity supplied increases by 2. Therefore,

$$\left(\frac{\Delta Q_S}{\Delta P}\right) = \frac{2}{20} = 0.1.$$

At $P = 80$, quantity supplied equals 16 and

$$E_S = \left(\frac{80}{16}\right)(0.1) = 0.5.$$

Similarly, at $P = 100$, quantity supplied equals 18 and

$$E_S = \left(\frac{100}{18}\right)(0.1) = 0.56.$$

c. **What are the equilibrium price and quantity?**

The equilibrium price and quantity are found where the quantity supplied equals the quantity demanded at the same price. As we see from the table, the equilibrium price is $100 and the equilibrium quantity is 18 million.

d. **Suppose the government sets a price ceiling of $80. Will there be a shortage, and, if so, how large will it be?**

With a price ceiling of $80, consumers would like to buy 20 million, but producers will supply only 16 million. This will result in a shortage of 4 million.

2. Refer to Example 2.4 on the market for wheat. At the end of 1998, both Brazil and Indonesia opened their wheat markets to U.S. farmers. (Source: http://www.fas.usda.gov/) Suppose that these

new markets add 200 million bushels to U.S. wheat demand. What will be the free market price of wheat and what quantity will be produced and sold by U.S. farmers in this case?

The following equations describe the market for wheat in 1998:

$$Q_S = 1944 + 207P$$

and

$$Q_D = 3244 - 283P.$$

If Brazil and Indonesia add an additional 200 million bushels of wheat to U.S. wheat demand, the new demand curve Q'_D, would be equal to $Q_D + 200$, or

$$Q'_D = (3244 - 283P) + 200 = 3444 - 283P.$$

Equating supply and the new demand, we may determine the new equilibrium price,

$$1944 + 207P = 3444 - 283P, \text{ or}$$

$$490P = 1500, \text{ or } P^* = \$3.06 \text{ per bushel.}$$

To find the equilibrium quantity, substitute the price into either the supply or demand equation, e.g.,

$$Q_S = 1944 + (207)(3.06) = 2,577.67$$

and

$$Q_D = 3444 - (283)(3.06) = 2,577.67$$

3. A vegetable fiber is traded in a competitive world market, and the world price is $9 per pound. Unlimited quantities are available for import into the United States at this price. The U.S. domestic supply and demand for various price levels are shown below.

Price	U.S. Supply (million lbs.)	U.S. Demand (million lbs.)
3	2	34
6	4	28
9	6	22
12	8	16
15	10	10
18	12	4

a. What is the equation for demand? What is the equation for supply?

The equation for demand is of the form Q=a-bP. First find the slope which is

$\dfrac{\Delta Q}{\Delta P} = \dfrac{-6}{3} = -2 = -b.$ You can figure this out by noticing that every time price increases by 3 quantity demanded falls by 6 million pounds. Demand is now Q=a-2P. To find a, plug in any of the price quantity demanded points from the table: Q=34=a-2*3 so that a=40 and demand is Q=40-2P.

The equation for supply is of the form Q=c+dP. First find the slope which is

$\dfrac{\Delta Q}{\Delta P} = \dfrac{2}{3}.$ You can figure this out by noticing that every time price increases by 3 quantity

supplied increases by 2 million pounds. Supply is now $Q = c + \dfrac{2}{3}P.$ To find c plug in any of the price quantity supplied points from the table: $Q = 2 = c + \frac{2}{3}(3)$ so that c=0 and

supply is $Q = \frac{2}{3}P$.

b. At a price of $9, what is the price elasticity of demand? At a price of $12?

Elasticity of demand at P=9 is $\frac{P}{Q}\frac{\Delta Q}{\Delta P} = \frac{9}{22}(-2) = \frac{-18}{22} = -0.82$.

Elasticity of demand at P=12 is $\frac{P}{Q}\frac{\Delta Q}{\Delta P} = \frac{12}{16}(-2) = \frac{-24}{16} = -1.5$.

c. What is the price elasticity of supply at $9? At $12?

Elasticity of supply at P=9 is $\frac{P}{Q}\frac{\Delta Q}{\Delta P} = \frac{9}{6}\left(\frac{2}{3}\right) = \frac{18}{18} = 1.0$.

Elasticity of supply at P=12 is $\frac{P}{Q}\frac{\Delta Q}{\Delta P} = \frac{12}{8}\left(\frac{2}{3}\right) = \frac{24}{24} = 1.0$.

d. In a free market, what will be the U.S. price and level of fiber imports?

With no restrictions on trade, world price will be the price in the United States, so that P=$9. At this price, the domestic supply is 6 million lbs, while the domestic demand is 22 million lbs. Imports make up the difference and are 16 million lbs.

4. The rent control agency of New York City has found that aggregate demand is

Q_D = 100 - 5P. **Quantity is measured in tens of thousands of apartments. Price, the average monthly rental rate, is measured in hundreds of dollars. The agency also noted that the increase in Q at lower P results from more three-person families coming into the city from Long Island and demanding apartments. The city's board of realtors acknowledges that this is a good demand estimate and has shown that supply is Q_S = 50 + 5P.**

a. **If both the agency and the board are right about demand and supply, what is the free market price? What is the change in city population if the agency sets a maximum average monthly rental of $100, and all those who cannot find an apartment leave the city?**

To find the free market price for apartments, set supply equal to demand:

$$100 - 5P = 50 + 5P, \text{ or } P = \$500,$$

since price is measured in hundreds of dollars. Substituting the equilibrium price into either the demand or supply equation to determine the equilibrium quantity:

$$Q_D = 100 - (5)(5) = 75$$

and

$$Q_S = 50 + (5)(5) = 75.$$

We find that at the rental rate of $500, 750,000 apartments are rented.

If the rent control agency sets the rental rate at $100, the quantity supplied would then be 550,000 (Q_S = 50 + (5)(1) = 55), a decrease of 200,000 apartments from the free market equilibrium. (Assuming three people per family per apartment, this would imply a loss of 600,000 people.) At the $100 rental rate, the demand for apartments is 950,000 units, and the resulting shortage is 400,000 units (950,000-550,000). The city population will only fall by 600,000 which is represented by the drop in the number of apartments from 750.000 to 550,000, or 200,000 apartments with 3 people each. These are the only people that were originally in the City to begin with.

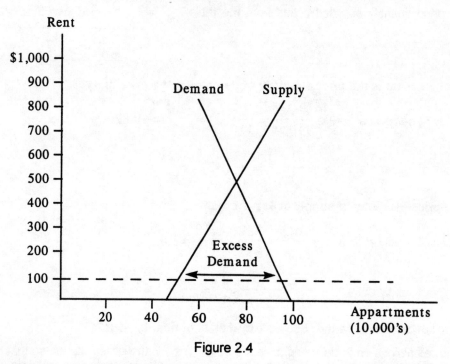

Figure 2.4

b. **Suppose the agency bows to the wishes of the board and sets a rental of $900 per month on all apartments to allow landlords a "fair" rate of return. If 50 percent of any long-run increases in apartment offerings comes from new construction, how many apartments are constructed?**

At a rental rate of $900, the supply of apartments would be 50 + 5(9) = 95, or 950,000 units, which is an increase of 200,000 units over the free market equilibrium. Therefore, (0.5)(200,000) = 100,000 units would be constructed. Note, however, that since demand is only 550,000 units, 400,000 units would go unrented.

5. Much of the demand for U.S. agricultural output has come from other countries. From Example 2.4, total demand is $Q = 3244 - 283P$. In addition, we are told that domestic demand is $Q_d = 1700 - 107P$. Domestic supply is $Q_s = 1944 + 207P$. Suppose the export demand for wheat falls by 40 percent.

a. **U.S. farmers are concerned about this drop in export demand. What happens to the free market price of wheat in the United States? Do the farmers have much reason to worry?**

Given total demand, $Q = 3244 - 283P$, and domestic demand, $Q_d = 1700 - 107P$, we may subtract and determine export demand, $Q_e = 1544 - 176P$.

The initial market equilibrium price is found by setting total demand equal to supply:

$$3244 - 283P = 1944 + 207P, \text{ or}$$

$$P = \$2.65.$$

The best way to handle the 40 percent drop in export demand is to assume that the export demand curve pivots down and to the left around the vertical intercept so that at all prices demand decreases by 40 percent, and the reservation price (the maximum price that the foreign country is willing to pay) does not change. If you instead shifted the demand curve down to the left in a parallel fashion the effect on price and quantity will be qualitatively the same, but will differ quantitatively.

The new export demand is $0.6Q_e = 0.6(1544 - 176P) = 926.4 - 105.6P$. Graphically, export demand has pivoted inwards as illustrated in figure 2.5a below.

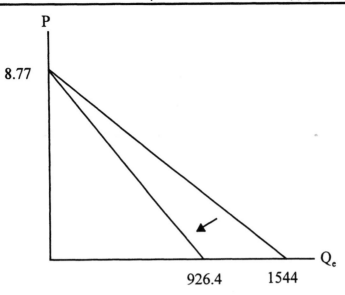

Figure 2.5a

Total demand becomes

$$Q_D = Q_d + 0.6Q_e = 1700 - 107P + (0.6)(1544 - 176P) = 2626.4 - 212.6P.$$

Equating total supply and total demand,

$$1944 + 207P = 2626.4 - 212.6P, \text{ or}$$

$$P = \$1.63,$$

which is a significant drop from the market-clearing price of $2.65 per bushel. At this price, the market-clearing quantity is 2280.65 million bushels. Total revenue has decreased from $6614.6 million to $3709.0 million. Most farmers would worry.

b.   **Now suppose the U.S. government wants to buy enough wheat each year to raise the price to $3.50 per bushel. With this drop in export demand, how much wheat would the government have to buy each year? How much would this cost the government?**

With a price of $3.50, the market is not in equilibrium. Quantity demanded and supplied are

$$Q_D = 2626.4 - 212.6(3.5) = 1882.3, \text{ and}$$

$$Q_S = 1944 + 207(3.5) = 2668.5.$$

Excess supply is therefore 2668.5-1882.3=786.2 million bushels. The government must purchase this amount to support a price of $3.5, and will spend

$3.5(786.2 million) = $2751.7 million per year.

6. In 1998, Americans smoked 470 billion cigarettes. The average retail price was $2 per pack. Statistical studies have shown that the price elasticity of demand is -0.4, and the price elasticity of supply is 0.5. Using this information, derive linear demand and supply curves for the cigarette market.

Let the demand curve be of the general form Q=a+bP and the supply curve be of the general form Q=c+dP, where a, b, c, and d are the constants that you have to find from the information given above. To begin, recall the formula for the price elasticity of demand

$$E_P^D = \frac{P}{Q}\frac{\Delta Q}{\Delta P}.$$

You are given information about the value of the elasticity, P, and Q, which means that you can solve for the slope which is b in the above formula for the demand curve.

$$-0.4 = \frac{2}{470}\frac{\Delta Q}{\Delta P}$$

$$\frac{\Delta Q}{\Delta P} = -0.4\left(\frac{470}{2}\right) = -94 = b.$$

To find the constant a, substitute for Q, P, and b into the above formula so that 470=a-94*2 and a=658. The equation for demand is therefore Q=658-94P. To find the supply curve, recall the formula for the elasticity of supply and follow the same method as above:

$$E_P^S = \frac{P}{Q}\frac{\Delta Q}{\Delta P}$$

$$0.5 = \frac{2}{470}\frac{\Delta Q}{\Delta P}$$

$$\frac{\Delta Q}{\Delta P} = 0.5\left(\frac{470}{2}\right) = 117.5 = d.$$

To find the constant c, substitute for Q, P, and d into the above formula so that 470=c+117.5*2 and c=235. The equation for supply is therefore Q=235+117.5P.

7. In Example 2.7 we examined the effect of a 20 percent decline in copper demand on the price of copper, using the linear supply and demand curves developed in Section 2.6. Suppose the long-run price elasticity of copper demand were -0.4 instead of -0.8.

a. Assuming, as before, that the equilibrium price and quantity are P* = 75 cents per pound and Q* = 7.5 million metric tons per year, derive the linear demand curve consistent with the smaller elasticity.

Following the method outlined in Section 2.6, we solve for a and b in the demand equation

$Q_D = a - bP$. First, we know that for a linear demand function $E_D = -b\left(\frac{P*}{Q*}\right)$. Here E_D = -

0.4 (the long-run price elasticity), $P*$ = 0.75 (the equilibrium price), and $Q*$ = 7.5 (the equilibrium quantity). Solving for b,

$$-0.4 = -b\left(\frac{0.75}{7.5}\right), \text{ or } b = 4.$$

To find the intercept, we substitute for b, Q_D (= $Q*$), and P (= $P*$) in the demand equation:

$$7.5 = a - (4)(0.75), \text{ or } a = 10.5.$$

The linear demand equation consistent with a long-run price elasticity of -0.4 is therefore

$$Q_D = 10.5 - 4P.$$

b. Using this demand curve, recalculate the effect of a 20 percent decline in copper demand on the price of copper.

The new demand is 20 percent below the original (using our convention that quantity demanded is reduced by 20% at every price):

$$Q_D' = (0.8)(10.5 - 4P) = 8.4 - 3.2P.$$

Equating this to supply,

$$8.4 - 3.2P = -4.5 + 16P, \text{ or}$$

$$P = 0.672.$$

With the 20 percent decline in the demand, the price of copper falls to 67.2 cents per pound.

8. Example 2.8 analyzes the world oil market. Using the data given in that example,

a.   Show that the short-run demand and competitive supply curves are indeed given by

$$D = 24.08 - 0.06P$$

$$S_c = 11.74 + 0.07P.$$

First, considering non-OPEC supply:

$$S_c = Q^* = 13.$$

With $E_S = 0.10$ and $P^* = \$18$, $E_S = d(P^*/Q^*)$ implies $d = 0.07$.

Substituting for d, S_c, and P in the supply equation, $c = 11.74$ and $S_c = 11.74 + 0.07P$.

Similarly, since $Q_D = 23$, $E_D = -b(P^*/Q^*) = -0.05$, and b = 0.06. Substituting for b, $Q_D = 23$, and $P = 18$ in the demand equation gives 23 = a - 0.06(18), so that a = 24.08.

Hence $Q_D = 24.08 - 0.06P$.

b.   Show that the long-run demand and competitive supply curves are indeed given by

$$D = 32.18 - 0.51P$$

$$S_c = 7.78 + 0.29P.$$

As above, $E_S = 0.4$ and $E_D = -0.4$: $E_S = d(P^*/Q^*)$ and $E_D = -b(P^*/Q^*)$, implying 0.4 = d(18/13) and -0.4 = -b(18/23). So d = 0.29 and b = 0.51.

Next solve for c and a:

$S_c = c + dP$ and $Q_D = a - bP$, implying 13 = c + (0.29)(18) and 23 = a - (0.51)(18).

So c = 7.78 and a = 32.18.

c.   During the late 1990s, Saudi Arabia accounted for 3 billion barrels per year of OPEC's production. Suppose that war or revolution caused Saudi Arabia to stop producing oil. Use the model above to calculate what would happen to the price of oil in the short run and the long run if OPEC's production were to drop by 3 billion barrels per year.

With OPEC's supply reduced from 10 bb/yr to 7 bb/yr, add this lower supply of 7 bb/yr to the short-run and long-run supply equations:

$$S_c' = 7 + S_c = 11.74 + 7 + 0.07P = 18.74 + 0.07P \text{ and } S'' = 7 + S_c = 14.78 + 0.29P.$$

These are equated with short-run and long-run demand, so that:

$$18.74 + 0.07P = 24.08 - 0.06P,$$

implying that $P = \$41.08$ in the short run; and

$$14.78 + 0.29P = 32.18 - 0.51P,$$

implying that $P = \$21.75$ in the long run.

9.   Refer to Example 2.9, which analyzes the effects of price controls on natural gas.

a.   Using the data in the example, show that the following supply and demand curves did indeed describe the market in 1975:

$$\text{Supply: } Q = 14 + 2P_G + 0.25P_O$$

$$\text{Demand: } Q = -5P_G + 3.75P_O$$

where P_G and P_O are the prices of natural gas and oil, respectively. **Also, verify that if the price of oil is \$8.00, these curves imply a free market price of \$2.00 for natural gas.**

To solve this problem, we apply the analysis of Section 2.6 to the definition of cross-price elasticity of demand given in Section 2.4. For example, the cross-price-elasticity of demand for natural gas with respect to the price of oil is:

$$E_{GO} = \left(\frac{\Delta Q_G}{\Delta P_O}\right)\left(\frac{P_O}{Q_G}\right).$$

$\left(\dfrac{\Delta Q_G}{\Delta P_O}\right)$ is the change in the quantity of natural gas demanded, because of a small change

in the price of oil. For linear demand equations, $\left(\dfrac{\Delta Q_G}{\Delta P_O}\right)$ is constant. If we represent

demand as:

$$Q_G = a - bP_G + eP_O$$

(notice that income is held constant), then $\left(\dfrac{\Delta Q_G}{\Delta P_O}\right) = e$. Substituting this into the cross-price

elasticity, $E_{PO} = e\left(\dfrac{P_O^*}{Q_G^*}\right)$, where P_O^* and Q_G^* are the equilibrium price and quantity. We know

that P_O^* = \$8 and Q_G^* = 20 trillion cubic feet (Tcf). Solving for e,

$$1.5 = e\left(\frac{8}{20}\right), \text{ or } e = 3.75.$$

Similarly, if the general form of the supply equation is represented as:

$$Q_G = c + dP_G + gP_O,$$

the cross-price elasticity of supply is $g\left(\dfrac{P_O^*}{Q_G^*}\right)$, which we know to be 0.1. Solving for g,

$$0.1 = g\left(\frac{8}{20}\right), \text{ or } g = 0.25.$$

The values for d and b may be found with equations 2.5a and 2.5b in Section 2.6. We know that E_s = 0.2, P^* = 2, and Q^* = 20. Therefore,

$$0.2 = d\left(\frac{2}{20}\right), \text{ or } d = 2.$$

Also, E_D = -0.5, so

$$-0.5 = b\left(\frac{2}{20}\right), \text{ or } b = -5.$$

By substituting these values for $d, g, b,$ and e into our linear supply and demand equations, we may solve for c and a:

$$20 = c + (2)(2) + (0.25)(8), \text{ or } c = 14,$$

and

$$20 = a - (5)(2) + (3.75)(8), \text{ or } a = 0.$$

If the price of oil is \$8.00, these curves imply a free market price of \$2.00 for natural gas. Substitute the price of oil in the supply and demand curves to verify these equations. Then set the curves equal to each other and solve for the price of gas.

$$14 + 2P_G + (0.25)(8) = -5P_G + (3.75)(8), \ 7P_G = 14, \text{ or}$$

$$P_G = \$2.00.$$

b. **Suppose the regulated price of gas in 1975 had been $1.50 per thousand cubic feet, instead of $1.00. How much excess demand would there have been?**

With a regulated price of $1.50 for natural gas and a price of oil equal to $8.00 per barrel,
$$\text{Demand: } Q_D = (-5)(1.50) + (3.75)(8) = 22.5, \text{ and}$$
$$\text{Supply: } Q_S = 14 + (2)(1.5) + (0.25)(8) = 19.$$

With a supply of 19 Tcf and a demand of 22.5 Tcf, there would be an excess demand of 3.5 Tcf.

c. **Suppose that the market for natural gas had *not* been regulated. If the price of oil had increased from $8 to $16, what would have happened to the free market price of natural gas?**

If the price of natural gas had not been regulated and the price of oil had increased from $8 to $16, then
$$\text{Demand: } Q_D = -5P_G + (3.75)(16) = 60 - 5P_G, \text{ and}$$
$$\text{Supply: } Q_S = 14 + 2P_G + (0.25)(16) = 18 + 2P_G.$$

Equating supply and demand and solving for the equilibrium price,
$$18 + 2P_G = 60 - 5P_G, \text{ or } P_G = \$6.$$

The price of natural gas would have tripled from $2 to $6.

10. **The table below shows the retail price and sales for instant coffee and roasted coffee for 1997 and 1998.**

Year	Retail Price of Instant Coffee ($/lb)	Sales of Instant Coffee (million lbs)	Retail Price of Roasted Coffee ($/lb)	Sales of Roasted Coffee (million lbs)
1997	10.35	75	4.11	820
1998	10.48	70	3.76	850

a. **Using this data alone, estimate the short-run price elasticity of demand for roasted coffee. Also, derive a linear demand curve for roasted coffee.**

To find elasticity, you must first estimate the slope of the demand curve:
$$\frac{\Delta Q}{\Delta P} = \frac{820 - 850}{4.11 - 3.76} = -\frac{30}{0.35} = -85.7.$$

Given the slope, we can now estimate elasticity using the price and quantity data from the above table. Since the demand curve is assumed to be linear, the elasticity will differ in 1997 and 1998 because price and quantity are different. You can calculate the elasticity at both points and at the average point between the two years:

$$E_p^{97} = \frac{P}{Q}\frac{\Delta Q}{\Delta P} = \frac{4.11}{820}(-85.7) = -0.43$$

$$E_p^{98} = \frac{P}{Q}\frac{\Delta Q}{\Delta P} = \frac{3.76}{850}(-85.7) = -0.38$$

$$E_p^{AVE} = \frac{\dfrac{P_{97}+P_{98}}{2}}{\dfrac{Q_{97}+Q_{98}}{2}}\frac{\Delta Q}{\Delta P} = \frac{3.935}{835}(-85.7) = -0.40.$$

To derive the demand curve for roasted coffee, note that the slope of the demand curve is -85.7=-b. To find the coefficient a, use either of the data points from the table above so that a=830+85.7*4.11=1172.3 or a=850+85.7*3.76=1172.3. The equation for the demand curve is therefore

Q=1172.3-85.7P.

b.   **Now estimate the short-run price elasticity of demand for instant coffee. Derive a   linear demand curve for instant coffee.**

To find elasticity, you must first estimate the slope of the demand curve:

$$\frac{\Delta Q}{\Delta P} = \frac{75-70}{10.35-10.48} = -\frac{5}{0.13} = -38.5.$$

Given the slope, we can now estimate elasticity using the price and quantity data from the above table. Since the demand curve is assumed to be linear, the elasticity will differ in 1997 and 1998 because price and quantity are different. You can calculate the elasticity at both points and at the average point between the two years:

$$E_p^{97} = \frac{P}{Q}\frac{\Delta Q}{\Delta P} = \frac{10.35}{75}(-38.5) = -5.31$$

$$E_p^{98} = \frac{P}{Q}\frac{\Delta Q}{\Delta P} = \frac{10.48}{70}(-38.5) = -5.76$$

$$E_p^{AVE} = \frac{\dfrac{P_{97}+P_{98}}{2}}{\dfrac{Q_{97}+Q_{98}}{2}}\frac{\Delta Q}{\Delta P} = \frac{10.415}{72.5}(-38.5) = -5.52.$$

To derive the demand curve for instant coffee, note that the slope of the demand curve is -38.5=-b. To find the coefficient a, use either of the data points from the table above so that a=75+38.5*10.35=473.1 or a=70+38.5*10.48=473.1. The equation for the demand curve is therefore

Q=473.1-38.5P.

c.   **Which coffee has the higher short-run price elasticity of demand? Why do you   think this is the case?**

Instant coffee is significantly more elastic than roasted coffee. In fact, the demand for roasted coffee is inelastic and the demand for instant coffee is elastic. Roasted coffee may have an inelastic demand in the short-run as many people think of coffee as a necessary good. Instant coffee on the other hand may be viewed by many people as a convenient, though imperfect substitute for roasted coffee. Given the higher price per pound for instant coffee, and the preference for roasted over instant coffee by many consumers, this will cause the demand for roasted coffee to be less elastic than the demand for instant coffee. Note also that roasted coffee is the premium good so that the demand for roasted coffee lies to the right of the demand for instant coffee. This will cause the demand for roasted coffee to be more inelastic because at any given price there will be a higher quantity demanded for roasted versus instant coffee, and this quantity difference will be large enough to offset the difference in the slope of the two demand curves.

PART II
PRODUCERS, CONSUMERS, AND COMPETITIVE MARKETS
CHAPTER 3
CONSUMER BEHAVIOR

TEACHING NOTES

Chapter 3 builds the foundation for deriving the demand curve in Chapter 4. In order to understand demand theory, students must have a firm grasp of indifference curves, the marginal rate of substitution, the budget line, and optimal consumer choice. It is possible to discuss consumer choice without going into extensive detail on utility theory. Many students find utility functions to be a more abstract concept than preference relationships. However, if you plan to discuss uncertainty in Chapter 5, you will need to cover marginal utility (section 3.5). Even if you cover utility theory only briefly, make sure students are comfortable with the term utility because it appears frequently in Chapter 4.

When introducing indifference curves, stress that physical quantities are represented on the two axes. After discussing supply and demand, students may think that price should be on the vertical axis. To illustrate the indifference curves, pick an initial bundle on the graph and ask which other bundles are likely to be more preferred and less preferred to the initial bundle. This will divide the graph into four quadrants, and it is then easier for students to figure out the set of bundles between which the consumer is indifferent. It is helpful to present a lot of examples with different types of goods and see if the class can figure out how to draw the indifference curves. The examples are also useful for explaining the significance of the assumptions made about preferences. In presenting different examples, you can ask which assumption would be violated.

Explaining utility follows naturally from the discussion of indifference curves. Though an abstract concept, it is possible to get students to understand the basic idea without spending too much time on the topic. You might point out that we as consumers have a goal in life which is to maximize our utility subject to our budget constraint. When we go to the store we pick the basket that we like best and that stays within our budget. From this we derive demand curves. Emphasize that it is the ranking that is important and not the utility number, and point out that if we can graph an indifference curve we can certainly find an equation to represent it. Finally, what is most important is the rate at which consumers are willing to exchange goods (the marginal rate of substitution) and this is based on the relative satisfaction that they derive from each good at any particular time.

The marginal rate of substitution, *MRS*, can be confusing to students. Some confuse the *MRS* with the ratio of the two quantities. If this is the case, point out that the slope is equal to the ratio of the rise, ΔY, and the run, ΔX. This ratio is equal to the ratio of the intercepts of a line just tangent to the indifference curve. As we move along a convex indifference curve, these intercepts and the *MRS* change. Another problem is the terminology "of *X* for *Y*." This is confusing because we are not substituting "*X* for *Y*," but *Y* for one unit of *X*. You may want to present a variety of examples in class to explain this important concept.

REVIEW QUESTIONS

1. What does *transitivity of preferences* mean?

Transitivity of preferences implies that if someone prefers *A* to *B* and prefers *B* to *C*, then he or she prefers *A* to *C*.

2. Suppose that a set of indifference curves was not negatively sloped. What could you say about the desirability of the two goods?

One major assumption of preference theory is that more is preferred to less. Thus, we can expect that consumers will experience a lower level of satisfaction if we take some of a good away from them. From this, we necessarily derive negatively sloped indifference curves. However, if one good is undesirable, then less of the undesirable good leaves the consumer better off, e.g., less toxic waste is preferred to more toxic waste. When one good is undesirable, the indifference curves showing the trade-off between that good and a desired good have positive slopes. In Figure 3.2 below, the indifference curve U_2 is preferred to the indifference curve U_1.

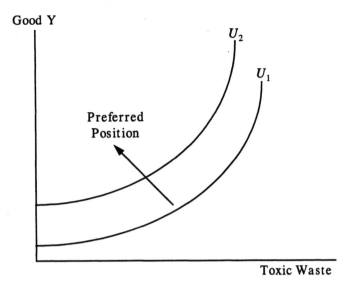

Figure 3.2

3. Explain why two indifference curves cannot intersect.

The explanation is most easily achieved with the aid of a graph such as Figure 3.3, which shows two indifference curves intersecting at point A. We know from the definition of an indifference curve that a consumer has the same level of utility along any given curve. In this case, the consumer is indifferent between bundles A and B because they both lie on indifference curve U_1. Similarly, the consumer is indifferent between bundles A and C because they both lie on indifference curve U_2. By the transitivity of preferences this consumer should also be indifferent between C and B. However, we see from the graph that C lies above B, so C must be preferred to B. Thus, the fact that indifference curves cannot intersect is proven.

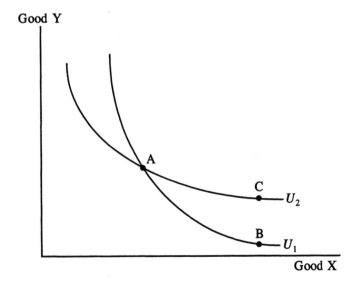

Figure 3.3

4. Draw a set of indifference curves for which the marginal rate of substitution is constant. Draw two budget lines with different slopes; show what the satisfaction-maximizing choice will be in each case. What conclusions can you draw?

In Figure 3.4, Good X and Good Y are perfect substitutes and, thus, the indifference curves are straight lines, U_1 and U_2, each with a slope of -1. For goods that are perfect substitutes, the consumer will always prefer to purchase the cheaper of the two goods to obtain maximum utility. For example, if Good Y is cheaper than Good X, the consumer would face the budget constraint L_2 and would maximize utility at point A. On the other hand, if Good X were cheaper than Good Y, the consumer would face the budget constraint L_1 and would maximize utility at point B. If Good X and Good Y have the same price, the budget constraint would coincide with the indifference curve, and the consumer would be indifferent between any point on the curve. To see this, recall that the slope of the budget line is $-\dfrac{P_x}{P_y}$.

More generallly, the slope of a linear indifference curve is the constant rate at which the consumer is willing to trade the two goods. If the slope of the budget line and the indifference curve are the same, then the consumer is indifferent between any point on the budget line. When the slopes are different, the consumer will choose one of the corners, depending on the respective slopes.

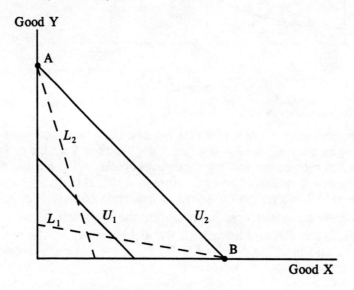

Figure 3.4

5. Explain why a person's marginal rate of substitution between two goods must equal the ratio of the price of the goods for the consumer to achieve maximum satisfaction.

The *MRS* describes the rate at which the *consumer* is willing to trade one good for another to maintain the same level of satisfaction. The ratio of prices describes the trade-off that the *market* is willing to make between the same two goods. The tangency of the indifference curve with the budget line represents the point at which the trade-offs are equal and consumer satisfaction is maximized. If the *MRS* between two goods is not equal to the ratio of prices, then the consumer could trade one good for another at market prices to obtain higher levels of satisfaction. This trading continues until the highest level of satisfaction is achieved.

6. Explain why consumers are likely to be worse off when a product that they consume is rationed.

If the maximum quantity of a good is fixed by decree and desired quantities are not available for purchase, then there is no guarantee that the highest level of satisfaction can be achieved. The consumer will not be able to give up the consumption of other goods in order to obtain more of the rationed good. Only if the amount rationed is greater than the desired level of consumption can the consumer still maximize satisfaction without constraint. (Note: rationing may imply a higher level of *social* welfare because of equity or fairness considerations across consumers.)

7. Upon merging with West Germany's economy, East German consumers indicated a preference for Mercedes-Benz automobiles over Volkswagen automobiles. However, when they converted their savings into deutsche marks, they flocked to Volkswagen dealerships. How can you explain this apparent paradox?

Three assumptions are required to address this question: 1) that a Mercedes costs more than a Volkswagen; 2) that the East German consumers' utility function comprises two goods, automobiles and all other goods evaluated in deutsche marks; and 3) that East Germans have incomes. Based on these assumptions, we can surmise that while once-East German consumers may prefer a Mercedes to a Volkswagen, they either cannot afford a Mercedes or they prefer a bundle of other goods plus a Volkswagen to a Mercedes alone. While the marginal utility of consuming a Mercedes exceeds the marginal utility of consuming a Volkswagon, the consumer will consider marginal utility per dollar for each good. This means the marginal utility per dollar must have been higher for the Volkswagon since consumers flocked to the Volkswagon dealerships and not the Mercedes dealerships.

8. Describe the equal marginal principle. Explain why this principle may not hold if increasing marginal utility is associated with the consumption of one or both goods.

The equal marginal principle states that the ratio of the marginal utility to price must be equal across all goods to obtain maximum satisfaction. This explanation follows from the same logic examined in Review Question 5. Utility maximization is achieved when the budget is allocated so that the marginal utility per dollar of expenditure is the same for each good.

If marginal utility is increasing, the consumer maximizes satisfaction by consuming ever larger amounts of the good. Thus, the consumer would spend all income on one good, assuming a constant price, resulting in a corner solution. With a corner solution, the equal marginal principle *cannot* hold.

9. What is the difference between ordinal utility and cardinal utility? Explain why the assumption of cardinal utility is not needed in order to rank consumer choices.

Ordinal utility implies an ordering among alternatives without regard for intensity of preference. For example, the consumer's first choice is preferred to their second choice. Cardinal utility implies that the intensity of preferences may be quantified. An ordinal ranking is all that is needed to rank consumer choices. It is not necessary to know how intensely a consumer prefers basket *A* over basket *B*; it is enough to know that *A* is preferred to *B*.

10. The price of computers has fallen substantially over the past two decades. Use this drop in price to explain why the Consumer Price Index is likely to substantially understate the cost-of-living index for individuals who use computers intensively.

The consumer price index measures the changes in the weighted average of the prices of the bundle of goods purchased by consumers. The weights equal the share of consumer's expenditures on all of the goods in the bundle. A base year is chosen, and the weights for that year are used to compute the CPI in that and subsequent years. When the price of a good falls substantially then a consumer will substitute towards that good, altering the share of that consumer's income spent on each good. By using the base year's weights the CPI does not take into account that large price changes alter these expenditure shares, and so gives an inaccurate measure of changes in the cost of living.

For example, assume Fred spends 10% of his income on computers in 1970, and that Fred's expenditure shares in 1970 were used as the weights to calculate Fred's CPI in subsequent years. If Fred's demand for computers was inelastic, then reductions in the price of computers (relative to other goods) would reduce the share of his income spent on computers. After 1970 a CPI that used Fred's 1970 expenditure shares as weights would give a 10% weight to the falling price of computers, even though Fred spent less that 10% of his income on computers. As long as the prices of other goods rose, or fell less than 10%, then the CPI gives too little weight to the changes in the prices of other goods, and understates the changes in Fred's cost of living.

EXERCISES

1. In this chapter, consumer preferences for various commodities did not change during the analysis. Yet in some situations, preferences do change as consumption occurs. Discuss why and how preferences might change over time with consumption of these two commodities:

a.   cigarettes

The assumption that preferences do not change is a reasonable one if choices are independent across time. It does not hold, however, when "habit-forming" or addictive behavior is involved, as in the case of cigarettes: the consumption of cigarettes in one period influences their consumption in the next period.

b.   dinner for the first time at a restaurant with a special cuisine

While there may not be anything physically addictive in dining at new and different restaurants, one can become better informed about a particular restaurant. One may enjoy choosing more new and different restaurants, or one may be tired of choosing another new and different place to eat. In either of these cases, choices change as consumption occurs.

2. Draw the indifference curves for the following individuals' preferences for two goods: hamburgers and beer.

a.   Al likes beer but hates hamburgers. He always prefers more beer no matter how many hamburgers he has.

For Al, hamburgers are a "bad." His indifference curves slope upward and to the right rather than downward and to the left. For Al, U_1 is preferred to U_2 and U_2 is preferred to U_3. See figure 3.2a. If you instead assumed that hamburgers were a neutral good, then the indifference curves would be vertical and utility is increasing to the right as more beer is consumed.

b.   Betty is indifferent between bundles of either three beers or two hamburgers. Her preferences do not change as she consumes any more of either food.

Since Betty is indifferent between three beers and two burgers, an indifference curve connects these two points. Betty's indifference curves are a series of parallel lines with slope of $-\frac{2}{3}$. See figure 3.2b.

c.   Chris eats one hamburger and washes it down with one beer. He will not consume an additional unit of one item without an additional unit of the other.

For Chris, hamburgers and beer are perfect complements, i.e., he always wants to consume the goods in fixed proportions to each other. The indifference curves are *L*-shaped, with corners on a 45-degree line out of the origin. See figure 3.2c.

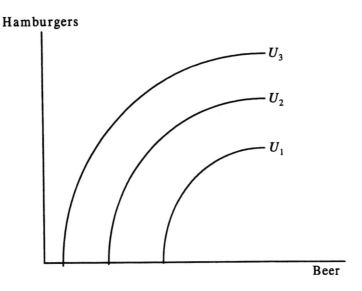

Figure 3.2.a

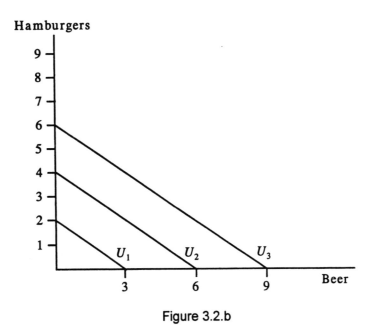

Figure 3.2.b

d. **Doreen loves beer but is allergic to beef. Every time she eats a hamburger she breaks out in hives.**

For Doreen, hamburgers are not considered a "good" but rather a "bad," and thus her preferred position is not upwards and to the right, but rather downward and to the right. For Doreen, U_1 is preferred to U_2 and U_2 is preferred to U_3. See figure 3.2d.

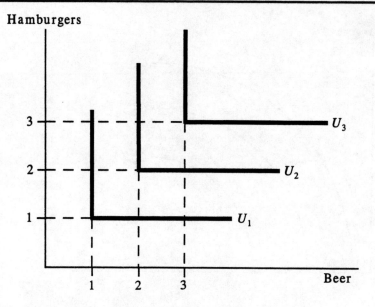

Figure 3.2.c

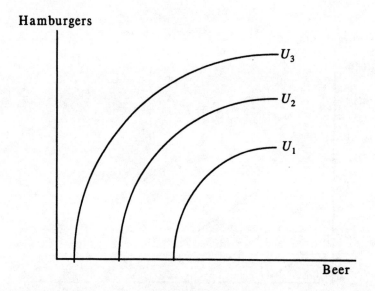

Figure 3.2.d

3. The price of tapes is $10 and the price of CD's is $15. Philip has a budget of $100 and has already purchased 3 tapes. He thus has $70 more to spend on additional tapes and CD's. Draw his budget line. If his remaining expenditure is made on 1 tape and 4 CD's, show Philip's consumption choice on the budget line.

Given Philip's remaining income of $70, he can afford 7 tapes if he spends the entire amount on tapes, and he can afford 4.7 CD's if he spends the entire amount on CD's. According to figure 3.3, his budget line therefore intersects the vertical axis at a quantity of 7 tapes and the horizontal axis at a quantity of 4.7 CD's. Since he faces constant prices, the budget line has a constant slope and is a straight line.

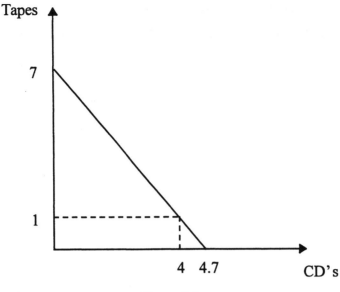

Figure 3.3

4. Debra usually buys a soft drink when she goes to a movie theater, where she has a choice of three sizes: the 8 ounce drink costs $1.50, the 12 ounce drink, $2.00, and the 16 ounce drink, $2.25. Describe the budget constraint that Debra faces when deciding how many ounces of the drink to purchase. (Assume that Debra can costlessly dispose of any of the soft drink that she does not want.

First notice that as the size of the drink increases, the price eper ounce decreases. When she buys the 8 ounce soft drink she pays $\dfrac{\$1.50}{8\ oz} = \$0.19$ per *oz*. When she buys the 12 ounce size she pays $0.17 per ounce, and when she buys the 16 ounce size, she pays $0.14 per ounce. Given that there are three different prices per ounce of soft drink, the budget line will have two kinks in it, as illustrated in figure 3.4.

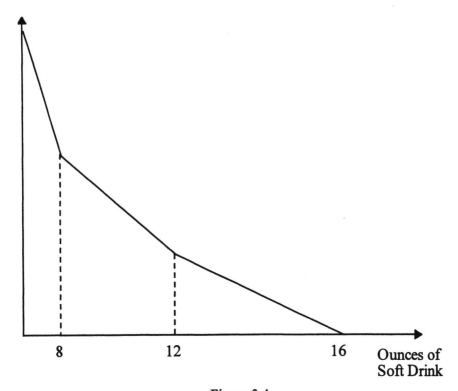

Figure 3.4

29

5. Suppose Bill views butter and margarine as perfectly substitutable for each other.

a. **Draw a set of indifference curves that describes Bill's preferences for butter and margarine.**

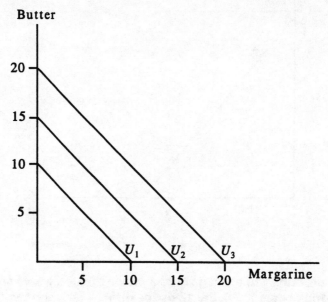

Figure 3.5.a

b. **Are these indifference curves convex? Why?**

Convexity implies that a line segment connecting any two points on a curve lies above the curve, i.e., the curve is "bowed inward." Because the consumer considers butter and margarine to be perfect substitutes, there is no diminishing marginal utility, and the resultant indifference curves are straight lines. *Straight-line indifference curves are not strictly convex.*

c. **If butter costs \$2 per package, while margarine costs only \$1, and Bill has a \$20 budget to spend for the month, which butter-margarine market basket will he choose? Can you show this graphically?**

Let Bill's income be represented by Y, the price of butter by P_B, the quantity of butter by B, the price of margarine by P_M, and the quantity of margarine by M. Then the general form of the budget constraint is:

$$Y = P_B B + P_M M.$$

Substituting for the given values of Y, P_B, and P_M, we obtain the specific representation of Bill's budget constraint:

$$20 = 2B + 1M, \text{ or } B = 10 - 0.5M.$$

Because Bill is indifferent between butter and margarine, and the price of butter is greater than the price of margarine, Bill will only buy margarine. This is a *corner solution*, because the optimal choice occurs on an axis. In Figure 3.5.c Bill's utility maximizing bundle is point *A*.

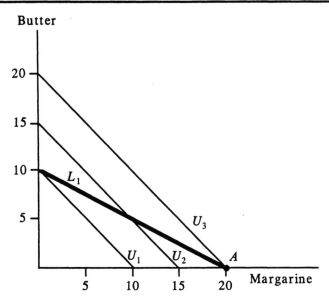

Figure 3.5.c

6. Suppose that Jones and Smith have decided to allocate $1,000 per year on liquid refreshments in the form of alcoholic or nonalcoholic drinks. Jones and Smith differ substantially in their preferences for these two forms of refreshment. Jones prefers alcoholic to nonalcoholic drinks, while Smith prefers the nonalcoholic option.

a.   Draw a set of indifference curves for Jones and a second set for Smith.

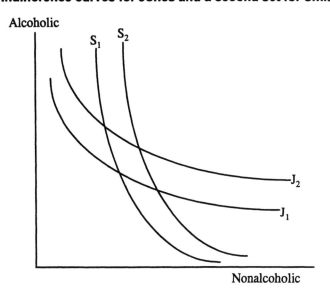

Figure 3.6.a

b.   Discuss why the two sets of curves are different from each other using the concept of marginal rate of substitution.

At any combination of alcoholic, *A*, and nonalcoholic, *N*, drinks, Jones is willing to give up a lot of *N* for an additional unit of *A*; whereas, Smith is willing to give up a lot of *A* for an additional unit of *N*. Because Jones needs more *N* to compensate him for giving up some *A*, he has a lower marginal rate of substitution of alcoholic for nonalcoholic beverages than Smith. With alcoholic beverages on the vertical axis, Jones' indifference curves are less steep than Smith's at any point on the graph.

c.   **If both Smith and Jones pay the same prices for their refreshments, will their marginal rates of substitution of alcoholic for nonalcoholic drinks be the same or different? Explain.**

In order to maximize utility, the consumer must consume quantities such that the *MRS* between any two commodities is equal to the ratio of prices. If Smith and Jones are rational consumers, their *MRS* must be equal because they face the same market prices. But because they have different preferences, they will consume different amounts of the two goods, alcoholic and nonalcoholic. At those different levels, however, their *MRS* are equal.

7.   Consumers in Georgia pay twice as much for avocados as they do for peaches. However, avocados and peaches are equally priced in California. If consumers in both states maximize utility, will the marginal rage of substitution of peaches for avocados be the same for consumers in both states? If not, which will be higher?

The marginal rate of substitution of peaches for avocados is the amount of avocados that a person is willing to give up to obtain one additional peach. When consumers maximize utility, they set their marginal rate of substitution equal to the price ratio, which in this case is $\dfrac{P_{peach}}{P_{avocado}}$.   In Georgia, $P_{avocado} = 2P_{peach}$, which means that when consumers are maximizing utility, $MRS = \dfrac{P_{peach}}{P_{avocado}} = \dfrac{1}{2}$.   In California, $P_{avocado} = P_{peach}$, which means that when consumers are maximizing utility, $MRS = \dfrac{P_{peach}}{P_{avocado}} = \dfrac{1}{1}$.   The marginal rate of substitution is therefore not the same in both states, and will be higher in California.

8.   Anne is a frequent flyer whose fares are reduced (through coupon giveaways) by 25 percent after she flies 25,000 miles a year, and then by 50 percent after she flies 50,000 miles. Can you graph the budget line that Anne faces in making her flight plans for the year?

In Figure 3.8, we plot miles flown, *M*, against all other goods, *G*, in dollars. The budget constraint is:

$$Y = P_M M + P_G G, \text{ or}$$

$$G = \frac{Y}{P_G} - M\left(\frac{P_M}{P_G}\right).$$

The slope of the budget line is $-\dfrac{P_M}{P_G}$. In this case, the price of miles flown changes as the number of miles flown changes, so the budget curve is kinked at 25,000 and at 50,000 miles. If we assume P_M is \$1 per mile for less than or equal to 25,000 miles, then P_M = \$0.75 for 25,000 < $M \geq$ 50,000, and P_M = \$0.50 for M > 50,000. Also, assume that P_G = \$1.00. The slope of the budget line from *A* to *B* is -1, the slope of the budget line from *B* to *C* is -0.75, and the slope of the budget line from *C* to *D* is -0.5.

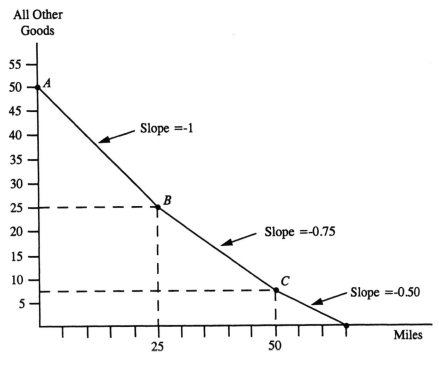

Figure 3.8

9. Antonio buys 8 new college textbooks during his first year at school at a cost of $50 each. Used books cost only $30 each. When the bookstore announces that there will be a 20 percent price increase in new texts and a 10 percent increase in used texts for the next year, Antonio's father offers him $80 extra. Is Antonio better off or worse off after the price change?

It follows from the axiom of revealed preferences that, since Antonio chose to purchase only new textbooks when both new and used textbooks were available, it must be the case that Antonio does not consider used textbooks substitutes for new textbooks at the old prices.

With the increase in price, however, to $60 for new textbooks and $33 for used texts, the relative price of new texts to used texts increases from $\frac{50}{30} = 1.67$ to $\frac{60}{33} = 1.82$. Antonio may react to the relative price increase in one of two ways:

(1) If new and used texts are *not* substitutes for Antonio (*L*-shaped indifference curves), then Antonio will be just as well off when the price of new texts rises and his father gives him $80 (= (60 - 50)8).

(2) If he chooses to buy a few used texts in response to the relative price increase (given the extra $80), he will move to a higher indifference curve and will therefore be better off. See Figures 3.9.a and 3.9.b.

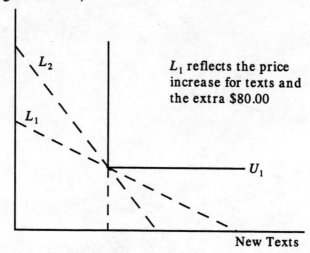

Figure 3.9.a

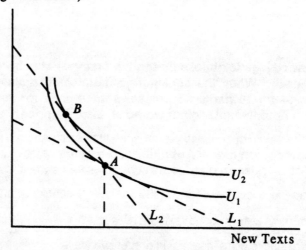

Figure 3.9.b

10. Suppose that Samantha and Jason both spend $24 per week on video and movie entertainment. When the prices of videos and movies are both $4, they both rent 3 videos and buy 3 movie tickets. Following a video price war and an increased cost of movie tickets, the video price falls to $2 and the movie ticket increases to $6. Samantha now rents 6 videos and buys 2 movie tickets; Jason, however, buys 1 movie ticket and rents 9 videos.

a.   **Is Samantha better off or worse off after the price change?**

Samantha's original point of utility maximization may be represented by point *A* on U_1 in Figure 3.10.a. With the new prices, Samantha could still afford to choose bundle *A*: $24 = $2(3 videos) + $6 (3 movies). The fact that she chose bundle *B* reveals she has obtained a higher level of utility, U_2. See Figure 3.10.a.

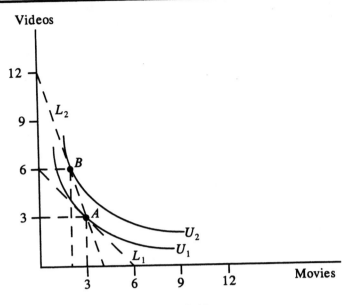

Figure 3.10.a

b.   Is Jason better off or worse off?

Similarly, Jason must also be better off.

11. Connie Consumer has a monthly income of $200 which she allocates among two goods: meat and potatoes.

a.   Suppose meat costs $4 per pound and potatoes cost $2 per pound.   Draw her budget constraint.

Let M = meat and P = potatoes. Connie's budget constraint is

$$\$200 = 4M + 2P, \text{ or}$$

$$M = 50 - 0.5P.$$

As shown in Figure 3.11.a, with M on the vertical axis, the vertical intercept is 50. The horizontal intercept may be found by setting $M = 0$ and solving for P.

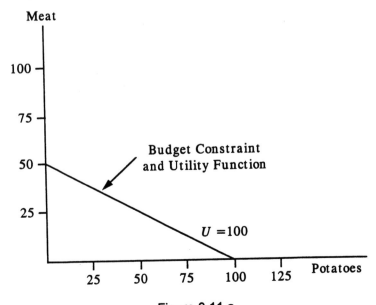

Figure 3.11.a

b. **Suppose also that her utility function is given by the equation u(M, P) = 2M + P. What combination of meat and potatoes should she buy to maximize her utility? (Hint: Meat and potatoes are perfect substitutes.)**

Connie's utility is equal to 100 when she buys 50 pounds of meat and no potatoes or no meat and 100 pounds of potatoes. The indifference curve for $U = 100$ coincides with her budget constraint. Any combination of meat and potatoes along this line will provide her with maximum utility.

c. **Connie's supermarket has a special promotion. If she buys 20 pounds of potatoes (at $2 per pound), she gets the next 10 pounds for free. This offer applies only to the first 20 pounds she buys. All potatoes in excess of the first 20 pounds (excluding bonus potatoes) are still $2 per pound. Draw her budget constraint.**

Figure 3.11.c represents Connie's budget constraint when the supermarket runs its special promotion on potatoes. Notice that her budget constraint has a slope of -2 until Connie has purchased twenty pounds of potatoes, is then flat, since the ten next pounds of potatoes are free, and then has a slope of -2 until it intercepts the potato axis at 110.

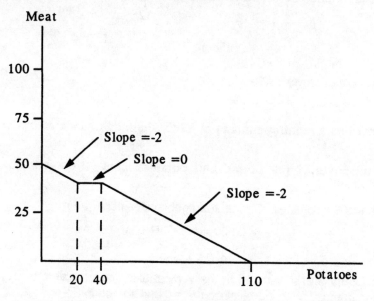

Figure 3.11.c

d. **An outbreak of potato rot raises the price of potatoes to $4 per pound. The supermarket ends its promotion. What does her budget constraint look like now? What combination of meat and potatoes maximizes her utility?**

With the price of potatoes at $4, Connie may buy either 50 pounds of meat or 50 pounds of potatoes, or some combination in between. See Figure 3.11.d. She maximizes utility at $U = 100$ at point *A* when she consumes 50 pounds of meat and no potatoes. *This is a corner solution.*

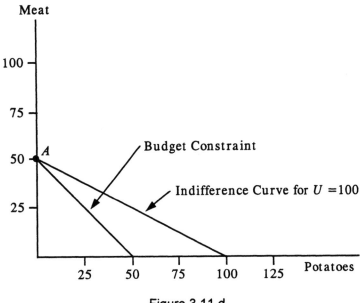

Figure 3.11.d

12. The utility that Jane receives by consuming food F and clothing C is given by: u(F,C) = FC.

a. Draw the indifference curve associated with a utility level of 12 and the indifference curve associated with a utility level of 24. Are the indifference curves convex?

To find the baskets of food, *F*, and clothing, *C*, which yield satisfactions of 12 and 24 solve the equations $C = \dfrac{12}{F}$ and $C = \dfrac{24}{F}$.

U = 12		U = 24	
Food	Clothing	Food	Clothing
1.0	12.0	1.0	24.0
1.5	8.0	2.0	12.0
2.0	6.0	3.0	8.0
3.0	4.0	4.0	6.0
4.0	3.0	6.0	4.0
6.0	2.0	8.0	3.0
8.0	1.5	12.0	2.0
12.0	1.0	24.0	1.0

The indifference curves are convex.

b. Suppose that food costs $1 a unit, clothing costs $3 a unit, and Jane has $12 to spend on food and clothing. Graph the budget line that she faces.

The budget constraint is:

$$Y = P_F F + P_C C, \text{ or}$$

$$12 = 1F + 3C, \text{ or } C = 4 - \left(\frac{1}{3}\right)F.$$

See Figure 3.12.a.

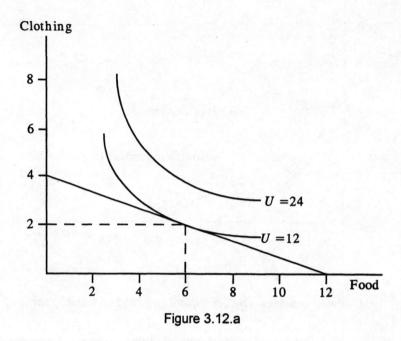

Figure 3.12.a

c.   **What is the utility-maximizing choice of food and clothing?   (Hint: Solve the problem graphically.)**

The highest level of satisfaction occurs where the budget line is tangent to the highest indifference curve. In Figure 3.12.a this is at the point $F = 6$ and $C = 2$. To check this answer, note that it exhausts Jane's income, $12 = 6P_F + 2P_C$. Also, this bundle yields a satisfaction of 12, as $(6)(2) = 12$. See Figure 3.12.a.

d.   **What is the marginal rate of substitution of food for clothing when utility is maximized?**

At the utility-maximizing level of consumption, the slope of the indifference curve is equal to the slope of the budget constraint. Since the MRS is equal to the negative slope of the indifference curve, the MRS in this problem is equal to one-third. Thus, Jane would be willing to give up one-third of a unit of clothing for one unit of food.

e.   **Suppose that Jane buys 3 units of food and 3 units of clothing with her $12 budget. Would her marginal rate of substitution of food for clothing be greater or less than 1/3? Explain.**

If Jane buys 3 units of food for $1.00 per unit and 3 units of clothing for $3.00 per unit, she would spend all her income. However, she would obtain a level of satisfaction of only 9, which represents a sub-optimal choice. At this point, the MRS is greater than one-third, and thus, at the prices she faces, she would welcome the opportunity to give up clothing to get more food. She is willing to trade clothing for food until her MRS is equal to the ratio of prices. See Figure 3.12.e.

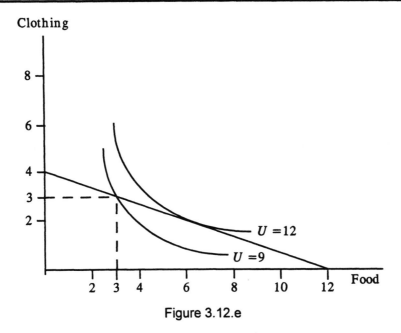

Figure 3.12.e

13. The utility that Meredith receives by consuming food F and clothing C is given by u(F,C) = FC. Suppose that Meredith's income in 1990 is $1,200 and the prices of food and clothing are $1 per unit for each. However, by 1995 the price of food has increased to $2 and the price of clothing to $3. Let 100 represent the cost of living index for 1990. Calculate the ideal and the Laspeyres cost-of-living index for Meredith for 1995. (Hint: Meredith will spend equal amounts on food and clothing with these preferences.)

Laspeyres Index

The Laspeyres index represents how much more Meredith would have to spend in 1995 versus 1990 if she consumed the same amounts of food and clothing in 1995 as she did in 1990. That is, the Laspeyres index for 1995 (L) is given by:

$$L = 100 \, (Y')/Y$$

where Y' represents the amount Meredith would spend at 1995 prices consuming the same amount of food and clothing as in 1990: $Y' = P'_F F + P'_C C = 2F + 3C$, where F and C represent the amounts of food and clothing consumed in 1990.

We thus need to calculate F and C, which make up the bundle of food and clothing which maximizes Meredith's utility given 1990 prices and her income in 1990. Use the hint to simplify the problem: Since she spends equal amounts on both goods, $P_F F = P_C C$. Or, you can derive this same equation mathematically: With this utility function, $MU_C = \Delta U/\Delta C = F$, and $MU_F = \Delta U/\Delta F = C$. To maximize utility, Meredith chooses a consumption bundle such that $MU_F/MU_C = P_F/P_C$, which again yields $P_F F = P_C C$.

From the budget constraint, we also know that:

$$P_F F + P_C C = Y.$$

Combining these two equations and substituting the values for the 1990 prices and income yields the system of equations:

$$C = F \text{ and } C + F = 1,200.$$

Solving these two equations, we find that:

$$C = 600 \text{ and } F = 600.$$

Therefore, the Laspeyres cost-of-living index is:

$$L = 100(2F + 3C)/Y = 100[(2)(600) + (3)(600)]/1200 = 250.$$

Ideal Index

The ideal index represents how much more Meredith would have to spend in 1995 versus 1990 if she consumed amounts of food and clothing in 1995 which would give her the same amount of utility as she had in 1990. That is, the ideal index for 1995 (I) is given by:

$$I = 100(Y'')/Y, \text{ where } Y'' = P'_F F + P'_C C' = 2F' + 3C'$$

where F' and C' are the amount of food and clothing which give Meredith the same utility as she had in 1990. F' and C' must also be such that Meredith spends the least amount of money at 1995 prices to attain the 1990 utility level.

The bundle (F',C') will be on the same indifference curve as (F,C) and the indifference curve at this point will be tangent to a budget line with slope $-(P'_F/P'_C)$, where P'_F and P'_C are the prices of food and clothing in 1995. Since Meredith spends equal amounts on the two goods, we know that $2F' = 3C'$. Since this bundle lies on the same indifference curve as the bundle F = 600, C = 600, we also know that $F'C' = (600)(600)$.

Solving for F' yields:

$$F'[(2/3)F'] = 360,000 \text{ or } F' = \sqrt{[(3/2)360,000]} = 734.8.$$

From this, we obtain C':

$$C' = (2/3)F' = (2/3)734.8 = 489.9.$$

We can now calculate the ideal index:

$$I = 100(2F' + 3C')/Y = 100[2(734.8) + (3)(489.9)]/1200 = 244.9.$$

CHAPTER 4
INDIVIDUAL AND MARKET DEMAND

TEACHING NOTES

Chapter 4 relies on two important ideas from Chapter 3: the influence of price and income changes on the budget line, and how to determine the optimal consumer choice. The chapter focuses on deriving individual demand graphically by changing either price or income, determining the income and substitution effects of a price change, deriving market demand, demand elasticity, and consumer surplus. These concepts are crucial to understanding the application of demand and supply analysis in Chapter 9 as well as the discussion of market failure in Parts III and IV. The analytical tools students learn in this chapter will be important for the discussion of factor supply and demand in Chapter 14.

When discussing the derivation of demand, review how the budget curve pivots around an intercept as price changes and how optimal quantities change as the budget line pivots. Once students understand the effect of price changes on consumer choice, they can grasp the derivation of the price consumption path and the individual demand curve. Remind students that the price a consumer is willing to pay is a measure of the marginal benefit of consuming another unit.

Income and substitution effects are often difficult for the student to understand, and they frequently have trouble remembering which effect is which on the graph. Emphasize that the substitution effect explains the portion of the change in demand caused by the change in relative prices (a pivot of the budget line) and the income effect explains the portion of the change in demand caused by a change in purchasing power (a shift of the budget line). The distinction between normal and inferior goods is used to determine the direction of the income effect. You might point out that the demand curve can only slope upwards if the good is inferior and the income effect is unusually large (a Giffen good). Doing a lot of examples is helpful. You might even skip the topic altogether if you are not prepared to devote some time to it. The labor leisure choice problem and derivation of the labor supply curve is a good illustration of income and substitution effects (see Chapter 14).

When covering the aggregation of individual demand curves, stress that this is equivalent to the summation of the individual demand curves horizontally. To obtain the market demand curve, you must have demand written in the form Q=f(P) as opposed to the inverse demand P=f(Q). The concept of a kink in the market demand curve is often new to students. Emphasize that this is because not all consumers are in the market at all prices.

The concept of elasticity is reintroduced and expanded upon. In particular, the relationship between elasticity and revenue, and arc versus point elasticity is explained. Many students find elasticity to be a mysterious and puzzling concept. Point out that it is merely a more precise measure than the slope of the curve to measure the response of quantity demanded to a change in price, because it is a unit free measure. One effective teaching method is to use a linear demand curve to show that while the slope is constant, the elasticity changes throughout the range of prices. The text relies on this relationship in the discussion of the monopolist's determination of the profit-maximizing quantity in Chapter 10.

Although this chapter introduces consumer surplus, it is not extensively discussed until Chapter 9; producer surplus is covered in Chapter 8. If you introduce it here, it may be necessary to review it again when you get to Chapter 9.

Finally, there are other special topics in this chapter and its Appendix that you might cover, time and interest permitting. An application of network externalities is given in Example 4.6. The first part of Section 4.6, "Empirical Estimation of Demand," is straightforward, particularly if you have covered the forecasting section of Chapter 2. However, the last part, "The Form of the Demand Relationship," is difficult for students who do not understand logarithms. The Appendix is intended for students with a background in calculus, and contains a brief mathematical treatment of demand theory.

REVIEW QUESTIONS

1. How is an individual demand curve different from a market demand curve? Which curve is likely to be more price elastic? (*Hint*: Assume that there are no network externalities.)

The market demand curve is the horizontal summation of the individual demand curves. The graph of market demand shows the relation between each price and the sum of individual quantities. Because price elasticities of demand may vary by individual, the price elasticity of demand is likely to be greater than some individual price elasticities and less than others.

2. Is the demand for a particular brand of product, such as Head skis, likely to be more price elastic or price inelastic than the demand for the aggregate of all brands, such as downhill skis? Explain.

Individual brands compete with other brands. If the two brands are similar, a small change in the price of one good will encourage many consumers to switch to the other brand. Because substitutes are readily available, the quantity response to a change in one brand's price is more elastic than the quantity response for all brands. Thus, the demand for Head skis is more elastic than the demand for downhill skis.

3. Tickets to a rock concert sell for $10. But at that price, the demand is substantially greater than the available number of tickets. Is the value or marginal benefit of an additional ticket greater than, less than, or equal to $10? How might you determine that value?

If, at $10, demand exceeds supply, then consumers are willing to bid up the market price to a level where the quantity demanded is equal to the quantity supplied. Since utility-maximizing consumers must be willing to pay more than $10, then the marginal increase in satisfaction (value) is greater than $10. One way to determine the value of tickets would be to auction off a block of tickets. The highest bid would determine the value of the tickets.

4. Suppose a person allocates a given budget between two goods, food and clothing. If food is an inferior good, can you tell whether clothing is inferior or normal? Explain.

If an individual consumes only food and clothing, then any increase in income must be spent on either food or clothing (Hint: we assume there are no savings). If food is an inferior good, then, as income increases, consumption falls. With constant prices, the extra income not spent on food must be spent on clothing. Therefore, as income increases, more is spent on clothing, i.e. clothing is a normal good.

5. Which of the following combinations of goods are complements and which are substitutes? Could they be either in different circumstances? Discuss.

a.   a mathematics class and an economics class

If the math class and the economics class do not conflict in scheduling, then the classes could be either complements or substitutes. The math class may illuminate economics, and the economics class can motivate mathematics. If the classes conflict, they are substitutes.

b.   tennis balls and a tennis racket

Tennis balls and a tennis racket are both needed to play a game of tennis, thus they are complements.

c.   steak and lobster

Foods can both complement and substitute for each other. Steak and lobster can compete, i.e., be substitutes, when they are listed as separate items on a menu. However, they can also function as complements because they are often served together.

d.   a plane trip and a train trip to the same destination

Two modes of transportation between the same two points are substitutes for one another.

e.   bacon and eggs

Bacon and eggs are often eaten together and are, therefore, complementary goods. By considering them in relation to something else, such as pancakes, bacon and eggs can function as substitutes.

6. Which of the following events would cause a movement along the demand curve for U.S.-produced clothing, and which would cause a shift in the demand curve?

a.   the removal of quotas on the importation of foreign clothes

The removal of quotas will shift the demand curve inward for domestically-produced clothes, because foreign-produced goods are substitutes for domestically-produced goods. Both the equilibrium price and quantity will fall as foreign clothes are traded in a free market environment.

b.   an increase in the income of U.S. citizens

When income rises, expenditures on normal goods such as clothing increase, causing the demand curve to shift out. The equilibrium quantity and price will increase.

c.   a cut in the industry's costs of producing domestic clothes that is passed on to the market in the form of lower clothing prices

A cut in an industry's costs will shift the supply curve out. The equilibrium price will fall and quantity will increase. There is a movement along the demand curve.

7. For which of the following goods is a price increase likely to lead to a substantial income (as well as substitution) effect?

a.   salt

Small Income effect, small substitution effect: The amount of income that is spent on salt is relatively small, but since there are few substitutes for salt, consumers will not readily substitute away from it. As the price of salt rises, real income will fall only slightly, thus leading to a small decline in consumption.

b.   housing

Large income effect, no substitution effect: The amount of income spent on housing is relatively large for most consumers. If the price of housing were to rise, real income would be reduced substantially, thereby reducing the consumption of all other goods. However, consumers would find it impossible to substitute for housing, in general.

c.   theater tickets

Small income effect, large substitution effect: The amount of income that is spent on theater tickets is relatively small, but consumers can substitute away from the theater tickets by choosing other forms of entertainment (e.g., television and movies). As the price of theater tickets rises, real income will fall only slightly, thus leading to a small decline in consumption.

d.   food

Large income effect, no substitution effect: As with housing, the amount of income spent on food is relatively large for most consumers. Price increases for food will reduce real income substantially, thereby reducing the consumption of all other commodities. Although consumers can substitute out of particular foods, they cannot substitute out of food in general.

8. Suppose that the average household in a state consumes 500 gallons of gasoline per year. A 10-cent gasoline tax is introduced, coupled with a $50 annual tax rebate per household. Will the household be better or worse off after the new program is introduced?

If the household does not change its consumption of gasoline, it will be unaffected by the tax-rebate program, because in this case the household pays 0.10*500=$50 in taxes and receives $50 as an annual tax rebate. The two effects would cancel each other out. To the extent that the household reduces its gas consumption through substitution, it must be better off. The new budget line (price change plus rebate) will pass through the old consumption point of 500 gallons of gasoline, and any now affordable bundle which contains less gasoline must be on a higher indifference curve. The household will not choose any bundle with more gasoline because these bundles are all inside the old budget line, and hence are inferior to the bundle with 500 gallons of gas.

9. Which of the following three groups is likely to have the most, and which the least, price-elastic demand for membership in the Association of Business Economists?

a.   students

The major difference among the groups is the level of income. We know that if the consumption of a good constitutes a large percentage of an individual's income, then the demand for the good will be relatively elastic. If we assume that a membership in the Association of Business Economists is likely to be a large expenditure for students, we may conclude that the demand will be relatively elastic for this group.

b.   junior executives

The level of income for junior executives will be larger than that of students, but smaller than that of senior executives. Therefore, the demand for a membership for this group will be less elastic than that of the students but more elastic than that of the senior executives.

c.   senior executives

The high earnings among senior executives will result in a relatively inelastic demand for membership.

EXERCISES

1. The ACME corporation determines that at current prices the demand for its computer chips has a price elasticity of -2 in the short run, while the price elasticity for its disk drives is -1.

a.   If the corporation decides to raise the price of both products by 10 percent, what will happen to its sales? To its sales revenue?

We know the formula for the elasticity of demand is:

$$E_P = \frac{\%\Delta Q}{\%\Delta P}.$$

For computer chips, $E_P = -2$, so a 10 percent increase in price will reduce the quantity sold by 20 percent. For disk drives, $E_P = -1$, so a 10 percent increase in price will reduce sales by 10 percent.

Sales revenue is equal to price times quantity sold. Let $TR_1 = P_1 Q_1$ be revenue before the price change and $TR_2 = P_2 Q_2$ be revenue after the price change.

For computer chips:

$$\Delta TR_{cc} = P_2 Q_2 - P_1 Q_1$$

$$\Delta TR_{cc} = (1.1 P_1)(0.8 Q_1) - P_1 Q_1 = -0.12 P_1 Q_1, \text{ or a 12 percent decline.}$$

For disk drives:

$$\Delta TR_{dd} = P_2 Q_2 - P_1 Q_1$$

$$\Delta TR_{dd} = (1.1 P_1)(0.9 Q_1) - P_1 Q_1 = -0.01 P_1 Q_1, \text{ or a 1 percent decline.}$$

Therefore, sales revenue from computer chips decreases substantially, -12 percent, while the sales revenue from disk drives is almost unchanged, -1 percent. Note that at the point on the demand curve where demand is unit elastic, total revenue is maximized.

b.   Can you tell from the available information which product will generate the most revenue for the firm? If yes, why? If not, what additional information would you need?

No. Although we know the responsiveness of demand to changes in price, we need to know both quantities and prices of the products to determine total sales revenue.

2. Refer to Example 4.3 on the aggregate demand for wheat in 1998. Consider 1996, at which time the domestic demand curve was Q_{DD} = 1560 - 60*P*. The export demand curve, however, was about the same as in 1998, i.e., $Q_{DE}=1544\text{-}176P$. Calculate and draw the aggregate demand curve for wheat in 1996.

Given the domestic demand curve for wheat is Q_{DD} = 1560-60P, we find an intercept of 1560 on the quantity axis and an intercept of $\dfrac{1560}{60} = 26$ on the price axis. The export demand curve for wheat, Q_{DE} = 1544 - 176P, has an intercept of 1544 on the quantity axis and an intercept of $\dfrac{1544}{176} = 8.77$ on the price axis. The total demand curve follows the domestic demand curve between the prices of $26 and $8.77 because the export demand is 0 in this range of prices. At $8.77 and a quantity of approximately 1033.7 = 1560 - (60)(8.77), the total demand curve kinks. As price drops below $8.77, total demand is domestic demand plus export demand, which is the horizontal sum of the two individual demand curves. Between a price of $26 and $8.77 the equation for total demand is Q_T=1560-60P and between a price of $8.77 and zero, the equation for total demand is $Q_T=Q_{DD}+Q_{DE}$=3104-236P. See figure 4.2.

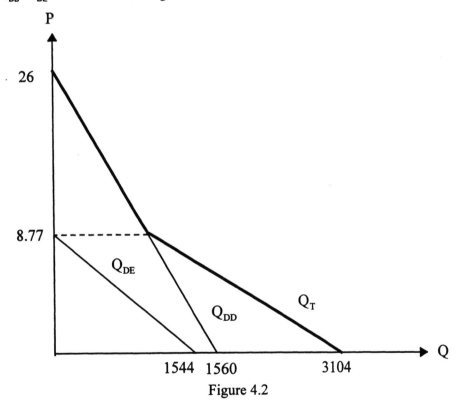

Figure 4.2

3. Judy has decided to allocate exactly $500 to textbooks at college every year, even though she knows that the prices are likely to increase by 5 to 10 percent per year and that she will be getting a substantial monetary gift from her grandparents next year. What is Judy's price elasticity of demand for textbooks? Income elasticity?

> Price elasticity of demand is percentage change in quantity for a given percentage change in price. Judy knows that prices will go up in the future. Given she is going to spend a fixed amount on books, this must mean that her quantity demanded will decrease as price increases. Since expenditure is constant the percentage change in quantity demanded must be equal to the percentage change in price, and price elasticity is -1. Income elasticity must be zero because although she expects a large monetary gift, she has no plans to purchase more books. Recall that income elasticity is defined as the percentage change in quantity demanded for a given percentage change in income, all else the same.

4. Vera has decided to upgrade the operating system on her new PC. She hears that the new Linux operating system is technologically superior to the Windows operating system and substantially lower in price. However, when she asks her friends it turns out they all use PCs with Windows. They agree that Linux is more appealing but add that they see relatively few copies of Linux on sale at the local retail software stores. Based on what she learns and observes, Vera chooses to upgrade her PC with Windows. Can you explain her decision?

> Vera is consuming under the influence of a positive network externality (not a bandwagon effect). When she hears that there are limited software choices that are compatible with the Linux operating system, she decides to go with Windows. If she had not been interested in acquiring much software, she may have gone with Linux. See Example 4.6 in the text. In the future, however, there may be a bandwagon effect, i.e., the purchase of Linux because almost everyone else has it. As more people use Linux, manufacturers might introduce more software that is compatible with the Linux operating system. As the Linux based software section at the local computer store gets larger and larger, this prompts more consumers to purchase Linux. Eventually, the Windows section shrinks as the Linux section becomes larger and larger.

5. Suppose you are in charge of a toll bridge that is essentially cost free. The demand for bridge crossings Q is given by $P = 12 - 2Q$.

a.   Draw the demand curve for bridge crossings.

> See figure 5.4a below.

b.   How many people would cross the bridge if there were no toll?

> At a price of zero, the quantity demanded would be 6.

c.   What is the loss of consumer surplus associated with the charge of a bridge toll of $6?

> The consumer surplus with no toll is equal to $(0.5)(6)(12) = 36$. Consumer surplus with a $6 toll is equal to $(0.5)(3)(6) = 9$, illustrated in Figure 4.4.a. Therefore, the loss of consumer surplus is $27.

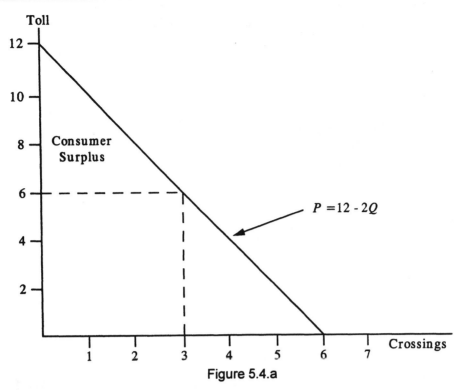

Figure 5.4.a

6.a. Orange juice and apple juice are known to be perfect substitutes. Draw the appropriate price-consumption (for a variable price of orange juice) and income-consumption curves.

We know that the indifference curves for perfect substitutes will be straight lines. In this case, the consumer will always purchase the cheaper of the two goods. If the price of orange juice is less than that of apple juice, the consumer will purchase only orange juice and the price consumption curve will be on the "orange juice axis" of the graph. If apple juice is cheaper, the consumer will purchase only apple juice and the price consumption curve will be on the "apple juice axis." If the two goods have the same price, the consumer will be indifferent between the two; the price consumption curve will coincide with the indifference curve. See Figure 4.6.a.i.

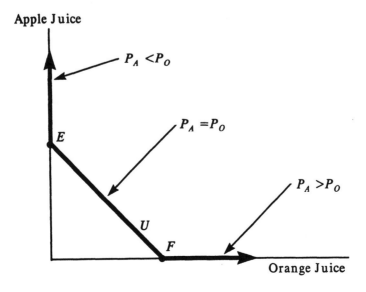

Figure 4.6.a.i

Assuming that the price of orange juice is less than the price of apple juice, the consumer will maximize her utility by consuming only orange juice. As the level of income varies, only the amount of orange juice varies. Thus, the income consumption curve will be the "orange juice axis" in Figure 4.6.a.ii.

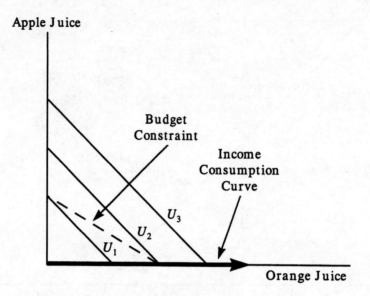

Figure 4.6.a.ii

5.b. Left shoes and right shoes are perfect complements. Draw the appropriate price-consumption and income-consumption curves.

For goods that are perfect complements, such as right shoes and left shoes, we know that the indifference curves are *L*-shaped. The point of utility maximization occurs when the budget constraints, L_1 and L_2 touch the kink of U_1 and U_2. See Figure 4.6.b.i.

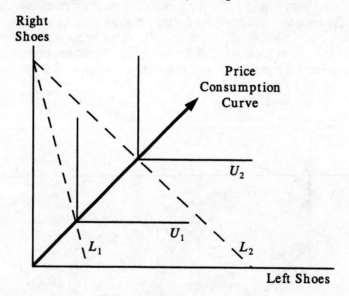

Figure 4.6.b.i

In the case of perfect complements, the income consumption curve is a line through the corners of the *L*-shaped indifference curves. See Figure 4.6.b.ii.

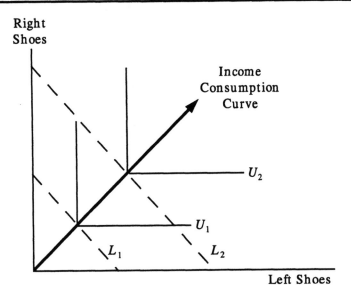

Figure 4.6.b.ii

7. Heather's marginal rate of substitution of movie tickets for rental videos is known to be the same no matter how many rental videos she wants. Draw Heather's income consumption curve and her Engel curve for videos.

If we let the price of movie tickets be less than the price of a video rental, the budget constraint, *L*, will be flatter than the indifference curve for the substitute goods, movie tickets and video rentals. The income consumption curve will be on the "video axis," since she only consumes videos. See Figure 4.7.a.

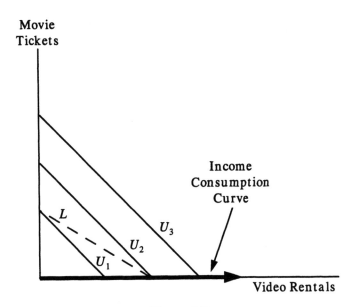

Figure 4.7.a

Heather's Engel curve shows that her consumption of video rentals increases as her income rises, and thus the slope of her Engel curve is equal to the price of a video rental. See Figure 4.7.b.

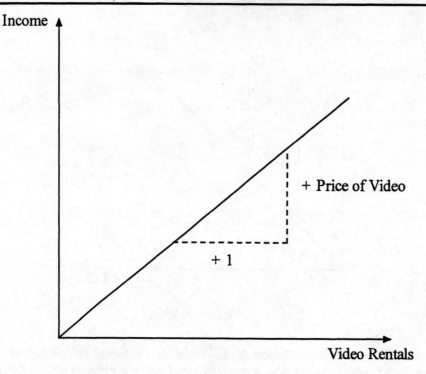

Figure 4.7.b

8. You are managing a $300,000 city budget in which monies are spent on schools and public safety only. You are about to receive aid from the federal government to support a special anti-drug law enforcement program. Two programs that are available are (1) a $100,000 grant that must be spent on law enforcement; and (2) a 100 percent matching grant, in which each dollar of local spending on law enforcement is matched by a dollar of federal money. The federal matching program limits its payment to each city to a maximum of $100,000.

a.   Complete the table below with the amounts available for safety.

SCHOOLS	SAFETY No Govt. Assistance	SAFETY Program (1)	SAFETY Program (2)
$0			
$50,000			
$100,000			
$150,000			
$200,000			
$250,000			
$300,000			

a. **See Table 4.8.a.**

SCHOOLS	SAFETY No Govt. Assistance	SAFETY Program (1)	SAFETY Program (2)
$0	$300,000	$400,000	$400,000
$50,000	$250,000	$350,000	$350,000
$100,000	$200,000	$300,000	$300,000
$150,000	$150,000	$250,000	$250,000
$200,000	$100,000	$200,000	$200,000
$250,000	$50,000	$150,000	$100,000
$300,000	$0	$100,000	$0

Table 4.8.a

b. **Which program would you (the manager) choose if you wish to maximize the satisfaction of the citizens if you allocate $50,000 of the $300,000 to schools? What about $250,000?**

With $50,000 to schools and $250,000 to law enforcement, both aid programs yield the same amount, $100,000, so you are indifferent between the programs. With $250,000 to schools and $50,000 to law enforcement, program (1) yields $100,000 (for a total of $150,000) and program (2) yields $50,000 (for a total of $100,000), so you prefer program (1).

c. **Draw the budget constraints for the three options: no aid, program (1), or program (2).**

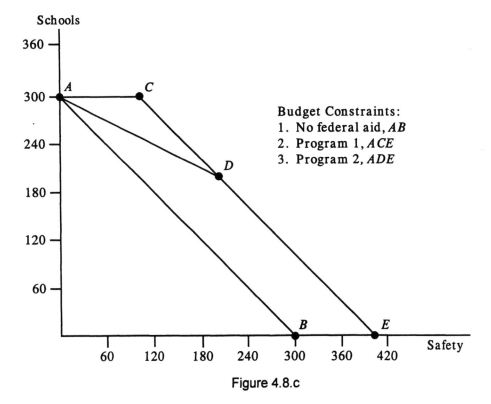

Figure 4.8.c

With no aid, the budget constraint is the line segment *AB*, from $300,000 for schools and nothing for law enforcement to $300,000 for law enforcement and nothing for schools. With program (1), the budget constraint, *ACE*, has two line segments, one parallel to the horizontal axis, until expenditures on safety equal $100,000, and a second sloping downward until $400,000 is spent on safety. With program (2), the budget constraint, *ADE*, has two line segments, one from ($0, $300,000) to ($200,000, $200,000) and another from ($200,000, $200,000) to ($400,000, $0).

9. By observing an individual's behavior in the situations outlined below, determine the relevant income elasticities of demand for each good (i.e., whether the good is normal or inferior). If you cannot determine the income elasticity, what additional information might you need?

a.   Bill spends all his income on books and coffee. He finds $20 while rummaging through a used paperback bin at the bookstore. He immediately buys a new hardcover book of poetry.

Books are a normal good since his consumption of books increases with income. Coffee is a normal or neutral good since consumption of coffee did not fall when income increased.

b.   Bill loses $10 he was going to use to buy a double espresso. He decides to sell his new book at a discount to his friend and use the money to buy coffee.

Coffee is clearly a normal good.

c.   Being bohemian becomes the latest teen fad. As a result, coffee and book prices rise by 25 percent. Bill lowers his consumption of both goods by the same percentage.

Books and coffee are both normal goods since his response to a decline in real income is to decrease consumption of both goods.

d.   Bill drops out of art school and gets an M.B.A. instead. He stops reading books and drinking coffee. Now he reads *The Wall Street Journal* and drinks bottled mineral water.

His tastes have changed completely, and we do not know why. We could use more information regarding his level of income, his desire for sleep, and maybe even a change in political affiliation.

10. Suppose the income elasticity of demand for food is 0.5, and the price elasticity of demand is -1.0. Suppose also that Felicia spends $10,000 a year on food, and that the price of food is $2 and her income is $25,000.

a.   If a $2 sales tax on food were to cause the price of food to double, what would happen to her consumption of food? (*Hint*: Since a large price change is involved, you should assume that the price elasticity measures an arc elasticity, rather than a point elasticity.)

The price of food doubles from $2 to $4, so arc elasticity should be used:

$$E_P = \left(\frac{\Delta Q}{\Delta P}\right)\left(\frac{\frac{P_1 + P_2}{2}}{\frac{Q_1 + Q_2}{2}}\right).$$

We know that $E_P = -1$, $P = 2$, $\Delta P = 2$, and Q=5000. We also know that Q_2, the new quantity, is $Q + \Delta Q$. Thus, if there is no change in income, we may solve for ΔQ:

$$-1 = \left(\frac{\Delta Q}{2}\right)\left(\frac{\frac{2+4}{2}}{\frac{5,000 + (5,000 + \Delta Q)}{2}}\right).$$

By cross-multiplying and rearranging terms, we find that $\Delta Q = -2,500$. This means that she decreases her consumption of food from 5,000 to 2,500 units.

b. **Suppose that she is given a tax rebate of $5,000 to ease the effect of the tax. What would her consumption of food be now?**

A tax rebate of $5,000 implies an income increase of $5,000. To calculate the response of demand to the tax rebate, use the definition of the arc elasticity of income.

$$E_I = \left(\frac{\Delta Q}{\Delta I}\right)\left(\frac{\frac{I_1 + I_2}{2}}{\frac{Q_1 + Q_2}{2}}\right).$$

We know that $E_I = 0.5$, $I = 25,000$, $\Delta I = 5,000$, $Q = 2,500$ (from the answer to 10.a). Assuming no change in price, we solve for ΔQ.

$$0.5 = \left(\frac{\Delta Q}{5,000}\right)\left(\frac{\frac{25,000 + 30,000}{2}}{\frac{2,500 + (2,500 + \Delta Q)}{2}}\right).$$

By cross-multiplying and rearranging terms, we find that $\Delta Q = 238$ (approximately). This means that she increases her consumption of food from 2,500 to 2,738 units.

c. **Is she better or worse off when given a rebate equal to the sales tax payments? Discuss.**

We want to know if her original indifference curve lies above or below her final indifference curve after the sales tax and after the tax rebate. On her final indifference curve, she chooses to consume 2,738 units of food (for $10,952) and $19,048 of other goods. Was this combination attainable with her original budget? At the original food price of $2, this combination would have cost her (2,738)($2) + $19,048 = $24,524, thus leaving her an extra $476 to spend on either food or other consumption. Therefore, she would have been better off before the sales tax and tax rebate. She could have purchased more of both food and other goods than she could have after the taxes.

11. Suppose that you are the consultant to an agricultural cooperative that is deciding whether members should cut their production of cotton in half next year. The cooperative wants your advice as to whether this will increase the farmers' revenues. Knowing that cotton (C) and watermelons (W) both compete for agricultural land in the South, you estimate the demand for cotton to be:

C=3.5-1.0P_C+0.25P_W+0.50I,

where P_C is the price of cotton, P_W the price of watermelon, and I income. Should you support or oppose the plan? Is there any additional information that would help you to provide a definitive answer?

If production of cotton is cut in half, then the price of cotton will increase, given that we see from the equation above that demand is downward sloping. With price increasing and quantity demanded decreasing, revenue could go either way. It depends on whether demand is inelastic or elastic at the current price. If demand is inelastic then a decrease in production and an increase in price could increase revenue. If demand is elastic then a decrease in production and an increase in price will clearly decrease revenue. You need to know the current price and/or quantity demanded to figure out the current level of elasticity.

CHAPTER 4
INDIVIDUAL AND MARKET DEMANDS, APPENDIX

EXERCISES

1. Which of the following utility functions are consistent with convex indifference curves, and which are not?

a.   **U(X, Y) = 2X + 5Y**

b.   **U(X, Y) = (XY)$^{0.5}$**

c.   **U(X, Y) = Min(X, Y), where Min is the minimum of the two values of X and Y**

The three utility functions are presented in Figures 4A.1.a, 4A.1.b, and 4A.1.c. The first may be represented as a series of straight lines; the second as a series of hyperbolas; and the third as a series of "*L*'s." Only the second utility function meets the definition of a strictly convex shape.

To graph the indifference curves which represent the preferences given by U(X,Y)=2X+5Y, set utility to some given level U_0 and solve for Y to get

$$Y = \frac{U_0}{5} - \frac{2}{5}X.$$

Since this is the equation for a straight line, the indifference curves are linear with intercept $\frac{U_0}{5}$ and slope $-\frac{2}{5}$.

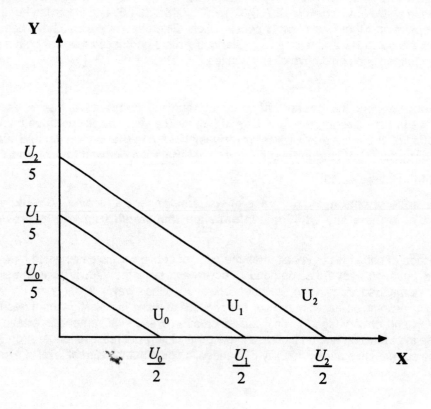

Figure 4A.1.a

To graph the indifference curves which represent the preferences given by $U(X,Y) = (XY)^{0.5}$, set utility to some given level U_0 and solve for Y to get

$$Y = \frac{U_0^2}{X}.$$

By plugging in a few values for X and solving for Y, you will be able to graph the indifference curve U_0, which is illustrated in Figure 4A.1.b, along with the indifference curve U_1.

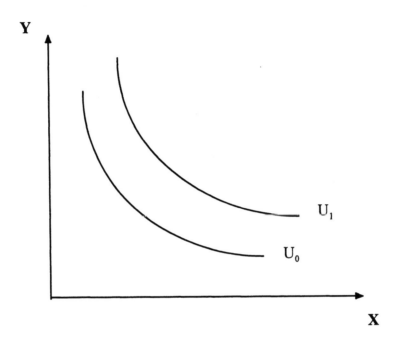

Figure 4A.1.b

To graph the indifference curves which represent the preferences given by $U(X,Y) = Min(X,Y)$, first note that utility functions of this form result in indifference curves which are L-shaped and represent a complementary relationship between X and Y. In this case, for any given level of utility U_0, the value of X and Y will also be equal to U_0. As X increases and Y does not change, utility will also not change. If both X and Y change, then utility will change and we will move to a different indifference curve. See the following table.

X	Y	U
10	10	10
10	11	10
10	9	9
11	10	10
9	10	9
9	9	9

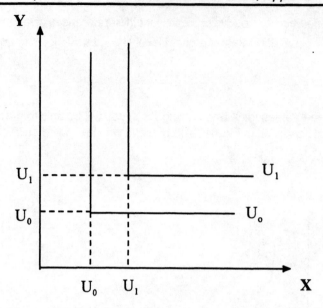

Figure 4A.1.c

2. Show that two utility functions given below generate the identical demand functions for goods X and Y:

a.   **U(X, Y) = log(X) + log(Y)**

b.   **U(X, Y) = (XY)⁰·⁵**

The Appendix discusses how to derive demand functions from utility functions. If we show that the two utility functions are equivalent, then we know that the demand functions derived from them are identical. We may show their equivalence by identifying a suitable transformation from one set of numbers into another set without changing their order.

Taking the logarithm of $U(X, Y) = (XY)^{0.5}$ we obtain:

$$\log U(X, Y) = 0.5\log(X) + 0.5\log(Y).$$

Now multiply both sides by 2:

$$2(\log U(X,Y) = \log(X) + \log(Y).$$

Therefore, the two utility functions are equivalent and will yield identical demand functions. However, we will solve for the demand functions in both cases to show that they are the same.

a. To find the demand functions for X and Y, corresponding to $U(X, Y) = \log(X) + \log(Y)$, given the usual budget constraint, write the Lagrangian:

$$\Phi = \log(X) + \log(Y) - \lambda(P_X X + P_Y Y - I)$$

Differentiating with respect to X, Y, λ, and setting the derivatives equal to zero:

$$\frac{\partial \Phi}{\partial X} = \frac{1}{X} - \lambda P_X = 0$$

$$\frac{\partial \Phi}{\partial Y} = \frac{1}{Y} - \lambda P_Y = 0$$

$$\frac{\partial \Phi}{\partial \lambda} = P_X X + P_Y Y - I = 0.$$

56

The first two conditions imply that $P_X X = \dfrac{1}{\lambda}$ and $P_Y Y = \dfrac{1}{\lambda}$.

The third condition implies that $\dfrac{1}{\lambda} + \dfrac{1}{\lambda} - I = 0$, or $\lambda = \dfrac{2}{I}$.

Substituting this expression into $P_X X = \dfrac{I}{\lambda}$ and $P_Y Y = \dfrac{I}{\lambda}$ gives the demand functions:

$$X = \left(\dfrac{0.5}{P_X}\right) I^2 \quad \text{and} \quad Y = \left(\dfrac{0.5}{P_Y}\right) I^2$$

Notice that the demand for each good depends only on the price of that good and on income, not on the price of the other good.

b. To find the demand functions for X and Y, corresponding to $U(X,Y) = (XY)^{0.5}$ given the usual budget constraint, first write the Lagrangian:

$$\Phi = 0.5(\log X) + (1 - 0.5)\log Y - \lambda(P_X X + P_Y Y - I)$$

Differentiating with respect to X, Y, λ and setting the derivatives equal to zero:

$$\dfrac{\partial \Phi}{\partial X} = \dfrac{0.5}{X} - \lambda P_X = 0$$

$$\dfrac{\partial \Phi}{\partial Y} = \dfrac{0.5}{Y} - \lambda P_Y = 0$$

$$\dfrac{\partial \Phi}{\partial \lambda} = P_X X + P_Y Y = 0.$$

The first two conditions imply that $P_X X = \dfrac{0.5}{\lambda}$ and $P_Y Y = \dfrac{0.5}{\lambda}$.

Combining these with the budget constraint gives: $\dfrac{0.5}{\lambda} + \dfrac{0.5}{\lambda} - I = 0$ or $\lambda = \dfrac{1}{I}$.

Now substituting this expression into $P_X X = \dfrac{0.5}{\lambda}$ and $P_Y Y = \dfrac{0.5}{\lambda}$ gives the demand functions:

$$X = \left(\dfrac{0.5}{P_X}\right) I \quad \text{and} \quad Y = \left(\dfrac{0.5}{P_Y}\right) I.$$

3. Assume that a utility function is given by Min(X, Y), as in Exercise 1(c). What is the Slutsky equation that decomposes the change in the demand for X in response to a change in its price? What is the income effect? What is the substitution effect?

The Slutsky equation is $\dfrac{\Delta X}{\Delta P_X} = \left.\dfrac{\Delta X}{\Delta P_X}\right|_{U=U^\bullet} - X\left(\dfrac{\Delta X}{\Delta I}\right)$,

where the first term represents the substitution effect and the second term represents the income effect. Because there is no substitution as prices change with this type of utility function, the substitution effect is zero. The income effect is the shift from U_1 to U_2.

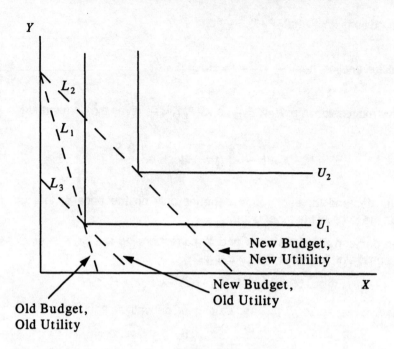

Figure 4A.3

4. Sharon has the following utility function:

$$U(X,Y) = \sqrt{X} + \sqrt{Y}$$

where X is her consumption of candy bars, with price P_X=\$1, and Y is her consumption of espressos, with P_Y=\$3.

    a. Derive Sharon's demand for candy bars and espressos.

Using the Lagrangian method, the Lagrangian equation is

$$\Phi = \sqrt{X} + \sqrt{Y} - \lambda(P_X X + P_Y Y - I).$$

To find the demand functions, we need to maximize the Lagrangian equation with respect to X, Y, and λ, which is the same as maximizing utility subject to the budget constraint. The necessary conditions for a maximum are

(1) $\dfrac{\partial \Phi}{\partial X} = \dfrac{1}{2} X^{-\frac{1}{2}} - P_X \lambda = 0$

(2) $\dfrac{\partial \Phi}{\partial Y} = \dfrac{1}{2} Y^{-\frac{1}{2}} - P_Y \lambda = 0$

(3) $\dfrac{\partial \Phi}{\partial \lambda} = P_X X + P_Y Y - I = 0.$

Combining necessary conditions (1) and (2) results in

$$\lambda = \frac{1}{2P_X\sqrt{X}} = \frac{1}{2P_Y\sqrt{Y}}$$

$$P_X X^{\frac{1}{2}} = P_Y Y^{\frac{1}{2}}$$

(4) $\quad X = \left(\frac{P_Y^2}{P_X^2}\right) Y.$

You can now substitute (4) into (3) and solve for Y. Once you have solved for Y, you can substitute Y back into (4) and solve for X. Note that algebraically there are several ways to solve this type of problem, and that it does not have to be done exactly as we have done here. The demand functions are

$$Y = \frac{P_X I}{P_Y^2 + P_Y P_X} \text{ or } Y = \frac{I}{12}$$

$$X = \frac{P_Y I}{P_X^2 + P_Y P_X} \text{ or } X = \frac{3I}{4}.$$

b. Assume that her income I=\$100. How many candy bars and espressos will Sharon consume?

Substitute the values for the two prices and income into the demand functions to find that she consumes X=75 candy bars and Y=8.3 espressos.

c. What is the marginal utility of income?

From part a $\lambda = \frac{1}{2P_X\sqrt{X}} = \frac{1}{2P_Y\sqrt{Y}}$. Substitute into either part of the equation to find

that λ=0.058. This is how much utility would increase by if Sharon had one more dollar to spend.

CHAPTER 5
CHOICE UNDER UNCERTAINTY

TEACHING NOTES

Choice under uncertainty is an important topic in microeconomic theory, but students find the concept difficult. The topic should be covered in business-oriented courses, particularly if you intend to cover the role of risk in capital markets, which is discussed in Chapter 15. The primary purpose of this chapter is to encourage students to think about the influence on behavior of attitudes toward risk. The first three sections of the chapter should be covered in at least two lectures, giving the students time to absorb the basic ideas.

If students have not been previously exposed to probability, expected value, and variance, they will have difficulty with this chapter, particularly with Exercises (1) through (5), which illustrate these concepts. Most students without a background in probability consider risk to be the possibility of loss or injury, instead of the probability of either loss or gain. Make sure they understand this distinction before further discussing uncertainty.

If students have had basic probability theory before and you have covered utility theory, they should easily grasp the definition of expected utility. However, they usually confuse the utility of an expected value with expected utility. Both concepts are needed to explain risk aversion in general and the subtleties of Exercise (7) in particular. For an empirical analysis of gambling, see Selby and Beranek, "Sweepstake Contests: Analysis, Strategies, and Survey," *American Economic Review* (March 1981) and Brunk, "A Test of the Friedman-Savage Gambling Model," *Quarterly Journal of Economics* (May 1981). In a more theoretical class, present the derivation of the Von Neumann-Morgenstern utility function. See Copeland and Weston's discussion of utility theory under uncertainty in Chapter 4, *Financial Theory and Corporate Policy* (Addison-Wesley, 1979).

Even if your students have not fully understood the technical aspects of choice under uncertainty, they should easily comprehend Examples 5.1 and 5.2 (the latter example leads to Exercise (8), which is easier than it looks). This is also true of the topics presented in Section 5.3, i.e., diversification and purchasing insurance and Examples 5.3 and 5.4. Also, you might mention the problems of adverse selection and moral hazard in insurance, to be discussed in Chapter 17.

The last section, 5.4, is more difficult and may be postponed until after the class has completed the discussion of risk and rates of return in Chapter 15.

REVIEW QUESTIONS

1. What does it mean to say that a person is risk averse? Why are some people likely to be risk averse, while others are risk lovers?

A risk-averse person has a diminishing marginal utility of income and prefers a certain income to a gamble with the same expected income. A risk lover has an increasing marginal utility of income and prefers an uncertain income to a certain income. The economic explanation of whether an individual is risk averse or risk loving depends on the shape of the individual's utility function for wealth. Also, a person's risk aversion (or risk loving) depends on the nature of the risk involved and on the person's income.

2. Why is the variance a better measure of variability than the range?

Range is the difference between the highest possible outcome and the lowest possible outcome. Range does not indicate the probabilities of observing these high or low outcomes. Variance weighs the difference of each outcome from the mean outcome by its probability and, thus, is a more useful measure of variability than the range.

3. What does it mean for consumers to maximize expected utility? Can you think of a case where a person might not maximize expected utility?

The expected utility is the sum of the utilities associated with all possible outcomes, weighted by the probability that each outcome will occur. To maximize expected utility means that the individual chooses the option that yields the highest average utility, where average utility is a probability-weighted sum of all utilities. This theory requires that the consumer knows the probability of every outcome. At times, consumers either do not know the relevant probabilities or have difficulty in evaluating low-probability, high-payoff events. In some cases, consumers cannot assign a utility level to these high-payoff events, such as when the payoff is the loss of the consumer's life.

4. Why do people want to fully insure against uncertain situations when insurance is actuarially fair?

If the cost of insurance is equal to the expected loss, (i.e., if the insurance is actuarially fair), risk-averse individuals will fully insure against monetary loss. The insurance premium assures the individual of having the *same income* regardless of whether or not a loss occurs. Because the insurance is actuarially fair, this certain income is equal to the *expected* income if the individual takes the risky option of not purchasing insurance. This guarantee of the same income, whatever the outcome, generates *more utility* for a risk-averse person than the average utility of a high income when there was no loss and the utility of a low income with a loss (i.e., because of risk aversion, $E[U(x)] \le U(E[x])$.

5. Why is an insurance company likely to behave *as if* it is risk neutral even if its managers are risk-averse individuals? (Hint: How many projects are insured by an entire insurance company? How many does each individual manager deal with?)

Most large companies have opportunities for diversifying risk. Managers acting for the owners of a company choose a portfolio of independent, profitable projects at different levels of risk. Of course, shareholders may diversify their risk by investing in several projects in the same way that the insurance company itself diversifies risk by insuring many people. By operating on a sufficiently large scale, insurance companies can assure themselves that over many outcomes the total premiums paid to the company will be equal to the total amount of money paid out to compensate the losses of the insured. Thus, the insurance company behaves as if it is risk neutral, while the managers, as individuals, might be risk averse.

6. When is it worth paying to obtain more information to reduce uncertainty?

Individuals are willing to pay more for information when the utility of the choice with more information, including the cost of gathering the information, is greater than the expected utility of the choice without the information.

7. How does the diversification of an investor's portfolio avoid risk?

An investor reduces risk by investing in many inversely related assets. For example, a mutual fund is a portfolio of stocks of independent companies. If the variance of the return on one company's stock is inversely related to the variance of the return on another company's stock, a portfolio of both stocks will have a lower variance than either stock held separately. As the number of stocks increases, the variance in the rate of return on the portfolio as a whole decreases. While there is less risk in a portfolio of stocks, risk is not eliminated altogether; there is still some market risk in holding such a portfolio, compared to a low-risk asset, such as a U.S. government savings bond.

8. Why do some investors put a large portion of their portfolios into risky assets, while others invest largely in risk-free alternatives? (Hint: Do the two investors receive exactly the same return on average? Why?)

In a market for risky assets, where investors are risk averse, investors demand a higher return on investments that have a higher level of risk (a higher variance in returns). Although some individuals are willing to accept a higher level of risk in exchange for a higher rate of return, this does not mean that these individuals are less risk averse. On the contrary, they will not invest in risky assets unless they are compensated for the increased risk.

EXERCISES

1. Consider a lottery with three possible outcomes: $100 will be received with probability .1, $50 with probability .2, and $10 with probability .7.

a.   What is the expected value of the lottery?

The expected value, *EV*, of the lottery is equal to the sum of the returns weighted by their probabilities:

$$EV = (0.1)(\$100) + (0.2)(\$50) + (0.7)(\$10) = \$27.$$

b.   What is the variance of the outcomes of the lottery?

The variance, σ^2, is the sum of the squared deviations from the mean, $27, weighted by their probabilities:

$$\sigma^2 = (0.1)(100 - 27)^2 + (0.2)(50 - 27)^2 + (0.7)(10 - 27)^2 = \$841.$$

c.   What would a risk-neutral person pay to play the lottery?

A risk-neutral person would pay the expected value of the lottery: $27.

2.   Suppose you have invested in a new computer company whose profitability depends on (1) whether the U.S. Congress passes a tariff that raises the cost of Japanese computers and (2) whether the U.S. economy grows slowly or quickly. What are the four mutually exclusive states of the world that you should be concerned about?

The four mutually exclusive states may be represented as:

	Congress passes tariff	Congress does not pass tariff
Slow growth rate	State 1: Slow growth with tariff	State 2: Slow growth without tariff
Fast growth rate	State 3: Fast growth with tariff	State 4: Fast growth without tariff

3. Richard is deciding whether to buy a state lottery ticket. Each ticket costs $1, and the probability of the following winning payoffs is given as follows:

Probability	Return
0.50	$0.00
0.25	$1.00
0.20	$2.00
0.05	$7.50

a.   What is the expected value of Richard's payoff if he buys a lottery ticket? What is the variance?

The expected value of the lottery is equal to the sum of the returns weighted by their probabilities:

$$EV = (0.5)(0) + (0.25)(\$1.00) + (0.2)(\$2.00) + (0.05)(\$7.50) = \$1.025$$

The variance is the sum of the squared deviation from the mean, $1.025, weighted by their probabilities:

$$\sigma^2 = (0.5)(0 - 1.025)^2 + (0.25)(1 - 1.025)^2 + (0.2)(2 - 1.025)^2 + (0.05)(7.5 - 1.025)^2, \text{ or}$$

$$\sigma^2 = \$2.812.$$

b. **Richard's nickname is "No-risk Rick." He is an extremely risk-averse individual. Would he buy the ticket?**

An extremely risk-averse individual will probably not buy the ticket, even though the expected outcome is higher than the price, $1.025 > $1.00. The difference in the expected return is not enough to compensate Rick for the risk. For example, if his wealth is $10 and he buys a $1.00 ticket, he would have $9.00, $10.00, $11.00, and $16.50, respectively, under the four possible outcomes. Let us assume that his utility function is $U = W^{0.5}$, where W is his wealth. Then his expected utility is:

$$EU = (0.5)(9^{0.5}) + (0.25)(10^{0.5}) + (0.2)(11^{0.5}) + (0.05)(16.5^{0.5}) = 3.157.$$

This is less than 3.162, which is the utility associated with not buying the ticket ($U(10) = 10^{0.5} = 3.162$). He would prefer the sure thing, i.e., $10.

c. **Suppose Richard was offered insurance against losing any money. If he buys 1,000 lottery tickets, how much would he be willing to pay to insure his gamble?**

If Richard buys 1,000 tickets, it is likely that he will have $1,025 minus the $1,000 he paid, or $25. He would not buy any insurance, as the expected return, $1,025, is greater than the cost, $1,000. He has insured himself by buying a large number of tickets. Given that Richard is risk averse though, he may still want to buy insurance. The amount he would be willing to pay is equal to the risk premium which is the amount of money that Richard would pay to avoid the risk. See figure 5.4 in the text. To calculate the risk premium, you need to know the utility function. If the utility function is $U = W^{0.5}$, then his expected utility from the 1,000 lottery tickets is

$$EU = (0.5)(0^{0.5}) + (0.25)(1000^{0.5}) + (0.2)(2000^{0.5}) + (0.05)(7500^{0.5}) = 21.18.$$

This is less than the utility he would get from keeping his $1000 which is $U=1000^{0.5}=31.62$. To find the risk premium, find the level of income that would guarantee him a utility of 21.18, which is $448.59. This means he would pay $1000-$448.59=$551.41 to insure his gamble.

d. **In the long run, given the price of the lottery ticket and the probability/return table, what do you think the state would do about the lottery?**

In the long run, the state lottery will be bankrupt! Given the price of the ticket and the probabilities, the lottery is a money loser. The state must either raise the price of a ticket or lower the probability of positive payoffs.

4. Suppose an investor is concerned about a business choice in which there are three prospects, whose probability and returns are given below:

Probability	Return
0.2	$100
0.4	50
0.4	-25

What is the expected value of the uncertain investment? What is the variance?

The expected value of the return on this investment is

$$EV = (0.2)(100) + (0.4)(50) + (0.4)(-25) = $30.$$

The variance is

$$\sigma^2 = (0.2)(100 - 30)^2 + (0.4)(50 - 30)^2 + (0.4)(-25 - 30)^2 = $2,350.$$

5. You are an insurance agent who has to write a policy for a new client named Sam. His company, Society for Creative Alternatives to Mayonnaise (SCAM), is working on a low-fat, low-cholesterol mayonnaise substitute for the sandwich condiment industry. The sandwich industry will pay top

dollar to whoever invents such a mayonnaise substitute first. Sam's SCAM seems like a very risky proposition to you. You have calculated his possible returns table as follows.

Probability	Return	
.999	-$1,000,000	(he fails)
.001	$1,000,000,000	(he succeeds and sells the formula)

a.   What is the expected return of his project? What is the variance?

The expected return, *ER*, of the investment is

$$ER = (0.999)(-1,000,000) + (0.001)(1,000,000,000) = \$1,000.$$

The variance is

$$\sigma^2 = (0.999)(-1,000,000 - 1,000)^2 + (0.001)(1,000,000,000 - 1,000)^2 \text{, or}$$

$$\sigma^2 = 1,000,998,999,000,000.$$

b.   What is the most Sam is willing to pay for insurance? Assume Sam is risk neutral.

Because Sam is risk neutral and because the expected outcome is $1,000, Sam is unwilling to buy insurance.

c.   Suppose you found out that the Japanese are on the verge of introducing their own mayonnaise substitute next month. Sam does not know this and has just turned down your final offer of $1,000 for the insurance. If Sam tells you his SCAM is only six months away from perfecting his mayonnaise substitute *and* knowing what you know about the Japanese, would you raise or lower your policy premium on any subsequent proposal to Sam? Based on his information, would Sam accept?

The entry of the Japanese lowers Sam's probability of a high payoff. For example, assume that the probability of the billion dollar payoff is lowered to zero. Then the expected outcome is:

$$(1.0)(-\$1,000,000) + (0.0)((\$1,000,000,000) = -\$1,000,000.$$

Therefore, you should raise the policy premium substantially. But Sam, not knowing about the Japanese entry, will continue to refuse your offers to insure his losses.

6. Suppose that Natasha's utility function is given by u(I) = I$^{0.5}$, where I represents annual income in thousands of dollars.

a.   Is Natasha risk loving, risk neutral, or risk averse? Explain.

Natasha is risk averse. To show this, assume that she has $10,000 and is offered a gamble of a $1,000 gain with 50 percent probability and a $1,000 loss with 50 percent probability. Her utility of $10,000 is 3.162, ($u(I) = 10^{0.5} = 3.162$). Her expected utility is:

$$EU = (0.5)(9^{0.5}) + (0.5)(11^{0.5}) = 3.158 < 3.162.$$

She would avoid the gamble. If she were risk neutral, she would be indifferent between the $10,000 and the gamble; whereas, if she were risk loving, she would prefer the gamble.

You can also see that she is risk averse by plotting the function for a few values (see Figure 5.6) and noting that it displays a diminishing marginal utility. (Or, note that the second derivative is negative, again implying diminishing marginal utility.)

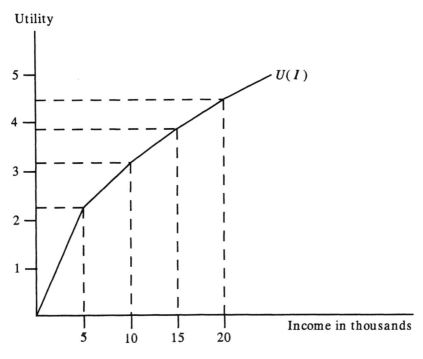

Figure 5.6

b. **Suppose that Natasha is currently earning an income of $10,000 (I = 10) and can earn that income next year with certainty. She is offered a chance to take a new job that offers a .5 probability of earning $16,000, and a .5 probability of earning $5,000. Should she take the new job?**

The utility of her current salary is $10^{0.5}$, which is 3.162. The expected utility of the new job is

$$EU = (0.5)(5^{0.5}) + (0.5)(16^{0.5}) = 3.118,$$

which is less than 3.162. Therefore, she should not take the job.

c. **In (b), would Natasha be willing to buy insurance to protect against the variable income associated with the new job? If so, how much would she be willing to pay for that insurance? (Hint: What is the risk premium?)**

Assuming that she takes the new job, Natasha would be willing to pay a risk premium equal to the difference between $10,000 and the utility of the gamble so as to ensure that she obtains a level of utility equal to 3.162. We know the utility of the gamble is equal to 3.118. Substituting into her utility function we have, $3.118 = I^{0.5}$, and solving for I we find the income associated with the gamble to be $9,722. Thus, Natasha would be willing to pay for insurance equal to the risk premium, $10,000 - $9,722 = $278.

7. Draw a utility function over income u(I) that has the property that a man is a risk lover when his income is low but a risk averter when his income is high. Can you explain why such a utility function might reasonably describe a person's tastes?

Consider an individual who needs a certain level of income, I^*, in order to stay alive. An increase in income above I^* will have a diminishing marginal utility. Below I^*, the individual will be a risk lover and will take unfair gambles in an effort to make large gains in income. Above I^*, the individual will purchase insurance against losses.

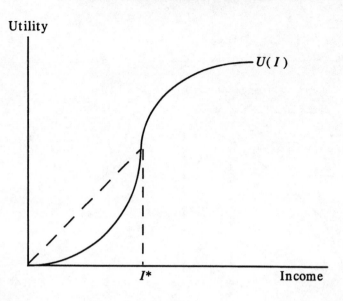

Figure 5.7

8. A city is considering how much to spend monitoring parking meters. The following information is available to the city manager:

> **i.   Hiring each meter-monitor costs $10,000 per year.**
>
> **ii.   With one monitoring person hired, the probability of a driver getting a ticket each time he or she parks illegally is equal to .25.**
>
> **iii.   With two monitors hired, the probability of getting a ticket is .5, with three monitors the probability is .75, and with four the probability is equal to 1.**
>
> **iv.   The current fine for overtime parking with two metering persons hired is $20.**

a.   Assume first that all drivers are risk-neutral. What parking fine would you levy and how many meter monitors would you hire (1, 2, 3, or 4) to achieve the current level of deterrence against illegal parking at the minimum cost?

If drivers are risk neutral, their behavior is only influenced by the expected fine. With two meter-monitors, the probability of detection is 0.5 and the fine is $20. So, the expected fine is $10 = (0.5)($20). To maintain this expected fine, the city can hire one meter-monitor and increase the fine to $40, or hire three meter-monitors and decrease the fine to $13.33, or hire four meter-monitors and decrease the fine to $10.

If the only cost to be minimized is the cost of hiring meter-monitors, i.e., $10,000 per year, you as the city manager, should minimize the number of meter-monitors. Hire only one monitor and increase the fine to $40 to maintain the current level of deterrence.

b.   Now assume that drivers are very risk averse. How would your answer to (a) change?

If drivers are risk averse, their utility of a certain outcome is greater than their utility of an expected value equal to the certain outcome. They will avoid the possibility of paying a parking fine more than would risk-neutral drivers. Therefore, a fine of less than $40 will maintain the current level of deterrence.

c.   (For discussion) What if drivers could insure themselves against the risk of parking fines? Would it make good public policy to allow such insurance to be available?

Drivers engage in many forms of behavior to insure themselves against the risk of parking fines, such as parking blocks away from their destination in a non-metered spot or taking public transportation. A private insurance firm could offer an insurance policy to pay fines if a ticket is received. Of course, the premium for such insurance would be based on each driver's probability of receiving a parking ticket and on the opportunity cost of providing service. (Note: full insurance leads to moral hazard problems, to be discussed in Chapter 17.)

Public policy should attempt to maximize the difference between the benefits and costs to all parties. Private insurance may not be optimal, because of the increase in transactions costs. Instead, as the city manager, consider offering another form of insurance, e.g., the selling of parking stickers, and give tickets for inappropriately parked cars.

9. A moderately risk-averse investor has 50 percent of her portfolio invested in stocks and 50 percent invested in risk-free Treasury bills. Show how each of the following events will affect the investor's budget line and the proportion of stocks in her portfolio:

a. The standard deviation of the return on the stock market increases, but the expected return on the stock market remains the same.

From section 5.4, the equation for the budget line is

$$R_p = \left[\frac{R_m - R_f}{\sigma_m}\right]\sigma_p + R_f,$$

where R_p is the expected return on the portfolio, R_m is the expected return on the risky asset, R_f is the expected return on the risk-free asset, σ_m is the standard deviation of the return on the risky asset, and σ_p is the standard deviation of the return on the portfolio. The budget line shows the positive relationship between the return on the portfolio, R_p, and the standard deviation of the return on the portfolio, σ_p.

In this case, if the standard deviation of the return on the stock market increases, σ_m, the slope of the budget line will change and the budget line will become flatter. At any given level of portfolio return, there is now a higher standard deviation associated with that level of return. You would expect the proportion of stocks in the portfolio to fall.

b. The expected return on the stock market increases, but the standard deviation of the stock market remains the same.

In this case, if the expected return on the stock market increases, R_m, then the slope of the budget line will change and the budget line will become steeper. At any given level of standard deviation of return, σ_p, there is now a higher level of return, R_p. You would expect the proportion of stocks in the portfolio to rise.

c. The return on risk-free Treasury bills increases.

In this case there is an increase in R_f. The budget line will pivot and shift, or in other words will shift up and become flatter. The proportion of stocks in the portfolio could go either way. On the one hand, Treasury bills now have a higher return and so are more attractive. On the other hand, the investor can now earn a higher return from each Treasury bill so could hold fewer Treasury bills and still maintain the same return in terms of the total flow or payment from the Treasury bills. In this second case, the investor may be willing to place more of his savings into the riskier asset. It will depend on the particular preferences of the investor, as well as the magnitude of the returns to the two assets. An analogy would be to consider what happens to savings when the interest rate increases. On the one hand it goes up because the return is higher, but on the other hand it can go down because a person can save less each period and still come out with the same accumulation of savings at some future date.

CHAPTER 6
PRODUCTION

TEACHING NOTES

Chapter 6 is the first of the three chapters which present the basic theory of supply. It may be beneficial to first review, or summarize, the derivation of demand and present an overview of the theory of competitive supply. The review can be beneficial given the similarities between the theory of demand and the theory of supply. Students often find that the theory of supply is easier to understand because it is less abstract, and the concepts are more familiar. This in turn can improve the students' understanding of the theory of demand when they go back and review it again.

In this chapter it is important to take the time to carefully go through the definitions, as this will be the foundation for what is done in the next two chapters. While the concept of a production function is not difficult, the mathematical and graphical representation can sometimes be confusing. It helps to take the time to do as many examples as you have time for. When describing and graphing the production function with output on the vertical axis and one input on the horizontal axis, point out that the production function is the equation for the boundary of the production set, and hence defines the highest level of output for any given level of inputs. Technical efficiency is assumed throughout the discussion of the theory of supply. At any time you can introduce a discussion of the importance of improving productivity and the concept of learning by doing. Examples 1 and 2 in the text are also good for discussion.

Graphing the production function leads naturally to a discussion of marginal product and diminishing returns. Emphasize that diminishing returns exist because some factors are fixed by definition, and that diminishing returns does not mean negative returns. If you have not discussed marginal utility, now is the time to make sure that the student knows the difference between average and marginal. An example that captures students' attention is the relationship between average and marginal test scores. If their latest mid-term grade is greater than their average grade to date, this will increase their average.

Though isoquants are defined in the first section of the chapter, they are examined in more detail in the last section of the chapter. Rely on the students' understanding of indifference curves when discussing isoquants, and point out that as with indifference curves, isoquants are a two-dimensional representation of a three-dimensional production function. Key concepts in this last section of the chapter are the marginal rate of technical substitution and returns to scale. Do as many concrete examples as you have time for to help explain these two important concepts. Examples 6.3 and 6.4 help to give concrete meaning to *MRTS* and returns to scale.

REVIEW QUESTIONS

1. What is a production function? How does a long-run production function differ from a short-run production function?

A production function represents how inputs are transformed into outputs by a firm. We focus on the firm with one output and aggregate all inputs or factors of production into one of several categories, such as labor, capital, and materials. In the short run, one or more factors of production cannot be changed. As time goes by, the firm has the opportunity to change the levels of all inputs. In the long-run production function, all inputs are variable.

2. Why is the marginal product of labor likely to increase and then decline in the short run?

When additional units of labor are added to a fixed quantity of capital, we see the marginal product of labor rise, reach a maximum, and then decline. The marginal product of labor increases because, as the first workers are hired, they may specialize in those tasks in which they have the greatest ability. Eventually, with the quantity of capital fixed, the workplace becomes congested and the productivity of additional workers declines.

3. Diminishing returns to a single factor of production and constant returns to scale are not inconsistent. Discuss.

Diminishing returns to a single factor are observable in all production processes at some level of inputs. This fact is so pervasive that economists have named it the "law of diminishing marginal productivity." By definition, the marginal product of an input is the additional output generated by employing one more unit of the input, all other inputs held fixed. The extra output, or returns, to the single input diminish because all other inputs are held fixed. For example, when holding the level of capital constant, each additional unit of labor has less capital to work with.

Unlike the returns to a single factor, returns to scale are proportional increases in *all* inputs. While each factor by itself exhibits diminishing returns, output may more than double, less than double, or exactly double when all the inputs are doubled. The distinction again is that with returns to scale, all inputs are increased in the same proportion and no input is held fixed.

4. You are an employer seeking to fill a vacant position on an assembly line. Are you more concerned with the average product of labor or the marginal product of labor for the last person hired? If you observe that your average product is just beginning to decline, should you hire any more workers? What does this situation imply about the marginal product of your last worker hired?

In filling a vacant position, you should be concerned with the marginal product of the last worker hired because the marginal product measures the effect on output, or total product, of hiring another worker. This in turn will help to determine the revenue generated by hiring another worker, which can then be compared to the cost of hiring another worker.

The point at which the average product begins to decline is the point where average product is equal to marginal product. Although adding more workers results in a further decline in average product, total product continues to increase, so it may still be advantageous to hire another worker.

When average product declines, the marginal product of the last worker hired is lower than the average product of previously hired workers.

5. Faced with constantly changing conditions, why would a firm ever keep *any* factors fixed? What determines whether a factor is fixed or variable?

Whether a factor is fixed or variable depends on the time horizon in consideration: all factors are fixed in the very short run; all factors are variable in the long run. As stated in the text: "All fixed inputs in the short run represent outcomes of previous long-run decisions based on firms' estimates of what they could profitably produce and sell." Some factors are fixed in the short run, whether the firm likes it or not, simply because it takes time to adjust the level of the variables. For example, the firm may be legally bound by a lease on a building, some employees may have contracts that must be upheld, or construction of a new facility may take some number of months. Recall that the short run is not defined as a specific number of months or years, but as that period of time where some inputs cannot be changed for reasons such as those given above.

6. How does the curvature of an isoquant relate to the marginal rate of technical substitution?

The isoquant identifies all the combinations of the two inputs which can produce the same level of output. The curvature of the isoquant is measured by the slope of the isoquant at any given point. The slope of the isoquant measures the rate at which the two inputs can be exchanged and still keep output constant, and this rate is called the marginal rate of technical substitution. Along the typical "bowed-in" or convex isoquant, the marginal rate of technical substitution diminishes as you move down along the isoquant.

7. Can a firm have a production function that exhibits increasing returns to scale, constant returns to scale, and decreasing returns to scale as output increases? Discuss.

Most firms have production functions that exhibit first increasing, then constant, and ultimately decreasing returns to scale. At low levels of output, a proportional increase in all inputs may lead to a larger-than-proportional increase in output, based on an increase in the opportunity for each factor to specialize. For example, if there are now two people and two computers, each person can specialize by completing those tasks that they are best at, which allows output to more than double. As the firm grows, the opportunities for specialization may diminish and a doubling of all inputs will lead to only a doubling of output. When there are constant returns to scale, the firm is replicating what it is already doing. At some level of production, the firm will be so large that when inputs are doubled, output will less than double, a situation that can arise from management diseconomies.

8. Give an example of a production process in which the short run involves a day or a week and the long run any period longer than a week.

Any small business where one input requires more than a week to change would be an example. The process of hiring more labor, which requires announcing the position, interviewing applicants, and negotiating terms of employment, can take a day, if done through a temporary employment agency. Usually, however, the process takes a week or more. Expansion, requiring a larger location, will also take longer than a week.

EXERCISES

---

1. Suppose a chair manufacturer is producing in the short run when equipment is fixed. The manufacturer knows that as the number of laborers used in the production process increases from 1 to 7, the number of chairs produced changes as follows: 10, 17, 22, 25, 26, 25, 23.

a. Calculate the marginal and average product of labor for this production function.

The average product of labor, AP_L, is equal to $\frac{Q}{L}$. The marginal product of labor, MP_L, is equal to $\frac{\Delta Q}{\Delta L}$, the change in output divided by the change in labor input. For this production process we have:

L	Q	AP_L	MP_L
0	0	—	—
1	10	10	10
2	17	8 1/2	7
3	22	7 1/3	5
4	25	6 1/4	3
5	26	5 1/5	1
6	25	4 1/6	-1
7	23	3 2/7	-2

b. Does this production function exhibit diminishing returns to labor? Explain.

This production process exhibits diminishing returns to labor. The marginal product of labor, the extra output produced by each additional worker, diminishes as workers are added, and is actually negative for the sixth and seventh workers.

c. Explain intuitively what might cause the marginal product of labor to become negative.

Labor's negative marginal product for $L > 5$ may arise from congestion in the chair manufacturer's factory. Since more laborers are using the same, fixed amount of capital, it is possible that they could get in each other's way, decreasing efficiency and the amount of output.

2. Fill in the gaps in the table below.

Quantity of Variable Input	Total Output	Marginal Product of Variable Input	Average Product of Variable Input
0	0	—	—
1	150		
2			200
3		200	
4	760		
5		150	
6			150

Quantity of Variable Input	Total Output	Marginal Product of Variable Input	Average Product of Variable Input
0	0	—	—
1	150	150	150
2	400	250	200
3	600	200	200
4	760	160	190
5	910	150	182
6	900	-10	150

3. A political campaign manager has to decide whether to emphasize television advertisements or letters to potential voters in a reelection campaign. Describe the production function for campaign votes. How might information about this function (such as the shape of the isoquants) help the campaign manager to plan strategy?

The output of concern to the campaign manager is the number of votes. The production function uses two inputs, television advertising and direct mail. The use of these inputs requires knowledge of the substitution possibilities between them. If the inputs are perfect substitutes, the resultant isoquants are line segments, and the campaign manager will use only one input based on the relative prices. If the inputs are not perfect substitutes, the isoquants will have a convex shape. The campaign manager will then use a combination of the two inputs.

4. A firm has a production process in which the inputs to production are perfectly substitutable in the long run. Can you tell whether the marginal rate of technical substitution is high or low, or is further information necessary? Discuss.

The marginal rate of technical substitution, MRTS, is the absolute value of the slope of an isoquant. If the inputs are perfect substitutes, the isoquants will be linear. To calculate the slope of the isoquant, and hence the MRTS, we need to know the rate at which one input may be substituted for the other.

5. The marginal product of labor is known to be greater than the average product of labor at a given level of employment. Is the average product increasing or decreasing? Explain.

If the marginal product of labor, MP_L, is greater than the average product of labor, AP_L, then each additional unit of labor is more productive than the average of the previous units.

71

Therefore, by adding the last unit, the overall average increases. If MP_L is greater than AP_L, then AP_L is increasing. If the MP_L is lower than the AP_L, then the last unit reduces the average. The AP_L is at a maximum when the productivity of the last unit is equal to the average of the previous units (i.e., when $MP_L = AP_L$).

6. The marginal product of labor in the production of computer chips is 50 chips per hour. The marginal rate of technical substitution of hours of labor for hours of machine-capital is 1/4. What is the marginal product of capital?

The marginal rate of technical substitution is defined at the ratio of the two marginal products. Here, we are given the marginal product of labor and the marginal rate of technical substitution. To determine the marginal product of capital, substitute the given values for the marginal product of labor and the marginal rate of technical substitution into the following formula:

$$\frac{MP_L}{MP_K} = MRTS, \text{ or } \frac{50}{MP_K} = \frac{1}{4}, \text{ or}$$

$MP_K = 200$ computer chips per hour.

7. Do the following production functions exhibit decreasing, constant or increasing returns to scale?

a.   Q = 0.5KL

Returns to scale refers to the relationship between output and proportional increases in all inputs. This concept may be represented in the following manner, where λ represents a proportional increase in inputs:

$F(\lambda K, \lambda L) > \lambda F(K, L)$ implies increasing returns to scale;

$F(\lambda K, \lambda L) = \lambda F(K, L)$ implies constant returns to scale; and

$F(\lambda K, \lambda L) < \lambda F(K, L)$ implies decreasing returns to scale.

Therefore, we can substitute λK for K and λL for L, and check the result against an equal increase in Q.

$$Q^* = 0.5(\lambda K)(\lambda L) = (0.5KL)\lambda^2 = Q\lambda^2 > \lambda Q$$

This production function exhibits increasing returns to scale.

b.   Q = 2K + 3L

$$Q^* = 2(\lambda K) + 3(\lambda L) = (2K + 3L)\lambda = Q\lambda = \lambda Q.$$

This production function exhibits constant returns to scale.

8. The production function for the personal computers of DISK, Inc., is given by

$Q = 10K^{0.5}L^{0.5}$, where Q is the number of computers produced per day, K is hours of machine time, and L is hours of labor input. DISK's competitor, FLOPPY, Inc., is using the production function $Q = 10K^{0.6}L^{0.4}$.

a.   If both companies use the same amounts of capital and labor, which will generate more output?

Let Q be the output of DISK, Inc., Q_2, be the output of FLOPPY, Inc., and X be the same equal amounts of capital and labor for the two firms. Then, according to their production functions,

$$Q = 10X^{0.5}X^{0.5} = 10X^{(0.5+0.5)} = 10X$$

and

$$Q_2 = 10X^{0.6}X^{0.4} = 10X^{(0.6+0.4)} = 10X.$$

Because $Q = Q_2$, both firms generate the same output with the same inputs. Note that if the two firms both used the same amount of capital and the same amount of labor, but the amount of capital was not equal to the amount of labor, then the two firms would not produce the same level of output. In fact, if K>L then Q_2>Q.

b.   **Assume that capital is limited to 9 machine hours but labor is unlimited in supply. In which company is the marginal product of labor greater? Explain.**

With capital limited to 9 machine units, the production functions become $Q = 30L^{0.5}$ and $Q_2 = 37.37L^{0.4}$. To determine the production function with the highest marginal productivity of labor, consider the following table:

L	Q Firm 1	MP_L Firm 1	Q Firm 2	MP_L Firm 2
0	0.0	—	0.00	—
1	30.00	30.00	37.37	37.37
2	42.43	12.43	49.31	11.94
3	51.96	9.53	58.00	8.69
4	60.00	8.04	65.07	7.07

For each unit of labor above 1, the marginal productivity of labor is greater for the first firm, DISK, Inc.

9. In Example 6.3, wheat is produced according to the production function

$Q = 100(K^{0.8}L^{0.2})$.

a.   **Beginning with a capital input of 4 and a labor input of 49, show that the marginal product of labor and the marginal product of capital are both decreasing.**

For fixed labor and variable capital:

$K = 4 \Rightarrow Q = (100)(4^{0.8})(49^{0.2}) = 660.21$

$K = 5 \Rightarrow Q = (100)(5^{0.8})(49^{0.2}) = 789.25 \Rightarrow MP_K = 129.04$

$K = 6 \Rightarrow Q = (100)(6^{0.8})(49^{0.2}) = 913.19 \Rightarrow MP_K = 123.94$

$K = 7 \Rightarrow Q = (100)(7^{0.8})(49^{0.2}) = 1,033.04 \Rightarrow MP_K = 119.85.$

For fixed capital and variable labor:

$L = 49 \Rightarrow Q = (100)(4^{0.8})(49^{0.2}) = 660.21$

$L = 50 \Rightarrow Q = (100)(4^{0.8})(50^{0.2}) = 662.89 \Rightarrow MP_L = 2.68$

$L = 51 \Rightarrow Q = (100)(4^{0.8})(51^{0.2}) = 665.52 \Rightarrow MP_L = 2.63$

$L = 52 \Rightarrow Q = (100)(4^{0.8})(52^{0.2}) = 668.11 \Rightarrow MP_L = 2.59.$

Notice that the marginal products of both capital and labor are decreasing as the variable input increases.

b.   **Does this production function exhibit increasing, decreasing, or constant returns to scale?**

Constant (increasing, decreasing) returns to scale imply that proportionate increases in inputs lead to the same (more than, less than) proportionate increases in output. If we were to increase labor and capital by the same proportionate amount (λ) in this production function, output would change by the same proportionate amount:

$$\lambda Q = 100(\lambda K)^{0.8}(\lambda L)^{0.2}, \text{ or}$$

$$\lambda Q = 100K^{0.8}L^{0.2}\lambda^{(0.8+0.2)} = Q\lambda$$

Therefore, this production function exhibits constant returns to scale.

CHAPTER 7
THE COST OF PRODUCTION

TEACHING NOTES

The key topics in this chapter are

- accounting versus economic costs of production,

- definitions of total, average, and marginal cost in the short run and long run,

- a graphical representation of total, average, and marginal cost, and

- cost minimization, graphically in the chapter, and mathematically in the appendix.

It is important to distinguish between accounting and economic costs so that students will understand that zero (economic) profit is a feasible long run equilibrium. It is important to spend time on the cost curve definitions and graph because they form the foundation for what will be covered in chapter 8 (firm supply). The cost minimization problem is useful for explaining which inputs the firm should use to produce a given quantity of output, and this discussion draws on the discussion of isoquants from chapter 6. It is also possible at this point to discuss the basic concept of hiring inputs until the wage is equal to the marginal revenue product of the input (chapter 14). The chapter also contains three sections which can be covered as special topics (production with two outputs, dynamic changes in costs, and estimating cost), or can be skipped altogether.

Opportunity cost forms the conceptual base of this chapter. While most students think of costs in accounting terms, they must develop an understanding of the distinction between accounting, economic, and opportunity costs. One source of confusion is the opportunity cost of capital, i.e., why the rental rate on capital must be considered explicitly by economists. It is important, for example, to distinguish between the purchase price of capital equipment and the opportunity cost of using the equipment. The opportunity cost of a person's time also leads to some confusion for students.

Following the discussion of opportunity cost, the chapter diverges in two directions: one path introduces types of cost and cost curves, and the other focuses on cost minimization. Both directions converge with the discussion of long-run average cost.

While the definitions of total cost, fixed cost, average cost, and marginal cost and the graphical relationships between them can seem tedious and/or uninteresting to the student, both are important in terms of understanding the derivation of the firm's supply curve in chapter 8. Doing algebraic or numerical examples in table form is helpful for some students in terms of seeing the relationships between the different costs. Explain that each firm has a unique set of cost curves based on its own particular production function and resulting total cost function. Discuss the importance of returns to scale and diminishing returns in explaining the shapes of the cost curves. Point out the clear rules that average cost tends to be u-shaped in the short run and marginal cost will hit average cost and average variable cost at their respective minimum points. Once you have successfully developed the cost curve graph, you can then take it and address the questions of finding the profit maximizing level of output and deriving the firm, and hence industry, supply curve.

The cost minimization problem is useful for addressing a different type of question, namely what quantity of the inputs should the firm use to produce a given level of output. Point out to students that the necessary condition for cost minimization, where the ratio of the marginal products is equal to the ratio of the input costs, is very similar to the necessary condition for profit maximization.

A clear understanding of short-run cost and cost minimization is necessary for the derivation of long-run average cost. With long-run costs, stress that firms are operating on short-run cost curves at each level of the fixed factor and that long-run costs do not exist separately from short-run costs. Exercise (6) illustrates the relationship between long-run cost and cost minimization, with an emphasis on the importance of the expansion path. Stress the connection between the shape of a long-run cost curve and returns to scale.

REVIEW QUESTIONS

1. A firms pays its accountant an annual retainer of $10,000. Is this an explicit or implicit cost?

Explicit costs are actual outlays. They include all costs that involve a monetary transaction. An implicit cost is an economic cost that does not necessarily involve a monetary transaction, but still involves the use of resources. When a firm pays an annual retainer of $10,000, there is a monetary transaction. The accountant trades his or her time in return for money. Therefore, an annual retainer is an explicit cost.

2. The owner of a small retail store does her own accounting work. How would you measure the opportunity cost of her work?

Opportunity costs are measured by comparing the use of a resource with its alternative uses. The opportunity cost of doing accounting work is the time *not spent in other ways*, i.e., time such as running a small business or participating in leisure activity. The economic cost of doing accounting work is measured by computing the monetary amount that the time would be worth in its *next best use*.

3. Suppose a chair manufacturer finds that the marginal rate of technical substitution of capital for labor in his production process is substantially greater than the ratio of the rental rate on machinery to the wage rate for assembly-line labor. How should he alter his use of capital and labor to minimize the cost of production?

To minimize cost, the manufacturer should use a combination of capital and labor so the rate at which he can trade capital for labor in his production process is the same as the rate at which he can trade capital for labor in external markets. The manufacturer would be better off if he increased his use of capital and decreased his use of labor, decreasing the marginal rate of technical substitution, *MRTS*. He should continue this substitution until his *MRTS* equals the ratio of the rental rate to the wage rate.

4. Why are isocost lines straight lines?

The isocost line represents all possible combinations of labor and capital that may be purchased for a given total cost. The slope of the isocost line is the ratio of the input prices of labor and capital. If input prices are fixed, then the ratio of these prices is clearly fixed and the isocost line is straight. Only when the ratio or factor prices change as the quantities of inputs change is the isocost line not straight.

5. If the marginal cost of production is increasing, does this tell you whether the average variable cost is increasing or decreasing? Explain.

Marginal cost can be increasing while average variable cost is either increasing or decreasing. If marginal cost is less (greater) than average variable cost, then each additional unit is adding less (more) to total cost than previous units added to the total cost, which implies that the *AVC* declines (increases). Therefore, we need to know whether marginal cost is greater than average variable cost to determine whether the *AVC* is increasing or decreasing.

6. If the marginal cost of production is greater than the average variable cost, does this tell you whether the average variable cost is increasing or decreasing? Explain.

If the average variable cost is increasing (decreasing), then the last unit produced is adding more (less) to total variable cost than the previous units did, on average. Therefore, marginal cost is above (below) average variable cost. If marginal cost is above average variable cost, average variable cost must be increasing. In order for the average variable cost to rise, the extra cost must come in above the current average variable cost.

7. If the firm's average cost curves are U-shaped, why does its average variable cost curve achieve its minimum at a lower level of output than the average total cost curve?

Total cost is equal to fixed plus variable cost. Average total cost is equal to average fixed plus average variable cost. When graphed, the difference between the *U*-shaped total cost and average variable cost curves is the average fixed cost curve. If fixed cost is greater than zero, the minimum of average variable cost must be less than the minimum average total cost. In addition, since average fixed cost continues to fall as more output is produced, average total cost will continue to fall even after average variable cost has reached its minimum because the drop in average fixed cost exceeds the increase in the average variable cost. Eventually, the fall in average fixed cost becomes small enough so that the rise in average variable cost causes average total cost to begin to rise.

8. If a firm enjoys increasing returns to scale up to a certain output level, and then constant returns to scale, what can you say about the shape of the firm's long-run average cost curve?

When the firm experiences increasing returns to scale, its long-run average cost curve is downward sloping. When the firm experiences constant returns to scale, its long-run average cost curve is horizontal. If the firm experiences increasing returns to scale, then constant returns to scale, its long-run average cost curve falls, then becomes horizontal.

9. How does a change in the price of one input change the firm's long-run expansion path?

The expansion path describes the combination of inputs that the firm chooses to minimize cost for every output level. This combination depends on the ratio of input prices: if the price of one input changes, the price ratio also changes. For example, if the price of an input increases, less of the input can be purchased for the same total cost, and the intercept of the isocost line on that input's axis moves closer to the origin. Also, the slope of the isocost line, the price ratio, changes. As the price ratio changes, the firm substitutes away from the now more expensive input toward the cheaper input. Thus, the expansion path bends toward the axis of the now cheaper input.

10. Distinguish between economies of scale and economies of scope. Why can one be present without the other?

Economies of scale refer to the production of *one* good and occur when proportionate increases in all inputs lead to a more-than-proportionate increase in output. Economies of scope refer to the production of *more than one good* and occur when joint output is less costly than the sum of the costs of producing each good or service separately. There is no direct relationship between increasing returns to scale and economies of scope, so production can exhibit one without the other. See Exercise (13) for a case with constant product-specific returns to scale and multiproduct economies of scope.

EXERCISES

1. Assume a computer firm's marginal costs of production are constant at $1,000 per computer. However, the fixed costs of production are equal to $10,000.

a.   Calculate the firm's average variable cost and average total cost curves.

The variable cost of producing an additional unit, marginal cost, is constant at $1,000, so $VC = \$1000Q$, and $AVC = \dfrac{VC}{Q} = \dfrac{\$1,000Q}{Q} = \$1,000$. Average fixed cost is $\dfrac{\$10,000}{Q}$.
Average total cost is the sum of average variable cost and average fixed cost:
$ATC = \$1,000 + \dfrac{\$10,000}{Q}$.

b.   If the firm wanted to minimize the average total cost of production, would it choose to be very large or very small? Explain.

The firm should choose a very large output because average total cost decreases with increase in Q. As Q becomes infinitely large, *ATC* will equal $1,000.

2. If a firm hires a currently unemployed worker, the opportunity cost of utilizing the worker's service is zero. Is this true? Discuss.

From the worker's perspective, the opportunity cost of his or her time is the time not spent in other ways, including time spent in personal or leisure activities. Certainly, the opportunity cost of hiring an unemployed mother of pre-school children is not zero! While it might be difficult to assign a monetary value to the time of an unemployed worker, we can not conclude that it is zero.

From the perspective of the firm, the opportunity cost of hiring the worker is not zero, and the firm could purchase a piece of machinery rather than hiring the worker.

3.a.   Suppose that a firm must pay an annual franchise fee, which is a fixed sum,   independent of whether it produces any output. How does this tax affect the firm's   fixed, marginal, and average costs?

Total cost, TC, is equal to fixed cost, FC, plus variable cost, VC. Fixed costs do not vary with the quantity of output. Because the franchise fee, FF, is a fixed sum, the firm's fixed costs increase by this fee. Thus, average cost, equal to $\dfrac{FC+VC}{Q}$, and average fixed cost, equal to $\dfrac{FC}{Q}$, increase by the average franchise fee $\dfrac{FF}{Q}$. Note that the franchise fee does not affect average variable cost. Also, because marginal cost is the *change* in total cost with the production of an additional unit and because the fee is constant, marginal cost is unchanged.

b.   Now suppose the firm is charged a tax that is proportional to the number of items it produces. Again, how does this tax affect the firm's fixed, marginal, and average   costs?

Let t equal the per unit tax. When a tax is imposed on each unit produced, variable costs increase by tQ. Average variable costs increase by t, and because fixed costs are constant, average (total) costs also increase by t. Further, because total cost increases by t with each additional unit, marginal costs increase by t.

4. A recent issue of *Business Week* reported the following:

> **During the recent auto sales slump, GM, Ford, and Chrysler decided it was cheaper to sell cars to rental companies at a loss than to lay off workers.   That's because closing and reopening plants is expensive, partly because the auto makers' current union contracts obligate them to pay many workers even if they're not working.**
>
> **When the article discusses selling cars "at a loss," is it referring to accounting profit or economic profit? How will the two differ in this case?   Explain briefly.**

When the article refers to the car companies selling at a loss, it is referring to accounting profit. The article is stating that the price obtained for the sale of the cars to the rental companies was less than their <u>accounting</u> cost. Economic profit would be measured by the difference of the price with the opportunity cost of the cars. This opportunity cost represents the market value of all the inputs used by the companies to produce the cars. The article mentions that the car companies must pay workers even if they are not working (and thus producing cars). This implies that the wages paid to these workers are sunk and are thus not part of the opportunity cost of production. On the other hand, the wages would still be included in the accounting costs. These accounting costs would then be higher than the opportunity costs and would make the accounting profit lower than the economic profit.

5. A chair manufacturer hires its assembly-line labor for $22 an hour and calculates that the rental cost of its machinery is $110 per hour. Suppose that a chair can be produced using 4 hours of labor or machinery in any combination. If the firm is currently using 3 hours of labor for each hour of

machine time, is it minimizing its costs of production? If so, why? If not, how can it improve the situation?

If the firm can produce one chair with either four hours of labor or four hours of capital, machinery, or any combination, then the isoquant is a straight line with a slope of -1 and intercept at $K = 4$ and $L = 4$, as depicted in Figure 7.5.

The isocost line, $TC = 22L + 110K$ has a slope of $-\dfrac{22}{110} = -0.2$ when plotted with capital on the vertical axis and has intercepts at $K = \dfrac{TC}{110}$ and $L = \dfrac{TC}{22}$. The cost minimizing point is a corner solution, where $L = 4$ and $K = 0$. At that point, total cost is $88.

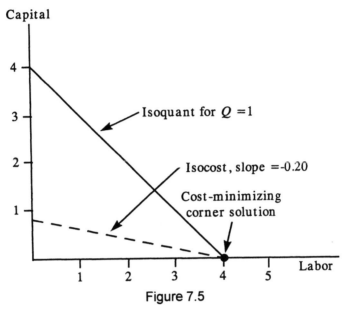

Figure 7.5

6. Suppose the economy takes a downturn, and that labor costs fall by 50 percent and are expected to stay at that level for a long time. Show graphically how this change in the relative price of labor and capital affects the firm's expansion path.

Figure 7.6 shows a family of isoquants and two isocost curves. Units of capital are on the vertical axis and units of labor are on the horizontal axis. (Note: In drawing this figure we have assumed that the production function underlying the isoquants exhibits constant returns to scale, resulting in linear expansion paths. However, the results do not depend on this assumption.)

If the price of labor decreases while the price of capital is constant, the isocost curve pivots outward around its intersection with the capital axis. Because the expansion path is the set of points where the *MRTS* is equal to the ratio of prices, as the isocost curves pivot outward, the expansion path pivots toward the labor axis. As the price of labor falls relative to capital, the firm uses more labor as output increases.

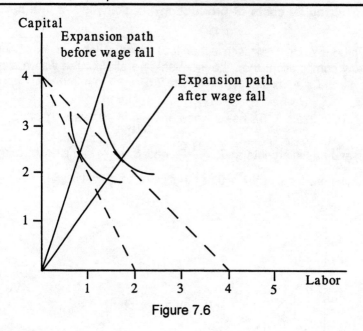

Figure 7.6

7. You are in charge of cost control in a large metropolitan transit district. A consultant you have hired comes to you with the following report:

> Our research has shown that the cost of running a bus for each trip down its line is $30, regardless of the number of passenger's it carries. Each bus can carry 50 people. At rush hour, when the buses are full, the average cost per passenger is 60 cents. However, during off-peak hours, average ridership falls to 18 people and average cost soars to $1.67 per passenger. As a result, we should encourage more rush-hour business when costs are cheaper and discourage off-peak business when costs are higher.

Do you follow the consultant's advice? Discuss.

> The consultant does not understand the definition of average cost. Encouraging ridership always decreases average costs, peak or off-peak. If ridership falls to 10, costs climb to $3.00 per rider. Further, during rush hour, the buses are full. How could more people get on? Instead, encourage passengers to switch from peak to off-peak times, for example, by charging higher prices during peak periods.

8. An oil refinery consists of different pieces of processing equipment, each of which differs in its ability to break down heavy sulfurized crude oil into final products. The refinery process is such that the marginal cost of producing gasoline is constant up to a point as crude oil is put through a basic distilling unit. However, as the unit fills up, the firm finds that in the short run the amount of crude oil that can be processed is limited. The marginal cost of producing gasoline is also constant up to a capacity limit when crude oil is put through a more sophisticated hydrocracking unit. Graph the marginal cost of gasoline production when a basic distilling unit and a hydrocracker are used.

> The production of gasoline involves two steps: (1) distilling crude oil and (2) refining the distillate into gasoline. Because the marginal cost of production is constant up to the capacity constraint for both processes, the marginal cost curves are "mirror" *L*-shapes.

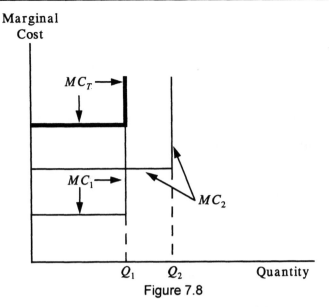

Figure 7.8

Total marginal cost, MC_T, is the sum of the marginal costs of the two processes, i.e., $MC_T = MC_1 + MC_2$, where MC_1 is the marginal cost of distilling crude oil up to the capacity constraint, Q_1, and MC_2 is the marginal cost of refining distillate up to the capacity constraint, Q_2. The shape of the total marginal cost curve is horizontal up to the lower capacity constraint. If the capacity constraint of the distilling unit is lower than that of the hydrocracking unit, MC_T is vertical at Q_1. If the capacity constraint of the hydrocracking unit is lower than that of the distilling unit, MC_T is vertical at Q_2.

9. You manage a plant that mass produces engines by teams of workers using assembly machines. The technology is summarized by the production function.

$$Q = 4\ KL$$

where Q is the number of engines per week, K is the number of assembly machines, and L is the number of labor teams. Each assembly machine rents for r = \$12,000 per week and each team costs w = \$3,000 per week. Engine costs are given by the cost of labor teams and machines, plus \$2,000 per engine for raw materials. Your plant has a fixed installation of 10 assembly machines as part of its design.

a. What is the cost function for your plant — namely, how much would it cost to produce Q engines? What are average and marginal costs for producing Q engines? How do average costs vary with output?

K is fixed at 10. The short-run production function then becomes Q = 40L. This implies that for any level of output Q, the number of labor teams hired will be $L = \dfrac{Q}{40}$. The total cost function is thus given by the sum of the costs of capital, labor, and raw materials:

TC(Q) = rK + wL + 2000Q = (12,000)(10) + (3,000)(Q/40) + 2,000 Q

= 120,000 + 2,075Q

The average cost function is then given by:

AC(Q) = TC(Q)/Q = 120,000/Q + 2,075

and the marginal cost function is given by:

$\partial\,$TC(Q) $/\,\partial\,$Q = 2,075

Marginal costs are constant and average costs will decrease as quantity increases (due to the fixed cost of capital).

b. **How many teams are required to produce 80 engines? What is the average cost per engine?**

To produce Q = 80 engines we need labor teams $L = \dfrac{Q}{40}$ or L=2. Average costs are given by

$$AC(Q) = 120{,}000/Q + 2{,}075 \qquad \text{or} \qquad AC = 3575.$$

c. **You are asked to make recommendations for the design of a new production facility. What would you suggest? In particular, what capital/labor (K/L) ratio should the new plant accommodate? If lower average cost were your only criterion, should you suggest that the new plant have more production capacity or less production capacity that the plant you currently manage?**

We no longer assume that K is fixed at 10. We need to find the combination of K and L which minimizes costs at any level of output Q. The cost-minimization rule is given by

$$\frac{MP_K}{r} = \frac{MP_L}{w}.$$

To find the marginal product of capital, observe that increasing K by 1 unit increases Q by 4L, so MP_K = 4L. Similarly, observe that increasing L by 1 unit increases Q by 4K, so MP_L = 4K. (Mathematically, $MP_K = \dfrac{\partial Q}{\partial K} = 4L$ and $MP_L = \dfrac{\partial Q}{\partial L} = 4K$.) Using these formulas in the cost-minimization rule, we obtain:

$$\frac{4L}{r} = \frac{4K}{w} \Rightarrow \frac{K}{L} = \frac{w}{r} = \frac{3000}{12{,}000} = \frac{1}{4}.$$

The new plant should accommodate a capital to labor ratio of 1 to 4.

The firm's capital-labor ratio is currently 10/2 or 5. To reduce average cost, the firm should either use more labor and less capital to produce the same output or it should hire more labor and increase output.

*10. A computer company's cost function, which relates its average cost of production AC to its cumulative output in thousands of computers CQ and its plant size in terms of thousands of computers produced per year Q, within the production range of 10,000 to 50,000 computers is given by

$$AC = 10 - 0.1CQ + 0.3Q.$$

a. **Is there a learning curve effect?**

The learning curve describes the relationship between the cumulative output and the inputs required to produce a unit of output. Average cost measures the input requirements per unit of output. Learning curve effects exist if average cost falls with increases in cumulative output. Here, average cost decreases as cumulative output, *CQ*, increases. Therefore, there are learning curve effects.

b. **Are there increasing or decreasing returns to scale?**

To measure scale economies, calculate the elasticity of total cost, *TC*, with respect to output, *Q*:

$$E_C = \frac{\dfrac{\Delta TC}{TC}}{\dfrac{\Delta Q}{Q}} = \frac{\dfrac{\Delta TC}{\Delta Q}}{\dfrac{TC}{Q}} = \frac{MC}{AC}.$$

If this elasticity is greater (less) than one, then there are decreasing (increasing) returns to scale, because total costs are rising faster (slower) than output. From average cost we can calculate total and marginal cost:

$$TC = Q(AC) = 10Q - (0.1)(CQ)(Q) + 0.3Q^2, \quad \text{therefore}$$

$$MC = \frac{dTC}{dQ} = 10 - 0.1CQ + 0.6Q .$$

Because marginal cost is greater than average cost (since $0.6Q > 0.3Q$), the elasticity, E_C, is greater than one; there are decreasing returns to scale. The production process exhibits a learning effect and decreasing returns to scale.

c.   **During its existence, the firm has produced a total of 40,000 computers and is producing 10,000 computers this year.   Next year it plans to increase its production to 12,000 computers. Will its average cost of production increase or decrease? Explain.**

First, calculate average cost this year:

$$AC_1 = 10 - 0.1CQ + 0.3Q = 10 - (0.1)(40) + (0.3)(10) = 9.$$

Second, calculate the average cost next year:

$$AC_2 = 10 - (0.1)(50) + (0.3)(12) = 8.6.$$

(Note: Cumulative output has increased from 40,000 to 50,000.)   The average cost will decrease because of the learning effect.

11. The short-run cost function of a company is given by the equation C=190+53Q, where C is the total cost and Q is the total quantity of output, both measured in tens of thousands.

a.   **What is the company's fixed cost?**

When $Q = 0$, $C = 190$, so fixed cost is equal to 190 (or $\$1,900,000$).

b.   **If the company produced 100,000 units of goods, what is its average variable cost?**

With 100,000 units, $Q = 10$. Variable cost is $53Q = (53)(10) = 530$ (or $\$5,300,000$). Average variable cost is $\dfrac{TVC}{Q} = \dfrac{\$530}{10} = \$53$. or $\$530,000$.

c.   **What is its marginal cost *per unit* produced?**

With constant average variable cost, marginal cost is equal to average variable cost, $\$53$ (or $\$530,000$).

d.   **What is its average fixed cost?**

At $Q = 10$, average fixed cost is $\dfrac{TFC}{Q} = \dfrac{\$190}{10} = \$19$ or ($\$190,000$).

e.   **Suppose the company borrows money and expands its factory. Its fixed cost rises by $50,000, but its variable cost falls to $45,000 per 10,000 units. The cost of interest (I) also enters into the equation. Each one-point increase in the interest rate raises costs by $30,000. Write the new cost equation.**

Fixed cost changes from 190 to 195. Variable cost decreases from 53 to 45. Fixed cost also includes interest charges: $3I$. The cost equation is

$$C = 195 + 45Q + 3I.$$

*12. Suppose the long-run total cost function for an industry is given by the cubic equation TC = a + bQ + cQ^2 + dQ^3. Show (using calculus) that this total cost function is consistent with a U-shaped average cost curve for at least some values of a, b, c, d.

To show that the cubic cost equation implies a *U*-shaped average cost curve, we use algebra, calculus, and economic reasoning to place sign restrictions on the parameters of the equation. These techniques are illustrated by the example below.

First, if output is equal to zero, then *TC* = *a*, where *a* represents fixed costs. In the short run, fixed costs are positive, *a* > 0, but in the long run, where all inputs are variable *a* = 0. Therefore, we restrict *a* to be zero.

Next, we know that average cost must be positive. Dividing *TC* by *Q*:

$$AC = b + cQ + dQ^2.$$

This equation is simply a quadratic function. When graphed, it has two basic shapes: a *U* shape and a hill shape. We want the *U* shape, i.e., a curve with a minimum (minimum average cost), rather than a hill shape with a maximum.

To the left of the minimum, the slope should be negative (downward sloping). At the minimum, the slope should be zero, and to the right of the minimum the slope should be positive (upward sloping). The first derivative of the average cost curve with respect to *Q* must be equal to zero at the minimum. For a *U*-shaped *AC* curve, the second derivative of the average cost curve must be positive.

The first derivative is *c* + 2*dQ*; the second derivative is 2*d*. If the second derivative is to be positive, then *d* > 0. If the first derivative is equal to zero, then solving for *c* as a function of *Q* and *d* yields: *c* = -2*dQ*. If *d* and *Q* are both positive, then *c* must be negative: *c* < 0.

To restrict *b*, we know that at its minimum, average cost must be positive. The minimum occurs when *c* + 2*dQ* = 0. We solve for *Q* as a function of *c* and *d*: $Q = -\dfrac{c}{2d} > 0$. Next, substituting this value for *Q* into our expression for average cost, and simplifying the equation:

$$AC = b + cQ + dQ^2 = b + c\left(\frac{-c}{2d}\right) + d\left(\frac{-c}{2d}\right)^2 \text{, or}$$

$$AC = b - \frac{c^2}{2d} + \frac{c^2}{4d} = b - \frac{2c^2}{4d} + \frac{c^2}{4d} = b - \frac{c^2}{4d} > 0.$$

implying $b > \dfrac{c^2}{4d}$. Because $c^2 > 0$ and *d* > 0, *b* must be positive.

In summary, for *U*-shaped long-run average cost curves, *a* must be zero, *b* and *d* must be positive, *c* must be negative, and $4db > c^2$. However, the conditions do not insure that marginal cost is positive. To insure that marginal cost has a *U* shape and that its minimum is positive, using the same procedure, i.e., solving for *Q* at minimum marginal cost $-c/3d$, and substituting into the expression for marginal cost $b + 2cQ + 3dQ^2$, we find that c^2 must be less than 3*bd*. Notice that parameter values that satisfy this condition also satisfy $4db > c^2$, but not the reverse.

For example, let *a* = 0, *b* = 1, *c* = -1, *d* = 1. Total cost is $Q - Q^2 + Q^3$; average cost is $1 - Q + Q^2$; and marginal cost is $1 - 2Q + 3Q^2$. Minimum average cost is *Q* = 1/2 and minimum marginal cost is 1/3 (think of *Q* as dozens of units, so no fractional units are produced). See Figure 7.12.

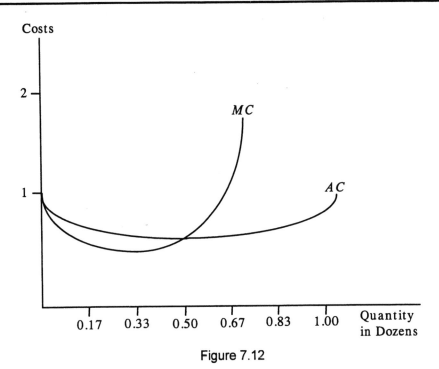

Figure 7.12

*13. A computer company produces hardware and software using the same plant and labor. The total cost of producing computer processing units H and software programs S is given by

$$TC = aH + bS - cHS,$$

where a, b, and c are positive. Is this total cost function consistent with the presence of economies or diseconomies of scale? With economies or diseconomies of scope?

There are two types of scale economies to consider: multiproduct economies of scale and product-specific returns to scale. From Section 7.5 we know that multiproduct economies of scale for the two-product case, $S_{H,S}$, are

$$S_{H,S} = \frac{TC\,(H,S)}{(H)(MC_H) + (S)(MC_S)}$$

where MC_H is the marginal cost of producing hardware and MC_S is the marginal cost of producing software. The product-specific returns to scale are:

$$S_H = \frac{TC\,(H,S) - TC\,(0,S)}{(H)(MC_H)} \quad \text{and}$$

$$S_S = \frac{TC\,(H,S) - TC\,(H,0)}{(S)(MC_S)}$$

where $TC(0,S)$ implies no hardware production and $TC(H,0)$ implies no software production. We know that the marginal cost of an input is the slope of the total cost with respect to that input. Since

$$TC = (a - cS)H + bS = aH + (b - cH)S,$$

we have $MC_H = a - cS$ and $MC_S = b - cH$.

Substituting these expressions into our formulas for $S_{H,S}$, S_H, and S_S:

$$S_{H,S} = \frac{aH + bS - cHS}{H(a - cS) + S(b - cH)} \quad \text{or}$$

85

$$S_{H,S} = \frac{aH + bS - cHS}{Ha + Sb - 2cHS} > 1 \text{, because } cHS > 0. \text{ Also,}$$

$$S_H = \frac{(aH + bS - cHS) - bS}{H(a - cS)} \text{, or}$$

$$S_H = \frac{(aH - cHS)}{H(a - cS)} = \frac{(a - cS)}{(a - cS)} = 1 \text{ and similarly}$$

$$S_S = \frac{(aH + bS - cHS) - aH}{S(b - cH)} = 1.$$

There are multiproduct economies of scale, $S_{H,S} > 1$, but constant product-specific returns to scale, $S_H = S_C = 1$.

Economies of scope exist if $S_C > 0$, where (from equation (7.8) in the text):

$$S_c = \frac{TC(H,0) + TC(0,S) - TC(H,S)}{TC(H,S)} \text{, or,}$$

$$S_c = \frac{aH + bS - (aH + bS - cHS)}{TC(H,S)} \text{, or}$$

$$S_c = \frac{cHS}{TC(H,S)} > 0.$$

Because *cHS* and *TC* are both positive, there are economies of scope.

CHAPTER 7
PRODUCTION AND COST THEORY—
A MATHEMATICAL TREATMENT

EXERCISES

1. Of the following production functions, which exhibit increasing, constant, or decreasing returns to scale?

a. $F(K, L) = K^2 L$

b. $F(K, L) = 10K + 5L$

c. $F(K, L) = (KL)^{0.5}$

Returns to scale refer to the relationship between output and proportional increases in all inputs. This is represented in the following manner:

$F(\lambda K, \lambda L) > \lambda F(K, L)$ implies increasing returns to scale;

$F(\lambda K, \lambda L) = \lambda F(K, L)$ implies constant returns to scale; and

$F(\lambda K, \lambda L) < \lambda F(K, L)$ implies decreasing returns to scale.

a. Applying this to $F(K, L) = K^2 L$,

$$F(\lambda K, \lambda L) = (\lambda K)^2 (\lambda L) = \lambda^3 K^2 L = \lambda^3 F(K, L).$$

This is greater than $\lambda F(K, L)$; therefore, this production function exhibits increasing returns to scale.

b. Applying the same technique to $F(K, L) = 10K + 5L$,

$$F(\lambda K, \lambda L) = 10 \lambda K + 5 \lambda L = \lambda F(K, L).$$

This production function exhibits constant returns to scale.

c. Applying the same technique to $F(K, L) = (KL)^{0.5}$,

$$F(\lambda K, \lambda L) = (\lambda K \, \lambda L)^{0.5} = (\lambda^2)^{0.5} (KL)^{0.5} = \lambda (KL)^{0.5} = \lambda F(K, L).$$

This production function exhibits constant returns to scale.

2. The production function for a product is given by Q = 100KL. If the price of capital is $120 per day and the price of labor $30 per day, what is the minimum cost of producing 1000 units of output?

The cost-minimizing combination of capital and labor is the one where

$$MRTS = \frac{MP_L}{MP_K} = \frac{w}{r}.$$

The marginal product of labor is $\dfrac{dQ}{dL} = 100K$. The marginal product of capital is $\dfrac{dQ}{dK} = 100L$. Therefore, the marginal rate of technical substitution is

$$\frac{100K}{100L} = \frac{K}{L}.$$

To determine the optimal capital-labor ratio set the marginal rate of technical substitution equal to the ratio of the wage rate to the rental rate of capital:

$$\frac{K}{L} = \frac{30}{120}, \text{ or } L = 4K.$$

Substitute for L in the production function and solve where K yields an output of 1,000 units:
$$1,000 = (100)(K)(4K), \text{ or } K = 1.58.$$

Because L equals $4K$ this means L equals 6.32.

With these levels of the two inputs, total cost is:

$$TC = wL + rK, \text{ or}$$

$$TC = (30)(6.32) + (120)(1.58) = \$379.20.$$

To see if $K = 1.58$ and $L = 6.32$ are the cost minimizing levels of inputs, consider small changes in K and L. around 1.58 and 6.32. At $K = 1.6$ and $L = 6.32$, total cost is \$381.60, and at $K = 1.58$ and $L = 6.4$, total cost is \$381.6, both greater than \$379.20. We have found the cost-minimizing levels of K and L.

3. Suppose a production function is given by F(K, L) = KL^2, the price of capital is \$10, and the price of labor \$15. What combination of labor and capital minimizes the cost of producing any given output?

The cost-minimizing combination of capital and labor is the one where

$$MRTS = \frac{MP_L}{MP_K} = \frac{w}{r}.$$

The marginal product of labor is $\frac{dQ}{dL} = 2KL$. The marginal product of capital is $\frac{dQ}{dK} = L^2$.

Set the marginal rate of technical substitution equal to the input price ratio to determine the optimal capital-labor ratio:

$$\frac{2KL}{L^2} = \frac{15}{10}, \text{ or } K = 0.75L.$$

Therefore, the capital-labor ratio should be 0.75 to minimize the cost of producing any given output.

4. Suppose the process of producing light-weight parkas by Polly's Parkas is described by the function:

$$Q = 10K^8(L - 40)^{.2}$$

where Q is the number of parkas produced, K the number of computerized stitching-machine hours, and L the number of person-hours of labor. In addition to capital and labor, \$10 worth of raw materials are used in the production of each parka.

We are given the production function: $Q = F(K,L) = 10K^8(L - 40)^{.2}$

We also know that the cost of production, in addition to the cost of capital and labor, includes \$10 of raw material per unit of output. This yields the following total cost function:

$$TC(Q) = wL + rK + 10Q$$

a. By minimizing cost subject to the production function, derive the cost-minimizing demands for K and L as a function of output (Q), wage rates (w), and rental rates on machines (r). Use these results to derive the total cost function, that is costs as a function of Q, r, w, and the constant \$10 per unit materials cost.

We need to find the combinations of K and L which will minimize this cost function for any given level of output Q and factor prices r and w. To do this, we set up the Lagrangian:

$$\Phi = wL + rK + 10Q - \lambda[10K^{.8}(L-40)^{.2} - Q]$$

Differentiating with respect to K, L, and λ, and setting the derivatives equal to zero:

(1) $$\frac{\partial \Phi}{\partial K} = r - 10\lambda(.8)K^{-.2}(L-40)^{.2} = 0$$

(2) $$\frac{\partial \Phi}{\partial L} = w - 10\lambda K^{.8}(.2)(L-40)^{-.8} = 0$$

(3) $$\frac{\partial \Phi}{\partial \lambda} = 10K^{8}(L-40)^{2} - Q = 0.$$

The first 2 equations imply:

$$r = 10\lambda(.8)K^{-.2}(L-40)^{.2} \quad \text{and} \quad w = 10\lambda K^{.8}(.2)(L-40)^{-.8}.$$

or

$$\frac{r}{w} = \frac{4(L-40)}{K}.$$

This further implies:

$$K = \frac{4w(L-40)}{r} \quad \text{and} \quad L - 40 = \frac{rK}{4w}..$$

Substituting the above equations for K and L-40 into equation (3) yields solutions for K and L:

$$Q = 10\left(\frac{4w}{r}\right)^{.8}(L-40)^{.8}(L-40)^{2} \quad \text{and} \quad Q = 10K^{.8}\left(\frac{rK}{4w}\right)^{.2}.$$

or

$$L = \frac{r^{8}Q}{30.3w^{.8}} + 40 \quad \text{and} \quad K = \frac{w^{2}Q}{7.6r^{.2}}.$$

We can now obtain the total cost function in terms of only r,w, and Q by substituting these cost-minimizing values for K and L into the total cost function:

$$TC(Q) = wL + rK + 10Q$$

$$TC(Q) = \frac{wr^{8}Q}{30.3w^{.8}} + 40w + \frac{rw^{2}Q}{7.6r^{.2}} + 10Q$$

$$TC(Q) = \frac{w^{2}r^{8}Q}{30.3} + 40w + \frac{r^{.8}w^{2}Q}{7.6} + 10Q.$$

b. This process requires skilled workers, who earn \$32 per hour. The rental rate on the machines used in the process is \$64 per hour. At these factor prices, what are total costs as a function of Q? Does this technology exhibit decreasing, constant, or increasing returns to scale?

Given the values w = 32 and r = 64, the total cost function becomes:

TC(Q)=19.2Q+1280.

The average cost function is then given by

AC(Q) = 19.2 + 1280/Q.

To find returns to scale, choose an input combination and find the level of output, and then double all inputs and compare the new and old output levels. Assume K=50 and L=60. Then $Q_1 = 10(50)^{0.8}(60-40)^{0.2} = 416.3$. When K=100 and L=120, $Q_2 = 10(100)^{0.8}(120-40)^{0.2} = 956$. Since $Q_2/Q_1 > 2$, the production function exhibits increasing returns to scale.

c. Polly's Parkas plans to produce 2000 parkas per week. At the factor prices given above, how many workers should the firm hire (at 40 hours per week) and how many machines should it rent (at 40 machines-hours per week)? What are the marginal and average costs at this level of production?

Given Q = 2,000 per week, we can calculate the required amount of inputs K and L using the formulas derived in part a:

$$L = \frac{r^{.8}Q}{30.3w^{.8}} + 40 \quad \text{and} \quad K = \frac{w^{.2}Q}{7.6r^{.2}}.$$

Thus L = 154.9 worker hours and K = 2,000/8.7 = 229.9 machine hours. Assuming a 40 hour week, L = 154.9/40 = 3.87 workers per week, and K = 229.9/40 = 5.74 machines per week. Polly's Parkas should hire 4 workers and rent 6 machines per week.

We know that the total cost and average cost functions are given by:

$$TC(Q) = 19.2Q + 1280$$

$$AC(Q) = 19.2 + 1280/Q,$$

so the marginal cost function is

$$MC(Q) = d\ TC(Q)\ /\ d\ Q = 19.2.$$

Marginal costs are constant at $19.2 per parka and average costs are 19.2+1280/2000 or $19.84 per parka.

CHAPTER 8
PROFIT MAXIMIZATION AND COMPETITIVE SUPPLY

TEACHING NOTES

This chapter identifies the behavioral incentives of the profit-maximizing firm and then explores the interaction of these firms in a competitive market. Each section of the chapter is important and builds a solid understanding of the supply side of the competitive market. It is necessary to build this foundation before moving on to the chapters in part III of the text. While the material in the chapter is written in a very clear, easy to understand manner, students still struggle with many of the concepts related to how the firm should choose the optimal quantity to produce, and how to apply the cost curve diagram learned in the previous chapter. One option for lecture is to spend time working with a table similar to the one used in the exercises at the end of the chapter. Working through many examples with this type of a table can help the students understand the different types of cost, as well as the firm's optimal level of production.

Section 8.1 identifies the three basic assumptions of perfect competition and section 8.2 discusses the assumption of profit maximization as the goal of the firm. Both sections are important in building the foundation for deriving the firm's supply curve, which is done in sections 8.3 to 8.5. Section 8.3 derives the general result that the firm should produce where marginal revenue is equal to marginal cost. The section then goes on to identify perfect competition as a special case where price is equal to marginal revenue, which follows directly from the assumption of price taker behavior in section 8.1. If your students have had calculus, it is helpful to derive the marginal revenue equals marginal cost rule by differentiating the profit function with respect to q. If your students have not had calculus then it is helpful to do some more work with the data tables so they understand that profit is maximized when marginal revenue equals marginal cost. Emphasize that the perfectly competitive firm chooses quantity and not price in order to maximize profit.

To put perfect competition in perspective, it can also be helpful to give a brief overview of monopoly, oligopoly, and monopolistic competition before presenting the assumptions of perfect competition. Restrict this discussion to identifying how many firms are in the industry, are there barriers to entry, is there product differentiation, and what assumptions does each firm make about how the other firms in the industry will react to their price and quantity decisions. This will stimulate the student's interest about upcoming lectures.

Sections 8.4 and 8.5 further explore the firm's decision to produce where price is equal to marginal cost, and show that the firm's supply curve is its marginal cost curve above its average variable cost curve. Although some students will understand references to second-order conditions, expect to be asked why q_0 in Figure 8.3 is not profit maximizing, although $MR = MC$. Two additional points warrant careful explanation: 1) why the firm would remain in business if the firm sustains a loss in the short run, and 2) that maximizing profit is the same as minimizing loss.

Although the summation of firm supply curves into a market supply curve is straightforward, the analysis of long-run competitive equilibrium is difficult. Difficult concepts include:

- why it may be optimal for the firm to incur losses in the short run but not the long run.

- why free entry and exit will reduce economic profit to zero in the long run.

- why price is equal to minimum average cost in the long run.

It can be helpful to present an example, algebraic and graphical, which starts out with only one firm in the industry that is earning positive economic profit, and then show how the market will converge on its long run equilibrium point. Explore changes in price, quantity produced, and the level of profits, and relate the changes to the firm's behavioral motivations.

This chapter introduces two other important topics that will be elaborated on in Chapter 9: producer surplus and economic rent. Students frequently confuse profit, producer surplus, and economic rent.

1. Why would a firm that incurs losses choose to produce rather than shut down?

Losses occur when revenues do not cover total costs. Revenues could be greater than variable costs, but not total costs, in which case the firm is better off producing in the short run rather than shutting down, even though they are incurring a loss. The firm should compare the level of loss with no production to the level of loss with positive production, and pick the option which results in the smallest loss. In the short run, losses will be minimized as long as the firm covers its variable costs. In the long run, all costs are variable, and thus, all costs must be covered if the firm is to remain in business.

2. The supply curve for a firm in the short run is the short-run marginal cost curve (above the point of minimum average variable cost). Why is the supply curve in the long run *not* the long-run marginal cost curve (above the point of minimum average total cost)?

In the short run, a change in the market price induces the profit-maximizing firm to change its optimal level of output. This optimal output occurs when price is equal to marginal cost, as long as marginal cost exceeds average variable cost. Therefore, the supply curve of the firm is its marginal cost curve, above average variable cost. (When the price falls below average variable cost, the firm will shut down.)

In the long run, the firm adjusts its inputs so that its long-run marginal cost is equal to the market price. At this level of output, it is operating on a short-run marginal cost curve where short-run marginal cost is equal to price. As the long-run price changes, the firm gradually changes its mix of inputs to minimize cost. Thus, the long-run supply response is this adjustment from one set of short-run marginal cost curves to another.

Note also that in the long run there will be entry and the firm will earn zero profit, so that any level of output where MC>AC is not possible.

3. In long-run equilibrium, all firms in the industry earn zero economic profit. Why is this true?

The theory of perfect competition explicitly assumes that there are no entry or exit barriers to new participants in an industry. With free entry, positive economic profits induce new entrants. As these firms enter, the supply curve shifts to the right, causing a fall in the equilibrium price of the product. Entry will stop, and equilibrium will be achieved, when economic profits have fallen to zero.

4. What is the difference between economic profit and producer surplus?

While economic profit is the difference between total revenue and total cost, producer surplus is the difference between total revenue and total variable cost. The difference between economic profit and producer surplus is the fixed cost of production.

5. Why do firms enter an industry when they know that in the long run economic profit will be zero?

Firms enter an industry when they expect to earn economic profit. These short-run profits are enough to encourage entry. Zero economic profits in the long run imply *normal* returns to the factors of production, including the labor and capital of the owners of firms. For example, the owner of a small business might experience positive accounting profits before the foregone wages from running the business are subtracted from these profits. If the revenue minus other costs is just equal to what could be earned elsewhere, then the owner is indifferent to staying in business or exiting.

6. At the beginning of the twentieth century, there were many small American automobile manufacturers. At the end of the century, there are only three large ones. Suppose that this situation is not the result of lax federal enforcement of antimonopoly laws. How do you explain the

decrease in the number of manufacturers? (Hint: What is the inherent cost structure of the automobile industry?)

Automobile plants are highly capital-intensive. Assuming there have been no impediments to competition, increasing returns to scale can reduce the number of firms in the long run. As firms grow, their costs decrease with increasing returns to scale. Larger firms are able to sell their product for a lower price and push out smaller firms in the long run. Increasing returns may cease at some level of output, leaving more than one firm in the industry.

7. Industry X is characterized by perfect competition, so every firm in the industry is earning zero economic profit. If the product price falls, no firms can survive. Do you agree or disagree? Discuss.

Disagree. As the market price falls, firms cut their production. If price falls below average total cost, firms continue to produce in the short run and cease production in the long run. If price falls below average variable costs, firms cease production in the short run. Therefore, with a small decrease in price, i.e., less than the difference between the price and average variable cost, the firm can survive. With larger price decrease, i.e., greater than the difference between price and minimum average cost, the firm cannot survive. In general, we would expect that some firms will survive and that just enough firms will leave to bring profit back up to zero.

8. An increase in the demand for video films also increases the salaries of actors and actresses. Is the long-run supply curve for films likely to be horizontal or upward sloping? Explain.

The long-run supply curve depends on the cost structure of the industry. If there is a fixed supply of actors and actresses, as more films are produced, higher salaries must be offered. Therefore, the industry experiences increasing costs. In an increasing-cost industry, the long-run supply curve is upward sloping. Thus, the supply curve for videos would be upward sloping.

9. True or false: A firm should always produce at an output at which long-run average cost is minimized. Explain.

False. In the long run, under perfect competition, firms should produce where average costs are minimized. The long-run average cost curve is formed by determining the minimum cost at every level of output. In the short run, however, the firm might not be producing the optimal long-run output. Thus, if there are any fixed factors of production, the firm does not always produce where long-run average cost is minimized.

10. Can there be constant returns to scale in an industry with an upward-sloping supply curve? Explain.

Constant returns to scale imply that proportional increases in all inputs yield the same proportional increase in output. Proportional increases in inputs can induce higher prices if the supply curves for these inputs are upward sloping. Therefore, constant returns to scale does not always imply long-run horizontal supply curves.

11. What assumptions are necessary for a market to be perfectly competitive? In light of what you have learned in this chapter, why is each of these assumptions important?

The two primary assumptions of perfect competition are (1) all firms in the industry are price takers, and (2) there is free entry and exit of firms from the market. This chapter discusses how competitive equilibrium is achieved under these assumptions. In particular, we have seen that in a competitive equilibrium, price is equal to marginal cost. Both assumptions insure this equilibrium condition in the long run. In the short run, price could be greater than average cost, implying positive economic profits. With free entry and exit, positive economic profits would encourage other firms to enter. This entry exerts downward pressure on price until price is equal to both marginal cost and minimum average cost.

12. Suppose a competitive industry faces an increase in demand (i.e., the curve shifts upward). What are the steps by which a competitive market insures increased output? Does your answer change if the government imposes a price ceiling?

If demand increases with fixed supply, price and profits increase. The price increase induces the firms in the industry to increase output. Also, with positive profit, firms enter the industry, shifting the supply curve to the right. With an effective price ceiling, profit will be lower than without the ceiling, reducing the incentive for firms to enter the industry. With zero economic profit, no firms enter and there is no shift in the supply curve.

13. The government passes a law that allows a substantial subsidy for every acre of land used to grow tobacco. How does this program affect the long-run supply curve for tobacco?

A subsidy on tobacco production decreases the firm's costs of production. These cost decreases encourage other firms to enter tobacco production, and the supply curve for the industry shifts out to the right.

EXERCISES

1. From the data in the following table, show what happens to the firm's output choice and profit if the price of the product falls from $40 to $35.

The table below shows the firm's revenue and cost information when the price falls to $35.

Q	P	TR P=40	TC	π P=40	MC P=40	MR P=40	TR P=35	MR P=35	π P=35
0	40	0	50	-50	—	—	0	—	-50
1	40	40	100	-60	50	40	35	35	-65
2	40	80	128	-48	28	40	70	35	-58
3	40	120	148	-28	20	40	105	35	-43
4	40	160	162	-2	14	40	140	35	-22
5	40	200	180	20	18	40	175	35	-5
6	40	240	200	40	20	40	210	35	10
7	40	280	222	58	22	40	245	35	23
8	40	320	260	60	38	40	280	35	20
9	40	360	305	55	45	40	315	35	10
10	40	400	360	40	55	40	350	35	-10
11	40	440	425	15	65	40	385	35	-40

At a price of $40, the firm should produce eight units of output to maximize profit because this is the point closest to where price equals marginal cost without having marginal cost exceed price. At a price of $35, the firm should produce seven units to maximize profit. When price falls from $40 to $35, profit falls from $60 to $23.

2. Again, from the data in the above table, show what happens to the firm's output choice and profit if the fixed cost of production increases from $50 to $100, and then to $150. What general conclusion can you reach about the effects of fixed costs on the firm's output choice?

The table below shows the firm's revenue and cost information for Fixed Cost, *FC* of 50, 100, and 150.

Q	P	TR	TC FC=50	π FC=50	MC	TC FC=100	π FC=100	TC FC=150	π FC=150
0	40	0	50	-50	—	100	-100	150	-120
1	40	40	100	-60	50	150	-110	200	-160
2	40	80	128	-48	28	178	-98	228	-148

3	40	120	148	-28	20	198	-78	248	-128
4	40	160	162	-2	14	212	-52	262	-102
5	40	200	180	20	18	230	-30	280	-80
6	40	240	200	40	20	250	-10	300	-60
7	40	280	222	58	22	272	8	322	-42
8	40	320	260	60	38	310	10	360	-40
9	40	360	305	55	45	355	5	405	-45
10	40	400	360	40	55	410	-10	460	-60
11	40	440	425	15	65	475	-35	525	-85

In all of the given cases, with fixed cost equal to 50, then 100, and then 150, the firm will produce 8 units of output because this is the point closest to where price equals marginal cost without having marginal cost exceed price. Fixed costs do not influence the optimal quantity, because they do not influence marginal cost.

3. **Suppose you are the manager of a watchmaking firm operating in a competitive market. Your cost of production is given by $C = 100 + Q^2$, where Q is the level of output and C is total cost. (The marginal cost of production is 2Q. The fixed cost of production is $100.)**

a. **If the price of watches is $60, how many watches should you produce to maximize profit?**

Profits are maximized where marginal cost is equal to marginal revenue. Here, marginal revenue is equal to $60; recall that price equals marginal revenue in a competitive market:
$$60 = 2Q, \text{ or } Q = 30.$$

b. **What will the profit level be?**

Profit is equal to total revenue minus total cost:
$$\pi = (60)(30) - (100 + 30^2) = \$800.$$

c. **At what minimum price will the firm produce a positive output?**

A firm will produce in the short run if the revenues it receives are greater than its variable costs. Remember that the firm's short-run supply curve is its marginal cost curve above the minimum of average variable cost. Here, average variable cost is $\frac{VC}{Q} = \frac{Q^2}{Q} = Q$. Also, MC is equal to 2Q. So, MC is greater than AVC for any quantity greater than 0. This means that the firm produces in the short run as long as price is positive.

4. **Use the same information as in Exercise 1 to answer the following.**

a. **Derive the firm's short-run supply curve. (Hint: you may want to plot the appropriate cost curves.)**

The firm's short-run supply curve is its marginal cost curve above average variable cost. The table below lists marginal cost, total cost, variable cost, fixed cost, and average variable cost. The firm will produce 8 or more units depending on the market price and will not produce in the 0-7 units of output range because in this range AVC is greater than MC. When AVC is greater than MC, the firm minimizes losses by producing nothing.

Q	TC	MC	TVC	TFC	AVC
0	50	—	0	50	—
1	100	50	50	50	50.0
2	128	28	78	50	39.0

3	148	20	98	50	32.7
4	162	14	112	50	28.0
5	180	18	130	50	26.0
6	200	20	150	50	25.0
7	222	22	172	50	24.6
8	260	38	210	50	26.3
9	305	45	255	50	28.3
10	360	55	310	50	31.0
11	425	65	375	50	34.1

b. **If 100 identical firms are in the market, what is the industry supply curve?**

For 100 firms with identical cost structures, the market supply curve is the horizontal summation of each firm's output at each price.

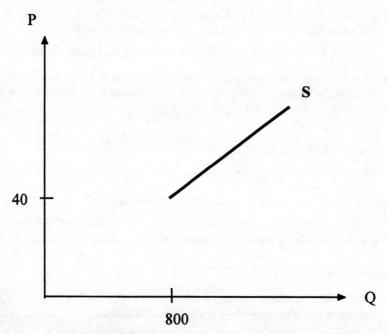

5. A sales tax of $1 per unit of output is placed on one firm whose product sells for $5 in a competitive industry.

a. **How will this tax affect the cost curves for the firm?**

With the imposition of a $1 tax on a single firm, all its cost curves shift up by $1.

b. **What will happen to the firm's price, output, and profit?**

Since the firm is a price-taker in a competitive market, the imposition of the tax on only one firm does not change the market price. Since the firm's short-run supply curve is its marginal cost curve above average variable cost and that marginal cost curve has shifted up (inward), the firm supplies less to the market at every price. Profits are lower at every quantity.

c. **Will there be entry or exit?**

If the tax is placed on a single firm, that firm will go out of business. In the long run, price in the market will be below the minimum average cost point of this firm.

6. **Suppose that a competitive firm's marginal cost of producing output q is given by MC(q) = 3 + 2q. Assume that the market price of the firm's product is $9:**

a. **What level of output will the firm produce?**

To maximize profits, the firm should set marginal revenue equal to marginal cost. Given the fact that this firm is operating in a competitive market, the market price it faces is equal to marginal revenue. Thus, the firm should set the market price equal to marginal cost to maximize its profits:

$$9 = 3 + 2q, \text{ or } q = 3.$$

b. **What is the firm's producer surplus?**

Producer surplus is equal to the area below the market price, i.e., $9.00, and above the marginal cost curve, i.e., 3 + 2q. Because MC is linear, producer surplus is a triangle with a base equal to $6 (9 - 3 = 6). The height of the triangle is 3, where P = MC. Therefore, producer surplus is

$$(0.5)(6)(3) = \$9.$$

See Figure 8.6.b.

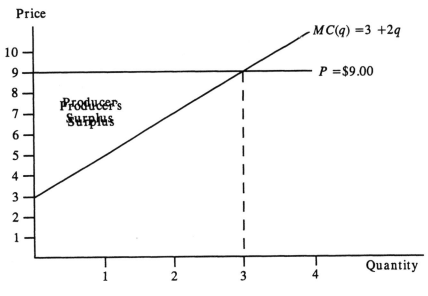

Figure 8.6.b

7. **Suppose that the average variable cost of the firm in Exercise (6) is given by AVC(q) = 3 + q. Suppose that the firm's fixed costs are known to be $3. Will the firm be earning a positive, negative, or zero profit in the short run?**

Profit is equal to total revenue minus total cost. Total cost is equal to total variable cost plus fixed cost. Total variable cost is equal to (AVC)(q). Therefore, at q = 3,

$$TVC = (3 + 3)(3) = \$18.$$

Fixed cost is equal to $3.

Therefore, total cost equals TVC plus TFC, or

$$TC = 18 + 3 = \$21.$$

Total revenue is price times quantity:

$$TR = (\$9)(3) = \$27.$$

Profit is total revenue minus total cost:

$$\pi = \$27 - \$21 = \$6.$$

Therefore, the firm is earning positive economic profits.

More easily, you might recall that profit equals surplus minus fixed cost. Since we found that surplus was \$9 in question 6, profit equals 9-3 or \$6.

8. A competitive industry is in long-run equilibrium. A sales tax is then placed on all firms in the industry. What do you expect to happen to the price of the product, the number of firms in the industry, and the output of each firm?

With the imposition of a sales tax on all firms, the marginal cost curve for each firm will shift up and to the left by the amount of the tax, and as a result the market supply curve shifts up and to the left. The shift in the market supply curve will increase the price of the product and decrease the quantity supplied by each firm. In the short run firms will continue to produce as long as price is above average variable cost. In the long run, some firms may exit if price falls below the new long run average cost curve, which has shifted up by the amount of the tax. As firms exit, the supply curve will shift up and to the left, resulting in a higher price and lower quantity supplied.

*9. A sales tax of 10 percent is placed on half the firms (the polluters) in a competitive industry. The revenue is paid to the remaining firms (the nonpolluters) as a 10 percent subsidy on the value of output sold.

a. **Assuming that all firms have identical constant long-run average costs before the sales tax-subsidy policy, what do you expect to happen to the price of the product, the output of each of the firms, and industry output, in the short run and the long run? (Hint: How does price relate to industry input?)**

The price of the product depends on the quantity produced by all firms in the industry. The immediate response to the sales-tax=subsidy policy is a reduction in quantity by polluters and an increase in quantity by non-polluters. If a long-run competitive equilibrium existed before the sales-tax=subsidy policy, price would have been equal to marginal cost and long-run minimum average cost. For the polluters, the price after the sales tax is below long-run average cost; therefore, in the long run, they will exit the industry. Furthermore, after the subsidy, the non-polluters earn economic profits that will encourage the entry of non-polluters. If this is a constant cost industry and the loss of the polluters' output is compensated by an increase in the non-polluters' output, the price will remain constant.

b. **Can such a policy *always* be achieved with a balanced budget in which tax revenues are equal to subsidy payments? Why? Explain.**

As the polluters exit and non-polluters enter the industry, revenues from polluters decrease and the subsidy to the non-polluters increases. This imbalance occurs when the first polluter leaves the industry and persists ever after.

CHAPTER 9
THE ANALYSIS OF COMPETITIVE MARKETS

TEACHING NOTES

With the exception of Chapter 1, Chapter 9 is the most straightforward and easily understood chapter in the text. The chapter begins with a review of consumer and producer surplus in section 9.1. If you have postponed these topics, you should carefully explain the definition of each. Section 9.2 discusses the basic concept of efficiency in competitive markets by comparing competitive outcomes with those under market failure. A more detailed discussion of efficiency is presented in Chapter 16.

Sections 9.3 to 9.6 present examples of government policies which cause the market equilibrium to differ from the competitive, efficient equilibrium. The instructor can pick and choose among sections 9.3 to 9.6 depending on time constraints and personal preference. The presentation in each of these sections follows the same format: there is a general discussion of why market intervention leads to deadweight loss, followed by the presentation of an important policy example. Each section is discussed in one review question and applied in at least one exercise. Exercise (1) focuses on minimum wages presented in Section 9.3. Exercises (4) and (5) reinforce discussion of price supports and production quotas from Section 9.4. The use of tariffs and quotas, presented in Section 9.5, can be found in Exercises (3), (6), (7), (10), and (12). Taxes and subsidies (Section 9.6) are discussed in Exercises (2), (8), and (14). Exercise (9) reviews natural gas price controls in Example 9.1, a continuation of Example 2.7. Exercise (4) may be compared to Example 9.4 and discussed as an extension of Example 2.2.

REVIEW QUESTIONS

1. What is meant by deadweight loss? Why does a price ceiling usually result in a deadweight loss?

Deadweight loss refers to the benefits lost to either consumers or producers when markets do not operate efficiently. The term deadweight denotes that these are benefits unavailable to any party. A price ceiling will tend to result in a deadweight loss because at any price below the market equilibrium price, quantity supplied will be below the market equilibrium quantity supplied, resulting in a loss of surplus to producers. Consumers will purchase less than the market equilibrium quantity, resulting in a loss of surplus to consumers. Consumers will also purchase less than the quantity they demand at the price set by the ceiling. The surplus lost by consumers and producers is not captured by either group, and surplus not captured by market participants is deadweight loss.

2. Suppose the supply curve for a good is completely inelastic. If the government imposed a price ceiling below the market-clearing level, would a deadweight loss result? Explain.

When the supply curve is completely inelastic, the imposition of an effective price ceiling transfers all loss in producer surplus to consumers. Consumer surplus increases by the difference between the market-clearing price and the price ceiling times the market-clearing quantity. Consumers capture all decreases in total revenue. Therefore, no deadweight loss occurs.

3. How can a price ceiling make consumers better off? Under what conditions might it make them worse off?

If the supply curve is perfectly inelastic a price ceiling will increase consumer surplus. If the demand curve is inelastic, price controls may result in a net loss of consumer surplus because consumers willing to pay a higher price are unable to purchase the price-controlled good or service. The loss of consumer surplus is greater than the transfer of producer surplus to consumers. If demand is elastic (and supply is relatively inelastic) consumers in the aggregate will enjoy an increase in consumer surplus.

4. Suppose the government regulates the price of a good to be no lower than some minimum level. Can such a minimum price make producers as a whole worse off? Explain.

Because a higher price increases revenue and decreases demand, some consumer surplus is transferred to producers but some producer revenue is lost because consumers purchase less. The problem with a price floor or minimum price is that it sends the wrong signal to producers. Thinking that more should be produced as the price goes up, producers incur extra cost to produce more than what consumers are willing to purchase at these higher prices. These extra costs can overwhelm gains captured in increased revenues. Thus, unless all producers decrease production, a minimum price can make producers as a whole worse off.

5. How are production limits used in practice to raise the prices of the following goods or services: (a) taxi rides, (b) drinks in a restaurant or bar, (c) wheat or corn?

Municipal authorities usually regulate the number of taxis through the issuance of licenses. When the number of taxis is less than it would be without regulation, those taxis in the market may charge a higher-than-competitive price.

State authorities usually regulate the number of liquor licenses. By requiring that any bar or restaurant that serves alcohol have a liquor license and then limiting the number of licenses available, the State limits entry by new bars and restaurants. This limitation allows those establishments that have a license to charge a higher price for alcoholic beverages.

Federal authorities usually regulate the number of acres of wheat or corn in production by creating acreage limitation programs that give farmers financial incentives to leave some of their acreage idle. This reduces supply, driving up the price of wheat or corn.

6. Suppose the government wants to increase farmers' incomes. Why do price supports or acreage limitation programs cost society more than simply giving farmers money?

Price supports and acreage limitations cost society more than the dollar cost of these programs because the higher price that results in either case will reduce quantity demanded and hence consumer surplus, leading to a deadweight loss because the farmer is not able to capture the lost surplus. Giving the farmers money does not result in any deadweight loss, but is merely a redistribution of surplus from one group to the other.

7. Suppose the government wants to limit imports of a certain good. Is it preferable to use an import quota or a tariff? Why?

Changes in domestic consumer and producer surpluses are the same under import quotas and tariffs. There will be a loss in (domestic) total surplus in either case. However, with a tariff, the government can collect revenue equal to the tariff times the quantity of imports and these revenues can be redistributed in the domestic economy to offset the domestic deadweight loss by, for example, reducing taxes. Thus, there is less of a loss to the domestic society as a whole. With the import quota, foreign producers can capture the difference between the domestic and world price times the quantity of imports. Therefore, with an import quota, there is a loss to the domestic society as a whole. If the national government is trying to increase welfare, it should use a tariff.

8. The burden of a tax is shared by producers and consumers. Under what conditions will consumers pay most of the tax? Under what conditions will producers pay most of it? What determines the share of a subsidy that benefits consumers?

The burden of a tax and the benefits of a subsidy depend on the elasticities of demand and supply. If the ratio of the elasticity of demand to the elasticity of supply is small, the burden of the tax falls mainly on consumers. On the other hand, if the ratio of the elasticity of demand to the elasticity of supply is large, the burden of the tax falls mainly on producers. Similarly, the benefit of a subsidy accrues mostly to consumers (producers) if the ratio of the elasticity of demand to the elasticity of supply is small (large).

9. Why does a tax create a deadweight loss? What determines the size of this loss?

A tax creates deadweight loss by artificially increasing price above the free market level, thus reducing the equilibrium quantity. This reduction in demand reduces consumer as well as producer surplus. The size of the deadweight loss depends on the elasticities of supply and demand. As the elasticity of demand increases and the elasticity of supply decreases, i.e., as supply becomes more inelastic, the deadweight loss becomes larger.

EXERCISES

1. In 1996, the U.S. Congress raised the minimum wage from $4.25 per hour to $5.15 per hour. Some people suggested that a government subsidy could help employers finance the higher wage. This exercise examines the economics of a minimum wage and wage subsidies. Suppose the supply of low-skilled labor is given by

$$L^S = 10w$$

where L^S is the quantity of low-skilled labor (in millions of persons employed each year) and w is the wage rate (in dollars per hour). The demand for labor is given by

$$L^D = 80 - 10w.$$

a. **What will the free market wage rate and employment level be? Suppose the government sets a minimum wage of $5 per hour. How many people would then be employed?**

In a free-market equilibrium, $L^S = L^D$. Solving yields $w = \$4$ and $L^S = L^D = 40$. If the minimum wage is $5, then $L^S = 50$ and $L^D = 30$. The number of people employed will be given by the labor demand, so employers will hire 30 million workers.

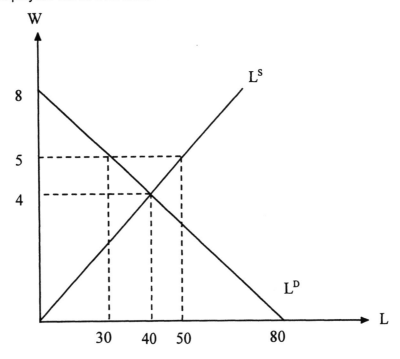

Figure 9.1.a

b. **Suppose that instead of a minimum wage, the government pays a subsidy of $1 per hour for each employee. What will the total level of employment be now? What will the equilibrium wage rate be?**

Let w denote the wage received by the employee. Then the employer receiving the $1 subsidy per worker hour only pays $w-1$ for each worker hour. As shown in Figure 9.1.b, the labor demand curve shifts to:

$$L^D = 80 - 10 (w-1) = 90 - 10w,$$

where w represents the wage received by the employee.

The new equilibrium will be given by the intersection of the old supply curve with the new demand curve, and therefore, $90-10_w{}^{**} = 10_w{}^{**}$, or $W^{**} = \$4.5$ per hour and

$L^{**} = 10(4.5) = 45$ million persons employed.

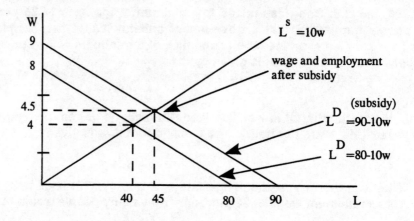

Figure 9.1.b

2. Suppose the market for widgets can be described by the following equations:

Demand: P = 10 - Q   **Supply: P = Q - 4**

where P is the price in dollars per unit and Q is the quantity in thousands of units.

a.   **What is the equilibrium price and quantity?**

To find the equilibrium price and quantity, equate supply and demand and solve for Q_{EQ}:

$$10 - Q = Q - 4, \text{ or } Q_{EQ} = 7.$$

Substitute Q_{EQ} into either the demand equation or the supply equation to obtain P_{EQ}.

$$P_{EQ} = 10 - 7 = 3,$$

or

$$P_{EQ} = 7 - 4 = 3.$$

b.   **Suppose the government imposes a tax of $1 per unit to reduce widget consumption and raise government revenues. What will the new equilibrium quantity be? What price will the buyer pay? What amount per unit will the seller receive?**

With the imposition of a $1.00 tax per unit, the demand curve for widgets shifts inward. At each price, the consumer wishes to buy less. Algebraically, the new demand function is:

$$P = 9 - Q.$$

The new equilibrium quantity is found in the same way as in (2a):

$$9 - Q = Q - 4, \text{ or } Q^* = 6.5.$$

To determine the price the buyer pays, P_B^*, substitute Q^* into the demand equation:

$$P_B^* = 10 - 6.5 = \$3.50.$$

To determine the price the seller receives, P_S^*, substitute Q^* into the supply equation:

$$P_S^* = 6.5 - 4 = \$2.50.$$

c. **Suppose the government has a change of heart about the importance of widgets to the happiness of the American public. The tax is removed and a subsidy of $1 per unit is granted to widget producers. What will the equilibrium quantity be? What price will the buyer pay? What amount per unit (including the subsidy) will the seller receive? What will be the total cost to the government?**

The original supply curve for widgets was $P = Q - 4$. With a subsidy of $1.00 to widget producers, the supply curve for widgets shifts outward. Remember that the supply curve for a firm is its marginal cost curve. With a subsidy, the marginal cost curve shifts down by the amount of the subsidy. The new supply function is:

$$P = Q - 5.$$

To obtain the new equilibrium quantity, set the new supply curve equal to the demand curve:
$$Q - 5 = 10 - Q, \text{ or } Q = 7.5.$$

The buyer pays $P = \$2.50$, and the seller receives that price plus the subsidy, i.e., $3.50. With quantity of 7,500 and a subsidy of $1.00, the total cost of the subsidy to the government will be $7,500.

3. **Japanese rice producers have extremely high production costs, in part due to the high opportunity cost of land and to their inability to take advantage of economies of large-scale production. Analyze two policies intended to maintain Japanese rice production: (1) a per-pound subsidy to farmers for each pound of rice produced, or (2) a per-pound tariff on imported rice. Illustrate with supply-and-demand diagrams the equilibrium price and quantity, domestic rice production, government revenue or deficit, and deadweight loss from each policy. Which policy is the Japanese government likely to prefer? Which policy are Japanese farmers likely to prefer?**

Figure 9.3.a shows the gains and losses from a per-pound subsidy with domestic supply, S, and domestic demand, D. P_S is the subsidized price, P_B is the price paid by the buyers, and P_{EQ} is the equilibrium price without the subsidy, assuming no imports. With the subsidy, buyers demand Q_1. Farmers gain amounts equivalent to areas A and B. This is the increase in producer surplus. Consumers gain areas C and F. This is the increase in consumer surplus. Deadweight loss is equal to the area E. The government pays a subsidy equal to areas $A + B + C + F + E$.

Figure 9.3.b shows the gains and losses from a per-pound tariff. P_W is the world price, and P_{EQ} is the equilibrium price. With the tariff, assumed to be equal to $P_{EQ} - P_W$, buyers demand Q_T, farmers supply Q_D, and $Q_T - Q_D$ is imported. Farmers gain a surplus equivalent to area A. Consumers lose areas A, B, C; this is the decrease in consumer surplus. Deadweight loss is equal to the areas B and C.

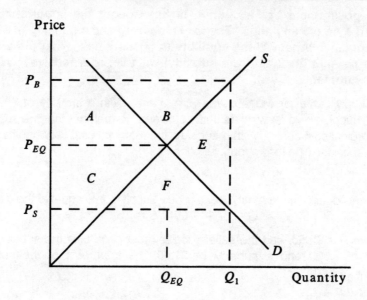

Figure 9.3.a

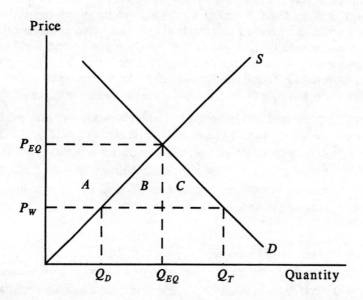

Figure 9.3.b

Without more information regarding the size of the subsidy and the tariff, and the specific equations for supply and demand, it seems sensible to assume that the Japanese government would avoid paying subsidies by choosing a tariff, but the rice farmers would prefer the subsidy.

4. In 1983, the Reagan Administration introduced a new agricultural program called the Payment-in-Kind Program. To see how the program worked, let's consider the wheat market.

a. Suppose the demand function is $Q^D = 28 - 2P$ and the supply function is $Q^S = 4 + 4P$, where P is the price of wheat in dollars per bushel and Q is the quantity in billions of bushels. Find the free-market equilibrium price and quantity.

Equating demand and supply, $Q^D = Q^S$,

$$28 - 2P = 4 + 4P, \text{ or } P = 4.$$

To determine the equilibrium quantity, substitute $P = 4$ into either the supply equation or the demand equation:

$$Q^S = 4 + 4(4) = 20$$

and

$$Q^D = 28 - 2(4) = 20.$$

b. **Now suppose the government wants to lower the supply of wheat by 25 percent from the free-market equilibrium by paying farmers to withdraw land from production. However, the payment is made in wheat rather than in dollars--hence the name of the program. The wheat comes from the government's vast reserves that resulted from previous price-support programs. The amount of wheat paid is equal to the amount that could have been harvested on the land withdrawn from production. Farmers are free to sell this wheat on the market. How much is now produced by farmers? How much is indirectly supplied to the market by the government? What is the new market price? How much do the farmers gain? Do consumers gain or lose?**

Because the free market supply by farmers is 20 billion bushels, the 25 percent reduction required by the new Payment-In-Kind (PIK) Program would imply that the farmers now produce 15 billion bushels. To encourage farmers to withdraw their land from cultivation, the government must give them 5 billion bushels, which they sell on the market.

Because the total supply to the market is still 20 billion bushels, the market price does not change; it remains at $4 per bushel. The farmers gain $20 billion, equal to ($4)(5 billion bushels), from the PIK Program, because they incur no costs in supplying the wheat (which they received from the government) to the market. The PIK program does not affect consumers in the wheat market, because they purchase the same amount at the same price as they did in the free market case.

c. **Had the government not given the wheat back to the farmers, it would have stored or destroyed it. Do taxpayers gain from the program? What potential problems does the program create?**

Taxpayers gain because the government is not required to store the wheat. Although everyone seems to gain from the PIK program, it can only last while there are government wheat reserves. The PIK program assumes that the land removed from production may be restored to production when stockpiles are exhausted. If this cannot be done, consumers may eventually pay more for wheat-based products. Finally, farmers are taxpayers too. Since producing the wheat must have cost something, the program offers them a windfall profit.

5. About 100 million pounds of jelly beans are consumed in the United States each year, and the price has been about 50 cents per pound. However, jelly bean producers feel that their incomes are too low, and they have convinced the government that price supports are in order. The government will therefore buy up as many jelly beans as necessary to keep the price at $1 per pound. However, government economists are worried about the impact of this program, because they have no estimates of the elasticities of jelly bean demand or supply.

a. **Could this program cost the government *more* than $50 million per year? Under what conditions? Could it cost *less* than $50 million per year? Under what conditions? Illustrate with a diagram.**

If the quantities demanded and supplied are very responsive to price changes, then a government program that doubles the price of jelly beans could easily cost more than $50 million. In this case, the change in price will cause a large change in quantity supplied, and a large change in quantity demanded. In Figure 9.5.a.i, the cost of the program is (Q_S-Q_D)*$1. Given Q_S-Q_D is larger than 50 million, then the government will pay more than 50 million dollars. If instead supply and demand were relatively price inelastic, then the change in price would result in very small changes in quantity supplied and quantity demanded and (Q_S-Q_D) would be less than $50 million, as illustrated in figure 9.5.a.ii.

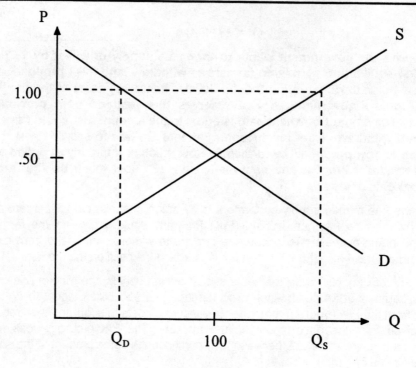

Figure 9.5.a.i

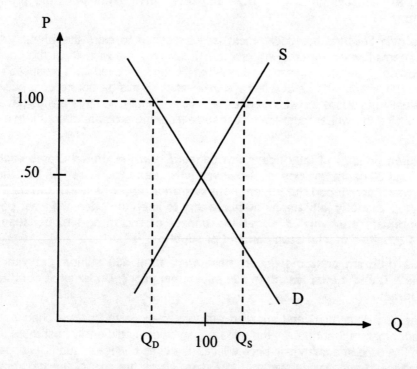

Figure 9.5.a.ii

b. **Could this program cost consumers (in terms of lost consumer surplus)** *more* **than $50 million per year? Under what conditions? Could it cost consumers** *less* **than $50 million per year? Under what conditions? Again, use a diagram to illustrate.**

When the demand curve is perfectly inelastic, the loss in consumer surplus is $50 million, equal to ($0.5)(100 million pounds). This represents the highest possible loss in consumer surplus. If the demand curve has any elasticity at all, the loss in consumer surplus would be less then $50 million. In Figure 9.5.b, the loss in consumer surplus is area A plus area B if the demand curve is D and only area A if the demand curve is D'.

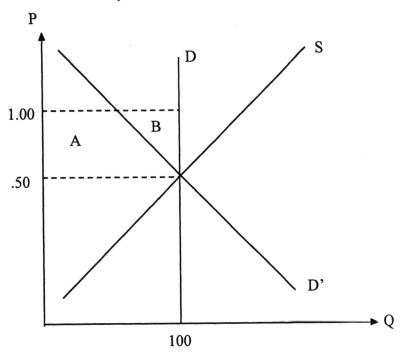

Figure 9.5.b

6. A vegetable fiber is traded in a highly competitive world market, and the world price is $9 per pound. Unlimited quantities are available for import into the United States at this price. The U.S. domestic supply and demand for various price levels are shown below.

Price	U.S. Supply (million pounds)	U.S. Demand (million pounds)
3	2	34
6	4	28
9	6	22
12	8	16
15	10	10
18	12	4

Answer the following questions about the U.S. market:

a. Confirm that the demand curve is given by $Q_D=40-2P$, and that the supply curve is given by $Q_S=2/3P$.

To find the equation for demand, we need to find a linear function $Q_D= a + bP$ such that the line it represents passes through two of the points in the table such as (15,10) and (12,16). First, the slope, b, is equal to the "rise" divided by the "run,"

$$\frac{\Delta Q}{\Delta P} = \frac{10-16}{15-12} = -2 = b.$$

Second, we substitute for b and one point, e.g., (15, 10), into our linear function to solve for the constant, a:

$$10 = a - 2(15), \text{ or } a = 40.$$

Therefore, $Q_D = 40 - 2P$.

Similarly, we may solve for the supply equation $Q_S = c + dP$ passing through two points such as (6,4) and (3,2). The slope, d, is

$$\frac{\Delta Q}{\Delta P} = \frac{4-2}{6-3} = \frac{2}{3}..$$

Solving for c:

$$4 = c + \left(\frac{2}{3}\right)(6), \text{ or } c = 0.$$

Therefore, $Q_S = \left(\frac{2}{3}\right)P$.

b. **Confirm that if there were no restrictions on trade, the U.S. would import 16 million pounds.**

If there are no trade restrictions, the world price of $9.00 will prevail in the U.S. From the table, we see that at $9.00 domestic supply will be 6 million pounds. Similarly, domestic demand will be 22 million pounds. Imports will provide the difference between domestic demand and domestic supply: 22 - 6 = 16 million pounds.

c. **If the United States imposes a tariff of $9 per pound, what will be the U.S. price and level of imports? How much revenue will the government earn from the tariff? How large is the deadweight loss?**

With a $9.00 tariff, the U.S. price will be $15 (the domestic equilibrium price), and there will be no imports. Because there are no imports, there is no revenue. The deadweight loss is equal to

(0.5)(16 million pounds)($6.00) = $48 million,

where 16 is the difference at a price of $9 between 22 demanded and 6 supplied, and $6 is the difference between $15 and $9.

d. **If the United States has no tariff but imposes an import quota of 8 million pounds, what will be the U.S. domestic price? What is the cost of this quota for U.S. consumers of the fiber? What is the gain for U.S. producers?**

With an import quota of 8 million pounds, the domestic price will be $12. At $12, the difference between domestic demand and domestic supply is 8 million pounds, i.e., 16 million pounds minus 8 million pounds. Note you can also find the equilibrium price by setting demand equal to supply plus the quota so that

$$40 - 2P = \frac{2}{3}P + 8.$$

The cost of the quota to consumers is equal to area A+B+C+D in Figure 9.6.f, which is

(12 - 9)(16) + (0.5)(12 - 9)(22 - 16) = $57 million.

The gain to domestic producers is equal to area A in Figure 9.6.d, which is

(12 - 9)(6) + (0.5)(8 - 6)(12 - 9) = $21 million.

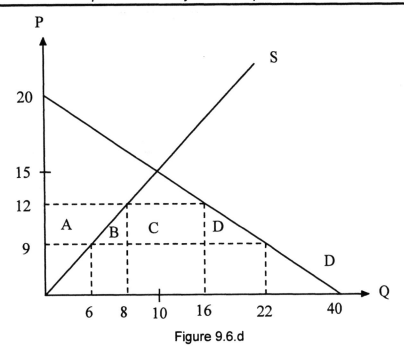

Figure 9.6.d

7. A particular metal is traded in a highly competitive world market at a world price of $9 per ounce. Unlimited quantities are available for import into the United States at this price. The supply of this metal from domestic U.S. mines and mills can be represented by the equation $Q^S = 2/3P$, where Q^S is U.S. output in million ounces and P is the domestic price. The demand for the metal in the United States is $Q^D = 40 - 2P$, where Q^D is the domestic demand in million ounces.

In recent years, the U.S. industry has been protected by a tariff of $9 per ounce. Under pressure from other foreign governments, the United States plans to reduce this tariff to zero. Threatened by this change, the U.S. industry is seeking a Voluntary Restraint Agreement that would limit imports into the United States to 8 million ounces per year.

.a.   **Under the $9 tariff, what was the U.S. domestic price of the metal?**

With a $9 tariff, the price of the imported metal on U.S. markets would be $18, the tariff plus the world price of $9. To determine the domestic equilibrium price, equate domestic supply and domestic demand:

$$\frac{2}{3}P = 40 - 2P, \text{ or } P = \$15.$$

The equilibrium quantity is found by substituting a price of $15 into either the demand or supply equations:

$$Q^D = 40 - (2)(15) = 10$$

and

$$Q^S = \left(\frac{2}{3}\right)(15) = 10.$$

The equilibrium quantity is 10 million ounces. Because the domestic price of $15 is less than the world price plus the tariff, $18, there will be no imports.

b.   **If the United States eliminates the tariff and the Voluntary Restraint Agreement is approved, what will be the U.S. domestic price of the metal?**

With the Voluntary Restraint Agreement, the difference between domestic supply and domestic demand would be limited to 8 million ounces, i.e. $Q^D - Q^S = 8$. To determine the domestic price of the metal, set $Q^D - Q^S = 8$ and solve for P:

$$(40 - 2P) - \frac{2}{3}P = 8, \text{ or } P = \$12.$$

At a price of \$12, Q^D = 16 and Q^S = 8; the difference of 8 million ounces will be supplied by imports.

8. Among the tax proposals regularly considered by Congress is an additional tax on distilled liquors. The tax would not apply to beer. The price elasticity of supply of liquor is 4.0, and the price elasticity of demand is -0.2. The cross-elasticity of demand for beer with respect to the price of liquor is 0.1.

a.   If the new tax is imposed, who will bear the greater burden, liquor suppliers or liquor consumers? Why?

Section 9.6 in the text provides a formula for the "pass-through" fraction, i.e., the fraction of the tax borne by the consumer. This fraction is $\frac{E_S}{E_S - E_D}$, where E_s is the own-price elasticity of supply and E_D is the own-price elasticity of demand. Substituting for E_s and E_D, the pass-through fraction is

$$\frac{4}{4 - (-0.2)} = \frac{4}{4.2} \approx 0.95.$$

Therefore, 95 percent of the tax is passed through to the consumers because supply is relatively elastic and demand is relatively inelastic.

b.   Assuming that beer supply is infinitely elastic, how will the new tax affect the beer market?

With an increase in the price of liquor (from the large pass-through of the liquor tax), some consumers will substitute away from liquor to beer, shifting the demand curve for beer outward. With an infinitely elastic supply for beer (a perfectly flat supply curve), there will be no change in the equilibrium price of beer.

9. In Example 9.1, we calculated the gains and losses from price controls on natural gas and found that there was a deadweight loss of \$1.4 billion. This calculation was based on a price of oil of \$8 per barrel. If the price of oil was \$12 per barrel, what would the free market price of gas be? How large a deadweight loss would result if the maximum allowable price of natural gas was \$1.00 per thousand cubic feet?

From Example 9.1, we know that the supply and demand curves for natural gas in the 1970s can be approximated as follows:

$$Q_S = 14 + 2P_G + 0.25P_O$$

and

$$Q_D = -5P_G + 3.75P_O,$$

where P_G is the price of gas and P_O is the price of oil.

With the price of oil at \$12 per barrel, these curves become,

$$Q_S = 17 + 2P_G$$

and

$$Q_D = 45 - 5P_G.$$

Setting quantity demanded equal to quantity supplied,

$$17 + 2P_G = 45 - 5P_G, \text{ or } P_G = \$4.$$

At this price, the equilibrium quantity is 25 thousand cubic feet (Tcf).

If a ceiling of \$1 is imposed, producers would supply 19 Tcf and consumers would demand 40 Tcf. Consumers gain area A - B = 57 - 3.6 = \$53.4 billion in the figure below. Producers lose the area -A - C = -57 - 9 = $66.0 billion. Deadweight loss is equal to the area C + B, which is equal to $12.6 billion.

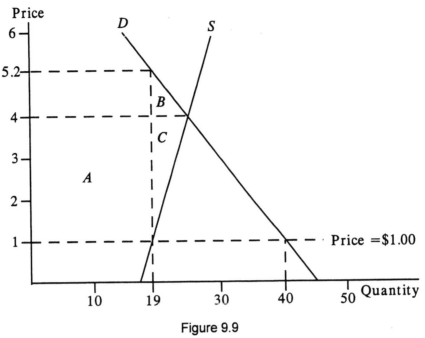

Figure 9.9

10. Example 9.5 describes the effects of the sugar quota. In 1997, imports were limited to 5.5 billion pounds, which pushed the domestic price to 22 cents per pound. Suppose imports were expanded to 6.5 billion pounds.

a. What would be the new U.S. domestic price?

We are given the equations for the total market demand for sugar in the U.S. and the supply of U.S. producers:

$$Q_D = 27.45 - .29P$$

$$Q_S = -7.83 + 1.07P.$$

The difference between the quantity demanded and supplied, Q_D-Q_S, is the amount of sugar imported which is restricted by the quota. If the quota is increased from 5.5 billion pounds to 6.5 billion pounds, then we will have $Q_D - Q_S = 6.5$ and we can solve for P:

$$(27.45-.29P)-(-7.83+1.07P)=6.5$$

$$35.28-1.36P=6.5$$

$$P=21.2 \text{ cents per pound.}$$

At a price of 21.2 cents per pound $Q_S = -7.83 + (1.07)(21.2) = 14.85$ billion pounds and $Q_D = Q_S + 6.5 = 21.35$ billion pounds.

b.   **How much would consumers gain and domestic producers lose?**

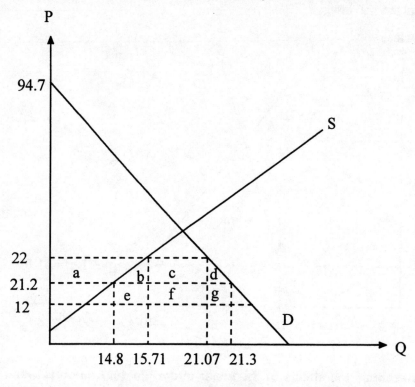

Figure 9.10.b

The gain in consumer surplus is area a+b+c+d in Figure 9.10.b. The loss to domestic producers is equal to area a.

Numerically:

a = (22-21.2)(14.8)+(15.71-14.8)(22-21.2)(.5)=12.2

b = (15.71-14.8)(22-21.2)(.5)=0.36

c = (22-21.2)(21.07-15.71)=4.3

d = (22-21.2)(21.3-21.07)(.5)=0.1.

These numbers are in billions of cents or tens of millions of dollars.

Thus, consumer surplus increases by $169.6 million, while domestic producer surplus decreases by $122 million.

c.   **What would be the effect on deadweight loss and foreign producers?**

When the quota is 5.5 billion pounds, the profit earned by foreign producers can be represented by the area c+f in Figure 9.10.b (the world price for sugar is assumed to be 12 cents per pound). When the quota increases to 6.5 billion, the profit can then be represented by the area e+f+g. The change in profit to foreign producers is thus (e+f+g)-(c+f) or e+g-c. Numerically:

e=(15.71-14.8)(21.2-12)=8.37

g=(21.3-21.07)(21.2-12)=2.12

c=(21.07-15.71)(22-21.2)=4.29.

Thus, the profit earned by foreign producers increases by $62 million. The deadweight loss of the quota decreases by area b+e+d+g, which is equal to $109.5 million.

11. Review Example 9.5 on the sugar quota. During the mid-1990's, U.S. sugar producers became more efficient, causing the domestic supply curve to shift to the right. We will examine the implications of this shift. Suppose that the supply curve shifts to the right by 5.5 billion pounds, so the new supply curve is given by

$$Q_s = -2.33 + 1.07P.$$

a. **Show that if the demand curve remains the same as in Example 9.5, domestic demand would equal domestic supply at a price of 21.9 cents per pound. Thus the U.S. price could be maintained at 21.9 cents with no imports.**

At a price P=21.9 cents per pound,

$$Q_D = 27.45 - .29(21.9) = 21.1 \text{ billion pounds, and}$$

$$Q_S = -2.33 + 1.07(21.9) = 21.1 \text{ billion pounds.}$$

b. **Suppose that, under pressure from foreign sugar producers, the U.S. government allows imports of 2.5 billion lbs. and requires domestic sugar producers to reduce their production by the same amount. Draw the supply and demand curves and calculate the resulting benefit to consumers, the cost to domestic producers, and the benefit to foreign producers. Is there any deadweight loss associated with this change in policy?**

If we simply allow for imports of 2.5 billion pounds, then the domestic price will fall until the difference between quantity supplied and quantity demanded is 2.5 billion pounds. As price falls, quantity supplied will fall and quantity demanded will increase, resulting in a change in quantity supplied that is less than 2.5 billion. To find the equilibrium price and quantity in this case, note again that quantity demanded will equal quantity supplied plus 2.5:

$$Q_D = 27.45 - 0.29P = -2.33 + 1.07P + 2.5 = Q_S + 2.5 \implies$$
$$P = 20 \text{ cents, } Q_S = 19.1, \text{ and } Q_D = 21.6.$$

Figure 9.11.b.i illustrates these results.

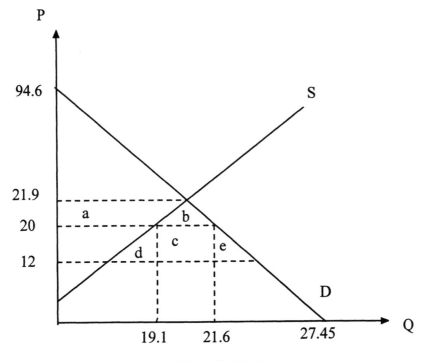

Figure 9.11.b.i

In figure 9.11.b.i, the gain to consumers is area a+b (38.7 or $387 million), the loss to producers is area b (1.4 or $14 million), and the gain to foreign producers is area c (20 or $200 million). There is actually a reduction in deadweight loss because there is an increase in imports. Assuming still that the world price is equal to 12, the deadweight loss associated with maintaining a price of 21.9 and excluding all imports is area b+c+d+e (65.3 or $653 million). When imports are 2.5 and the price drops to 20, deadweight loss is reduced to area d+e (43.84 or $438.4 million).

If the government wanted to reduce domestic production by exactly 2.5 billion pounds then the situation is a little bit different. The supply curve is the domestic supply curve up to a quantity of 21.1-2.5=18.6, at which point the supply curve becomes horizontal out to a quantity of 18.6+2.5=21.1, at which point the supply curve becomes vertical because there are no more imports and no more domestic production is allowed. If total quantity supplied is 21.6 billion pounds, domestic and foreign firms can sell their output for a price of 21.9. In this case there is no change in consumer surplus, producers lose area a, foreign firms gain area a+b+c, and deadweight loss is reduced by area b+c, as illustrated in figure 9.11.b.ii.

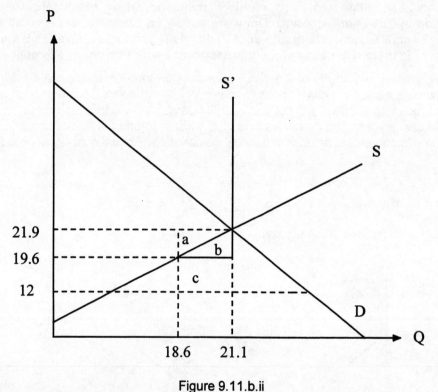

Figure 9.11.b.ii

12. The domestic supply and demand curves for hula beans are as follows:

Supply: P = 50 + Q   Demand: P = 200 - 2Q

where P is the price in cents per pound and Q is the quantity in millions of pounds. The U.S. is a small producer in the world hula bean market, where the current price (which will not be affected by anything we do) is 60 cents per pound. Congress is considering a tariff of 40 cents per pound. Find the domestic price of hula beans that will result if the tariff is imposed. Also compute the dollar gain or loss to domestic consumers, domestic producers, and government revenue from the tariff.

To analyze the influence of a tariff on the domestic hula bean market, start by solving for domestic equilibrium price and quantity. First, equate supply and demand to determine equilibrium quantity:

$$50 + Q = 200 - 2Q, \text{ or } Q_{EQ} = 50.$$

Thus, the equilibrium quantity is 50 million pounds. Substituting Q_{EQ} equals 50 into either the supply or demand equation to determine price, we find:

$$P_S = 50 + 50 = 100 \text{ and } P_D = 200 - (2)(50) = 100.$$

The equilibrium price P is \$1 (100 cents). However, the world market price is 60 cents. At this price, the domestic quantity supplied is $60 = 50 - Q_S$, or $Q_S = 10$, and similarly, domestic demand at the world price is $60 = 200 - 2Q_D$, or $Q_D = 70$. Imports are equal to the difference between domestic demand and supply, or 60 million pounds. If Congress imposes a tariff of 40 cents, the effective price of imports increases to \$1. At \$1, domestic producers satisfy domestic demand and imports fall to zero.

As shown in Figure 9.12, consumer surplus before the imposition of the tariff is equal to area a+b+c, or $(0.5)(200 - 60)(70) = 4,900$ million cents or \$49 million. After the tariff, the price rises to \$1.00 and consumer surplus falls to area a, or

$(0.5)(200 - 100)(50) = \$25$ million, a loss of \$24 million. Producer surplus will increase by area b, or $(100-60)(10)+(.5)(100-60)(50-10)=\$12$ million.

Finally, because domestic production is equal to domestic demand at \$1, no hula beans are imported and the government receives no revenue. The difference between the loss of consumer surplus and the increase in producer surplus is deadweight loss which in this case is equal to \$12 million. See Figure 9.12.

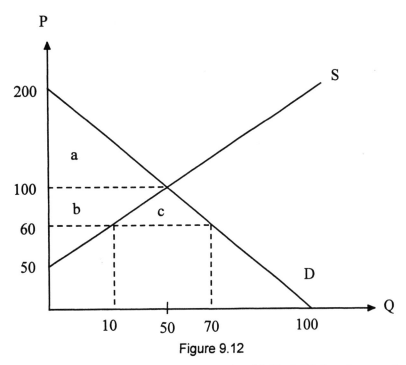

Figure 9.12

13. Currently, the social security payroll tax in the United States is evenly divided between employers and employees. Employers must pay the government a tax of 6.2 percent of the wages they pay, and employees must pay 6.2 percent of the wages they receive. Suppose the tax was changed so that employers paid the full 12.4 percent and employees paid nothing. Would employees then be better off?

If the labor market is competitive, that is, both employers and employees take the wage as given, then shifting an equal tax amount from the employee to the employer will have no effect on the amount of labor employed and on the wage kept by the employee after taxes. The equilibrium amount of labor employed is determined by the total amount of tax paid by both employees and employers. This is represented by the difference between the wage paid by the employer and the wage received by the employee. As long as the total tax doesn't change, the same amount of labor is employed and the wages paid by the employer and received by the employee (after tax) will not change. Hence, employees would be no better or worse off if the employers paid the full amount of the social security tax.

14. You know that if a tax is imposed on a particular product, the burden of the tax is shared by producers and consumers. You also know that the demand for automobiles is characterized by a stock adjustment process. Suppose a special 20 percent sales tax is suddenly imposed on automobiles. Will the share of the tax paid by consumers rise, fall, or stay the same over time? Explain briefly. Repeat for a 50-cents-per-gallon gasoline tax.

For products with demand characterized by a stock adjustment process, the short-run demand curve is more elastic than the long-run demand curve because consumers can delay their purchases of these goods in the short run. For example, when price rises, consumers may continue using the older version of the product, which they currently own. However, in the long run, a new product will be purchased. Thus, the long-run demand curve is more inelastic than the short-run one.

Consider the effect of imposing a 20 percent sales tax on automobiles in the short and long run. To analyze the influence of the tax, we can shift the demand curves because consumers are forced to pay a higher price. Notice that this tax is an ad valorem tax. The demand curve does not shift parallel to the old one, but pivots to reflect the higher tax paid per unit at higher prices.

The burden of the tax shifts from producers to consumers as we move from the short run (Figure 9.14.a) to the long run (Figure 9.14.b). In these figures, P_O is the consumer's price, P_S is the producer's price, and $P_O - P_S$ is the value of the tax. Intuitively, we may assume consumers have a more inelastic demand curve in the long run. They are less able to adjust their demand to price changes and must carry a larger burden of the tax. In both figures, the supply curve is the same in the long and short run. If the supply curve is more elastic in the long run, then even more of the tax burden is shifted to consumers.

Short Run

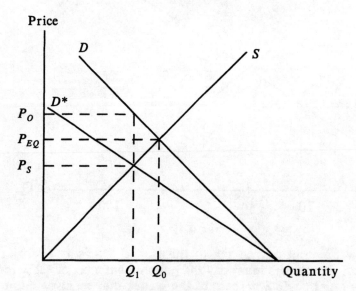

Figure 9.14.a

116

Long Run

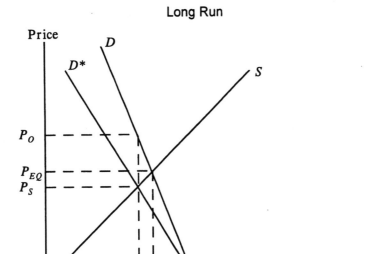

Figure 9.14.b

Unlike the automobile market, the gasoline demand curve is not characterized by a stock adjustment effect. The long-run demand curve will be more elastic than the short-run one, because in the long run substitutes (e.g., gasohol or propane) will become available for gasoline. We may analyze the effect of the tax on gasoline in the same manner as the tax on automobiles. However, the gasoline tax is a per unit or specific tax, so the demand curves exhibit a parallel shift.

In Figures 9.14.c and 9.14.d, the tax burden shifts from consumers to producers as we move from the short to the long run. Now the elasticity of demand increases from the short run to the long run (the usual case), resulting in less gasoline consumption. Also, if the supply curve is more elastic in the long run, some of the burden would again be shifted back to consumers. Note that we have drawn demand curve shifts in both cases, assuming the consumers pay the tax. The same results may be obtained by shifting the supply curve, assuming the firms pay the tax.

Short Run

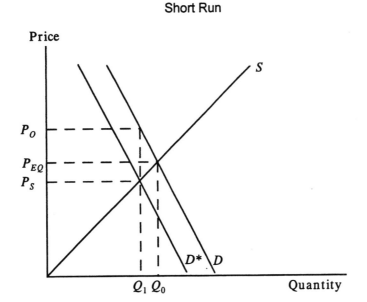

Figure 9.14.c

Long Run

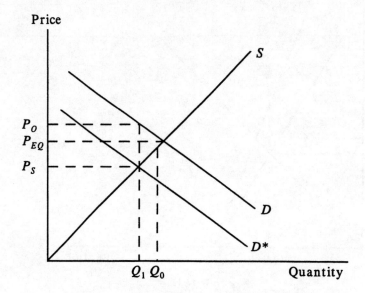

Figure 9.14.d

15. In 1998, Americans smoked 23.5 billion packs of cigarettes. They paid an average retail price of $2 per pack.

a.   Given that the elasticity of supply is 0.5 and the elasticity of demand is -0.4,   derive linear demand and supply curves for cigarettes.

Let the demand curve be of the general form Q=a+bP and the supply curve be of the general form Q=c+dP, where a, b, c, and d are the constants that you have to find from the information given above. To begin, recall the formula for the price elasticity of demand

$$E_P^D = \frac{P}{Q}\frac{\Delta Q}{\Delta P}.$$

You are given information about the value of the elasticity, P, and Q, which means that you can solve for the slope which is b in the above formula for the demand curve.

$$-0.4 = \frac{2}{23.5}\frac{\Delta Q}{\Delta P}$$

$$\frac{\Delta Q}{\Delta P} = -0.4\left(\frac{23.5}{2}\right) = -4.7 = b.$$

To find the constant a, substitute for Q, P, and b into the above formula so that 23.5=a-4.7*2 and a=32.9. The equation for demand is therefore Q=32.9-4.7P. To find the supply curve, recall the formula for the elasticity of supply and follow the same method as above:

$$E_P^S = \frac{P}{Q}\frac{\Delta Q}{\Delta P}$$

$$0.5 = \frac{2}{23.5}\frac{\Delta Q}{\Delta P}$$

$$\frac{\Delta Q}{\Delta P} = 0.5\left(\frac{23.5}{2}\right) = 5.875 = d.$$

To find the constant c, substitute for Q, P, and d into the above formula so that 23.5=c+5.875*2 and c=11.75. The equation for supply is therefore Q=11.75+5.875P.

b. **In November 1998, after settling a lawsuit filed by 46 states, the three major tobacco companies raised the retail price of a pack of cigarettes by 45 cents.   What is the new equilibrium price and quantity? How many fewer packs of   cigarettes are sold?**

The new price of cigarettes would be $2.45. Plugging $2.45 into the demand curve results in a quantity demanded of 21.39 billion packs, which represents a decrease of 2.11 billion packs of cigarettes. Note that you could also use the formula for elasticity to come up with the answer:

$$\varepsilon_p^D = \frac{\%\Delta Q}{\%\Delta P} = \frac{\%\Delta Q}{22.5\%} \Rightarrow \%\Delta Q = 9\%.$$

The new quantity demanded is then 23.5*.91=21.39 billion packs.

c. **Cigarettes are subject to a Federal tax, which was about 25 cents per pack in   1998. This tax will increase by 15 cents in 2002. What will this increase do to the   market-clearing price and quantity?**

The tax of 15 cents will shift the supply curve up by 15 cents. To find the new supply curve, first rewrite the equation for the supply curve as a function of Q instead of P:

$$Q_S = 11.75 + 5.875P \Rightarrow P = \frac{Q_S}{5.875} - \frac{11.75}{5.875}.$$

The new supply curve is now

$$P = \frac{Q_S}{5.875} - \frac{11.75}{5.875} + .15 = 0.17Q_S - 1.85.$$

To equate the new supply with the equation for demand, first rewrite demand as a function of Q instead of P:

$$Q_D = 32.9 - 4.7P \Rightarrow P = 7 - .21Q_D.$$

Now equate supply and demand and solve for the equilibrium quantity:

$$0.17Q - 1.85 = 7 - .21Q \Rightarrow Q = 23.12.$$

Plugging the equilibrium quantity into the equation for demand gives a market price of $2.09.

Note that we assume that part c is independent of part b. If we incorporate information from part b, the supply curve in part c is 60 cents (45+15) higher vertically than the supply curve from part a.

d. **How much of the Federal tax will consumers pay? What part will producers pay?**

Since the price went up by 9 cents, consumers pay 9 of the 15 cents or 60% of the tax, and producers will pay the remaining 40% or 6 cents.

PART III
FIRM STRUCTURE
CHAPTER 10
MARKET POWER: MONOPOLY AND MONOPSONY

TEACHING NOTES

This chapter covers both monopoly and monopsony in order to highlight the similarity between the two types of market power. The chapter begins with a discussion of monopoly in sections 1-4. Section 5 first discusses monopsony, and then offers an instructive comparison of monopoly and monopsony. Section 6 discusses sources of monopsony power and the social costs of monopsony power, while section 7 concludes with a discussion of antitrust law. If you are pressed for time you might choose to only cover the first four sections on monopoly and skip the remainder of the chapter. Section 7 can be covered even if you choose to skip sections 5 and 6. The last part of section 1 on the multiplant firm can also be skipped if you are pressed for time.

Although chapter 8 presented the general rule for profit maximization, you should review marginal revenue and price elasticity of demand through a careful derivation of Equation 10.1. A discussion of the derivation of Equation 10.1 will elucidate the geometry of Figure 10.3. Point out that because marginal revenue is positive at the profit maximizing level of price and quantity for a monopolist, demand at that quantity is elastic. Equation 10.1 also leads directly to the Lerner Index in Section 10.2. This provides fruitful ground for a discussion of a monopolist's market power. For example, if E_d is large (e.g., because of close substitutes), then (1) the demand curve is relatively flat, (2) the marginal revenue curve is relatively flat (although steeper than the demand curve), and (3) the monopolist has little power to raise price above marginal cost. To reinforce these points, introduce a non-linear demand curve by, for example, showing the location of the marginal revenue curve for a unit-elastic demand curve. Once this concept has been clearly presented, the discussion of the effect of an excise tax on a monopolist with non-linear demand (Figure 10.5) will not seem out of place.

The social costs of market power are a good topic for class discussion, and this topic can be introduced by comparing the deadweight loss associated with monopoly with the analysis of market intervention given in Chapter 9. For example, compare Figure 10.10 with Figure 9.5. Given that Exercises (9), (13), and (15) involve "kinked marginal revenue curves," you should present Figure 10.11 if you plan to assign those problems. Although Figure 10.11 is complicated, exposure to it here will help when it reappears in Chapter 12.

REVIEW QUESTIONS

1. A monopolist is producing at a point at which marginal cost exceeds marginal revenue. How should it adjust its output to increase profit?

When marginal cost is greater than marginal revenue, the incremental cost of the last unit produced is greater than incremental revenue. The firm would increase its profit by not producing the last unit. It should continue to reduce production, thereby decreasing marginal cost and increasing marginal revenue, until marginal cost is equal to marginal revenue.

2. We write the percentage markup of prices over marginal cost as (P - MC)/P. For a profit-maximizing monopolist, how does this markup depend on the elasticity of demand? Why can this markup be viewed as a measure of monopoly power?

We can show that this measure of market power is equal to the negative inverse of the price elasticity of demand.

$$\frac{P - MC}{P} = -\frac{1}{E_D}$$

The equation implies that, as the elasticity increases (demand becomes more elastic), the inverse of elasticity decreases and the measure of market power decreases. Therefore, as elasticity increases (decreases), the firm has less (more) power to increase price above marginal cost.

3. Why is there no market supply curve under conditions of monopoly?

The monopolist's output decision depends not only on marginal cost, but also on the demand curve. Shifts in demand do not trace out a series of prices and quantities that we can identify as the supply curve for the firm. Instead, shifts in demand lead to changes in price, output, or both. Thus, there is no one-to-one correspondence between the price and the seller's quantity; therefore, a monopolized market lacks a supply curve.

4. Why might a firm have monopoly power even if it is not the only producer in the market?

The degree of monopoly power or market power enjoyed by a firm depends on the elasticity of the demand curve that it faces. As the elasticity of demand increases, i.e., as the demand curve becomes flatter, the inverse of the elasticity approaches zero and the monopoly power of the firm decreases. Thus, if the firm's demand curve has any elasticity less than infinity, the firm has some monopoly power.

5. What are some of the sources of monopoly power? Give an example of each.

The firm's exploitation of its monopoly power depends on how easy it is for other firms to enter the industry. There are several barriers to entry, including exclusive rights (e.g., patents, copyrights, and licenses) and economies of scale. These two barriers to entry are the most common. Exclusive rights are legally granted property rights to produce or distribute a good or service. Positive economies of scale lead to "natural monopolies" because the largest producer can charge a lower price, driving competition from the market. For example, in the production of aluminum, there is evidence to suggest that there are scale economies in the conversion of bauxite to alumina. (See *U.S. v. Aluminum Company of America*, 148 F.2d 416 [1945], discussed in Exercise 8, below.)

6. What factors determine the amount of monopoly power an individual firm is likely to have? Explain each one briefly.

Three factors determine the firm's elasticity of demand: (1) the elasticity of market demand, (2) the number of firms in the market, and (3) interaction among the firms in the market. The elasticity of market demand depends on the uniqueness of the product, i.e., how easy it is for consumers to substitute away from the product. As the number of firms in the market increases, the demand elasticity facing each firm increases because customers may shift to the firm's competitors. The number of firms in the market is determined by how easy it is to enter the industry (the height of barriers to entry). Finally, the ability to raise the price above marginal cost depends on how other firms react to the firm's price changes. If other firms match price changes, customers will have little incentive to switch to another supplier.

7. Why is there a social cost to monopoly power? If the gains to producers from monopoly power could be redistributed to consumers, would the social cost of monopoly power be eliminated? Explain briefly.

When the firm exploits its monopoly power to raise the price above marginal cost, consumers buy less at the higher price. Consumers enjoy less surplus, the difference between the price they are willing to pay and the market price on each unit consumed. Some of the lost consumer surplus is not captured by the seller and is a deadweight loss to society. Therefore, if the gains to producers were redistributed to consumers, society would still suffer the deadweight loss.

8. Why will a monopolist's output increase if the government forces it to lower its price? If the government wants to set a price ceiling that maximizes the monopolist's output, what price should it set?

By restricting price below the monopolist's profit-maximizing price, the government can change the shape of the firm's marginal revenue, *MR*, curve. When a price ceiling is imposed, *MR* is equal to the price ceiling for all quantities lower than the quantity demanded at the price ceiling. If the government wants to maximize output, it should set a price equal to marginal cost. Prices below this level induce the firm to decrease production, assuming the marginal cost curve is upward sloping. The regulator's problem is to determine the shape of the monopolist's marginal cost curve. This task is difficult given the monopolist's incentive to hide or distort this information.

9. How should a monopsonist decide how much of a product to buy? Will it buy more or less than a competitive buyer? Explain briefly.

The marginal expenditure is the change in the total expenditure as the purchased quantity changes. For a firm competing with many firms for inputs, the marginal expenditure is equal to the average expenditure (price). For a monopsonist, the marginal expenditure curve lies above the average expenditure curve because the decision to buy an extra unit raises the price that must be paid for all units, including the last unit. All firms should buy inputs so that the marginal value of the last unit is equal to the marginal expenditure on that unit. This is true for both the competitive buyer and the monopsonist. However, because the monopsonist's marginal expenditure curve lies above the average expenditure curve and because the marginal value curve is downward sloping, the monopsonist buys less than a firm would buy in a competitive market.

10. What is meant by the term "monopsony power"? Why might a firm have monopsony power even if it is not the only buyer in the market?

Monopsony power is the power in the factor market held by the buyer. A buyer facing an upward-sloping factor supply curve has some monopsony power. In a competitive market, the seller faces a perfectly-elastic market curve and the buyer faces a perfectly-elastic supply curve. Thus, any characteristic of the market (e.g., when there is a small number of buyers or if buyers engage in collusive behavior) that leads to a less-than-perfectly-elastic supply curve gives the buyer some monopsony power.

11. What are some sources of monopsony power? What determines the amount of monopsony power an individual firm is likely to have?

The individual firm's monopsony power depends on the characteristics of the "buying-side" of the market. There are three characteristics that enhance monopsony power: (1) the elasticity of market supply, (2) the number of buyers, and (3) how the buyers interact. The elasticity of market supply depends on how responsive producers are to changes in price. If, in the short run, supply is relatively fixed, then supply is relatively inelastic. For example, since tobacco farmers can sell their crop to only a handful of tobacco product producers, the power to buy at a price below marginal value is increased.

12. Why is there a social cost to monopsony power? If the gains to buyers from monopsony power could be redistributed to sellers, would the social cost of monopsony power be eliminated? Explain briefly.

With monopsony power, the price is lower and the quantity is less than under competitive buying conditions. Because of the lower price and reduced sales, sellers lose revenue. Only part of this lost revenue is transferred to the buyer as consumer surplus, and the net loss in total surplus is deadweight loss. Even if the consumer surplus could be redistributed to sellers, the deadweight loss persists. This inefficiency will remain because quantity is reduced below a level where price is equal to marginal cost.

13. How do the antitrust laws limit market power in the United States? Give examples of major provisions of the laws.

Antitrust laws, which are subject to interpretation by the courts, limit market power by proscribing a firm's behavior in attempting to maximize profit. Section 1 of the Sherman Act prohibits *every* restraint of trade, including any attempt to fix prices by buyers or sellers. Section 2 of the Sherman Act prohibits behavior that leads to monopolization. The Clayton Act, with the Robinson-Patman Act, prohibits price discrimination and exclusive dealing (sellers prohibiting buyers from buying goods from other sellers). The Clayton Act also limits mergers when they could substantially lessen competition. The Federal Trade Commission Act makes it illegal to use unfair or deceptive practices.

14. Explain briefly how the U.S. antitrust laws are actually enforced.

Antitrust laws are enforced in three ways: (1) through the Antitrust Division of the Justice Department, whenever firms violate federal statutes, (2) through the Federal Trade Commission, whenever firms violate the Federal Trade Commission Act, and (3) through civil suits. The Justice Department can seek to impose fines or jail terms on managers or owners involved or seek to reorganize the firm, as it did in its case against A.T.& T. The FTC can seek a voluntary understanding to comply with the law or a formal Commission order. Individuals or companies can sue in federal court for awards equal to three times the damage arising from the anti-competitive behavior.

EXERCISES

1. Will an increase in the demand for a monopolist's product always result in a higher price? Explain. Will an increase in the supply facing a monopsonist buyer always result in a lower price? Explain.

As illustrated in Figure 10.4b in the textbook, an increase in demand need not *always* result in a higher price. Under the conditions portrayed in Figure 10.4b, the monopolist supplies different quantities at the same price. Similarly, an increase in supply facing the monopsonist need not *always* result in a higher price. Suppose the average expenditure curve shifts from AE_1 to AE_2, as illustrated in Figure 10.1. With the shift in the average expenditure curve, the marginal expenditure curve shifts from ME_1 to ME_2. The ME_1 curve intersects the marginal value curve (demand curve) at Q_1, resulting in a price of P. When the AE curve shifts, the ME_2 curve intersects the marginal value curve at Q_2 resulting in the same price at P.

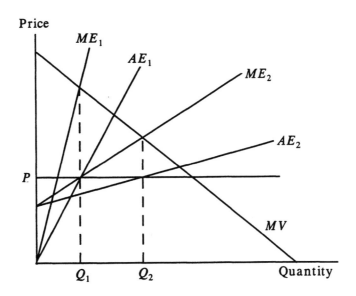

Figure 10.1

2. Caterpillar Tractor, one of the largest producers of farm machinery in the world, has hired you to advise them on pricing policy. One of the things the company would like to know is how much a 5 percent increase in price is likely to reduce sales. What would you need to know to help the company with this problem? Explain why these facts are important.

As a large producer of farm equipment, Caterpillar Tractor has market power and should consider the entire demand curve when choosing prices for its products. As their advisor, you should focus on the determination of the elasticity of demand for each product. There are three important factors to be considered. First, how similar are the products offered by

Caterpillar's competitors? If they are close substitutes, a small increase in price could induce customers to switch to the competition. Secondly, what is the age of the existing stock of tractors? With an older population of tractors, a 5 percent price increase induces a smaller drop in demand. Finally, because farm tractors are a capital input in agricultural production, what is the expected profitability of the agricultural sector? If farm incomes are expected to fall, an increase in tractor prices induces a greater decline in demand than one would estimate with information on only past sales and prices.

3. A monopolist firm faces a demand with constant elasticity of -2.0. It has a constant marginal cost of $20 per unit and sets a price to maximize profit. If marginal cost should increase by 25 percent, would the price charged also rise by 25 percent?

Yes. The monopolist's pricing rule as a function of the elasticity of demand for its product is:

$$\frac{(P - MC)}{P} = -\frac{1}{E_d}$$

or alternatively,

$$P = \frac{MC}{\left(1 + \left(\frac{1}{E_d}\right)\right)}$$

In this example $E_d = -2.0$, so $1/E_d = -1/2$; price should then be set so that:

$$P = \frac{MC}{\left(\frac{1}{2}\right)} = 2MC$$

Therefore, if MC rises by 25 percent price, then price will also rise by 25 percent. When MC = $20, P = $40. When MC rises to $20(1.25) = $25, the price rises to $50, a 25% increase.

4. A firm faces the following average revenue (demand) curve:

$$P = 100 - 0.01Q$$

where Q is weekly production and P is price, measured in cents per unit. The firm's cost function is given by C = 50Q + 30,000. Assuming the firm maximizes profits,

a.   What is the level of production, price, and total profit per week?

The profit-maximizing output is found by setting marginal revenue equal to marginal cost. Given a linear demand curve in inverse form, $P = 100 - 0.01Q$, we know that the marginal revenue curve will have twice the slope of the demand curve. Thus, the marginal revenue curve for the firm is $MR = 100 - 0.02Q$. Marginal cost is simply the slope of the total cost curve. The slope of $TC = 30,000 + 50Q$ is 50. So MC equals 50. Setting $MR = MC$ to determine the profit-maximizing quantity:

$$100 - 0.02Q = 50, \text{ or}$$

$$Q = 2,500.$$

Substituting the profit-maximizing quantity into the inverse demand function to determine the price:

$$P = 100 - (0.01)(2,500) = 75 \text{ cents.}$$

Profit equals total revenue minus total cost:

$$\pi = (75)(2,500) - (30,000 + (50)(2,500)), \text{ or}$$

$$\pi = \$325 \text{ per week.}$$

b. **If the government decides to levy a tax of 10 cents per unit on this product, what will be the new level of production, price, and profit?**

Suppose initially that the consumers must pay the tax to the government. Since the total price (including the tax) consumers would be willing to pay remains unchanged, we know that the demand function is

$$P^* + T = 100 - 0.01Q, \text{ or}$$
$$P^* = 100 - 0.01Q - T,$$

where P^* is the price received by the suppliers. Because the tax increases the price of each unit, total revenue for the monopolist decreases by TQ, and marginal revenue, the revenue on each additional unit, decreases by T:

$$MR = 100 - 0.02Q - T$$

where $T = 10$ cents. To determine the profit-maximizing level of output with the tax, equate marginal revenue with marginal cost:

$$100 - 0.02Q - 10 = 50, \text{ or}$$
$$Q = 2,000 \text{ units.}$$

Substituting Q into the demand function to determine price:

$$P^* = 100 - (0.01)(2,000) - 10 = 70 \text{ cents.}$$

Profit is total revenue minus total cost:

$$\pi = (70)(2,000) - \big((50)(2,000) + 30,000\big) = 10,000 \text{ cents, or}$$

$$\$100 \text{ per week.}$$

Note: The price facing the consumer after the imposition of the tax is 80 cents. The monopolist receives 70 cents. Therefore, the consumer and the monopolist each pay 5 cents of the tax.

If the monopolist had to pay the tax instead of the consumer, we would arrive at the same result. The monopolist's cost function would then be

$$TC = 50Q + 30,000 + TQ = (50 + T)Q + 30,000.$$

The slope of the cost function is $(50 + T)$, so $MC = 50 + T$. We set this MC to the marginal revenue function from part (a):

$$100 - 0.02Q = 50 + 10, \text{ or}$$
$$Q = 2,000.$$

Thus, it does not matter who sends the tax payment to the government. The burden of the tax is reflected in the price of the good.

5. The following table shows the demand curve facing a monopolist who produces at a constant marginal cost of \$10.

Price	Quantity
27	0
24	2
21	4
18	6
15	8
12	10
9	12
6	14

3	16
0	18

a.   Calculate the firm's marginal revenue curve.

To find the marginal revenue curve, we first derive the inverse demand curve. The intercept of the inverse demand curve on the price axis is 27. The slope of the inverse demand curve is the change in price divided by the change in quantity. For example, a decrease in price from 27 to 24 yields an increase in quantity from 0 to 2. Therefore, the slope is $-\frac{3}{2}$ and the demand curve is

$$P = 27 - 1.5Q.$$

The marginal revenue curve corresponding to a linear demand curve is a line with the same intercept as the inverse demand curve and a slope that is twice as steep. Therefore, the marginal revenue curve is

$$MR = 27 - 3Q.$$

b.   What are the firm's profit-maximizing output and price? What is its profit?

The monopolist's maximizing output occurs where marginal revenue equals marginal cost. Marginal cost is a constant $10. Setting *MR* equal to *MC* to determine the profit-maximizing quantity:

$$27 - 3Q = 10, \text{ or } Q = 5.67.$$

To find the profit-maximizing price, substitute this quantity into the demand equation:

$$P = 27 - (1.5)(5.67) = \$18.5.$$

Total revenue is price times quantity:

$$TR = (18.5)(5.67) = \$104.83.$$

The profit of the firm is total revenue minus total cost, and total cost is equal to average cost times the level of output produced. Since marginal cost is constant, average variable cost is equal to marginal cost. Ignoring any fixed costs, total cost is $10Q$ or 56.67, and profit is

$$104.83 - 56.67 = \$48.17.$$

c.   What would the equilibrium price and quantity be in a competitive industry?

For a competitive industry, price would equal marginal cost at equilibrium. Setting the expression for price equal to a marginal cost of 10:

$$27 - 1.5Q = 10 \Rightarrow Q = 11.3 \Rightarrow P = 10.$$

Note the increase in the equilibrium quantity compared to the monopoly solution.

d.   What would the social gain be if this monopolist were forced to produce and price at the competitive equilibrium? Who would gain and lose as a result?

The social gain arises from the elimination of deadweight loss. Deadweight loss in this case is equal to the triangle above the constant marginal cost curve, below the demand curve, and between the quantities 5.67 and 11.3, or numerically

(18.5-10)(11.3-5.67)(.5)=$24.10.

Consumers gain this deadweight loss plus the monopolist's profit of $48.17. The monopolist's profits are reduced to zero, and the consumer surplus increases by $72.27.

6. A firm has two factories for which costs are given by:

$$\text{Factory \#1: } C_1(Q_1) = 10Q_1^2$$

$$\text{Factory \#2: } C_2(Q_2) = 20Q_2^2$$

The firm faces the following demand curve:

$$P = 700 - 5Q$$

where Q is total output, i.e. Q = Q$_1$ + Q$_2$.

a.   **On a diagram, draw the marginal cost curves for the two factories, the average and marginal revenue curves, and the total marginal cost curve (i.e., the marginal cost of producing Q = Q$_1$ + Q$_2$). Indicate the profit-maximizing output for each factory, total output, and price.**

The average revenue curve is the demand curve,

$$P = 700 - 5Q.$$

For a linear demand curve, the marginal revenue curve has the same intercept as the demand curve and a slope that is twice as steep:

$$MR = 700 - 10Q.$$

Next, determine the marginal cost of producing Q. To find the marginal cost of production in Factory 1, take the first derivative of the cost function with respect to Q:

$$\frac{dC_1(Q_1)}{dQ} = 20Q_1.$$

Similarly, the marginal cost in Factory 2 is

$$\frac{dC_2(Q_2)}{dQ} = 40Q_2.$$

Rearranging the marginal cost equations in inverse form and horizontally summing them, we obtain total marginal cost, MC_T:

$$Q = Q_1 + Q_2 = \frac{MC_1}{20} + \frac{MC_2}{40} = \frac{3MC_T}{40}, \text{ or}$$

$$MC_T = \frac{40Q}{3}.$$

Profit maximization occurs where $MC_T = MR$. See Figure 10.6.a for the profit-maximizing output for each factory, total output, and price.

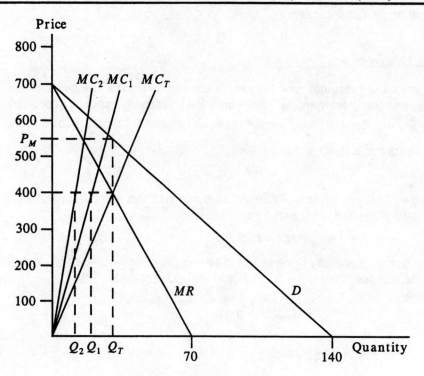

Figure 10.6.a

b. **Calculate the values of Q_1, Q_2, Q, and P that maximize profit.**

Calculate the total output that maximizes profit, i.e., Q such that $MC_T = MR$:

$$\frac{40Q}{3} = 700 - 10Q, \text{ or } Q = 30.$$

Next, observe the relationship between *MC* and *MR* for multiplant monopolies:

$$MR = MC_T = MC_1 = MC_2.$$

We know that at $Q = 30$, $MR = 700 - (10)(30) = 400$.

Therefore,

$$MC_1 = 400 = 20Q_1, \text{ or } Q_1 = 20 \text{ and}$$

$$MC_2 = 400 = 40Q_2, \text{ or } Q_2 = 10.$$

To find the monopoly price, P_M, substitute for Q in the demand equation:

$$P_M = 700 - (5)(30), \text{ or}$$

$$P_M = 550.$$

c. **Suppose labor costs increase in Factory 1 but not in Factory 2. How should the firm adjust the following(i.e., raise, lower, or leave unchanged): Output in Factory 1? Output in Factory 2? Total output? Price?**

An increase in labor costs will lead to a horizontal shift to the left in MC_1, causing MC_T to shift to the left as well (since it is the horizontal sum of MC_1 and MC_2). The new MC_T curve intersects the MR curve at a lower quantity and higher marginal revenue. At a higher level of marginal revenue, Q_2 is greater than at the original level for MR. Since Q_T falls and Q_2 rises, Q_1 must fall. Since Q_T falls, price must rise.

7. A drug company has a monopoly on a new patented medicine. The product can be made in either of two plants. The costs of production for the two plants are

$MC_1 = 20 + 2Q_1$, and $MC_2 = 10 + 5Q_2$. The firm's estimate of the demand for the product is

$P = 20 - 3(Q_1 + Q_2)$. How much should the firm plan to produce in each plant, and at what price should it plan to sell the product?

First, notice that *only MC_2* is relevant because the marginal cost curve of the first plant lies above the demand curve.

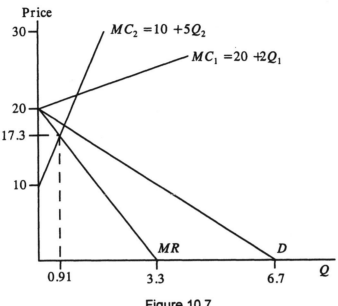

Figure 10.7

· This means that the demand curve becomes $P = 20 - 3Q_2$. With an inverse linear demand curve, we know that the marginal revenue curve has the same vertical intercept but twice the slope, or $MR = 20 - 6Q_2$. To determine the profit-maximizing level of output, equate MR and MC_2:

$$20 - 6Q_2 = 10 + 5Q_2, \text{ or}$$

$$Q = Q_2 = 0.91.$$

Price is determined by substituting the profit-maximizing quantity into the demand equation:
$$P = 20 - 3(0.91) = 17.3.$$

8. One of the more important antitrust cases of this century involved the Aluminum Company of America (Alcoa) in 1945. At that time, Alcoa controlled about 90 percent of primary aluminum production in the United States, and the company had been accused of monopolizing the aluminum market. In its defense, Alcoa argued that although it indeed controlled a large fraction of the primary market, secondary aluminum (i.e., aluminum produced from the recycling of scrap) accounted for roughly 30 percent of the total supply of aluminum, and many competitive firms were engaged in recycling. Therefore, Alcoa argued, it did not have much monopoly power.

a.   Provide a clear argument *in favor* of Alcoa's position.

Although Alcoa controlled about 90 percent of primary aluminum production in the United States, secondary aluminum production by recyclers accounted for 30 percent of the total aluminum supply. Therefore, with a higher price, a much larger proportion of aluminum supply could come from secondary sources. This assertion is true because there is a large stock of potential supply in the economy. Therefore, the price elasticity of demand for Alcoa's primary aluminum is much higher (in absolute value) than we would expect, given Alcoa's dominant position in primary aluminum production. In many applications, other metals such as copper and steel are feasible substitutes for aluminum. Again, the demand elasticity Alcoa faces might be higher than we would otherwise expect.

b.   Provide a clear argument *against* Alcoa's position.

While Alcoa could not raise its price by very much at any one time, the stock of potential aluminum supply is limited. Therefore, by keeping a stable high price, Alcoa could reap monopoly profits. Also, since Alcoa had originally produced the metal reappearing as recycled scrap, it would have considered the effect of scrap reclamation on future prices. Therefore, it exerted effective monopolistic control over the secondary metal supply.

c.   The 1945 decision by Judge Learned Hand has been called "one of the most celebrated judicial opinions of our time." Do you know what Judge Hand's ruling was?

Judge Hand ruled against Alcoa but did not order it to divest itself of any of its United States production facilities. The two remedies imposed by the court were (1) that Alcoa was barred from bidding for two primary aluminum plants constructed by the government during World War II (they were sold to Reynolds and Kaiser) and (2) that it divest itself of its Canadian subsidiary, which became Alcan.

9. A monopolist faces the demand curve P = 11 - Q, where P is measured in dollars per unit and Q in thousands of units. The monopolist has a constant average cost of $6 per unit.

a.   Draw the average and marginal revenue curves and the average and marginal cost curves. What are the monopolist's profit-maximizing price and quantity? What is the resulting profit? Calculate the firm's degree of monopoly power using the Lerner index.

Because demand (average revenue) may be described as $P = 11 - Q$, we know that the marginal revenue function is $MR = 11 - 2Q$. We also know that if average cost is constant, then marginal cost is constant and equal to average cost: $MC = 6$.

To find the profit-maximizing level of output, set marginal revenue equal to marginal cost:
$$11 - 2Q = 6, \text{ or } Q = 2.5.$$

That is, the profit-maximizing quantity equals 2,500 units. Substitute the profit-maximizing quantity into the demand equation to determine the price:

$$P = 11 - 2.5 = \$8.50.$$

Profits are equal to total revenue minus total cost,

$$\pi = TR - TC = (AR)(Q) - (AC)(Q), \text{ or}$$

$$\pi = (8.5)(2.5) - (6)(2.5) = 6.25, \text{ or } \$6,250.$$

The degree of monopoly power is given by the Lerner Index:

$$\frac{P - MC}{P} = \frac{8.5 - 6}{8.5} = 0.294.$$

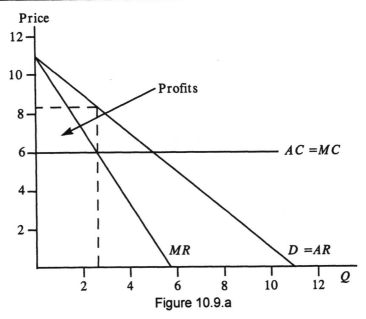

Figure 10.9.a

b. **A government regulatory agency sets a price ceiling of $7 per unit. What quantity will be produced, and what will the firm's profit be? What happens to the degree of monopoly power?**

To determine the effect of the price ceiling on the quantity produced, substitute the ceiling price into the demand equation.

$$7 = 11 - Q, \text{ or}$$

$$Q = 4{,}000.$$

The monopolist will pick the price of $7 because it is the highest price that it can charge, and this price is still greater than the constant marginal cost of $6, resulting in positive monopoly profit.

Profits are equal to total revenue minus total cost:

$$\pi = (7)(4{,}000) - (6)(4{,}000) = \$4{,}000.$$

The degree of monopoly power is:

$$\frac{P - MC}{P} = \frac{7 - 6}{7} = 0.143.$$

c. **What price ceiling yields the largest level of output? What is that level of output? What is the firm's degree of monopoly power at this price?**

If the regulatory authority sets a price below $6, the monopolist would prefer to go out of business instead of produce because it cannot cover its average costs. At any price above $6, the monopolist would produce less than the 5,000 units that would be produced in a competitive industry. Therefore, the regulatory agency should set a price ceiling of $6, thus making the monopolist face a horizontal effective demand curve up to Q = 5,000. To ensure a positive output (so that the monopolist is not indifferent between producing 5,000 units and shutting down), the price ceiling should be set at $6 + δ, where δ is small.

Thus, 5,000 is the maximum output that the regulatory agency can extract from the monopolist by using a price ceiling. The degree of monopoly power is

$$\frac{P - MC}{P} = \frac{6 + \delta - 6}{6} = \frac{\delta}{6} \to 0 \text{ as } \delta \to 0.$$

131

10. Michelle's Monopoly Mutant Turtles (MMMT) has the exclusive right to sell Mutant Turtle t-shirts in the United States. The demand for these t-shirts is Q = 10,000/P². The firm's short-run cost is SRTC = 2,000 + 5Q, and its long-run cost is LRTC = 6Q.

a. What price should MMMT charge to maximize profit in the short run? What quantity does it sell, and how much profit does it make? Would it be better off shutting down in the short run?

MMMT should offer enough t-shirts such that $MR = MC$. In the short run, marginal cost is the change in $SRTC$ as the result of the production of another t-shirt, i.e., $SRMC = 5$, the slope of the $SRTC$ curve. Demand is:

$$Q = \frac{10,000}{P^2},$$

or, in inverse form,

$$P = 100Q^{-1/2}.$$

Total revenue (PQ) is $100Q^{1/2}$. Taking the derivative of TR with respect to Q, $MR = 50Q^{-1/2}$. Equating MR and MC to determine the profit-maximizing quantity:

$$5 = 50Q^{-1/2}, \text{ or } Q = 100.$$

Substituting $Q = 100$ into the demand function to determine price:

$$P = (100)(100^{-1/2}) = 10.$$

The profit at this price and quantity is equal to total revenue minus total cost:

$$\pi = (10)(100) - (2000 + (5)(100)) = -\$1,500.$$

Although profit is negative, price is above the average variable cost of 5 and therefore, the firm should not shut down in the short run. Since most of the firm's costs are fixed, the firm loses $2,000 if nothing is produced. If the profit-maximizing quantity is produced, the firm loses only $1,500.

b. What price should MMMT charge in the long run? What quantity does it sell and how much profit does it make? Would it be better off shutting down in the long run?

In the long run, marginal cost is equal to the slope of the $LRTC$ curve, which is 6.

Equating marginal revenue and long run marginal cost to determine the profit-maximizing quantity:

$$50Q^{-1/2} = 6 \text{ or } Q = 69.44$$

Substituting $Q = 69.44$ into the demand equation to determine price:

$$P = (100)[(50/6)^2]^{-1/2} = (100)(6/50) = 12$$

Therefore, total revenue is $833.33 and total cost is $416.67. Profit is $416.67. The firm should remain in business.

c. Can we expect MMMT to have lower marginal cost in the short run than in the long run? Explain why.

In the long run, MMMT must replace all fixed factors. Therefore, we can expect $LRMC$ to be higher than $SRMC$.

11. You produce widgets to sell in a perfectly competitive market at a market price of $10 per widget. Your widgets are manufactured in two plants, one in Massachusetts and the other in Connecticut. Because of labor problems in Connecticut, you are forced to raise wages there, so marginal costs in that plant increase. In response to this, should you shift production and produce more in the Massachusetts plant?

No, production should not shift to the Massachusetts plant, although production in the Connecticut plant should be reduced. In order to maximize profits, a multiplant firm will schedule production at all plants so that the following two conditions are met:

- Marginal costs of production at each plant are equal.

- Marginal revenue of the total amount produced is equal to the marginal cost at each plant.

These two rules can be summarized as $MR=MC_1=MC_2=MC_T$, where the subscript indicates the plant.

The firm in this example has two plants and is in a perfectly competitive market. In a perfectly competitive market $P = MR$. To maximize profits, production among the plants should be allocated such that:

$$P = MC_c(Q_c) = MC_m(Q_m),$$

where the subscripts denote plant locations (c for Connecticut, etc.). The marginal costs of production have increased in Connecticut but have not changed in Massachusetts. Since costs have not changed in Massachusetts, the level of Q_m that sets $MC_m(Q_m) = P$, has not changed.

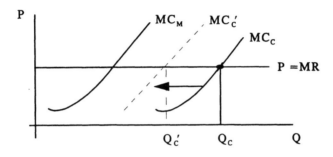

Figure 10.11

12. The employment of teaching assistants (TAs) by major universities can be characterized as a monopsony. Suppose the demand for TAs is W = 30,000 - 125n, where W is the wage (as an annual salary), and n is the number of TAs hired. The supply of TAs is given by W = 1,000 + 75n.

a. **If the university takes advantage of its monopsonist position, how many TAs will it hire? What wage will it pay?**

The supply curve is equivalent to the average expenditure curve. With a supply curve of $W = 1,000 + 75n$, the total expenditure is $Wn = 1,000n + 75n^2$. Taking the derivative of the total expenditure function with respect to the number of TAs, the marginal expenditure curve is $1,000 + 150n$. As a monopsonist, the university would equate marginal value (demand) with marginal expenditure to determine the number of TAs to hire:

$$30,000 - 125n = 1,000 + 150n, \text{ or}$$

$$n = 105.5.$$

Substituting $n = 105.5$ into the supply curve to determine the wage:

$$1,000 + (75)(105.5) = \$8,909 \text{ annually.}$$

b. **If, instead, the university faced an infinite supply of TAs at the annual wage level of $10,000, how many TAs would it hire?**

With an infinite number of TAs at $10,000, the supply curve is horizontal at $10,000. Total expenditure is $(10,000)(n)$, and marginal expenditure is 10,000. Equating marginal value and marginal expenditure:

$$30,000 - 125n = 10,000, \text{ or}$$

$$n = 160.$$

13. **Dayna's Doorstops, Inc. (DD), is a monopolist in the doorstop industry. Its cost is $C = 100 - 5Q + Q^2$, and demand is $P = 55 - 2Q$.**

a. **What price should DD set to maximize profit? What output does the firm produce? How much profit and consumer surplus does DD generate?**

To maximize profits, DD should equate marginal revenue and marginal cost. Given a demand of $P = 55 - 2Q$, we know that total revenue, PQ, is $55Q - 2Q^2$. Marginal revenue is found by taking the first derivative of total revenue with respect to Q or:

$$MR = \frac{dTR}{dQ} = 55 - 4Q.$$

Similarly, marginal cost is determined by taking the first derivative of the total cost function with respect to Q or:

$$MC = \frac{dTC}{dQ} = 2Q - 5.$$

Equating MC and MR to determine the profit-maximizing quantity,

$$55 - 4Q = 2Q - 5, \text{ or}$$

$$Q = 10.$$

Substituting $Q = 10$ into the demand equation to determine the profit-maximizing price:

$$P = 55 - (2)(10) = \$35.$$

Profits are equal to total revenue minus total cost:

$$\pi = (35)(10) - (100 - (5)(10) + 10^2) = \$200.$$

Consumer surplus is equal to one-half times the profit-maximizing quantity, 10, times the difference between the demand intercept (the maximum price anyone is willing to pay) and the monopoly price:

$$CS = (0.5)(10)(55 - 35) = \$100.$$

b. **What would output be if DD acted like a perfect competitor and set MC = P? What profit and consumer surplus would then be generated?**

In competition, profits are maximized at the point where price equals marginal cost, where price is given by the demand curve:

$$55 - 2Q = -5 + 2Q, \text{ or}$$

$$Q = 15.$$

Substituting $Q = 15$ into the demand equation to determine the price:

$$P = 55 - (2)(15) = \$25.$$

Profits are total revenue minus total cost or:

$$\pi = (25)(15) - (100 - (5)(15) + 15^2) = \$125.$$

Consumer surplus is

$$CS = (0.5)(55 - 25)(15) = \$225.$$

c.   What is the deadweight loss from monopoly power in part (a)?

The deadweight loss is equal to the area below the demand curve, above the marginal cost curve, and between the quantities of 10 and 15, or numerically

$$DWL = (0.5)(35 - 15)(15 - 10) = \$50.$$

d.   Suppose the government, concerned about the high price of doorstops, sets a maximum price at \$27. How does this affect price, quantity, consumer surplus, and DD's profit? What is the resulting deadweight loss?

With the imposition of a price ceiling, the maximum price that DD may charge is \$27.00. Note that when a ceiling price is set above the competitive price the ceiling price is equal to marginal revenue for all levels of output sold up to the competitive level of output.

Substitute the ceiling price of \$27.00 into the demand equation to determine the effect on the equilibrium quantity sold:

$$27 = 55 - 2Q, \text{ or } Q = 14.$$

Consumer surplus is

$$CS = (0.5)(55 - 27)(14) = \$196.$$

Profits are

$$\pi = (27)(14) - (100 - (5)(14) + 14^2) = \$152.$$

The deadweight loss is \$2.00 This is equivalent to a triangle of

$$(0.5)(15 - 14)(27 - 23) = \$2$$

e.   Now suppose the government sets the maximum price at \$23. How does this affect price, quantity, consumer surplus, DD's profit, and deadweight loss?

With a ceiling price set below the competitive price, DD will decrease its output. Equate marginal revenue and marginal cost to determine the profit-maximizing level of output:

$$23 = -5 + 2Q, \text{ or } Q = 14.$$

With the government-imposed maximum price of \$23, profits are

$$\pi = (23)(14) - (100 - (5)(14) + 14^2) = \$96.$$

Consumer surplus is realized on only 14 doorsteps. Therefore, it is equal to the consumer surplus in part *d*., i.e. \$196, plus the savings on each doorstep, i.e.,

$$CS = (27 - 23)(14) = \$56.$$

Therefore, consumer surplus is \$252. Deadweight loss is the same as before, \$2.00.

f.   Finally, consider a maximum price of \$12. What will this do to quantity, consumer surplus, profit, and deadweight loss?

With a maximum price of only \$12, output decreases even further:

$$12 = -5 + 2Q, \text{ or } Q = 8.5.$$

Profits are

$$\pi = (12)(8.5) - (100 - (5)(8.5) + 8.5^2) = -\$27.75.$$

Consumer surplus is realized on only 8.5 units, which is equivalent to the consumer surplus associated with a price of \$38 (38 = 55 - 2(8.5)), i.e.,

$$(0.5)(55 - 38)(8.5) = \$72.25$$

plus the savings on each doorstep, i.e.,

$$(38 - 12)(8.5) = \$221.$$

Therefore, consumer surplus is $293.25. Total surplus is $265.50, and deadweight loss is $84.50.

*14. There are 10 households in Lake Wobegon, Minnesota, each with a demand for electricity of Q = 50 - P. Lake Wobegon Electric's (LWE) cost of producing electricity is TC = 500 + Q.

a. **If the regulators of LWE want to make sure that there is no deadweight loss in this market, what price will they force LWE to charge? What will output be in that case? Calculate consumer surplus and LWE's profit with that price.**

The first step in solving the regulator's problem is to determine the market demand for electricity in Lake Wobegon. The quantity demanded in the market is the sum of the quantity demanded by each individual at any given price. Graphically, we horizontally sum each household's demand for electricity to arrive at market demand, and mathematically

$$Q_M = \sum_{i=1}^{10} Q_i = 10(50 - P) = 500 - 10P \Rightarrow P = 50 - .1Q.$$

To avoid deadweight loss, the regulators will set price equal to marginal cost. Given

$TC = 500+Q$, $MC = 1$ (the slope of the total cost curve). Setting price equal to marginal cost, and solving for quantity:

$$50 - 0.1Q = 1, \text{ or}$$

$$Q = 490.$$

Profits are equal to total revenue minus total costs:

$$\pi = (1)(490) - (500+490), = -\$500.$$

Total consumer surplus is:

$$CS = (0.5)(50 - 1)(490) = 12{,}005, \text{ or } \$1{,}200.50 \text{ per household.}$$

b. **If regulators want to ensure that LWE doesn't lose money, what is the lowest price they can impose? Calculate output, consumer surplus, and profit. Is there any deadweight loss?**

To guarantee that LWE does not lose money, regulators will allow LWE to charge the average cost of production, where

$$AC = \frac{TC}{Q} = \frac{500}{Q} + 1.$$

To determine the equilibrium price and quantity under average cost pricing, set price equal to average cost:

$$50 - 0.1Q = \frac{500}{Q} + 1.$$

Solving for Q yields the following quadratic equation:

$$0.1Q^2 - 49Q + 500 = 0.$$

Note: if $Q^2 + bQ + c = 0$, then

$$Q = \frac{-b \pm \sqrt{b^2 - 4ac}}{2a}.$$

Using the quadratic formula:

$$Q = \frac{49 \pm \sqrt{49^2 - (4)(0.1)(500)}}{(2)(0.1)},$$

there are two solutions: 10.4 and 479.6. Note that at a quantity of 10.4, marginal revenue is greater than marginal cost, and the firm will gain by producing more output. Also, note that the larger quantity results in a lower price and hence a larger consumer surplus. Therefore, Q=479.6 and P=$2.04. At this quantity and price, profit is zero (given some slight rounding error). Consumer surplus is

$$CS = (0.5)(50 - 2.04)(479.6) = \$11,500.$$

Deadweight loss is

$$DWL = (2.04 - 1)(490 - 479.6)(0.5) = \$5.40.$$

c. **Kristina knows that deadweight loss is something that this small town can do without. She suggests that each household be required to pay a fixed amount just to receive any electricity at all, and then a per-unit charge for electricity. Then LWE can break even while charging the price you calculated in part (a). What fixed amount would each household have to pay for Kristina's plan to work? Why can you be sure that no household will choose instead to refuse the payment and go without electricity?**

Fixed costs are $500. If each household pays $50, the fixed costs are covered and the utility can charge marginal cost for electricity. Because consumer surplus per household under marginal cost pricing is $1200.50, each would be willing to pay the $50.

15. A monopolist faces the following demand curve:

$$Q = 144/P^2$$

where Q is the quantity demanded and P is price. Its *average variable* cost is

$$AVC = Q^{1/2},$$

and its *fixed cost* is 5.

a. **What are its profit-maximizing price and quantity? What is the resulting profit?**

The monopolist wants to choose the level of output to maximize its profits, and it does this by setting marginal revenue equal to marginal cost. To find marginal revenue, first rewrite the demand function as a function of Q so that you can then express total revenue as a function of Q, and calculate marginal revenue:

$$Q = \frac{144}{P^2} \Rightarrow P^2 = \frac{144}{Q} \Rightarrow P = \sqrt{\frac{144}{Q}} = \frac{12}{\sqrt{Q}}$$

$$R = P * Q = \frac{12}{\sqrt{Q}} * Q = 12\sqrt{Q}$$

$$MR = \frac{\Delta R}{\Delta Q} = 0.5 * \frac{12}{\sqrt{Q}} = \frac{6}{\sqrt{Q}}.$$

To find marginal cost, first find total cost, which is equal to fixed cost plus variable cost. You are given fixed cost of 5. Variable cost is equal to average variable cost times Q so that total cost and marginal cost are:

$$TC = 5 + Q * Q^{\frac{1}{2}} = 5 + Q^{\frac{3}{2}}$$

$$MC = \frac{\Delta TC}{\Delta Q} = \frac{3\sqrt{Q}}{2}.$$

To find the profit-maximizing level of output, we set marginal revenue equal to marginal cost:

$$\frac{6}{\sqrt{Q}} = \frac{3\sqrt{Q}}{2} \Rightarrow Q = 4.$$

You can now find price and profit:

$$P = \frac{12}{\sqrt{Q}} = \frac{12}{\sqrt{4}} = \$6$$

$$\Pi = PQ - TC = 6*4 - (5 + 4^{\frac{3}{2}}) = \$11.$$

b. **Suppose the government regulates the price to be no greater than $4 per unit. How much will the monopolist produce? What will its profit be?**

The price ceiling truncates the demand curve that the monopolist faces at $P=4$ or $Q = \frac{144}{16} = 9$. Therefore, if the monopolist produces 9 units or less, the price must be $4. Because of the regulation, the demand curve now has two parts:

$$P = \begin{cases} \$4, & \text{if } Q \le 9 \\ 12Q^{-1/2}, & \text{if } Q > 9. \end{cases}$$

Thus, total revenue and marginal revenue also should be considered in two parts

$$TR = \begin{cases} 4Q, & \text{if } Q \le 9 \\ 12Q^{1/2}, & \text{if } Q > 9 \end{cases} \quad \text{and}$$

$$MR = \begin{cases} \$4, & \text{if } Q \le 9 \\ 6Q^{-1/2}, & \text{if } Q > 9. \end{cases}$$

To find the profit-maximizing level of output, set marginal revenue equal to marginal cost, so that for $P = 4$,

$$4 = \frac{3}{2}\sqrt{Q}, \text{ or } \sqrt{Q} = \frac{8}{3}, \text{ or } Q = 7.11.$$

If the monopolist produces an integer number of units, the profit-maximizing production level is 7 units, price is $4, revenue is $28, total cost is $23.52, and profit is $4.48. There is a shortage of two units, since the quantity demanded at the price of $4 is 9 units.

c. **Suppose the government wants to set a ceiling price that induces the monopolist to produce the largest possible output. What price will do this?**

To maximize output, the regulated price should be set so that demand equals marginal cost, which implies;

$$\frac{12}{\sqrt{Q}} = \frac{3\sqrt{Q}}{2} \Rightarrow Q = 8 \text{ and } P = \$4.24.$$

The regulated price becomes the monopolist's marginal revenue curve, which is a horizontal line with an intercept at the regulated price. To maximize profit, the firm produces where marginal cost is equal to marginal revenue, which results in a quantity of 8 units.

CHAPTER 11
PRICING WITH MARKET POWER

TEACHING NOTES

The chapter begins with a discussion of the basic objective of every pricing strategy which is to capture as much consumer surplus as possible and convert it into additional profit for the firm. The remainder of the chapter explores different methods of capturing the surplus. Section 11.2 discusses first, second, and third degree price discrimination, section 11.3 discusses intertemporal price discrimination and peak load pricing, section 11.4 discusses the two-part tariff, section 11.5 discusses bundling, and section 11.6 discusses advertising. If you are pressed for time you can pick and choose between sections 11.3 to 11.6. The chapter contains an excellent array of examples of how price discrimination is applied in different types of markets, not only in the formal examples but also in the body of the text. Although the graphs can seem very complicated to students, the challenge of figuring out how to price discriminate in a specific case can be quite stimulating and can promote many interesting class discussions. The Appendix to the chapter can be difficult for most students and should not be covered in class unless you are teaching a mathematical or business-oriented course. Should you choose to include the Appendix, make sure students have an intuitive feel for the model before presenting the algebra or geometry.

When introducing this chapter, highlight the requirements for profitable price discrimination: (1) supply-side market power, (2) the ability to separate customers, and (3) differing demand elasticities for different classes of customers. The discussion of first-degree price discrimination begins with the concept of a reservation price. The text uses reservation prices throughout the chapter. Since the discussion of Figure 11.2 may be confusing to students, an alternative presentation could begin with a diagram similar to Figure 9.1, with the addition of information from Figure 10.10. Show that with first-degree price discrimination the monopolist captures deadweight loss and all consumer surplus. Also, stress that with perfect price discrimination the marginal revenue curve coincides with the demand curve.

First-degree price discrimination is best followed by the discussion on third-degree, rather than second-degree, price discrimination. When you do cover second-degree price discrimination, note that many utilities currently charge higher prices for larger blocks. (Use your own electricity bill as an example.) The geometry of third-degree price discrimination is too difficult for most students; therefore, they need a careful explanation of the intuition behind the model. Slowly introduce the algebra so that students can see that the profit-maximizing quantities in each market are those where marginal revenue equals marginal cost. This section concludes with Examples 11.1 and 11.2. Because of the prevalence of coupons, rebates, and airline travel, all students will be able to relate to these examples.

When presenting intertemporal price discrimination and peak-load pricing, begin by comparing the similarities in the analysis with third-degree price discrimination. Discuss the difference between these forms of exploiting monopoly power and third-degree price discrimination. Here, marginal revenue and cost are equal within customer class but need not be equal across classes.

Students easily grasp the case of a two-part tariff with a single customer. Fewer will understand the case for two customers. Fewer still will understand the case of many different customers. Instead of moving directly into a discussion of more than one customer, you could introduce Example 11.4 to give concrete meaning to entry and usage fees. Then return to the cases dealing with more than one customer.

When discussing bundling, point out that in Figure 11.12 prices are on both axes. To introduce bundling, consider starting with Example 11.6 and a menu from a local restaurant. Make sure students understand when bundling is profitable (when demands are negatively correlated) and that mixed bundling can be more profitable than either selling separately or pure bundling (demands are only somewhat negatively correlated and/or when marginal production costs are significant). To distinguish tying, from bundling, point out that with tying the first product is useless without the second product.

REVIEW QUESTIONS

1. Suppose a firm can practice perfect, first-degree price discrimination. What is the lowest price it will charge, and what will its total output be?

When the firm is able to practice perfect first-degree price discrimination, each unit is sold at the reservation price of each consumer, assuming each consumer purchases one unit. Because each unit is sold at the consumer's reservation price, marginal revenue is simply the price of the last unit. We know that firms maximize profits by producing an output such that marginal revenue is equal to marginal cost. For the perfect price discriminator, that point is where the marginal cost curve intersects the demand curve. Increasing output beyond that point would imply that $MR < MC$, and the firm would lose money on each unit sold. For lower quantities, $MR > MC$, and the firm should increase its output.

2. How does a car salesperson practice price discrimination? How does the ability to discriminate correctly affect his or her earnings?

The relevant range of the demand curve facing the car salesperson is bounded above by the manufacturer's suggested retail price plus the dealer's markup and bounded below by the dealer's price plus administrative and inventory overhead. By sizing up the customer, the salesperson determines the customer's reservation price. Through a process of bargaining, a sales price is determined. If the salesperson has misjudged the reservation price of the customer, either the sale is lost because the customer's reservation price is lower than the salesperson's guess or profit is lost because the customer's reservation price is higher than the salesperson's guess. Thus, the salesperson's commission is positively correlated to his or her ability to determine the reservation price of each customer.

3. Electric utilities often practice second-degree price discrimination. Why might this improve consumer welfare?

Consumer surplus is higher under block pricing than under monopoly pricing because more output is produced. For example, assume there are two prices P_1 and P_2, with P_1 greater than P_2. Customers with reservation prices above P_1 pay P_1, capturing surplus equal to the area bounded by the demand curve and P_1. This also would occur with monopoly pricing. Under block pricing, customers with reservation prices between P_1 and P_2 capture surplus equal to the area bounded by the demand curve, the difference between P_1 and P_2, and the difference between Q_1 and Q_2. This quantity is greater than the surplus captured under monopoly, hence block pricing, under these assumptions, improves consumer welfare.

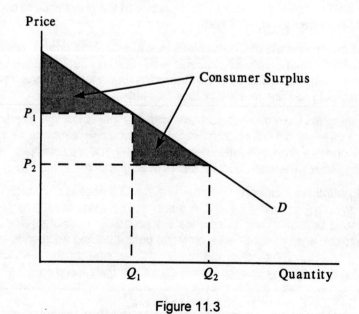

Figure 11.3

4. Give some examples of third-degree price discrimination. Can third-degree price discrimination be effective if the different groups of consumers have different levels of demand but the same price elasticities?

To engage in third-degree price discrimination, the producer must separate customers into distinct markets (sorting) and prevent the reselling of the product from customers in one market to customers in another market (arbitrage). While examples in this chapter stress the techniques for separating customers, there are also techniques for preventing resale. For example, airlines restrict the use of their tickets by printing the name of the passenger on the ticket. Other examples include dividing markets by age and gender, e.g., charging different prices for movie tickets to different age groups. If customers in the separate markets have the same price elasticities, then from equation 11.2 we know that the prices are the same in all markets. While the producer can effectively separate the markets, there is little profit incentive to do so.

5. Show why optimal, third-degree price discrimination requires that marginal revenue for each group of consumers equals marginal cost. Use this condition to explain how a firm should change its prices and total output if the demand curve for one group of consumers shifted outward, so that marginal revenue for that group increased.

We know that firms maximize profits by choosing output so marginal revenue is equal to marginal cost. If *MR* for one market is greater than *MC*, then the firm should increase sales to maximize profit, thus lowering the price on the last unit and raising the cost of producing the last unit. Similarly, if *MR* for one market is less than *MC*, the firm should decrease sales to maximize profit, thereby raising the price on the last unit and lowering the cost of producing the last unit. By equating *MR* and *MC* in each market, marginal revenue is equal in all markets.

If the quantity demanded increased, the marginal revenue at each price would also increase. If *MR* = *MC* before the demand shift, *MR* would be greater than *MC* after the demand shift. To lower *MR* and raise *MC*, the producer should increase sales to this market by lowering price, thus increasing output. This increase in output would increase *MC* of the last unit sold. To maximize profit, the producer must increase the *MR* on units sold in other markets, i.e., increase price in these other markets. The firm shifts sales to the market experiencing the increase in demand and away from other markets.

6. When pricing automobiles, American car companies typically charge a much higher percentage markup over cost for "luxury option" items (such as leather trim, etc.) than for the car itself or for more "basic" options such as power steering and automatic transmission. Explain why.

This can be explained as an instance of third-degree price discrimination. In order to use the model of third-degree price discrimination presented in the text, we need to assume that the costs of producing car options is a function of the total number of options produced and the production of each type of options affects costs in the same way. For simplicity, we can assume that there are two types of option packages, "luxury" and "basic," and that these two types of packages are purchased by two different types of consumers. In this case, the relationship across product types $MR_1 = MR_2$ must hold, which implies that:

$$P_1 / P_2 = (1 + 1/E_2) / (1 + 1/E_1)$$

where 1 and 2 denote the luxury and basic products types.

This means that the higher price is charged for the package with the lower elasticity of demand. Thus the pricing of automobiles can be explained if the "luxury" options are purchased by consumers with low elasticities of demand relative to consumers of more "basic" packages.

7. How is peak-load pricing a form of price discrimination? Can it make consumers better off? Give an example.

Price discrimination involves separating customers into distinct markets. There are several ways of segmenting markets: by customer characteristics, by geography, and by time. In peak-load pricing, sellers charge different prices to customers at different times. When there is a higher quantity demanded at each price, a higher price is charged. Peak-load pricing can increase total consumer surplus by charging a lower price to customers with elasticities greater than the average elasticity of the market as a whole. Most telephone companies charge a different price during normal business hours, evening hours, and night and weekend hours. Callers with more elastic demand wait until the period when the charge is closest to their reservation price.

8. How can a firm determine an optimal two-part tariff if it has two customers with different demand curves? (Assume that it knows the demand curves.)

If all customers had the same demand curve, the firm would set a price equal to marginal cost and a fee equal to consumer surplus. When consumers have different demand curves and, therefore, different levels of consumer surplus, the firm is faced with the following problem. If it sets the user fee equal to the larger consumer surplus, the firm will earn profits only from the consumers with the larger consumer surplus because the second group of consumers will not purchase any of the good. On the other hand, if the firm sets the fee equal to the smaller consumer surplus, the firm will earn revenues from both types of consumers.

9. Why is the pricing of a Gillette safety razor a form of a two-part tariff? Must Gillette be a monopoly producer of its blades as well as its razors? Suppose you were advising Gillette on how to determine the two parts of the tariff. What procedure would you suggest?

By selling the razor and the blades separately, the pricing of a Gillette safety razor can be thought of as a two-part tariff, where the entry fee is the cost of the razor and the usage fee is the cost of the blades. Gillette does not need to be a monopoly producer of its blades. In the simplest case where all consumers have identical demand curves, Gillette should set the blade price to marginal cost, and the razor cost to total consumer surplus for each consumer. Since blade price is set to marginal cost it does not matter if Gillette has a monopoly or not. The determination of the two parts of the tariff becomes more complicated the greater the variety of consumers with different demands, and there is no simple formula to calculate the optimal two part tariff. The key point to consider is that as the entry fee becomes smaller, the number of entrants will rise, and the profit from the entry fee will fall. Arriving at the optimal two part tariff might involve some amount of iteration over different entry and usage fees.

10. Why did Loews bundle *Gone with the Wind* and *Getting Gertie's Garter*? What characteristic of demands is needed for bundling to increase profits?

Loews bundled its film *Gone with the Wind* and *Getting Gertie's Garter* to maximize revenues. Because Loews could not price discriminate by charging a different price to each customer according to the customer's price elasticity, it chose to bundle the two films and charge theaters for showing both films. The price would have been the combined reservation prices of the last theater that Loews wanted to attract. Of course, this tactic would only maximize revenues if demands for the two films were negatively correlated, as discussed in the chapter.

11. How does mixed bundling differ from pure bundling? Under what conditions is mixed bundling preferable to pure bundling? Why do many restaurants practice mixed bundling (by offering complete dinners as well as an à la carte menu) instead of pure bundling?

Pure bundling involves selling products only as a package. Mixed bundling allows the consumer to purchase the products either separately or together. Mixed bundling yields higher profits than pure bundling when demands for the individual products do not have a strong negative correlation, marginal costs are high, or both. Restaurants can maximize profits with mixed bundling by offering both à la carte and full dinners by charging higher prices for individual items to capture the consumers' willingness to pay and lower prices for full dinners to induce customers with lower reservation prices to purchase more dinners.

12. How does tying differ from bundling? Why might a firm want to practice tying?

Tying involves the sale of two or more goods or services that must be used as complements. Bundling can involve complements or substitutes. Tying allows the firm to

142

monitor customer demand and more effectively determine profit-maximizing prices for the tied products. For example, a microcomputer firm might sell its computer, the tying product, with minimum memory and a unique architecture, then sell extra memory, the tied product, above marginal cost.

13. Why is it incorrect to advertise up to the point that the last dollar of advertising expenditures generates another dollar of sales? What is the correct rule for the marginal advertising dollar?

If the firm increases advertising expenditures to the point that the last dollar of advertising generates another dollar of sales, it will not be maximizing profits, because the firm is ignoring additional advertising costs. The correct rule is to advertise so that the marginal revenue of an additional dollar of advertising equals the additional dollars spent on advertising plus the marginal production cost of the increased sales.

14. How can a firm check that its advertising-to-sales ratio is not too high or too low? What information does it need?

The firm can check whether its advertising-to-sales ratio is profit maximizing by comparing it with the negative of the ratio of the advertising elasticity of demand to the price elasticity of demand. The firm must know both the advertising elasticity of demand and the price elasticity of demand.

EXERCISES

1. Price discrimination requires the ability to sort customers and the ability to prevent arbitrage. Explain how the following can function as price discrimination schemes and discuss both sorting and arbitrage:

a. Requiring airline travelers to spend at least one Saturday night away from home to qualify for a low fare.

The requirement of staying over Saturday night separates business travelers, who prefer to return for the weekend, from tourists, who travel on the weekend. Arbitrage is not possible when the ticket specifies the name of the traveler.

b. Insisting on delivering cement to buyers and basing prices on buyers' locations.

By basing prices on the buyer's location, customers are sorted by geography. Prices may then include transportation charges. These costs vary from customer to customer. The customer pays for these transportation charges whether delivery is received at the buyer's location or at the cement plant. Since cement is heavy and bulky, transportation charges may be large. This pricing strategy leads to "based-point-price systems," where all cement producers use the same base point and calculate transportation charges from this base point. Individual customers are then quoted the same price. For example, in *FTC v. Cement Institute*, 333 U.S. 683 [1948], the Court found that sealed bids by eleven companies for a 6,000-barrel government order in 1936 all quoted $3.286854 per barrel.

c. Selling food processors along with coupons that can be sent to the manufacturer to obtain a $10 rebate.

Rebate coupons with food processors separate consumers into two groups: (1) customers who are less price sensitive, i.e., those who have a lower elasticity of demand and do not request the rebate; and (2) customers who are more price sensitive, i.e., those who have a higher demand elasticity and do request the rebate. The latter group could buy the food processors, send in the rebate coupons, and resell the processors at a price just below the retail price without the rebate. To prevent this type of arbitrage, sellers could limit the number of rebates per household.

d. Offering temporary price cuts on bathroom tissue.

A temporary price cut on bathroom tissue is a form of intertemporal price discrimination. During the price cut, price-sensitive consumers buy greater quantities of tissue than they would otherwise. Non-price-sensitive consumers buy the same amount of tissue that they would buy without the price cut. Arbitrage is possible, but the profits on reselling bathroom tissue probably cannot compensate for the cost of storage, transportation, and resale.

e.   Charging high-income patients more than low-income patients for plastic surgery.

The plastic surgeon might not be able to separate high-income patients from low-income patients, but he or she can guess. One strategy is to quote a high price initially, observe the patient's reaction, and then negotiate the final price. Many medical insurance policies do not cover elective plastic surgery. Since plastic surgery cannot be transferred from low-income patients to high-income patients, arbitrage does not present a problem.

2. If the demand for drive-in movies is more elastic for couples than for single individuals, it will be optimal for theaters to charge one admission fee for the driver of the car and an extra fee for passengers. True or False? Explain.

True. Approach this question as a two-part tariff problem where the entry fee is a charge for the car plus the driver and the usage fee is a charge for each additional passenger other than the driver. Assume that the marginal cost of showing the movie is zero, i.e., all costs are fixed and do not vary with the number of cars. The theater should set its entry fee to capture the consumer surplus of the driver, a single viewer, and should charge a positive price for each passenger.

3. In Example 11.1, we saw how producers of processed foods and related consumer goods use coupons as a means of price discrimination. Although coupons are widely used in the United States, that is not the case in other countries. In Germany, the use of coupons is prohibited by law.

a.   Does prohibiting the use of coupons in Germany make German *consumers* better off or worse off?

In general, we cannot tell whether consumers will be better off or worse off. Total consumer surplus can increase or decrease with price discrimination, depending on the number of different prices charged and the distribution of consumer demand. Note, for example, that the use of coupons can increase the market size and therefore increase the total surplus of the market. Depending on the relative demand curves of the consumer groups and the producer's marginal cost curve, the increase in total surplus can be big enough to increase both producer surplus and consumer surplus. Consider the simple example depicted in Figure 11.3.a.

In this case there are two consumer groups with two different demand curves. Assuming marginal cost is zero, without price discrimination, consumer group 2 is left out of the market and thus has no consumer surplus. With price discrimination, consumer 2 is included in the market and collects some consumer surplus. At the same time, consumer 1 pays the same price under discrimination in this example, and therefore enjoys the same consumer surplus. The use of coupons (price discrimination) thus increases total consumer surplus in this example.

Furthermore, although the net change in consumer surplus is ambiguous in general, there is a transfer of consumer surplus from price-insensitive to price-sensitive consumers. Thus, price-sensitive consumers will benefit from coupons, even though on net consumers as a whole can be worse off.

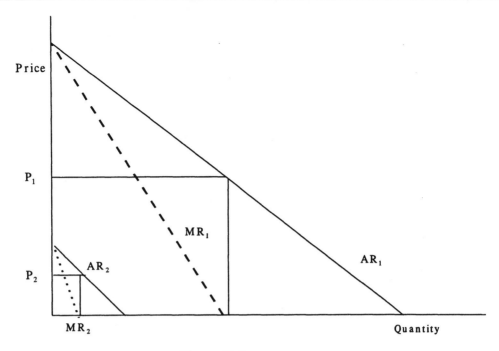

Figure 11.3.a

b. **Does prohibiting the use of coupons make German *producers* better off or worse off?**

Prohibiting the use of coupons will make the German producers worse off, or at least not better off. If firms can successfully price discriminate (i.e. they can prevent resale, there are barriers to entry, etc.), price discrimination can never make a firm worse off.

4. Suppose that BMW can produce any quantity of cars at a constant marginal cost equal to $15,000 and a fixed cost of $20 million. You are asked to advise the CEO as to what prices and quantities BMW should set for sales in Europe and in the U.S. The demand for BMWs in each market is given by:

$$Q_E = 18,000 - 400\,P_E \quad \text{and} \quad Q_U = 5500 - 100P_U$$

where the subscript *E* denotes Europe, the subscript *U* denotes the United States, and all prices and costs are in thousands of dollars. Assume that BMW can restrict U.S. sales to authorized BMW dealers only.

a. **What quantity of BMWs should the firm sell in each market, and what will the price be in each market? What will the total profit be?**

With separate markets, BMW chooses the appropriate levels of Q_E and Q_U to maximize profits, where profits are:

$$\pi = TR - TC = \left(Q_E P_E + Q_U P_U\right) - \left\{\left(Q_E + Q_U\right)15 + 20,000\right\}.$$

Solve for P_E and P_U using the demand equations, and substitute the expressions into the profit equation:

$$\pi = Q_E\left(45 - \frac{Q_E}{400}\right) + Q_U\left(55 - \frac{Q_U}{100}\right) - \left\{\left(Q_E + Q_U\right)15 + 20,000\right\}.$$

Differentiating and setting each derivative to zero to determine the profit-maximizing quantities:

$$\frac{\partial \pi}{\partial Q_E} = 45 - \frac{Q_E}{200} - 15 = 0, \text{ or } Q_E = 6,000 \text{ cars}$$

and

$$\frac{\partial \pi}{\partial Q_U} = 55 - \frac{Q_U}{50} - 15 = 0, \text{ or } Q_U = 2,000 \text{ cars.}$$

Substituting Q_E and Q_U into their respective demand equations, we may determine the price of cars in each market:

$$6,000 = 18,000 - 400P_E, \text{ or } P_E = \$30,000 \text{ and}$$

$$2,000 = 5,500 - 100P_U, \text{ or } P_U = \$35,000.$$

Substituting the values for Q_E, Q_U, P_E, and P_U into the profit equation, we have

$$\pi = \{(6,000)(30) + (2,000)(35)\} - \{(8,000)(15)) + 20,000\}, \text{ or}$$

$$\pi = \$110,000,000.$$

b.   If BMW were forced to charge the same price in each market, what would be the quantity sold in each market, the equilibrium price, and the company's profit?

If BMW charged the same price in both markets, we substitute $Q = Q_E + Q_U$ into the demand equation and write the new demand curve as

$$Q = 23,500 - 500P, \text{ or in inverse for as } P = 47 - \frac{Q}{500}.$$

Since the marginal revenue curve has twice the slope of the demand curve:

$$MR = 47 - \frac{Q}{250}.$$

To find the profit-maximizing quantity, set marginal revenue equal to marginal cost:

$$47 - \frac{Q}{250} = 15, \text{ or } Q^* = 8,000.$$

Substituting Q^* into the demand equation to determine price:

$$P = 47 - \left(\frac{8,000}{500}\right) = \$31,000.$$

Substituting into the demand equations for the European and American markets to find the quantity sold

$$Q_E = 18,000 - (400)(31), \text{ or } Q_E = 5,600 \text{ and}$$

$$Q_U = 5,500 - (100)(31), \text{ or } Q_U = 2,400.$$

Substituting the values for Q_E, Q_U, and P into the profit equation, we find

$$\pi = \{(5,600)(31) + (2,400)(31)\} - \{(8,000)(15)) + 20,000\}, \text{ or}$$

$$\pi = \$108,000,000.$$

5. A monopolist is deciding how to allocate output between two markets. The two markets are separated geographically (East Coast and Midwest). Demand and marginal revenue for the two markets are:

$$P_1 = 15 - Q_1 \qquad\qquad\qquad MR_1 = 15 - 2Q_1$$

$$P_2 = 25 - 2Q_2 \qquad\qquad\qquad MR_2 = 25 - 4Q_2.$$

The monopolist's total cost is C = 5 + 3(Q$_1$ + Q$_2$). What are price, output, profits, marginal revenues, and deadweight loss (i) if the monopolist can price discriminate? (ii) if the law prohibits charging different prices in the two regions?

With price discrimination, the monopolist chooses quantities in each market such that the marginal revenue in each market is equal to marginal cost. The marginal cost is equal to 3 (the slope of the total cost curve).

In the first market

$$15 - 2Q_1 = 3, \text{ or } Q_1 = 6.$$

In the second market

$$25 - 4Q_2 = 3, \text{ or } Q_2 = 5.5.$$

Substituting into the respective demand equations, we find the following prices for the two markets:

$$P_1 = 15 - 6 = \$9 \text{ and}$$
$$P_2 = 25 - 2(5.5) = \$14.$$

Noting that the total quantity produced is 11.5, then

$$\pi = ((6)(9) + (5.5)(14)) - (5 + (3)(11.5)) = \$91.5.$$

The monopoly deadweight loss in general is equal to

$$DWL = (0.5)(Q_C - Q_M)(P_M - P_C).$$

Here,

$$DWL_1 = (0.5)(12 - 6)(9 - 3) = \$18 \text{ and}$$
$$DWL_2 = (0.5)(11 - 5.5)(14 - 3) = \$30.25.$$

Therefore, the total deadweight loss is $48.25.

Without price discrimination, the monopolist must charge a single price for the entire market. To maximize profit, we find quantity such that marginal revenue is equal to marginal cost. Adding demand equations, we find that the total demand curve has a kink at $Q = 5$:

$$P = \begin{cases} 25 - 2Q, & \text{if } Q \le 5 \\ 18.33 - 0.67Q, & \text{if } Q > 5. \end{cases}$$

This implies marginal revenue equations of

$$MR = \begin{cases} 25 - 4Q, & \text{if } Q \le 5 \\ 18.33 - 1.33Q, & \text{if } Q > 5. \end{cases}$$

With marginal cost equal to 3, $MR = 18.33 - 1.33Q$ is relevant here because the marginal revenue curve "kinks" when $P = \$15$. To determine the profit-maximizing quantity, equate marginal revenue and marginal cost:

$$18.33 - 1.33Q = 3, \text{ or } Q = 11.5.$$

Substituting the profit-maximizing quantity into the demand equation to determine price:

$$P = 18.33 - (0.67)(11.5) = \$10.6.$$

With this price, $Q_1 = 4.3$ and $Q_2 = 7.2$. (Note that at these quantities $MR_1 = 6.3$ and $MR_2 = -3.7$).

Profit is

$$(11.5)(10.6) - (5 + (3)(11.5)) = \$83.2.$$

Deadweight loss in the first market is

$$DWL_1 = (0.5)(10.6-3)(12-4.3) = \$29.26.$$

Deadweight loss in the second market is

$$DWL_2 = (0.5)(10.6\text{-}3)(11\text{-}7.2) = \$14.44.$$

Total deadweight loss is $43.7. Note it is always possible to observe slight rounding error. With price discrimination, profit is higher, deadweight loss is smaller, and total output is unchanged. This difference occurs because the quantities in each market change depending on whether the monopolist is engaging in price discrimination.

*6. Elizabeth Airlines (EA) flies only one route: Chicago-Honolulu. The demand for each flight on this route is Q = 500 - P. Elizabeth's cost of running each flight is $30,000 plus $100 per passenger.

a. **What is the profit-maximizing price EA will charge? How many people will be on each flight? What is EA's profit for each flight?**

To find the profit-maximizing price, first find the demand curve in inverse form:

$$P = 500 - Q.$$

We know that the marginal revenue curve for a linear demand curve will have twice the slope, or

$$MR = 500 - 2Q.$$

The marginal cost of carrying one more passenger is $100, so $MC = 100$. Setting marginal revenue equal to marginal cost to determine the profit-maximizing quantity, we have:

$$500 - 2Q = 100, \text{ or } Q = 200 \text{ people per flight.}$$

Substituting Q equals 200 into the demand equation to find the profit-maximizing price for each ticket,

$$P = 500 - 200, \text{ or } P = \$300.$$

Profit equals total revenue minus total costs,

$$\pi = (300)(200) - \{30,000 + (200)(100)\} = \$10,000.$$

Therefore, profit is $10,000 per flight.

b. **Elizabeth learns that the fixed costs per flight are in fact $41,000 instead of $30,000. Will she stay in this business long? Illustrate your answer using a graph of the demand curve that EA faces, EA's average cost curve when fixed costs are $30,000, and EA's average cost curve when fixed costs are $41,000.**

An increase in fixed costs will not change the profit-maximizing price and quantity. If the fixed cost per flight is $41,000, EA will lose $1,000 on each flight. The revenue generated, $60,000, would now be less than total cost, $61,000. Elizabeth would shut down as soon as the fixed cost of $41,000 came due.

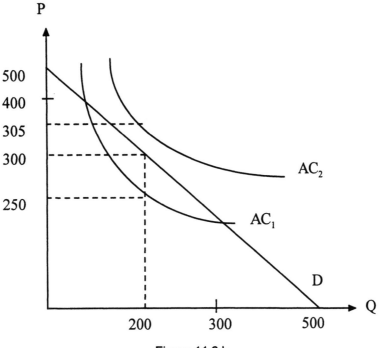

Figure 11.6.b

c. **Wait! EA finds out that two different types of people fly to Honolulu. Type A is business people with a demand of Q_A = 260 - 0.4P. Type B is students whose total demand is Q_B = 240 - 0.6P. The students are easy to spot, so EA decides to charge them different prices. Graph each of these demand curves and their horizontal sum. What price does EA charge the students? What price does EA charge other customers? How many of each type are on each flight?**

Writing the demand curves in inverse form, we find the following for the two markets:

$$P_A = 650 - 2.5Q_A \quad \text{and}$$
$$P_B = 400 - 1.67Q_B.$$

Using the fact that the marginal revenue curves have twice the slope of a linear demand curve, we have:

$$MR_A = 650 - 5Q_A \quad \text{and}$$
$$MR_B = 400 - 3.34Q_B.$$

To determine the profit-maximizing quantities, set marginal revenue equal to marginal cost in each market:

$$650 - 5Q_A = 100, \text{ or } Q_A = 110 \text{ and}$$
$$400 - 3.34Q_B = 100, \text{ or } Q_B = 90.$$

Substitute the profit-maximizing quantities into the respective demand curve to determine the appropriate price in each sub-market:

$$P_A = 650 - (2.5)(110) = \$375 \text{ and}$$
$$P_B = 400 - (1.67)(90) = \$250.$$

When she is able to distinguish the two groups, Elizabeth finds it profit-maximizing to charge a higher price to the Type A travelers, i.e., those who have a less elastic demand at any price.

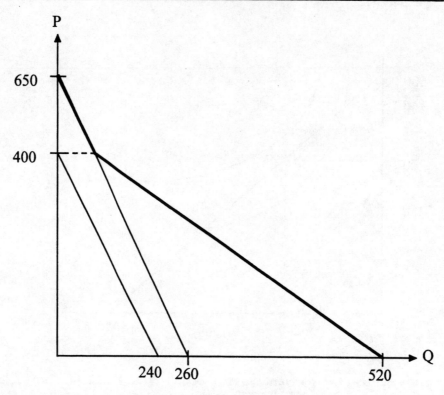

Figure 11.6.c

d. **What would EA's profit be for each flight? Would she stay in business? Calculate the consumer surplus of each consumer group. What is the total consumer surplus?**

With price discrimination, total revenue is

$$(90)(250) + (110)(375) = \$63{,}750.$$

Total cost is

$$41{,}000 + (90 + 110)(100) = \$61{,}000.$$

Profits per flight are

$$\pi = 63{,}750 - 61{,}000 = \$2{,}750.$$

Consumer surplus for Type A travelers is

$$(0.5)(650 - 375)(110) = \$15{,}125.$$

Consumer surplus for Type B travelers is

$$(0.5)(400 - 250)(90) = \$6{,}750$$

Total consumer surplus is $21,875.

e. **Before EA started price discriminating, how much consumer surplus was the Type A demand getting from air travel to Honolulu? Type B? Why did total surplus decline with price discrimination, even though the total quantity sold was unchanged?**

When price was $300, Type A travelers demanded 140 seats; consumer surplus was

$$(0.5)(650 - 300)(140) = \$24{,}500.$$

Type B travelers demanded 60 seats at P = $300; consumer surplus was

$$(0.5)(400 - 300)(60) = \$3{,}000.$$

Consumer surplus was therefore $27,500, which is greater than consumer surplus of $21,875 with price discrimination. Although the total quantity is unchanged by price discrimination, price discrimination has allowed EA to extract consumer surplus from those passengers who value the travel most.

7. **Many retail video stores offer two alternative plans for renting films:**

- **A *two-part tariff*: Pay an annual membership fee (e.g., $40) and then pay a small fee for the daily rental of each film (e.g., $2 per film per day).**

- **A *straight rental fee*: Pay no membership fee, but pay a higher daily rental fee (e.g., $4 per film per day).**

What is the logic behind the two-part tariff in this case? Why offer the customer a choice of two plans rather than simply a two-part tariff?

By employing this strategy, the firm allows consumers to sort themselves into two groups, or markets (assuming that subscribers do not rent to non-subscribers): high-volume consumers who rent many movies per year (here, more than 20) and low-volume consumers who rent only a few movies per year (less than 20). If only a two-part tariff is offered, the firm has the problem of determining the profit-maximizing entry and rental fees with many different consumers. A high entry fee with a low rental fee discourages low-volume consumers from subscribing. A low entry fee with a high rental fee encourages membership, but discourages high-volume customers from renting. Instead of forcing customers to pay both an entry and rental fee, the firm effectively charges two different prices to two types of customers.

8. **Sal's satellite company broadcasts TV to subscribers in Los Angeles and New York. The demand functions for each of these two groups are**

$$Q_{NY} = 50 - (1/3)P_{NY} \qquad\qquad Q_{LA} = 80 - (2/3)P_{LA}$$

where Q is in thousands of subscriptions per year and P is the subscription price per year. The cost of providing Q units of service is given by

$$C = 1,000 + 30Q$$

where $Q = Q_{NY} + Q_{LA}$.

a. **What are the profit-maximizing prices and quantities for the New York and Los Angeles markets?**

We know that a monopolist with two markets should pick quantities in each market so that the marginal revenues in both markets are equal to one another and equal to marginal cost. Marginal cost is $30 (the slope of the total cost curve). To determine marginal revenues in each market, we first solve for price as a function of quantity:

$$P_{NY} = 150 - 3Q_{NY} \quad \text{and}$$
$$P_{LA} = 120 - (3/2)Q_{LA}.$$

Since the marginal revenue curve has twice the slope of the demand curve, the marginal revenue curves for the respective markets are:

$$MR_{NY} = 150 - 6Q_{NY} \quad \text{and}$$
$$MR_{LA} = 120 - 3Q_{LA}.$$

Set each marginal revenue equal to marginal cost, and determine the profit-maximizing quantity in each submarket:

$$30 = 150 - 6Q_{NY}, \text{ or } Q_{NY} = 20 \text{ and}$$
$$30 = 120 - 3Q_{LA}, \text{ or } Q_{LA} = 30.$$

Determine the price in each submarket by substituting the profit-maximizing quantity into the respective demand equation:

$$P_{NY} = 150 - (3)(20) = \$90 \text{ and}$$

$$P_{LA} = 120 - (3/2)(30) = \$75.$$

b. **As a consequence of a new satellite that the Pentagon recently deployed, people in Los Angeles receive Sal's New York broadcasts, and people in New York receive Sal's Los Angeles broadcasts. As a result, anyone in New York or Los Angeles can receive Sal's broadcasts by subscribing in either city. Thus Sal can charge only a single price. What price should he charge, and what quantities will he sell in New York and Los Angeles?**

Given this new satellite, Sal can no longer separate the two markets. Since the total demand function is the horizontal summation of the LA and NY demand functions above a price of 120 (the vertical intercept of the demand function for Los Angeles viewers), the total demand is just the New York demand function. Below a price of 120, we add the two demands:

$$Q_T = 50 - (1/3)P + 80 - (2/3)P, \text{ or } Q_T = 130 - P.$$

Total revenue = $PQ = (130 - Q)Q$, or $130Q - Q^2$, and therefore, $MR = 130 - 2Q$.

Setting marginal revenue equal to marginal cost to determine the profit-maximizing quantity:

$$130 - 2Q = 30, \text{ or } Q = 50.$$

Substitute the profit-maximizing quantity into the demand equation to determine price:

$$50 = 130 - P, \text{ or } P = \$80.$$

Although a price of $80 is charged in both markets, different quantities are purchased in each market.

$$Q_{NY} = 50 - \left(\frac{1}{3}\right)(80) = 23\frac{1}{3} \quad \text{and}$$

$$Q_{LA} = 80 - \left(\frac{2}{3}\right)(80) = 26\frac{2}{3}.$$

Together, 50 units are purchased at a price of $80.

c. **In which of the above situations, (a) or (b), is Sal better off? In terms of consumer surplus, which situation do people in New York prefer and which do people in Los Angeles prefer? Why?**

Sal is better off in the situation with the highest profit. Under the market condition in 8a, profit is equal to:

$$\pi = Q_{NY}P_{NY} + Q_{LA}P_{LA} - (1{,}000 + 30(Q_{NY} + Q_{LA})), \text{ or}$$

$$\pi = (20)(90) + (30)(75) - (1{,}000 + 30(20 + 30)) = \$1{,}550.$$

Under the market conditions in 8b, profit is equal to:

$$\pi = Q_T P - (1{,}000 + 30Q_T), \text{ or}$$

$$\pi = (50)(80) - (1{,}000 + (30)(50)) = \$1{,}500.$$

Therefore, Sal is better off when the two markets are separated.

Consumer surplus is the area under the demand curve above price. Under the market conditions in 8a, consumer surpluses in New York and Los Angeles are:

$$CS_{NY} = (0.5)(150 - 90)(20) = \$600 \text{ and}$$
$$CS_{LA} = (0.5)(120 - 75)(30) = \$675.$$

Under the market conditions in 8b the respective consumer surpluses are:

$$CS_{NY} = (0.5)(150 - 80)(23.33) = \$816 \text{ and}$$
$$CS_{LA} = (0.5)(120 - 80)(26.67) = \$533.$$

The New Yorkers prefer 8*b* because the equilibrium price is $80 instead of $90, thus giving them a higher consumer surplus. The customers in Los Angeles prefer 8*a* because the equilibrium price is $75 instead of $80.

*9. You are an executive for Super Computer, Inc. (SC), which rents out super computers. SC receives a fixed rental payment per time period in exchange for the right to unlimited computing at a rate of P cents per second. SC has two types of potential customers of equal number--10 businesses and 10 academic institutions. Each business customer has the demand function Q = 10 - P, where Q is in millions of seconds per month; each academic institution has the demand Q = 8 - P. The marginal cost to SC of additional computing is 2 cents per second, regardless of the volume.

a. **Suppose that you could separate business and academic customers. What rental fee and usage fee would you charge each group? What are your profits?**

For academic customers, consumer surplus at a price equal to marginal cost is

$$(0.5)(8 - 2)(6) = 18 \text{ million cents per month or } \$180,000 \text{ per month.}$$

Therefore, charge $180,000 per month in rental fees and two cents per second in usage fees, i.e., the marginal cost. Each academic customer will yield a profit of $180,000 per month for total profits of $1,800,000 per month.

For business customers, consumer surplus is

$$(0.5)(10 - 2)(8) = 32 \text{ million cents or } \$320,000 \text{ per month.}$$

Therefore, charge $320,000 per month in rental fees and two cents per second in usage fees. Each business customer will yield a profit of $320,000 per month for total profits of $3,200,000 per month.

Total profits will be $5 million per month minus any fixed costs.

b. **Suppose you were unable to keep the two types of customers separate and charged a zero rental fee. What usage fee maximizes your profits? What are your profits?**

Total demand for the two types of customers with ten customers per type is

$$Q = (10)(10 - P) + (10)(8 - P) = 180 - 20P.$$

Solving for price as a function of quantity:

$$P = 9 - \frac{Q}{20}, \text{ which implies } MR = 9 - \frac{Q}{10}.$$

To maximize profits, set marginal revenue equal to marginal cost,

$$9 - \frac{Q}{10} = 2, \text{ or } Q = 70.$$

At this quantity, the profit-maximizing price, or usage fee, is 5.5 cents per second.

$$\pi = (5.5 - 2)(70) = \$2.45 \text{ million per month.}$$

c. **Suppose you set up one two-part tariff- that is, you set one rental and one usage fee that both business and academic customers pay. What usage and rental fees will you set? What are your profits? Explain why price is not equal to marginal cost.**

With a two-part tariff and no price discrimination, set the rental fee (RENT) to be equal to the consumer surplus of the academic institution (if the rental fee were set equal to that of business, academic institutions would not purchase any computer time):

$$\text{RENT} = CS_A = (0.5)(8 - P^*)(8 - P) = (0.5)(8 - P^*)^2.$$

Total revenue and total costs are:

$$TR = (20)(\text{RENT}) + (Q_A + Q_B)(P^*)$$

$$TC = 2(Q_A + Q_B).$$

Substituting for quantities in the profit equation with total quantity in the demand equation:

$$\pi = (20)(RENT) + (Q_A + Q_B)(P^*) - (2)(Q_A + Q_B), \text{ or}$$

$$\pi = (10)(8 - P^*)^2 + (P^* - 2)(180 - 20P^*).$$

Differentiating with respect to price and setting it equal to zero:

$$\frac{d\pi}{dP^*} = -20P^* + 60 = 0.$$

Solving for price, $P^* = 3$ cent per second. At this price, the rental fee is

$$(0.5)(8 - 3)^2 = 12.5 \text{ million cents or } \$125,000 \text{ per month.}$$

At this price

$$Q_A = (10)(8 - 3) = 50$$

$$Q_B = (10)(10 - 3) = 70.$$

The total quantity is 120 million seconds. Profits are rental fees plus usage fees minus total cost, i.e., (12.5)(20) plus (120)(3) minus 240, or 370 million cents, or $3.7 million per month. Price does not equal marginal cost, because SC can make greater profits by charging a rental fee and a higher-than-marginal-cost usage fee.

10. As the owner of the only tennis club in an isolated wealthy community, you must decide on membership dues and fees for court time. There are two types of tennis players. "Serious" players have demand

$$\mathbf{Q_1 = 6 - P}$$

where Q_1 is court hours per week and P is the fee per hour for each individual player. There are also "occasional" players with demand

$$\mathbf{Q_2 = 3 - (1/2)P.}$$

Assume that there are 1,000 players of each type. Because you have plenty of courts, the marginal cost of court time is zero. You have fixed costs of $5,000 per week. Serious and occasional players look alike, so you must charge them the same prices.

a. **Suppose that to maintain a "professional" atmosphere, you want to limit membership to serious players. How should you set the *annual* membership dues and court fees (assume 52 weeks per year) to maximize profits, keeping in mind the constraint that only serious players choose to join? What are profits (per week)?**

In order to limit membership to serious players, the club owner should charge an entry fee, T, equal to the total consumer surplus of serious players. With individual demands of $Q_1 = 6 - P$, individual consumer surplus is equal to:

$$(0.5)(6 - 0)(6 - 0) = \$18, \text{ or}$$

$$(18)(52) = \$936 \text{ per year.}$$

An entry fee of $936 maximizes profits by capturing all consumer surplus. The profit-maximizing court fee is set to zero, because marginal cost is equal to zero. The entry fee of $936 is higher than the occasional players are willing to pay (higher than their consumer surplus at a court fee of zero); therefore, this strategy will limit membership to the serious player. Weekly profits would be

$$\pi = (18)(1,000) - 5,000 = \$13,000.$$

b. **A friend tells you that you could make greater profits by encouraging both types of players to join. Is the friend right? What annual dues and court fees would maximize weekly profits? What would these profits be?**

When there are two classes of customers, serious and occasional players, the club owner maximizes profits by charging court fees above marginal cost and by setting the entry fee (annual dues) equal to the remaining consumer surplus of the consumer with the lesser demand, in this case, the occasional player. The entry fee, *T*, is equal to the consumer surplus remaining after the court fee is assessed:

$$T = (0.5)(Q_2)(6 - P),$$

where

$$Q_2 = 3 - \left(\frac{1}{2}\right)P, \text{ or}$$

$$T = (0.5)\left(3.0 - \frac{1}{2}P\right)(6 - P) = 9 - 3P + \frac{P^2}{4}.$$

The entry fees generated by all of the 2,000 players would be

$$(2,000)\left(9 - 3P + \frac{P^2}{4}\right) = 18,000 - 6,000P + 500P^2.$$

On the other hand, revenues from court fees are equal to

$$P(Q_1 + Q_2).$$

We can substitute demand as a function of price for Q_1 and Q_2:

$$P\left[(6 - P)(1,000) + \left(3 - \frac{P}{2}\right)(1,000)\right] = 9,000P - 1,500P^2.$$

Then total revenue from both entry and user fees is equal to

$$TR = 18,000 + 3,000P - 1,000P^2.$$

To maximize profits, the club owner should choose a price such that marginal revenue is equal to marginal cost, which in this case is zero. Marginal revenue is given by the slope of the total revenue curve:

$$MR = 3,000 - 2,000P.$$

Equating marginal revenue and marginal cost to maximize profits:

$$3,000 - 2,000P = 0, \text{ or } P = \$1.50.$$

Total revenue is equal to price time quantity, or:

$$TR = \$20,250.$$

Total cost is equal to fixed costs of $5,000. Profit with a two-part tariff is $15,250 per week, which is greater than the $13,000 per week generated when only professional players are recruited to be members.

c. **Suppose that over the years young, upwardly mobile professionals move to your community, all of whom are serious players. You believe there are now 3,000 serious players and 1,000 occasional players. Is it still profitable to cater to the occasional player? What are the profit-maximizing annual dues and court fees? What are profits per week?**

An entry fee of $18 per week would attract only serious players. With 3,000 serious players, total revenues would be $54,000 and profits would be $49,000 per week. With both serious and occasional players, we may follow the same procedure as in 10*b*. Entry fees would be equal to 4,000 times the consumer surplus of the occasional player:

$$T = 4,000\left(9 - 3P + \frac{P^2}{4}\right).$$

Court fees are:

$$P\left[(6-P)(3,000) + \left(3 - \frac{P}{2}\right)(1,000)\right] = \left(21P - 3.5P^2\right)(1,000).$$

Total revenue from both entry and user fees is equal to

$$TR = \left[4\left(9 - 3P + \frac{P^2}{4}\right) + \left(21P - 3.5P^2\right)\right](1,000) \text{ or}$$

$$TR = (36 + 9P - 2.5P^2)(1,000), \text{ or } TR = 36,000 + 9,000P - 2,500P^2.$$

This implies

$$MR = 9,000 - 5,000P.$$

Equate marginal revenue to marginal cost, which is zero, to determine the profit-maximizing price:

$$9,000 - 5,000P = 0, \text{ or } P = \$1.80.$$

Total revenue is equal to $44,100. Total cost is equal to fixed costs of $5,000. Profit with a two-part tariff is $39,100 per week, which is less than the $49,000 per week with only serious players. The club owner should set annual dues at $936 and earn profits of $2.548 million per year.

11. Look again at Figure 11.12, which shows the reservation prices of three consumers for two goods. Assuming that the marginal production cost is zero for both goods, can the producer make the most money by selling the goods separately, by bundling, or by using "mixed" bundling (i.e., offering the goods separately or as a bundle)? What prices should be charged?

The following tables summarize the reservation prices of the three consumers and the profits from the three strategies as shown in Figure 11.12 in the text:

	Reservation Price		
	For 1	For 2	Total
Consumer A	$ 3.25	$ 6.00	$ 9.25
Consumer B	$ 8.25	$ 3.25	$11.50
Consumer C	$10.00	$10.00	$20.00

	Price 1	Price 2	Bundled	Profit
Sell Separately	$ 8.25	$6.00	—	$28.50
Pure Bundling	—	—	$ 9.25	$27.75
Mixed Bundling	$10.00	$6.00	$11.50	$29.00

The profit-maximizing strategy is to use mixed bundling. When each item is sold separately, two of Product 1 are sold at $8.25, and two of Product 2 are sold at $6.00. In the pure bundling case, three bundles are purchased at a price of $9.25. The bundle price is determined by the lowest reservation price. With mixed bundling, one Product 2 is sold at $6.00 and two bundles at $11.50. Mixed bundling is often the ideal strategy when demands are only somewhat negatively correlated and/or when marginal production costs are significant.

12. Look again at Figure 11.17. Suppose the marginal costs c_1 and c_2 were zero. Show that in this case, pure bundling and not mixed bundling, is the most profitable pricing strategy. What price should be charged for the bundle? What will the firm's profit be?

Figure 11.17 in the text is reproduced as Figure 11.12 here. With marginal costs both equal to zero, the firm wants to sell as many units as possible to maximize profit. Here, revenue maximization is the same as profit maximization. The firm should set a price just under the sum of the reservation prices ($100), e.g. 99.95. At this price all customers purchase the bundle, and the firm's revenues are $399.80. This revenue is greater than setting $P_1 = P_2 = $89.95 and setting $P_B = $100 with the mixed bundling strategy. With mixed bundling, the firm sells one unit of Product 1, one unit of Product 2, and two bundles. Total revenue is $379.90, which is less than $399.80.

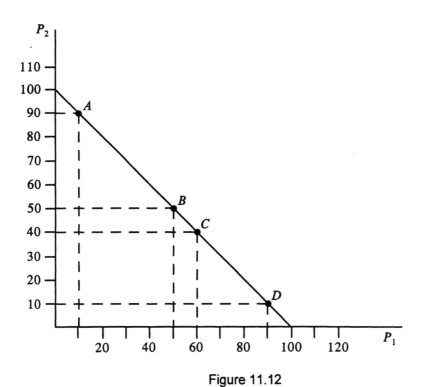

Figure 11.12

13. Some years ago, an article appeared in *The New York Times* about IBM's pricing policy. The previous day IBM had announced major price cuts on most of its small and medium-sized computers. The article said:

"IBM probably has no choice but to cut prices periodically to get its customers to purchase more and lease less. If they succeed, this could make life more difficult for IBM's major competitors. Outright purchases of computers are needed for ever larger IBM revenues and profits, says Morgan Stanley's Ulric Weil in his new book,

Information Systems in the '80's. **Mr. Weil declares that IBM cannot revert to an emphasis on leasing."**

a. **Provide a brief but clear argument *in support* of the claim that IBM should try "to get its customers to purchase more and lease less."**

If we assume there is no resale market, there are at least three arguments that could be made in support of the claim that IBM should try to "get its customers to purchase more and lease less." First, when customers purchase computers, they are "locked into" the product. They do not have the option of not renewing the lease when it expires. Second, by getting customers to purchase a computer instead of leasing it, IBM leads customers to make a stronger economic decision for IBM and against its competitors. Thus, it would be easier for IBM to eliminate its competitors if all its customers purchased, rather than leased, computers. Third, computers have a high obsolescence rate. If IBM believes that this rate is higher than what their customers perceive it is, the lease charges would be higher than what the customers would be willing to pay and it would be more profitable to sell the computers instead.

b. **Provide a brief but clear argument *against* this claim.**

The primary argument for leasing computers to customers, instead of selling the computers, is that because IBM has monopoly power on computers, it might be able to charge a two-part tariff and therefore extract some of the consumer surplus and increase its profits. For example, IBM could charge a fixed leasing fee plus a charge per unit of computing time used. Such a scheme would not be possible if the computers were sold outright.

c. **What factors determine whether leasing or selling is preferable for a company like IBM? Explain briefly.**

There are at least three factors that could determine whether leasing or selling is preferable for IBM. The first factor is the amount of consumer surplus that IBM could extract if the computer were leased and a two-part tariff scheme were applied. The second factor is the relative discount rates on cash flows: if IBM has a higher discount rate than its customers, it might prefer to sell; if IBM has a lower discount rate than its customers, it might prefer to lease. A third factor is the vulnerability of IBM's competitors. Selling computers would force customers to make more of a financial commitment to one company over the rest, while with a leasing arrangement the customers have more flexibility. Thus, if IBM feels it has the requisite market power, it should prefer to sell computers instead of lease them.

14. You are selling two goods, 1 and 2, to a market consisting of three consumers with reservation prices as follows:

Reservation Price ($)

Consumer	For 1	For 2
A	10	70
B	40	40
C	70	10

The unit cost of each product is $20.

a. **Compute the optimal prices and profits for (i) selling the goods separately, (ii) pure bundling, and (iii) mixed bundling.**

The prices and profits for each strategy are

	Price 1	Price 2	Bundled Price	Profit

Sell Separately	$50.00	$50.00	—	$100.00
Pure Bundling	—	—	$80.00	$120.00
Mixed Bundling	$69.95	$69.95	$80.00	$139.90

b. **Which strategy is most profitable? Why?**

Mixed bundling is best because, for each good, marginal production cost ($20) exceeds the reservation price for one consumer. Consumer A has a reservation price of $70 for good 2 and only $10 for good 1. Because the cost of producing a unit of good 1 is $20, Consumer A would buy only good 2, not the bundle. The firm responds by offering good 2 at a price just below Consumer A's reservation price and by charging a price for the bundle, so that the difference between the bundle price and the price of good 2 is above Consumer A's reservation price of good 1 ($10.05). Consumer C's choice is symmetric to Consumer A's choice. Consumer B chooses the bundle because the bundle's price is just below the reservation price and the separate prices for the goods are both above the reservation price for either good.

15. **Your firm produces two products, the demands for which are independent. Both products are produced at zero marginal cost. You face four consumers (or groups of consumers) with the following reservation prices:**

Consumer	Good 1 ($)	Good 2 ($)
A	30	90
B	40	60
C	60	40
D	90	30

a. **Consider three alternative pricing strategies: (i) selling the goods separately; (ii) pure bundling; (iii) mixed bundling. For *each strategy*, determine the optimal prices to be charged and the resulting profits. Which strategy is best?**

For each strategy, the optimal prices and profits are

	Price 1	Price 2	Bundled Price	Profit
Sell Separately	$40.00	$40.00	—	$240.00
Pure Bundling	—	—	$100.00	$400.00
Mixed Bundling	$69.95	$69.95	$100.00	$339.90

Pure bundling dominates mixed bundling, because with marginal costs of zero there is no reason to exclude purchases of both goods by all consumers.

b. **Now suppose that the production of each good entails a marginal cost of $35. How does this information change your answers to (a)? Why is the optimal strategy now different?**

With marginal cost of $35, the optimal prices and profits are:

	Price 1	Price 2	Bundled Price	Profit
Sell Separately	$90.00	$90.00	—	$110.00
Pure Bundling	—	—	$100.00	$120.00
Mixed Bundling	$69.95	$69.95	$100.00	$129.90

Mixed bundling is the best strategy.

16. A cable TV company offers, in addition to its basic service, two products: a Sports Channel (Product 1) and a Movie Channel (Product 2). Subscribers to the basic service can subscribe to these additional services individually at the monthly prices P_1 and P_2, respectively, or they can buy the two as a bundle for the price P_B, where $P_B < P_1 + P_2$. (They can also forego the additional services and simply buy the basic service.) The company's marginal cost for these additional services is *zero*. Through market research, the cable company has estimated the reservation prices for these two services for a representative group of consumers in the company's service area. These reservation prices are plotted (as *x*'s) in Figure 11.16, as are the prices P_1, P_2, and P_B that the cable company is currently charging. The graph is divided into regions, I, II, III, and IV.

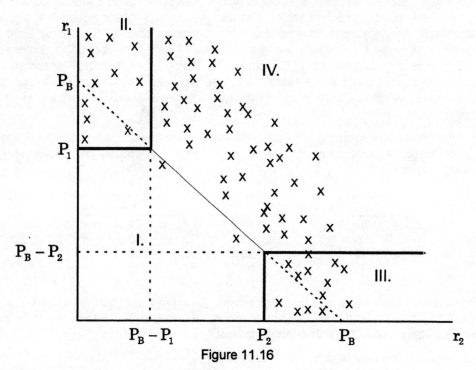

Figure 11.16

a. Which products, if any, will be purchased by the consumers in region I? In region II? In region III? In region IV? Explain briefly.

Product 1 = sports channel. Product 2 = movie channel.

Region	Purchase	Reservation Prices
I	nothing	$r_1 < P_1, r_2 < P_2, r_1 + r_2 < P_B$
II	sports channel	$r_1 > P_1, r_2 < P_B - P_1$
III	movie channel	$r_2 > P_2, r_1 < P_B - P_2$
IV	both channels	$r_1 > P_B - P_2, r_2 > P_B - P_1, r_1 + r_2 > P_B$

To see why consumers in regions II and III do not buy the bundle, reason as follows: For region II, $r_1 > P_1$, so the consumer will buy product 1. If she bought the bundle, she would pay an additional $P_B - P_1$. Since her reservation price for product 2 is less than $P_B - P_1$, she will choose only to buy product 1. Similar reasoning applies to region III.

Consumers in region I purchase nothing because the sum of their reservation values are less than the bundling price and each reservation value is lower than the respective price.

In region IV the sum of the reservation values for the consumers are higher than the bundle price, so these consumers would rather purchase the bundle than nothing. To see why the consumers in this region cannot do better than purchase either of the products separately, reason as follows: since $r_1 > P_B - P_2$ the consumer is better off purchasing both products than just product 2, likewise since $r_2 > P_B - P_1$, the consumer is better off purchasing both products rather than just product 1.

b.   **Note that the reservation prices for the Sports Channel and the Movie Channel, as drawn in the figure, are negatively correlated. Why would you, or would you not, expect consumers' reservation prices for cable TV channels to be negatively correlated?**

Prices may be negatively correlated if people's tastes differ in the following way: the more avidly a person likes sports, the less he or she will care for movies, and vice versa. Reservation prices would not be negatively correlated if people who were willing to pay a lot of money to watch sports were also willing to pay a lot of money to watch movies.

c.   **The company's vice president has said: "Because the marginal cost of providing an additional channel is zero, mixed bundling offers no advantage over pure bundling. Our profits would be just as high if we offered the Sports Channel and the Movie Channel together as a bundle, and only as a bundle." Do you agree or disagree? Explain why.**

It depends. By offering only the bundled product, the company would lose customers below the bundle price in regions II and III. At the same time, those consumers above the bundling price line in these regions would only buy one service, rather than the bundled service. The net effect on revenues is indeterminate. The exact solution depends on the distribution of consumers in those regions.

d.   **Suppose the cable company continues to use mixed bundling as a way of selling these two services. Based on the distribution of reservation prices shown in Figure 11.21, do you think the cable company should alter any of the prices it is now charging? If so, how?**

The cable company could raise P_B, P_1, and P_2 slightly without losing any customers. Alternatively, it could raise prices even past the point of losing customers as long as the additional revenue from the remaining customers made up for the revenue loss from the lost customers.

17. **Consider a firm with monopoly power that faces the demand curve**

$$P = 100 - 3Q + 4A^{1/2}$$

and has the total cost function

$$C = 4Q^2 + 10Q + A,$$

where A is the level of advertising expenditures, and P and Q are price and output.

a.   **Find the values of A, Q, and P that maximize the firm's profit.**

Profit (π) is equal to total revenue, *TR*, minus total cost, *TC*. Here,

$$TR = PQ = (100 - 3Q + 4A^{1/2})Q = 100Q - 3Q^2 + 4QA^{1/2} \text{ and}$$

$$TC = 4Q^2 + 10Q + A.$$

Therefore,

$$\pi = 100Q - 3Q^2 + 4QA^{1/2} - 4Q^2 - 10Q - A, \text{ or}$$

$$\pi = 90Q - 7Q^2 + 4QA^{1/2} - A.$$

The firm wants to choose its level of output and advertising expenditures to maximize its profits:

$$\text{Max } \pi = 90Q - 7Q^2 + 4QA^{1/2} - A$$

The necessary conditions for an optimum are:

(1) $\quad\quad \dfrac{\partial \pi}{\partial Q} = 90 - 14Q + 4A^{1/2} = 0,$ and

(2) $\quad\quad \dfrac{\partial \pi}{\partial A} = 2QA^{-1/2} - 1 = 0.$

From equation (2), we obtain

$$A^{1/2} = 2Q.$$

Substituting this into equation (1), we obtain

$$90 - 14Q + 4(2Q) = 0, \text{ or } Q^* = 15.$$

Then,

$$A^* = (4)(15^2) = 900,$$

which implies

$$P^* = 100 - (3)(15) + (4)(900^{1/2}) = \$175.$$

b. **Calculate the Lerner index of monopoly power, L = (P - MC)/P, for this firm at its profit-maximizing levels of A, Q, and P.**

The degree of monopoly power is given by the formula $\dfrac{P - MC}{P}$. Marginal cost is $8Q + 10$ (the derivative of total cost with respect to quantity). At the optimum, where $Q = 15$, $MC = (8)(15) + 10 = 130$. Therefore, the Lerner index is

$$L = \frac{175 - 130}{175} = 0.257.$$

CHAPTER 11
PRICING WITH MARKET POWER, APPENDIX

EXERCISES

1. **Review the numerical example about Race Car Motors. Calculate the profit earned by the upstream division, the downstream division, and the firm as a whole in each of the three cases examined: (a) no outside market for engines; (b) a competitive market for engines in which the market price is $6,000; and (c) the firm is a monopoly supplier of engines to an outside market. In which case does Race Car Motors earn the most profit? In which case does the upstream division earn the most? the downstream division?**

We shall examine each case, then compare profits. We are given the following information about Race Car Motors:

The demand for its automobiles is

$$P = 20,000 - Q.$$

Therefore its marginal revenue is

$$MR = 20,000 - 2Q.$$

The downstream division's cost of assembling cars is

$$C_A(Q) = 8,000Q,$$

so the division's marginal cost is $MC_A = 8,000$. The upstream division's cost of producing engines is

$$C_E(Q_E) = 2Q_E^2,$$

so division's marginal cost is $MC_E(Q_E) = 4Q_E$.

Case (a): To determine the profit-maximizing quantity of output, set the net marginal revenue for engines equal to the marginal cost of producing engines. Because each car has one engine, Q_E equals Q, and the net marginal revenue of engines is

$$NMR_E = MR - MC_A, \text{ or}$$
$$NMR_E = (20,000 - 2Q) - 8,000 = 12,000 - 2Q_E.$$

Setting NMR_E equal to MC_E:

$$12,000 - 2Q_E = 4Q_E, \text{ or } Q_E = 2,000.$$

The firm should produce 2,000 engines and 2,000 cars. The optimal transfer price is the marginal cost of the 2,000 engines:

$$MC_E = 4Q_E = (4)(2,000) = \$8,000.$$

The profit-maximizing price of the cars is found by substituting the profit-maximizing quantity into the demand function:

$$P = 20,000 - Q, \text{ or } P - 20,000 - 2,000 = \$18,000.$$

The profits for each division are equal to

$$\pi_E = (8,000)(2,000) - (2)(2,000)^2 = \$8,000,000,$$

and

$$\pi_C = (18,000)(2,000) - ((8,000)(2,000) + 16,000,000) = \$4,000,000.$$

Total profits are equal to $\pi_E + \pi_C = \$12,000,000$.

Case (b): To determine the profit-maximizing level of output when an outside market for engines exists, first note that the competitive price for engines on the outside market is $6,000, which is less than the transfer price of $8,000. With the market price less than the transfer price, this means that the firm will buy some of its engines on the outside market. To determine how many cars the firm should produce, set the market price of engines equal to net marginal revenue. We use the market price, since it is now the marginal cost of engines, and the optimal transfer price

$$6,000 = 12,000 - 2Q_E, \text{ or } Q_E = 3,000.$$

The total quantity of engines and automobiles is 3,000. The price of the cars is determined by substituting Q_E into the demand function for cars:

$$P = 20,000 - 3,000, \text{ or } P = \$17,000.$$

The company now produces more cars and sells them at a lower price. To determine the number of engines that the firm will produce and how many the firm will buy on the market, set the marginal cost of engine production equal to 6,000, solve for Q_E, and then find the difference between this number and the 3,000 cars to be produced:

$$MC_E = 4Q_E = 6,000, \text{ or } Q_E = 1,500.$$

Thus, 1,500 engines will be bought on the external market.

For the engine-building division, profits are found by subtracting total costs from total revenue:

$$\pi_E = TR_E - TC_E = (\$6,000)(1,500) - (2)(1,500)^2 = \$4,500,000.$$

For the automobile-assembly division, profits are found by subtracting total costs from total revenue:

$$\pi_A = TR_A - TC_A = (\$17,000)(3,000) - (8,000 + 6,000)(3,000) = \$9,000,000.$$

Total profits for the firm are the sum of the two divisions,

$$\pi_T = \$13,500,000.$$

Case (c): In the case where the firm is a monopoly supplier of engines to the outside market, the demand in the outside market for engines is:

$$P_{E,M} = 10,000 - Q_E,$$

which means that the marginal revenue curve for engines in the outside market is:

$$MR_{E,M} = 10,000 - 2Q_E.$$

To determine the optimal transfer price, find the *total* net marginal revenue by horizontally summing $MR_{E,M}$ with the net marginal revenue from "sales" to the downstream division, $12,000 - 2Q_E$. For output of Q_E greater than 1,000, this is:

$$NMR_{E, Total} = 11,000 - Q_E.$$

Set $NMR_{E, Total}$ equal to the marginal cost of producing engines to determine the optimal quantity of engines:

$$11,000 - Q_E = 4Q_E, \text{ or } Q_E = 2,200.$$

Now we must determine how many of the 2,200 engines produced will be sold to the downstream division and how may will be sold on the external market. First, note that the marginal cost of producing these 2,200 engines, and therefore the optimal transfer price, is $4Q_E = \$8,800$. Set the optimal transfer price equal to the marginal revenue from sales in the outside market:

$$8,800 = 10,000 - 2Q_E, \text{ or } Q_E = 600.$$

Therefore, 600 engines should be sold in the external market.

To determine the price at which these engines should be sold, substitute 600 into demand in the outside market for engines and solve for P:

$$P_{E,M} = 10,000 - 600 = \$9,400.$$

Finally, set the \$8,800 transfer price equal to the net marginal revenue from the "sales" to the downstream division:

$$8,800 = 12,000 - 2Q_E, \text{ or } Q_E = 1,600.$$

Thus, 1,600 engines should be sold to the downstream division for use in the production of 1,600 cars.

To determine the sale price of the cars, substitute 1,600 into the demand curve for automobiles:

$$P = 20,000 - 1,600 = \$18,400.$$

To determine the level of profits for each division, subtract total costs from total revenue:

$$\pi_E = \{(\$8,800)(1,600) + (\$9,400)(600)\} - (2)(2,200)^2 = \$10,040,000,$$

and

$$\pi_A = (\$18,400)(1,600) - [(8,000 + 8,800)(1,600)] = \$2,560,000.$$

Total profits are equal to the sum of the profits from the two divisions, or

$$\pi_T = \$12,600,000.$$

The table gives profits earned by each division and the firm for each case.

Profits with	Upstream Division	Downstream Division	Total
(a) No outside market	8,000,000	4,000,000	12,000,000
(b) Competitive market	4,500,000	9,000,000	13,500,000
(c) Monopolized market	10,000,000	2,600,000	12,600,000

The upstream division, building engines, earns the most profit when it has a monopoly on engines. The downstream division, building automobiles, earns the most when there is a competitive market for engines. Because of the high cost of engines, the firm does best when engines are produced at the lowest cost by an outside, competitive market.

2. Ajax Computer makes a computer for climate control in office buildings. The company uses a microprocessor, produced by its upstream division, along with other parts bought in outside competitive markets. The microprocessor is produced at a constant marginal cost of \$500, and the marginal cost of assembling the computer (including the cost of the other parts) by the downstream division is a constant \$700. The firm has been selling the computer for \$2,000, and until now there has been no outside market for the microprocessor.

a.   Suppose an outside market for the microprocessor develops and Ajax has monopoly power in that market, selling microprocessors for \$1,000 each. Assuming that demand for the microprocessor is unrelated to the demand for the Ajax computer, what transfer price should Ajax apply to the microprocessor for its use by the downstream division? Should its production of computers be increased, decreased, or left unchanged? Explain briefly.

Ajax should exploit its monopoly power in the processor market by charging its downstream firm a transfer price equal to the marginal cost of \$500. Although its production of processors will be greater than when there was no outside market, this will not affect the production of computers, because the extra production of processors does not increase their marginal cost.

b.   How would your answer to (a) change if the demands for the computer and the microprocessors were competitive; i.e., some of the people who buy the microprocessors use them to make climate control systems of their own?

Suppose that the demand for processors comes from a firm that produces a competing computer. Extra processors sold imply a reduced demand for computers, which means that *fewer* computers will be sold. However, the firm should still charge an efficient transfer price of $500, and it would probably want to raise the price that it charges on microprocessors to the outside firm and lower the price that it charges for its computer.

3.   Reebok produces and sells running shoes. It faces a market demand schedule P = 11 - 1.5Q$_s$, where Q$_s$ is the number of pairs of shoes sold (in thousands) and P is the price in dollars per thousand pairs of shoes. Production of each pair of shoes requires 1 square yard of leather. The leather is shaped and cut by the Form Division of Reebok. The cost function for leather is

$$TC_L = 1 + Q_L + 0.5Q_L^2,$$

where Q$_L$ is the quantity of leather (in thousands of square yards) produced. The cost function for running shoes is (excluding the leather)

$$TC_S = 2Q_S.$$

a.   What is the optimal transfer price?

With demand of $P = 11 - 1.5Q_S$, we have $TR = 11Q_S - 1.5Q_S^2$; therefore $MR = 11 - 3Q_S$. With total cost for shoes equal to $2Q_S$, the marginal cost of shoe production is 2. The marginal product of leather is 1; i.e., 1,000 square yards of leather makes 1,000 pairs of shoes. Therefore, the net marginal revenue is

$$(MR_S - MC_S)(MP_L) = (11 - 3Q_S - 2)(1) = 9 - 3Q_L.$$

For the optimal transfer price, choose the quantity so that

$$NMR_L = MC_L = P_L.$$

With the total cost for leather equal to $1 + Q_L + 0.5Q_L^2$, the marginal cost is $1 + Q_L$.

Therefore, set

$$MC_L = NMR_L,$$

$1 + Q_L = 9 - 3Q_L$, or $Q_L = 2$ yards.

With this quantity, the optimal transfer price is equal to $MC_L = 1 + 2 = \$3$ per square yard.

b.   Leather can be bought and sold in a competitive market at the price of P$_F$ = 1.5. In this case, how much leather should the Form Division supply internally? How much should it supply to the outside market? Will Reebok buy any leather in the outside market? Find the optimal transfer price.

If the transfer price is $1.5, the leather producer sets price equal to marginal cost: i.e.,

$1.5 = 1 + Q_L$, or $Q_L = 0.5$ square yards.

For the optimal transfer quantity, set

$$NMR_L = P_L,$$

$1.5 = 9 - 3Q$, or $Q = 2.5$ square yards.

Therefore, the shoe division should buy $2.5 - 0.5 = 2.0$ square yards from the outside market, and the leather division should sell nothing to the outside market.

c. **Now suppose the leather is unique and of extremely high quality. Therefore, the Form Division may act as a monopoly supplier to the outside market as well as a supplier to the downstream division. Suppose the outside demand for leather is given by P = 32 - Q_L. What is the optimal transfer price for the use of leather by the downstream division? At what price, if any, should leather be sold to the outside market? What quantity, if any, will be sold to the outside market?**

For the outside market, the leather division can determine the optimal amount of leather to produce by setting marginal cost equal to marginal revenue,

$$1 + Q_L = 32 - 2Q_L, \text{ or } Q_L = 10.67.$$

At that quantity, $MC_L = \$11.67$ per square yard. At this marginal cost, the shoe division would optimally demand a negative amount; i.e., the shoe division should stop making shoes and the firm should confine itself to selling leather. At this quantity, the outside market is willing to pay

$$P_L = 32 - Q_L, \text{ or } P_L = \$21.33 \text{ per square yard.}$$

4. The House Products Division of Acme Corporation manufactures and sells digital clock radios. A major component for these is supplied by the Electronic Division of Acme. The cost functions for the radio and the electronic component divisions are, respectively,

$$TC_r = 30 + 2Q_r$$

$$TC_C = 70 + 6Q_C + Q_C^2$$

(Note that TC_r does not include the cost of the component.) Manufacture of one radio set requires the use of one electronic component. Market studies show that the firm's demand curve for the digital clock radio is given by:

$$P_r = 108 - Q_r$$

a. **Assuming no outside market for the components, how many of them should be produced in order to maximize profits for Acme on a whole? What is the optimal transfer price?**

Radios require exactly one component and assembly.

radio assembly cost: $TC_r = 30 + 2Q_r$

component cost: $TC_c = 70 + 6Q_c + Q_c^2$

radio demand: $P_r = 108 - Q_r$

First we must solve for the profit-maximizing number of radios to produce. We must then set the transfer price that induces the internal supplier of components to provide the profit-maximizing level of components.

Profits are given by: $p = (108 - Q_c)Q_c - (30 + 2Q_c) - (70 + 6Q_c + Q_c^2)$.

Since one and only one component is used in each radio, we can set $Q_c = Q_r$:

$$\pi = (108 - Q_c)Q_c - (30 + 2Q_c) - (70 + 6Q_c + Q_c^2).$$

Profit maximization implies: $\partial\pi/\partial Qc = 108 - 2Q_c - 2 - 6 - 2Q_c = 0$ or $Q_c = 25$.

We must now calculate the transfer price that will induce the internal supplier to supply exactly 25 components. This will be the price for which $MC_c(Q_c = 25) = P_t$ or

$$MC_c(Q_c = 25) = 6 + 2Q_c = \$56.$$

We can check our solution as follows:

Component division: $\text{Max } \pi_c = 56Q_c - 70 - 6Q_c - Q_c^2$

$$d\pi_c/dQ_c = 0 \Leftrightarrow 56 - 6 - 2Q_c = 0 \Leftrightarrow Q_c = 25.$$

Radio assembly division: $\text{Max } \pi = (108 - Q_r)Q_r - (30 + 2Q_r) - 56Q_r$

$$d\pi/dQ_r = 0 \Leftrightarrow 108 - 2Q_r - 2 - 56 = 0 \Leftrightarrow Q_r = 25.$$

b.   **If other firms are willing to purchase in the outside market the component manufactured by the electronics division (which is the only supplier of this product), what is the optimal transfer price? Why? What price should be charged in the outside market? Why? How many units will the electronics division supply internally and to the outside market? Why? (Note: The demand for components in the outside market is: $P_c = 72 - 1.5Q_c$.)**

We now assume there is an outside market for components; the firm has market power in this outside market with market demand:

$$P_c = 72 - 3(Q_c/2)$$

First we solve for the profit-maximizing level of outside and internal sales. Then, we set the transfer price that induces the component division to supply the total output (sum of internal and external supply). We define Q_c as the outside sales of components and Q_i as components used inside.

Profits are given by:

$$\pi = (108 - Q_i)Q_i + (72 - (3/2)Q_c)Q_c - (30 + 2Q_i) - (70 + 6(Q_i + Q_c) + (Q_i + Q_c)^2).$$

Profit maximization implies:

$$\partial\pi/\partial Q_i = 108 - 2Q_c - 2 - 6 - 2(Q_i + Q_c) = 0$$

$$\partial\pi/\partial Q_{ic} = 72 - 3Q_c - 6 - 2(Q_i + Q_c) = 0$$

which yields:

$$Q_i + Q_c/2 = 25$$

$$5Q_c + 2Q_i = 66$$

and

$$Q_c = 4$$

$$Q_i = 23.$$

Thus, total components will be $23 + 4$, or 27.

As in part a, we solve for the transfer price by finding the marginal cost of the component division of producing the profit-maximizing level of output:

$$P_t = MC_c(Q_i^* + Q_c^*) = \$60.$$

The outside price will be: $P_c = 72 - (3/2)Q_c = \$66$ (this should actually be greater than the internal price since the firm has market power in the external price and, therefore, $MR_c < P_c$).

CHAPTER 12
MONOPOLISTIC COMPETITION AND OLIGOPOLY

TEACHING NOTES

Students viewing this material for the first time can be overwhelmed because of the number of models presented. Chapter 12 discusses seven models: monopolistic competition, Cournot-Nash, Stackelberg, Bertrand, non-cooperative game, kinked demand, and price leadership. You might want to concentrate your attention in class on the more basic models, e.g., monopolistic competition, Cournot-Nash, non-cooperative game, and price leadership. You can otherwise pick and choose among the models as time permits.

When introducing the material in this chapter, start by reviewing the basic results of the models of competition and monopoly. When presenting monopolistic competition, focus on why positive profits encourage entry and on the similarities and differences of this model with competition and monopoly. The example of brand competition in cola and coffee markets presented at the end of Section 12.2 facilitates a class discussion of the costs and benefits of freedom of choice among a vast array of brand names and trademarks. The chapter ends with two topics that invoke opinions from almost every student: an application on OPEC and Example 12.5, "The Cartelizaton of Intercollegiate Athletics."

Students may find the Cournot-Nash duopoly model to be a drastic change from the worlds of competition and monopoly. The key to understanding Cournot-Nash is a grasp of reaction functions. Stress that reaction functions are being graphed on axes that represent quantities (see Figure 12.4). Once they understand reaction functions, they will be able to follow the assumptions, reasoning, and results of the Cournot-Nash, Stackelberg, and Bertrand models. Although they might not comprehend the algebraic derivation of the Cournot-Nash equilibrium, point out the representations in Figure 12.5 of the competitive, Cournot-Nash, and collusive (monopoly) equilibria. Figure 12.5 gives the impression that the duopolists always have symmetric reaction curves. Exercise (2) shows that if the cost structures are not identical, the reaction curves are asymmetric.

While the Nash equilibrium, payoff matrices, and the Prisoners' Dilemma are introduced in this chapter, more attention is allotted to them in Chapter 13. If you will be covering Chapter 13, you can postpone discussion of Section 12.5, using it as a bridge between oligopoly theory and game theory. The discussion of a non-cooperative game is intuitive, but some students find payoff matrices difficult to read quickly. Example 12.3, "Procter & Gamble in a Prisoners' Dilemma," is an excellent representation of the pricing problems facing U.S. firms in foreign markets.

Sections 12.6 and 12.7 discuss price rigidity and price leadership. Students who have understood kinked marginal revenue curves in previous chapters will find the analysis of price rigidity easy. Those who have not mastered this concept will find Figure 12.7 difficult unless it is derived slowly. It is best to proceed as follows: (1) discuss a kinked demand curve; (2) add a kinked *MR* curve; (3) add a *MC* curve; and (4) derive profit-maximizing output.

REVIEW QUESTIONS

1. What are the characteristics of a monopolistically competitive market? What happens to the equilibrium price and quantity in such a market if one firm introduces a new, improved product?

The two primary characteristics of a monopolistically competitive market are (1) that firms compete by selling differentiated products which are highly, but not perfectly, substitutable and (2) that there is free entry and exit from the market. When a new firm enters a monopolistically competitive market (seeking positive profits), the demand curve for each of the incumbent firms shifts inward, thus reducing the price and quantity received by the incumbents. Thus, the introduction of a new product by a firm will reduce the price received and quantity sold of existing products.

2. Why is the firm's demand curve flatter than the total market demand curve in monopolistic competition? Suppose a monopolistically competitive firm is making a profit in the short run. What will happen to its demand curve in the long run?

The flatness or steepness of the firm's demand curve is a function of the elasticity of demand for the firm's product. The elasticity of the firm's demand curve is greater than the elasticity of market demand because it is easier for consumers to switch to another firm's highly substitutable product than to switch consumption to an entirely different product. Profit in the short run induces other firms to enter; as firms enter the incumbent firm's demand and marginal revenue curves shift inward, reducing the profit-maximizing quantity. Eventually, profits fall to zero, leaving no incentive for more firms to enter.

3. Some experts have argued that too many brands of breakfast cereal are on the market. Give an argument to support this view. Give an argument against it.

Pro: Too many brands of any single product signals excess capacity, implying an output level smaller than one that would minimize average cost.

Con: Consumers value the freedom to choose among a wide variety of competing products.

(Note: In 1972 the Federal Trade Commission filed suit against Kellogg, General Mills, and General Foods. It charged that these firms attempted to suppress entry into the cereal market by introducing 150 heavily advertised brands between 1950 and 1970, crowding competitors off grocers' shelves. This case was eventually dismissed in 1982.)

4. Why is the Cournot equilibrium stable (i.e., why don't firms have any incentive to change their output levels once in equilibrium)? Even if they can't collude, why don't firms set their outputs at the joint profit-maximizing levels (i.e., the levels they would have chosen had they colluded)?

A Cournot equilibrium is stable because each firm is producing the amount that maximizes its profits, *given what its competitors are producing*. If all firms behave this way, no firm has an incentive to change its output. Without collusion, firms find it difficult to agree tacitly to reduce output. Once one firm reduces its output, other firms have an incentive to increase output and increase profits at the expense of the firm that is limiting its sales.

5. In the Stackelberg model, the firm that sets output first has an advantage. Explain why.

The Stackelberg leader gains the advantage because the second firm must accept the leader's large output as given and produce a smaller output for itself. If the second firm decided to produce a larger quantity, this would reduce price and profit. The first firm knows that the second firm will have no choice but to produce a smaller output in order to maximize profit, and thus, the first firm is able to capture a larger share of industry profits.

6. Explain the meaning of a Nash equilibrium when firms are competing with respect to price. Why is the equilibrium stable? Why don't the firms raise prices to the level that maximizes joint profits?

A Nash equilibrium in price competition occurs when each firm chooses its price, assuming *its competitor's price as fixed*. In equilibrium, each firm does the best it can, conditional on its competitors' prices. The equilibrium is stable because firms are maximizing profit and no firm has an incentive to raise or lower its price.

Firms do not always collude: a cartel agreement is difficult to enforce because each firm has an incentive to cheat. By lowering price, the cheating firm can increase its market share and profits. A second reason that firms do not collude is that such collusion violates antitrust laws. In particular, price fixing violates Section 1 of the Sherman Act. Of course, there are attempts to circumvent antitrust laws through tacit collusion.

7. The kinked demand curve describes price rigidity. Explain how the model works. What are its limitations? Why does price rigidity arise in oligopolistic markets?

According to the kinked-demand curve model, each firm faces a demand curve that is kinked at the currently prevailing price. If a firm raises its price, most of its customers would shift their purchases to its competitors. This reasoning implies a highly elastic demand for price increases. If the firm lowers its price, however, its competitors would also lower their prices. This implies a demand curve that is more inelastic for price decreases than for price increases. This kink in the demand curve implies a discontinuity in the marginal revenue curve, so only large changes in marginal cost lead to changes in price. However accurate it is in pointing to price rigidity, this model does not explain *how* the rigid price is determined. The origin of the rigid price is explained by other models, such as the firms' desire to avoid mutually destructive price competition.

8. Why does price leadership sometimes evolve in oligopolistic markets? Explain how the price leader determines a profit-maximizing price.

Since firms cannot explicitly coordinate on setting price, they use implicit means. One form of implicit collusion is to follow a price leader. The price leader, often the dominant firm in the industry, determines its profit-maximizing price by calculating the demand curve it faces: it subtracts the quantity supplied at each price by all other firms from the market demand, and the residual is its demand curve. The leader chooses the quantity that equates its marginal revenue with marginal cost. The market price is the price at which the leader's profit-maximizing quantity sells in the market. At that price, the followers supply the remainder of the market.

9. Why has the OPEC oil cartel succeeded in raising prices substantially, while the CIPEC copper cartel has not? What conditions are necessary for successful cartelization? What organizational problems must a cartel overcome?

Successful cartelization requires two characteristics: demand should be inelastic, and the cartel must be able to control most of the supply. OPEC succeeded in the short run because the short-run demand and supply of oil were both inelastic. CIPEC has not been successful because both demand and non-CIPEC supply were highly responsive to price. A cartel faces two organizational problems: agreement on a price and a division of the market among cartel members; and monitoring and enforcing the agreement.

EXERCISES

1. Suppose all firms in a monopolistically competitive industry were merged into one large firm. Would that new firm produce as many different brands? Would it produce only a single brand? Explain.

Monopolistic competition is defined by product differentiation. Each firm earns economic profit by distinguishing its brand from all other brands. This distinction can arise from underlying differences in the product or from differences in advertising. If these competitors merge into a single firm, the resulting monopolist would not produce as many brands, since too much brand competition is internecine (mutually destructive). However, it is unlikely that only one brand would be produced after the merger. Producing several brands with different prices and characteristics is one method of splitting the market into sets of customers with different price elasticities, which may also stimulate overall demand.

2. Consider two firms facing the demand curve $P = 10 - Q$, where $Q = Q_1 + Q_2$. The firms' cost functions are $C_1(Q_1) = 4 + 2Q_1$ and $C_2(Q_2) = 3 + 3Q_2$.

a. Suppose both firms have entered the industry. What is the joint profit-maximizing level of output? How much will each firm produce? How would your answer change if the firms have not yet entered the industry?

If both firms enter the market, and they collude, they will face a marginal revenue curve with twice the slope of the demand curve:

$$MR = 10 - 2Q.$$

Setting marginal revenue equal to marginal cost (the marginal cost of Firm 1, since it is lower than that of Firm 2) to determine the profit-maximizing quantity, Q:

$$10 - 2Q = 2, \text{ or } Q = 4.$$

Substituting $Q = 4$ into the demand function to determine price:

$$P = 10 - 4 = \$6.$$

The profit for Firm 1 will be:

$$\pi_1 = (6)(4) - (4 + (2)(4)) = \$12.$$

The profit for Firm 2 will be:

$$\pi_2 = (6)(0) - (3 + (3)(0)) = -\$3.$$

Total industry profit will be:

$$\pi_T = \pi_1 + \pi_2 = 12 - 3 = \$9.$$

If Firm 1 were the only entrant, its profits would be $12 and Firm 2's would be 0.

If Firm 2 were the only entrant, then it would equate marginal revenue with its marginal cost to determine its profit-maximizing quantity:

$$10 - 2Q_2 = 3, \text{ or } Q_2 = 3.5.$$

Substituting Q_2 into the demand equation to determine price:

$$P = 10 - 3.5 = \$6.5.$$

The profits for Firm 2 will be:

$$\pi_2 = (6.5)(3.5) - (3 + (3)(3.5)) = \$9.25.$$

b. **What is each firm's equilibrium output and profit if they behave noncooperatively? Use the Cournot model. Draw the firms' reaction curves and show the equilibrium.**

In the Cournot model, Firm 1 takes Firm 2's output as given and maximizes profits. The profit function derived in 2.a becomes

$$\pi_1 = (10 - Q_1 - Q_2)Q_1 - (4 + 2Q_1), \text{ or}$$

$$\pi = -4 + 8Q_1 - Q_1^2 - Q_1 Q_2.$$

Setting the derivative of the profit function with respect to Q_1 to zero, we find Firm 1's reaction function:

$$\frac{\partial \pi}{\partial Q_1} = 8 - 2Q_1 - Q_2 = 0, \text{ or } Q_1 = 4 - \left(\frac{Q_2}{2}\right).$$

Similarly, Firm 2's reaction function is

$$Q_2 = 3.5 - \left(\frac{Q_1}{2}\right).$$

To find the Cournot equilibrium, we substitute Firm 2's reaction function into Firm 1's reaction function:

$$Q_1 = 4 - \left(\frac{1}{2}\right)\left(3.5 - \frac{Q_1}{2}\right), \text{ or } Q_1 = 3.$$

Substituting this value for Q_1 into the reaction function for Firm 2, we find $Q_2 = 2$.

Substituting the values for Q_1 and Q_2 into the demand function to determine the equilibrium price:

$$P = 10 - 3 - 2 = \$5.$$

The profits for Firms 1 and 2 are equal to

$$\pi_1 = (5)(3) - (4 + (2)(3)) = 5 \text{ and}$$

172

$$\pi_2 = (5)(2) - (3 + (3)(2)) = 1.$$

Reaction Functions

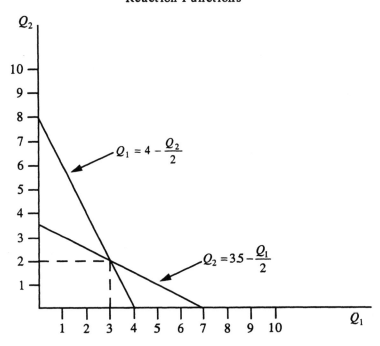

Figure 12.2.b

c. **How much should Firm 1 be willing to pay to purchase Firm 2 if collusion is illegal but the takeover is not?**

In order to determine how much Firm 1 will be willing to pay to purchase Firm 2, we must compare Firm 1's profits in the monopoly situation versus those in an oligopoly. The difference between the two will be what Firm 1 is willing to pay for Firm 2.

Substitute the profit-maximizing quantity from part *a* to determine the price:

$$P = 10 - 4 = \$6.$$

The profits for the firm are determined by subtracting total costs from total revenue:

$$\pi_1 = (6)(4) - (4 + (2)(4)), \text{ or}$$

$$\pi_1 = \$12.$$

We know from part b that the profits for Firm 1 in the oligopoly situation will be $5; therefore, Firm 1 should be willing to pay up to $7, which is the difference between its monopoly profits ($12) and its oligopoly profits ($5). (Note that any other firm would pay only the value of Firm 2's profit, i.e., $1.)

Note, Firm 1 might be able to accomplish its goal of maximizing profit by acting as a Stackelberg leader. If Firm 1 is aware of Firm 2's reaction function, it can determine its profit-maximizing quantity by substituting for Q_2 in its profit function and maximizing with respect to Q_1:

$$\pi_1 = -4 + 8Q_1 - Q_1^2 - Q_1 Q_2 \text{, or } \pi = -4 + 8Q_1 - \left(3.5 - \frac{Q_1}{2}\right)Q_1 \text{, or}$$

$$\pi = -4 + 4 5Q_1 - \frac{Q_1^2}{2}.$$

Therefore

$$\frac{\partial \pi}{\partial Q_1} = 45 - Q_1 = 0, \text{ or } Q_1 = 45.$$

$$Q_2 = 3.5 - \left(\frac{4.5}{2}\right) = 1.25.$$

Substituting Q_1 and Q_2 into the demand equation to determine the price:

$$P = 10 - 4.5 - 1.25 = \$4.25.$$

Profits for Firm 1 are:

$$\pi_1 = (4.25)(4.5) - (4 + (2)(4.5)) = \$6.125,$$

and profits for Firm 2 are:

$$\pi_2 = (4.25)(1.25) - (3 + (3)(1.25)) = -\$1.4375.$$

Although Firm 2 covers average variable costs in the short run, it will go out of business in the long run. Therefore, Firm 1 should drive Firm 2 out of business instead of buying it. If this is illegal, Firm 1 would have to resort to purchasing Firm 2, as discussed above.

3. A monopolist can produce at a constant average (and marginal) cost of AC = MC = 5. It faces a market demand curve given by Q = 53 - P.

a. **Calculate the profit-maximizing price and quantity for this monopolist. Also calculate its profits.**

The monopolist wants to choose quantity to maximize its profits:

$$\max \pi = PQ - C(Q),$$

$$\pi = (53 - Q)(Q) - 5Q, \text{ or } \pi = 48Q - Q^2.$$

To determine the profit-maximizing quantity, set the change in π with respect to the change in Q equal to zero and solve for Q:

$$\frac{d\pi}{dQ} = -2Q + 48 = 0, \text{ or } Q = 24.$$

Substitute the profit-maximizing quantity, $Q = 24$, into the demand function to find price:
$$24 = 53 - P, \text{ or } P = \$29.$$

Profits are equal to

$$\pi = TR - TC = (29)(24) - (5)(24) = \$576.$$

b. **Suppose a second firm enters the market. Let Q_1 be the output of the first firm and Q_2 be the output of the second. Market demand is now given by**

$$Q_1 + Q_2 = 53 - P.$$

Assuming that this second firm has the same costs as the first, write the profits of each firm as functions of Q_1 and Q_2.

When the second firm enters, price can be written as a function of the output of two firms: $P = 53 - Q_1 - Q_2$. We may write the profit functions for the two firms:

$$\pi_1 = PQ_1 - C(Q_1) = (53 - Q_1 - Q_2)Q_1 - 5Q_1, \text{ or } \pi_1 = 53Q_1 - Q_1^2 - Q_1Q_2 - 5Q_1$$

and

$$\pi_2 = PQ_2 - C(Q_2) = (53 - Q_1 - Q_2)Q_2 - 5Q_2, \text{ or } \pi_2 = 53Q_2 - Q_2^2 - Q_1Q_2 - 5Q_2.$$

c. **Suppose (as in the Cournot model) that each firm chooses its profit-maximizing level of output on the assumption that its competitor's output is fixed. Find each firm's "reaction curve" (i.e., the rule that gives its desired output in terms of its competitor's output).**

Under the Cournot assumption, Firm 1 treats the output of Firm 2 as a constant in its maximization of profits. Therefore, Firm 1 chooses Q_1 to maximize π_1 in b with Q_2 being treated as a constant. The change in π_1 with respect to a change in Q_1 is

$$\frac{\partial \pi_1}{\partial Q_1} = 53 - 2Q_1 - Q_2 - 5 = 0, \text{ or } Q_1 = 24 - \frac{Q_2}{2}.$$

This equation is the reaction function for Firm 1, which generates the profit- maximizing level of output, given the constant output of Firm 2. Because the problem is symmetric, the reaction function for Firm 2 is

$$Q_2 = 24 - \frac{Q_1}{2}.$$

d. **Calculate the Cournot equilibrium (i.e., the values of Q_1 and Q_2 for which both firms are doing as well as they can given their competitors' output). What are the resulting market price and profits of each firm?**

To find the level of output for each firm that would result in a stationary equilibrium, we solve for the values of Q_1 and Q_2 that satisfy both reaction functions by substituting the reaction function for Firm 2 into the one for Firm 1:

$$Q_1 = 24 - \left(\frac{1}{2}\right)\left(24 - \frac{Q_1}{2}\right), \text{ or } Q_1 = 16.$$

By symmetry, $Q_2 = 16$.

To determine the price, substitute Q_1 and Q_2 into the demand equation:

$$P = 53 - 16 - 16 = \$21.$$

Profits are given by

$$\pi_i = PQ_i - C(Q_i) = \pi_i = (21)(16) - (5)(16) = \$256.$$

Total profits in the industry are $\pi_1 + \pi_2 = \$256 + \$256 = \$512$.

*e. **Suppose there are N firms in the industry, all with the same constant marginal cost, MC = 5. Find the Cournot equilibrium. How much will each firm produce, what will be the market price, and how much profit will each firm earn? Also, show that as N becomes large the market price approaches the price that would prevail under perfect competition.**

If there are N identical firms, then the price in the market will be

$$P = 53 - (Q_1 + Q_2 + \cdots + Q_N).$$

Profits for the ith firm are given by

$$\pi_i = PQ_i - C(Q_i),$$

$$\pi_i = 53Q_i - Q_1Q_i - Q_2Q_i - \cdots - Q_i^2 - \cdots - Q_NQ_i - 5Q_i.$$

Differentiating to obtain the necessary first-order condition for profit maximization,

$$\frac{d\pi}{dQ_i} = 53 - Q_1 - \cdots - 2Q_i - \cdots - Q_N - 5 = 0.$$

Solving for Q_i,

$$Q_i = 24 - \frac{1}{2}\left(Q_1 + \cdots + Q_{i-1} + Q_{i+1} + \cdots + Q_N\right).$$

If all firms face the same costs, they will all produce the same level of output, i.e., $Q_i = Q^*$. Therefore,

$$Q^* = 24 - \frac{1}{2}(N-1)Q^*, \text{ or } 2Q^* = 48 - (N-1)Q^*, \text{ or}$$

$$(N+1)Q^* = 48, \text{ or } Q^* = \frac{48}{(N+1)}.$$

We may substitute for $Q = NQ^*$, total output, in the demand function:

$$P = 53 - N\left(\frac{48}{N+1}\right).$$

Total profits are

$$\pi_T = PQ - C(Q) = P(NQ^*) - 5(NQ^*)$$

or

$$\pi_T = \left[53 - N\left(\frac{48}{N+1}\right)\right](N)\left(\frac{48}{N+1}\right) - 5N\left(\frac{48}{N+1}\right) \text{ or}$$

$$\pi_T = \left[48 - (N)\left(\frac{48}{N+1}\right)\right](N)\left(\frac{48}{N+1}\right)$$

or

$$\pi_T = (48)\left(\frac{N+1-N}{N+1}\right)(48)\left(\frac{N}{N+1}\right) = (2,304)\left(\frac{N}{(N+1)^2}\right).$$

Notice that with *N* firms

$$Q = 48\left(\frac{N}{N+1}\right)$$

and that, as *N* increases ($N \rightarrow \infty$)

$$Q = 48.$$

Similarly, with

$$P = 53 - 48\left(\frac{N}{N+1}\right),$$

as $N \rightarrow \infty$,

$$P = 53 - 48 = 5.$$

With $P = 5$, $Q = 53 - 5 = 48$.

Finally,

$$\pi_T = 2,304\left(\frac{N}{(N+1)^2}\right),$$

so as $N \rightarrow \infty$,

$$\pi_T = \$0.$$

In perfect competition, we know that profits are zero and price equals marginal cost. Here, $\pi_T = \$0$ and $P = MC = 5$. Thus, when *N* approaches infinity, this market approaches a perfectly competitive one.

4. This exercise is a continuation of Exercise 3. We return to two firms with the same constant average and marginal cost, AC = MC = 5, facing the market demand curve

$Q_1 + Q_2 = 53 - P$. **Now we will use the Stackelberg model to analyze what will happen if one of the firms makes its output decision before the other.**

a. **Suppose Firm 1 is the Stackelberg leader (i.e., makes its output decisions before Firm 2). Find the reaction curves that tell each firm how much to produce in terms of the output of its competitor.**

Firm 1, the Stackelberg leader, will choose its output, Q_1, to maximize its profits, subject to the reaction function of Firm 2:

$$\max \pi_1 = PQ_1 - C(Q_1),$$

subject to

$$Q_2 = 24 - \left(\frac{Q_1}{2}\right).$$

Substitute for Q_2 in the demand function and, after solving for P, substitute for P in the profit function:

$$\max \pi_1 = \left(53 - Q_1 - \left(24 - \frac{Q_1}{2}\right)\right)(Q_1) - 5Q_1.$$

To determine the profit-maximizing quantity, we find the change in the profit function with respect to a change in Q_1:

$$\frac{d\pi_1}{dQ_1} = 53 - 2Q_1 - 24 + Q_1 - 5.$$

Set this expression equal to 0 to determine the profit-maximizing quantity:

$53 - 2Q_1 - 24 + Q_1 - 5 = 0$, or $Q_1 = 24$.

Substituting $Q_1 = 24$ into Firm 2's reaction function gives Q_2:

$$Q_2 = 24 - \frac{24}{2} = 12.$$

Substitute Q_1 and Q_2 into the demand equation to find the price:

$P = 53 - 24 - 12 = \$17$.

Profits for each firm are equal to total revenue minus total costs, or

$$\pi_1 = (17)(24) - (5)(24) = \$288 \text{ and}$$
$$\pi_2 = (17)(12) - (5)(12) = \$144.$$

Total industry profit, $\pi_T = \pi_1 + \pi_2 = \$288 + \$144 = \$432$.

Compared to the Cournot equilibrium, total output has increased from 32 to 36, price has fallen from \$21 to \$17, and total profits have fallen from \$512 to \$432. Profits for Firm 1 have risen from \$256 to \$288, while the profits of Firm 2 have declined sharply from \$256 to \$144.

b. **How much will each firm produce, and what will its profit be?**

If *each* firm believes that it is the Stackelberg leader, while the other firm is the Cournot follower, they both will initially produce 24 units, so total output will be 48 units. The market price will be driven to \$5, equal to marginal cost. It is impossible to specify exactly where the new equilibrium point will be, because no point is stable when both firms are trying to be the Stackelberg leader.

5. Two firms compete in selling identical widgets. They choose their output levels Q_1 and Q_2 simultaneously and face the demand curve

$$P = 30 - Q,$$

where $Q = Q_1 + Q_2$. **Until recently, both firms had *zero marginal costs*. Recent environmental regulations have increased Firm 2's marginal cost to \$15. Firm 1's marginal cost remains constant at zero. True or false: As a result, the market price will rise to the *monopoly* level.**

True.

If only one firm were in this market, it would charge a price of \$15 a unit. Marginal revenue for this monopolist would be

$$MR = 30 - 2Q,$$

Profit maximization implies MR = MC, or

30 - 2Q = 0, Q = 15, (using the demand curve) P = 15.

The current situation is a Cournot game where Firm 1's marginal costs are zero and Firm 2's marginal costs are 15. We need to find the best response functions:

Firm 1's revenue is

$$PQ_1 = (30 - Q_1 - Q_2)Q_1 = 30Q_1 - Q_1^2 - Q_1Q_2,$$

and its marginal revenue is given by:

$$MR_1 = 30 - 2Q_1 - Q_2.$$

Profit maximization implies $MR_1 = MC_1$, or

$$30 - 2Q_1 - Q_2 = 0 \Rightarrow Q_1 = 15 - \frac{Q_2}{2},$$

which is Firm 1's best response function.

Firm 2's revenue function is symmetric to that of Firm 1 and hence

$$MR_2 = 30 - Q_1 - 2Q_2.$$

Profit maximization implies $MR_2 = MC_2$, or

$$30 - 2Q_2 - Q_1 = 15 \Rightarrow Q_2 = 7.5 - \frac{Q_1}{2},$$

which is Firm 2's best response function.

Cournot equilibrium occurs at the intersection of best response functions. Substituting for Q_1 in the response function for Firm 2 yields:

$$Q_2 = 7.5 - 0.5(15 - \frac{Q_2}{2}).$$

Thus $Q_2 = 0$ and $Q_1 = 15$. P = 30 - Q_1 + Q_2 = 15, which is the monopoly price.

6. Suppose that two identical firms produce widgets and that they are the only firms in the market. Their costs are given by $C_1 = 30Q_1$ and $C_2 = 30Q_2$, where Q_1 is the output of Firm 1 and Q_2 the output of Firm 2. Price is determined by the following demand curve:

P = 150 - Q

where $Q = Q_1 + Q_2$.

a.   Find the Cournot-Nash equilibrium. Calculate the profit of each firm at this equilibrium.

To determine the Cournot-Nash equilibrium, we first calculate the reaction function for each firm, then solve for price, quantity, and profit. Profit for Firm 1, $TR_1 - TC_1$, is equal to

$$\pi_1 = 150Q_1 - Q_1^2 - Q_1Q_2 - 30Q_1 = 120Q_1 - Q_1^2 - Q_1Q_2.$$

Therefore,

$$\frac{\partial \pi_1}{\partial Q_1} = 120 - 2Q_1 - Q_2.$$

Setting this equal to zero and solving for Q_1 in terms of Q_2:

$$Q_1 = 60 - 0.5Q_2.$$

This is Firm 1's reaction function. Because Firm 2 has the same cost structure, Firm 2's reaction function is

$$Q_2 = 60 - 0.5Q_1.$$

Substituting for Q_2 in the reaction function for Firm 1, and solving for Q_1, we find

$$Q_1 = 60 - (0.5)(60 - 0.5Q_1), \text{ or } Q_1 = 40.$$

By symmetry, $Q_2 = 40$.

Substituting Q_1 and Q_2 into the demand equation to determine the price at profit maximization:

$$P = 150 - 40 - 40 = \$70.$$

Substituting the values for price and quantity into the profit function,

$$\pi_1 = (70)(40) - (30)(40) = \$1,600 \text{ and}$$

$$\pi_2 = (70)(40) - (30)(40) = \$1,600.$$

Therefore, profit is $1,600 for both firms in Cournot-Nash equilibrium.

b.   **Suppose the two firms form a cartel to maximize joint profits. How many widgets will be produced? Calculate each firm's profit.**

Because marginal cost is the same for both firms and is constant for all output, we may determine the joint profit-maximizing output by considering only one firm, i.e., let

$$Q_1 = Q \text{ and } Q_2 = 0.$$

Profit is

$$\pi = 150Q - Q^2 - 30Q.$$

Therefore,

$$\frac{d\pi}{dQ} = 120 - 2Q.$$

Solving for the profit-maximizing level of output,

$$120 - 2Q = 0, \text{ or } Q = 60.$$

Substituting $Q = 60$ into the demand function to determine price:

$$P = 150 - 60 = \$90.$$

Substituting P and Q into the profit function:

$$\pi = (90)(60) - (30)(60) = \$3,600.$$

Because MC is constant, the firms may split quantities and profits. If they split quantity equally, then $Q_1 = Q_2 = 30$ and profits are $1,800 for each firm.

c.   **Suppose Firm 1 were the only firm in the industry. How would the market output and Firm 1's profit differ from that found in part (b) above?**

If Firm 1 were the only firm, it would solve the profit-maximization problem as in 6.*b*, i.e., Q_1 = 60 and π_1 = \$3,600.

d. **Returning to the duopoly of part (b), suppose Firm 1 abides by the agreement, but Firm 2 cheats by increasing production. How many widgets will Firm 2 produce? What will be each firm's profits?**

Assuming their agreement is to split the market equally, Firm 1 produces 30 widgets. Firm 2 cheats by producing its profit-maximizing level, given Q_1 = 30. Substituting Q_1 = 30 into Firm 2's reaction function:

$$Q_2 = 60 - \frac{30}{2} = 45.$$

Total industry output, Q_T, is equal to Q_1 plus Q_2:

$$Q_T = 30 + 45 = 75.$$

Substituting Q_T into the demand equation to determine price:

$$P = 150 - 75 = \$75.$$

Substituting Q_1, Q_2, and P into the profit function:

$$\pi_1 = (75)(30) - (30)(30) = \$1,350 \quad \text{and}$$
$$\pi_2 = (75)(45) - (30)(45) = \$2,025.$$

Firm 2 has increased its profits at the expense of Firm 1 by cheating on the agreement.

7. Suppose that two competing firms, A and B, produce a homogeneous good. Both firms have a marginal cost of M=\$50. Describe what would happen to output and price in each of the following situations if the firms are at (i) Cournot equilibrium, (ii) collusive equilibrium, and (iii) Bertrand equilibrium.

a. **Firm A must increase wages and its MC increases to \$80.**

(i) In a Cournot equilibrium you must think about the effect on the reaction functions, as illustrated in figure 12.4 of the text. When firm A experiences an increase in marginal cost, their reaction function will shift inwards. The quantity produced by firm A will decrease and the quantity produced by firm B will increase. Total quantity produced will tend to decrease and price will increase.

(ii) In a collusive equilibrium, the two firms will collectively act like a monopolist. When the marginal cost of firm A increases, firm A will reduce their production. This will increase price and cause firm B to increase production. Price will be higher and total quantity produced will be lower.

(iii) Given that the good is homogeneous, both will produce where price equals marginal cost. Firm A will increase price to \$80 and firm B will keep its price at \$50. Assuming firm B can produce enough output, they will supply the entire market.

b. **The marginal cost of both firms increases.**

(i) Again refer to figure 12.4. The increase in the marginal cost of both firms will shift both reaction functions inwards. Both firms will decrease quantity produced and price will increase.

(ii) When marginal cost increases, both firms will produce less and price will increase, as in the monopoly case.

(iii) As in the above cases, price will increase and quantity produced will decrease.

c. **The demand curve shifts to the right.**

(i) This is the opposite of the above case in part b. In this case, both reaction functions will shift outwards and both will produce a higher quantity. Price will tend to increase.

(ii) Both firms will increase the quantity produced as demand and marginal revenue increase. Price will also tend to increase.

(iii) Both firms will supply more output. Given that marginal cost is constant, the price will not change.

8. Suppose the airline industry consisted of only two firms: American and Texas Air Corp. Let the two firms have identical cost functions, C(q) = 40q. Assume the demand curve for the industry is given by P = 100 - Q and that each firm expects the other to behave as a Cournot competitor.

a. **Calculate the Cournot-Nash equilibrium for each firm, assuming that each chooses the output level that maximizes its profits when taking its rival's output as given. What are the profits of each firm?**

To determine the Cournot-Nash equilibrium, we first calculate the reaction function for each firm, then solve for price, quantity, and profit. Profit for Texas Air, π_1, is equal to total revenue minus total cost:

$$\pi_1 = (100 - Q_1 - Q_2)Q_1 - 40Q_1, \text{ or}$$

$$\pi_1 = 100Q_1 - Q_1^2 - Q_1Q_2 - 40Q_1, \text{ or } \pi_1 = 60Q_1 - Q_1^2 - Q_1Q_2.$$

The change in π_1 with respect to Q_1 is

$$\frac{\partial \pi_1}{\partial Q_1} = 60 - 2Q_1 - Q_2.$$

Setting the derivative to zero and solving for Q_1 in terms of Q_2 will give Texas Air's reaction function:

$$Q_1 = 30 - 0.5Q_2.$$

Because American has the same cost structure, American's reaction function is

$$Q_2 = 30 - 0.5Q_1.$$

Substituting for Q_2 in the reaction function for Texas Air,

$$Q_1 = 30 - 0.5(30 - 0.5Q_1) = 20.$$

By symmetry, $Q_2 = 20$. Industry output, Q_T, is Q_1 plus Q_2, or

$$Q_T = 20 + 20 = 40.$$

Substituting industry output into the demand equation, we find $P = 60$. Substituting Q_1, Q_2, and P into the profit function, we find

$$\pi_1 = \pi_2 = 60(20) - 20^2 - (20)(20) = \$400$$

for both firms in Cournot-Nash equilibrium.

b. **What would be the equilibrium quantity if Texas Air had constant marginal and average costs of 25, and American had constant marginal and average costs of 40?**

By solving for the reaction functions under this new cost structure, we find that profit for Texas Air is equal to

$$\pi_1 = 100Q_1 - Q_1^2 - Q_1Q_2 - 25Q_1 = 75Q_1 - Q_1^2 - Q_1Q_2.$$

The change in profit with respect to Q_1 is

$$\frac{\partial \pi_1}{\partial Q_1} = 75 - 2Q_1 - Q_2.$$

Set the derivative to zero, and solving for Q_1 in terms of Q_2,

$$Q_1 = 37.5 - 0.5Q_2.$$

This is Texas Air's reaction function. Since American has the same cost structure as in 8.*a*., American's reaction function is the same as before:

$$Q_2 = 30 - 0.5Q_1.$$

To determine Q_1, substitute for Q_2 in the reaction function for Texas Air and solve for Q_1:

$$Q_1 = 37.5 - (0.5)(30 - 0.5Q_1) = 30.$$

Texas Air finds it profitable to increase output in response to a decline in its cost structure.

To determine Q_2, substitute for Q_1 in the reaction function for American:

$$Q_2 = 30 - (0.5)(37.5 - 0.5Q_2) = 15.$$

American has cut back slightly in its output in response to the increase in output by Texas Air.

Total quantity, Q_T, is $Q_1 + Q_2$, or

$$Q_T = 30 + 15 = 45.$$

Compared to 8*a*, the equilibrium quantity has risen slightly.

c. **Assuming that both firms have the original cost function, C(q) = 40q, how much should Texas Air be willing to invest to lower its marginal cost from 40 to 25, assuming that American will not follow suit? How much should American be willing to spend to reduce its marginal cost to 25, assuming that Texas Air will have marginal costs of 25 regardless of American's actions?**

Recall that profits for both firms were $400 under the original cost structure. With constant average and marginal costs of 25, Texas Air's profits will be

$$(55)(30) - (25)(30) = \$900.$$

The difference in profit is $500. Therefore, Texas Air should be willing to invest up to $500 to *lower costs* from 40 to 25 per unit (assuming American does not follow suit).

To determine how much American would be willing to spend to reduce its average costs, we must calculate the difference in profits, assuming Texas Air's average cost is 25. First, without investment, American's profits would be:

$$(55)(15) - (40)(15) = \$225.$$

Second, with investment by both firms, the reaction functions would be:

$$Q_1 = 37.5 - 0.5Q_2 \text{ and}$$
$$Q_2 = 37.5 - 0.5Q_1.$$

To determine Q_1, substitute for Q_2 in the first reaction function and solve for Q_1:

$$Q_1 = 37.5 - (0.5)(37.5 - 0.5Q_1) = 25.$$

Substituting for Q_1 in the second reaction function to find Q_2:

$$Q_2 = 37.5 - 0.5(37.5 - 0.5Q_2) = 25.$$

Substituting industry output into the demand equation to determine price:

$$P = 100 - 50 = \$50.$$

Therefore, American's profits if $Q_1 = 30$ and $Q_2 = 15$ are

$$\pi_2 = (100 - 30 - 15)(15) - (40)(15) = \$225.$$

American's profits if $Q_1 = Q_2 = 25$ (when both firms have $MC = AC = 25$) are

$$\pi_2 = (100 - 25 - 25)(25) - (25)(25) = \$625.$$

Therefore, the difference in profit with and without the cost-saving investment for American is $400. American should be willing to invest up to $400 to reduce its marginal cost to 25 if Texas Air also has marginal costs of 25.

*9. Demand for light bulbs can be characterized by Q = 100 - P, where Q is in millions of lights sold, and P is the price per box. There are two producers of lights: Everglow and Dimlit. They have identical cost functions:

$$C_i = 10Q_i + 1/2Q_i^2 \, (i = E, D) \qquad\qquad Q = Q_E + Q_D.$$

a. **Unable to recognize the potential for collusion, the two firms act as short-run perfect competitors. What are the equilibrium values of Q_E, Q_D, and P? What are each firm's profits?**

Given that the total cost function is $C_i = 10Q_i + 1/2Q_i^2$, the marginal cost curve for each firm is $MC_i = 10 + Q_i$. In the short run, perfectly competitive firms determine the optimal level of output by taking price as given and setting price equal to marginal cost. There are two ways to solve this problem. One way is to set price equal to marginal cost for each firm so that:

$$P = 100 - Q_1 - Q_2 = 10 + Q_1$$
$$P = 100 - Q_1 - Q_2 = 10 + Q_2.$$

Given we now have two equations and two unknowns, we can solve for Q_1 and Q_2. Solve the second equation for Q_2 to get

$$Q_2 = \frac{90 - Q_1}{2},$$

and substitute into the other equation to get

$$100 - Q_1 - \frac{90 - Q_1}{2} = 10 + Q_1.$$

This yields a solution where $Q_1=30$, $Q_2=30$, and P=40. You can verify that P=MC for each firm. Profit is total revenue minus total cost or

$$\Pi = 40 * 30 - (10 * 30 + 0.5 * 30 * 30) = \$450 \text{ million.}$$

The other way to solve the problem and arrive at the same solution is to find the market supply curve by summing the marginal cost curves, so that $Q_M=2P-20$ is the market supply. Setting supply equal to demand results in a quantity of 60 in the market, or 30 per firm since they are identical.

b. **Top management in both firms is replaced. Each new manager independently recognizes the oligopolistic nature of the light bulb industry and plays Cournot. What are the equilibrium values of Q_E, Q_D, and P? What are each firm's profits?**

To determine the Cournot-Nash equilibrium, we first calculate the reaction function for each firm, then solve for price, quantity, and profit. Profits for Everglow are equal to $TR_E - TC_E$, or

$$\pi_E = (100 - Q_E - Q_D)Q_E - (10Q_E + 0.5Q_E^2) = 90Q_E - 1.5Q_E^2 - Q_EQ_D.$$

The change in profit with respect to Q_E is

$$\frac{\partial \pi_E}{\partial Q_E} = 90 - 3Q_E - Q_D.$$

To determine Everglow's reaction function, set the change in profits with respect to Q_E equal to 0 and solve for Q_E:

$$90 - 3Q_E - Q_D = 0, \text{ or}$$

$$Q_E = \frac{90 - Q_D}{3}.$$

Because Dimlit has the same cost structure, Dimlit's reaction function is

$$Q_D = \frac{90 - Q_E}{3}.$$

Substituting for Q_D in the reaction function for Everglow, and solving for Q_E:

$$Q_E = \frac{90 - \dfrac{90 - Q_E}{3}}{3}$$

$$3Q_E = 90 - 30 + \frac{Q_E}{3}$$

$$Q_E = 22.5.$$

By symmetry, $Q_D = 22.5$, and total industry output is 45.

Substituting industry output into the demand equation gives P:

$$45 = 100 - P, \text{ or } P = \$55.$$

Substituting total industry output and P into the profit function:

$$\Pi_i = 22.5 * 55 - (10 * 22.5 + 0.5 * 22.5 * 22.5) = \$759.375 \text{ million}.$$

c. **Suppose the Everglow manager guesses correctly that Dimlit has a Cournot conjectural variation, so Everglow plays Stackelberg. What are the equilibrium values of Q_E, Q_D, and P? What are each firm's profits?**

Recall Everglow's profit function:

$$\pi_E = (100 - Q_E - Q_D)Q_E - (10Q_E + 0.5Q_E^2)$$

If Everglow sets its quantity first, knowing Dimlit's reaction function $\left(\text{i.e., } Q_D = 30 - \dfrac{Q_E}{3}\right)$, we may determine Everglow's reaction function by substituting for Q_D in its profit function. We find

$$\pi_E = 60Q_E - \frac{7Q_E^2}{6}.$$

To determine the profit-maximizing quantity, differentiate profit with respect to Q_E, set the derivative to zero and solve for Q_E:

$$\frac{\partial \pi_E}{\partial Q_E} = 60 - \frac{7Q_E}{3} = 0, \text{ or } Q_E = 25.7.$$

Substituting this into Dimlit's reaction function, we find $Q_D = 30 - \frac{25.7}{3} = 21.4$. Total industry output is 47.1 and P = $52.90. Profit for Everglow is $772.29 million. Profit for Dimlit is $689.08 million.

d. **If the managers of the two companies collude, what are the equilibrium values of Q_E, Q_D, and P? What are each firm's profits?**

If the firms split the market equally, total cost in the industry is $10Q_T + \frac{Q_T^2}{2}$; therefore, $MC = 10 + Q_T$. Total revenue is $100Q_T - Q_T^2$; therefore, $MR = 100 - 2Q_T$. To determine the profit-maximizing quantity, set $MR = MC$ and solve for Q_T:

$$100 - 2Q_T = 10 + Q_T, \text{ or } Q_T = 30.$$

This means $Q_E = Q_D$ = 15.

Substituting Q_T into the demand equation to determine price:

$$P = 100 - 30 = \$70.$$

The profit for each firm is equal to total revenue minus total cost:

$$\pi_i = (70)(15) - \left((10)(15) + \frac{15^2}{2} \right) = \$787.50 \text{ million.}$$

10. Two firms produce luxury sheepskin auto seat covers, Western Where (WW) and B.B.B. Sheep (BBBS). Each firm has a cost function given by:

$$C(q) = 20q + q^2$$

The market demand for these seat covers is represented by the inverse demand equation:

$$P = 200 - 2Q,$$

where $Q = q_1 + q_2$, total output.

a. **If each firm acts to maximize its profits, taking its rival's output as given (i.e., the firms behave as Cournot oligopolists), what will be the equilibrium quantities selected by each firm? What is total output, and what is the market price? What are the profits for each firm?**

We are given each firm's cost function $C(q) = 20q + q^2$ and the market demand function

$P = 200 - 2Q$ where total output Q is the sum of each firm's output q_1 and q_2. We find the best response functions for both firms by setting marginal revenue equal to marginal cost (alternatively you can set up the profit function for each firm and differentiate with respect to the quantity produced for that firm):

$$R_1 = P q_1 = (200 - 2(q_1 + q_2)) q_1 = 200q_1 - 2q_1^2 - 2q_1q_2.$$

$$MR_1 = 200 - 4q_1 - 2q_2$$

$$MC_1 = 20 + 2q_1$$

$$200 - 4q_1 - 2q_2 = 20 + 2q_1$$

$$q_1 = 30 - (1/3)q_2.$$

By symmetry, BBBS's best response function will be:

$$q_2 = 30 - (1/3)q_1.$$

Cournot equilibrium occurs at the intersection of these two best response functions, given by:

$$q_1 = q_2 = 22.5.$$

Thus,

$$Q = q_1 + q_2 = 45$$

$$P = 200 - 2(45) = \$110.$$

Profit for both firms will be equal and given by:

$$R - C = (110)(22.5) - (20(22.5) + 22.5^2) = \$1518.75$$

b. **It occurs to the managers of WW and BBBS that they could do a lot better by colluding. If the two firms collude, what would be the profit-maximizing choice of output? The industry price? The output and the profit for each firm in this case?**

If firms can collude, they should each produce half the quantity that maximizes total industry profits (i.e. half the monopoly profits).

Joint profits will be $(200-2Q)Q - 2(20(Q/2) + (Q/2)^2) = 180Q - 2.5Q^2$ and will be maximized at $Q = 36$. You can find this quantity by differentiating the above profit function with respect to Q, setting the resulting first order condition equal to zero, and then solving for Q.

Thus, we will have $q_1 = q_2 = 36 / 2 = 18$ and $\quad P = 200 - 2(36) = \$128$

Profit for each firm will be $18(128) - (20(18) + 18^2) = \$1,620$

c. **The managers of these firms realize that explicit agreements to collude are illegal. Each firm must decide on its own whether to produce the Cournot quantity or the cartel quantity. To aid in making the decision, the manager of WW constructs a payoff matrix like the real one below. Fill in each box with the (profit of WW, profit of BBBS). Given this payoff matrix, what output strategy is each firm likely to pursue?**

If WW produces the Cournot level of output (22.5) and BBBS produces the collusive level (18), then:

$$Q = q_1 + q_2 = 22.5 + 18 = 40.5$$

$$P = 200 - 2(40.5) = \$119.$$

Profit for WW $= 22.5(119) - (20(22.5) + 22.5^2) = \$1721.25.$

Profit for BBBS $= 18(119) - (20(18) + 18^2) = \$1458.$

Both firms producing at the Cournot output levels will be the only Nash Equilibrium in this industry, given the following payoff matrix. (Note: not only is this a Nash Equilibrium, but it is an equilibrium in dominant strategies.)

Profit Payoff Matrix (WW profit, BBBS profit)		BB Produce Cournot *q*	BS Produce Cartel *q*
WW	Produce Cournot *q*	1518, 1518	1721, 1458
	Produce Cartel *q*	1458, 1721	1620, 1620

d.   **Suppose WW can set its output level *before* BBBS does. How much will WW choose to produce in this case? How much will BBBS produce? What is the market price, and what is the profit for each firm? Is WW better off by choosing its output first? Explain why or why not.**

WW is now able to set quantity first. WW knows that BBBS will choose a quantity q_2 which will be its best response to q_1 or:

$$q_2 = 30 - \frac{1}{3}q_1.$$

WW profits will be:

$$\Pi = P_1 q_1 - C_1 = (200 - 2q_1 - 2q_2)q_1 - (20q_1 + q_1^2)$$
$$\Pi = 180q_1 - 3q_1^2 - 2q_1 q_2$$
$$\Pi = 180q_1 - 3q_1^2 - 2q_1(30 - \frac{1}{3}q_1)$$
$$\Pi = 120q_1 - \frac{7}{3}q_1^2.$$

Profit maximization implies:

$$\frac{\partial \Pi}{\partial q_1} = 120 - \frac{14}{3}q_1 = 0.$$

This results in q_1=25.7 and q_2=21.4. The equilibrium price and profits will then be:

P = 200 - 2(q_1 + q_2) = 200 - 2(25.7 + 21.4) = \$105.80

π_1 = (105.80) (25.7) - (20) (25.7) - 25.7^2 = \$1544.57

π_2 = (105.80) (21.4) - (20) (21.4) - 21.4^2 = \$1378.16.

WW is able to benefit from its first mover advantage by committing to a high level of output. Since firm 2 moves after firm 1 has selected its output, firm 2 can only react to the output decision of firm 1. If firm 1 produces its Cournot output as a leader, firm 2 produces its Cournot output as a follower. Hence, firm 1 cannot do worse as a leader than it does in the Cournot game. When firm 1 produces more, firm 2 produces less, raising firm 1's profits.

*11. Two firms compete by choosing price. Their demand functions are

Q_1 = 20 - P_1 + P_2 and Q_2 = 20 + P_1 - P_2

where P_1 and P_2 are the prices charged by each firm respectively and Q_1 and Q_2 are the resulting demands. Note that the demand for each good depends only on the difference in prices; if the two firms colluded and set the same price, they could make that price as high as they want, and earn infinite profits. Marginal costs are zero.

a.   **Suppose the two firms set their prices at the *same time*. Find the resulting Nash equilibrium. What price will each firm charge, how much will it sell, and what will its profit be? (Hint: Maximize the profit of each firm with respect to its price.)**

To determine the Nash equilibrium, we first calculate the reaction function for each firm, then solve for price. With zero marginal cost, profit for Firm 1 is:

$$\pi_1 = P_1 Q_1 = P_1(20 - P_1 + P_2) = 20P_1 - P_1^2 + P_2 P_1.$$

The marginal revenue is the slope of the total revenue function (here it is the slope of the profit function because total cost is equal to zero):

$$MR_1 = 20 - 2P_1 + P_2.$$

At the profit-maximizing price, $MR_1 = 0$. Therefore,

$$P_1 = \frac{20 + P_2}{2}.$$

This is Firm 1's reaction function. Because Firm 2 is symmetric to Firm 1, its reaction function is $P_2 = \frac{20 + P_1}{2}$. Substituting Firm 2's reaction function into that of Firm 1:

$$P_1 = \frac{20 + \dfrac{20 + P_1}{2}}{2} = 10 + 5 + \frac{P_1}{4} = \$20.$$

By symmetry, $P_2 = \$20$.

To determine the quantity produced by each firm, substitute P_1 and P_2 into the demand functions:

$$Q_1 = 20 - 20 + 20 = 20 \text{ and}$$
$$Q_2 = 20 + 20 - 20 = 20.$$

Profits for Firm 1 are $P_1 Q_1 = \$400$, and, by symmetry, profits for Firm 2 are also $400.

b.   **Suppose Firm 1 sets its price *first* and then Firm 2 sets its price. What price will each firm charge, how much will it sell, and what will its profit be?**

If Firm 1 sets its price first, it takes Firm 2's reaction function into account. Firm 1's profit function is:

$$\pi_1 = P_1\left(20 - P_1 + \frac{20 + P_1}{2}\right) = 30P_1 - \frac{P_1^2}{2}.$$

To determine the profit-maximizing price, find the change in profit with respect to a change in price:

$$\frac{d\pi_1}{dP_1} = 30 - P_1.$$

Set this expression equal to zero to find the profit-maximizing price:

$$30 - P_1 = 0, \text{ or } P_1 = \$30.$$

Substitute P_1 in Firm 2's reaction function to find P_2:

$$P_2 = \frac{20 + 30}{2} = \$25.$$

At these prices,

$$Q_1 = 20 - 30 + 25 = 15 \text{ and}$$
$$Q_2 = 20 + 30 - 25 = 25.$$

Profits are

$$\pi_1 = (30)(15) = \$450 \text{ and}$$
$$\pi_2 = (25)(25) = \$625.$$

If Firm 1 must set its price first, Firm 2 is able to undercut Firm 1 and gain a larger market share.

c. **Suppose you are one of these firms, and there are three ways you could play the game: (i) Both firms set price at the same time. (ii) You set price first. (iii) Your competitor sets price first. If you could choose among these options which would you prefer? Explain why.**

Your first choice should be (iii), and your second choice should be (ii). (Compare the Nash profits in part 11.a, $400, with profits in part 11.b., $450 and $625.) From the reaction functions, we know that the price leader provokes a price increase in the follower. By being able to move second, however, the follower increases price by less than the leader, and hence undercuts the leader. Both firms enjoy increased profits, but the follower does best.

*12. The dominant firm model can help us understand the behavior of some cartels. Let's apply this model to the OPEC oil cartel. We shall use isoelastic curves to describe world demand *W* and noncartel (competitive) supply *S*. Reasonable numbers for the price elasticities of world demand and non-cartel supply are -1/2 and 1/2, respectively. Then, expressing *W* and *S* in millions of barrels per day (mb/d), we could write

$$W = 160P^{-\frac{1}{2}} \qquad \text{and} \qquad S = 3\frac{1}{3}P^{\frac{1}{2}}.$$

Note that OPEC's net demand is D = W - S.

a. **Sketch the world demand curve *W*, the non-OPEC supply curve *S*, OPEC's net demand curve *D*, and OPEC's marginal revenue curve. For purposes of approximation, assume OPEC's production cost is zero. Indicate OPEC's optimal price, OPEC's optimal production, and non-OPEC production on the diagram. Now, show on the diagram how the various curves will shift, and how OPEC's optimal price will change if non-OPEC supply becomes more expensive because reserves of oil start running out.**

OPEC's net demand curve, *D*, is:

$$D = 160P^{-1/2} - 3\frac{1}{3}P^{1/2}.$$

OPEC's marginal revenue curve starts from the same point on the vertical axis as its net demand curve and is twice as steep. OPEC's optimal production occurs where *MR* = 0 (since production cost is assumed to be zero), and OPEC's optimal price in Figure 12.12.a.i is found from the net demand curve at Q_{OPEC}. Non-OPEC production can be read off of the non-OPEC supply curve at a price of *P**. Note that in the two figures below, the demand and supply curves are actually non-linear. They have been drawn in a linear fashion for ease of accuracy.

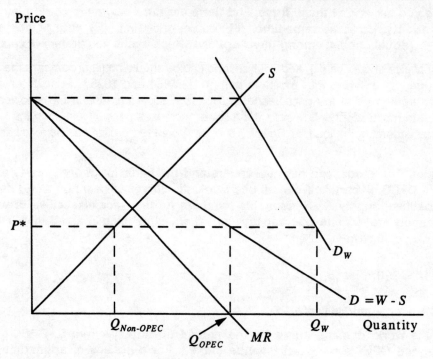

Figure 12.12.a.i

Next, suppose non-OPEC oil becomes more expensive. Then the supply curve S shifts to S^*. This changes OPEC's net demand curve from D to D^*, which in turn creates a new marginal revenue curve, MR^*, and a new optimal OPEC production level of Q_D^*, yielding a new higher price of P^*. At this new price, non-OPEC production is $Q_{Non-OPEC}^*$. Notice that the curves must be drawn accurately to give this result, and again have been drawn in a linear fashion as opposed to non-linear for ease of accuracy.

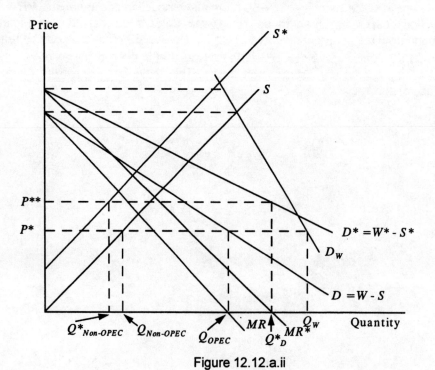

Figure 12.12.a.ii

b. **Calculate OPEC's optimal (profit-maximizing) price. (Hint: Because OPEC's cost is zero, just write the expression for OPEC revenue and find the price that maximizes it.)**

Since costs are zero, OPEC will choose a price that maximizes total revenue:

$$\text{Max } \pi = PQ = P(W - S)$$

$$\pi = P\left(160P^{-1/2} - 3\frac{1}{3}P^{1/2}\right) = 160P^{1/2} - 3\frac{1}{3}P^{3/2}.$$

To determine the profit-maximizing price, we find the change in the profit function with respect to a change in price and set it equal to zero:

$$\frac{\partial \pi}{\partial P} = 80P^{-1/2} - \left(3\frac{1}{3}\right)\left(\frac{3}{2}\right)P^{1/2} = 80P^{-1/2} - 5P^{1/2} = 0.$$

Solving for *P*,

$$5P^{\frac{1}{2}} = \frac{80}{P^{\frac{1}{2}}}, \text{ or } P = \$16.$$

c. **Suppose the oil-consuming countries were to unite and form a "buyers' cartel" to gain monopsony power. What can we say, and what can't we say, about the impact this would have on price?**

If the oil-consuming countries unite to form a buyers' cartel, then we have a monopoly (OPEC) facing a monopsony (the buyers' cartel). As a result, there is no well-defined demand or supply curve. We expect that the price will fall below the monopoly price when the buyers also collude, because monopsony power offsets monopoly power. However, economic theory cannot determine the exact price that results from this bilateral monopoly because the price depends on the bargaining skills of the two parties, as well as on other factors, such as the elasticities of supply and demand.

13. A lemon-growing cartel consists of four orchards. Their total cost functions are:

$$TC_1 = 20 + 5Q_1^2$$
$$TC_2 = 25 + 3Q_2^2$$
$$TC_3 = 15 + 4Q_3^2$$
$$TC_4 = 20 + 6Q_4^2$$

(TC is in hundreds of dollars, Q is in cartons per month picked and shipped.)

a. **Tabulate total, average, and marginal costs for each firm for output levels between 1 and 5 cartons per month (i.e., for 1, 2, 3, 4, and 5 cartons).**

The following tables give total, average, and marginal costs for each firm.

Units	Firm 1 TC	AC	MC	Firm 2 TC	AC	MC
0	20	—	—	25	—	—
1	25	25	5	28	28	3
2	40	20	15	37	18.5	9
3	65	21.67	25	52	17.3	15
4	100	25	35	73	18.25	21
5	145	29	45	100	20	27

Firm 3   Firm 4

Units	TC	AC	MC	TC	AC	MC
0	15			20		
1	19	19	4	26	26	6
2	31	15.5	12	44	22	18
3	51	17	20	74	24.67	30
4	79	19.75	28	116	29	42
5	115	23	36	170	34	54

b.   **If the cartel decided to ship 10 cartons per month and set a price of 25 per carton, how should output be allocated among the firms?**

The cartel should assign production such that the lowest marginal cost is achieved for each unit, i.e.,

Cartel Unit Assigned	Firm Assigned	MC
1	2	3
2	3	4
3	1	5
4	4	6
5	2	9
6	3	12
7	1	15
8	2	15
9	4	18
10	3	20

Therefore, Firms 1 and 4 produce 2 units each and Firms 2 and 3 produce 3 units each.

c.   **At this shipping level, which firm has the most incentive to cheat? Does any firm *not* have an incentive to cheat?**

At this level of output, Firm 2 has the lowest marginal cost for producing one more unit beyond its allocation, i.e., $MC = 21$ for the fourth unit for Firm 2. In addition, $MC = 21$ is less than the price of $25. For all other firms, the next unit has a marginal cost equal to or greater than $25. Firm 2 has the most incentive to cheat, while Firms 3 and 4 have no incentive to cheat, and Firm 1 is indifferent.

CHAPTER 13
GAME THEORY AND COMPETITIVE STRATEGY

Chapter 13 continues the discussion of competitive firms in the context of two-player games, with the first three sections covering topics introduced in Chapter 12. If you did not present Section 12.5, you should do so after discussing Sections 13.1 and 13.2. Sections 13.4 through 13.8 introduce advanced topics, as does section 13.9 on auctions, which is new to this edition. The presentation throughout the chapter focuses on the intuition behind each model or strategy. The exercises focus on relating Chapter 13 to Chapter 12 and on behavior in repeated games.

Two concepts pervade this chapter: rationality and equilibrium. Assuming the players are rational means that each player maximizes his or her own payoff whether it hurts or helps other players. Rationality underlies many of the equilibria in the chapter. Underlying all these models is the definition of a Nash equilibrium, which the students will find esoteric. When presenting each model, ask whether a unique Nash equilibrium exists. If there is more than one, discuss the conditions that will favor each equilibrium.

The analysis in the last five sections of the chapter is more demanding, but the examples are more detailed. Section 13.4 examines repeated games, and it will be important to discuss the role of rationality in the achievement of an equilibrium in both finite- and infinite-horizon games. Example 13.2 points out conditions that lead to stability in repeated games, while Example 13.3 presents an unstable case. Sections 13.5, 13.6, and 13.7 introduce strategy in the context of sequential games. To capture the students' attention, discuss the phenomenal success of Wal-Mart in its attempt to preempt the entry of other discount stores in rural areas (see Example 13.4). First, define a strategic move; second, discuss the advantage of moving first; third, present Example 13.4; and fourth, continue with other forms of strategic behavior, including the use of new capacity and R&D to deter entry (see Examples 13.5 and 13.6). You may wish to reintroduce the case of bilateral monopoly during the discussion of strategic behavior in cooperative games.

REVIEW QUESTIONS

1. What is the difference between a cooperative and a noncooperative game? Give an example of each.

In a noncooperative game the players do not formally communicate in an effort to coordinate their actions. They are aware of one another's existence, but act independently. The primary difference between a cooperative and a noncooperative game is that a binding contract, i.e., an agreement between the parties to which both parties must adhere, is possible in the former, but not in the latter. An example of a cooperative game would be a formal cartel agreement, such as OPEC, or a joint venture. An example of a noncooperative game would be a race in research and development to obtain a patent.

2. What is a dominant strategy? Why is an equilibrium stable in dominant strategies?

A dominant strategy is one that is best no matter what action is taken by the other party to the game. When both players have dominant strategies, the outcome is stable because neither party has an incentive to change.

3. Explain the meaning of a Nash equilibrium. How does it differ from an equilibrium in dominant strategies?

A Nash equilibrium is an outcome where both players correctly believe that they are doing the best they can, *given the action of the other player*. A game is in equilibrium if neither player has an incentive to change his or her choice, unless there is a change by the other player. The key feature that distinguishes a Nash equilibrium from an equilibrium in dominant strategies is the *dependence* on the opponent's behavior. An equilibrium in dominant strategies results if each player has a best choice, regardless of the other player's choice. Every dominant strategy equilibrium is a Nash equilibrium but the reverse does not hold.

4. How does a Nash equilibrium differ from a game's maximin solution? In what situations is a maximin solution a more likely outcome than a Nash equilibrium?

A maximin strategy is one in which each player determines the worst outcome for each of the opponent's actions and chooses the option that maximizes the minimum gain that can be earned. Unlike the Nash equilibrium, the maximin solution does not require players to react to an opponent's choice. If no dominant strategy exists (in which case outcomes depend on the opponent's behavior), players can reduce the uncertainty inherent in relying on the opponent's rationality by conservatively following a maximin strategy. The maximin solution is more likely than the Nash solution in cases where there is a higher probability of irrational (non-optimizing) behavior.

5. What is a "tit-for-tat" strategy? Why is it a rational strategy for the infinitely repeated prisoners' dilemma?

A player following a "tit-for-tat" strategy will cooperate as long as his or her opponent is cooperating and will switch to a noncooperative strategy if their opponent switches strategies. When the competitors assume that they will be repeating their interaction in *every* future period, the long-term gains from cooperating will outweigh any short-term gains from not cooperating. Because the "tit-for-tat" strategy encourages cooperation in infinitely repeated games, it is rational.

6. Consider a game in which the prisoners' dilemma is repeated 10 times and both players are rational and fully informed. Is a tit-for-tat strategy optimal in this case? Under what conditions would such a strategy be optimal?

Since cooperation will unravel from the last period back to the first period, the "tit-for-tat" strategy is not optimal when there is a finite number of periods and both players anticipate the competitor's response in *every* period. Given that there is no response possible in the eleventh period for action in the tenth (and last) period, cooperation breaks down in the last period. Then, knowing that there is no cooperation in the last period, players should maximize their self-interest by not cooperating in the second-to-last period. This unraveling occurs because both players assume that the other player has considered *all* consequences in *all* periods. However, if there is some doubt about whether the opponent has fully anticipated the consequences of the "tit-for-tat" strategy in the final period, the game will not unravel and the "tit-for-tat" strategy can be optimal.

7. Suppose you and your competitor are playing the pricing game shown in Table 13.8. Both of you must announce your prices at the same time. Can you improve your outcome by promising your competitor that you will announce a high price?

If the game is to be played only a few times, there is little to gain. If you are Firm 1 and promise to announce a high price, Firm 2 will undercut you and you will end up with a payoff of -50. However, next period you will undercut too, and both firms will earn 10. If the game is played many times, there is a better chance that Firm 2 will realize that if it matches your high price, the long-term payoff of 50 each period is better than 100 at first and 10 thereafter.

8. What is meant by "first-mover advantage"? Give an example of a gaming situation with a first-mover advantage.

A "first-mover" advantage can occur in a game where the first player to act receives the highest payoff. The first-mover signals his or her choice to the opponent, and the opponent must choose a response, *given this signal*. The first-mover goes on the offensive and the second-mover responds defensively. In many recreational games, from chess to football, the first-mover has an advantage. In many markets, the first firm to introduce a product can set the standard for competitors to follow. In some cases, the standard-setting power of the first mover becomes so pervasive in the market that the brand name of the product becomes synonymous with the product, e.g., "Kleenex," the name of Kleenex-brand facial tissue, is used by many consumers to refer to facial tissue of any brand.

9. What is a "strategic move"? How can the development of a certain kind of reputation be a strategic move?

A strategic move involves a commitment to reduce one's options. The strategic move might not seem rational outside the context of the game in which it is played, but it is rational given the anticipated response of the other player. Random responses to an opponent's action may not appear to be rational, but developing a reputation of being unpredictable could lead to higher payoffs in the long run. Another example would be making a promise to give a discount to all previous consumers if you give a discount to one. Such a move makes the firm vulnerable, but the goal of such a strategic move is to signal to rivals that you *won't* be discounting price and hope that your rivals follow suit.

10. Can the threat of a price war deter entry by potential competitors? What actions might a firm take to make this threat credible?

Both the incumbent and the potential entrant know that a price war will leave their firms worse off. Normally, such a threat is not credible. Thus, the incumbent must make his or her threat of a price war believable by signaling to the potential entrant that a price war *will* result if entry occurs. One strategic move is to increase capacity, signaling a lower future price, and another is to engage in apparently irrational behavior. Both types of strategic behavior might deter entry, but for different reasons. While an increase in capacity reduces expected profits by reducing prices, irrational behavior reduces expected profits by increasing uncertainty, hence increasing the rate at which future profits must be discounted into the present.

11. A strategic move limits one's flexibility and yet gives one an advantage. Why? How might a strategic move give one an advantage in bargaining?

A strategic move influences conditional behavior by the opponent. If the game is well understood and the opponent's reaction can be predicted, a strategic move leaves the player better off. Economic transactions involve a bargain, whether implicit or explicit. In every bargain, we assume that both parties attempt to maximize their self-interest. Strategic moves by one player provide signals to which another player reacts. If a bargaining game is played only once (so no reputations are involved), the players might act strategically to maximize their payoffs. If bargaining is repeated, players might act strategically to establish reputations for expected negotiations.

12. Why is the winner's curse potentially a problem for a bidder in a common value auction but not in a private value auction?

The winner's curse states that "The winner of a common value auction is likely to be made worse off (than not winning) because the winner was overly optimistic and, as a consequence, bid more for the item than it was actually worth." In a private value auction, you are aware of your own reservation price, and will bid accordingly. Once the price has escalated above your reservation price, you will no longer bid. If you win, it is because the winning bid was below your reservation price. In a common value auction, you do not know the exact value of the good you are bidding on. The winner will tend to be the person who has most overestimated the value of the good, assuming that some bidders overestimate and some underestimate. If all bids are below the actual value, then there is no winner's curse.

EXERCISES

1. In many oligopolistic industries, the same firms compete over a long period of time, setting prices and observing each other's behavior repeatedly. Given that the number of repetitions is large, why don't collusive outcomes typically result?

If games are repeated indefinitely and all players know all payoffs, rational behavior will lead to apparently collusive outcomes, i.e., the same outcomes that would result if firms were actively colluding. All payoffs, however, might not be known by all players. Sometimes the payoffs of other firms can only be known by engaging in extensive (and costly) information exchanges or by making a move and observing rivals' responses. Also, successful collusion encourages entry. Perhaps the greatest problem in maintaining a collusive outcome is that changes in market conditions change the collusive price and quantity. The firms then have to repeatedly change their agreement on price and quantity, which is costly, and this increases the ability of one firm to cheat without being discovered.

2. Many industries are often plagued by overcapacity--firms simultaneously make major investments in capacity expansion, so total capacity far exceeds demand. This happens not only in industries in which demand is highly volatile and unpredictable, but also in industries in which demand is fairly stable. What factors lead to overcapacity? Explain each briefly.

In Chapter 12, we found that excess capacity may arise in industries with easy entry and differentiated products. In the monopolistic competition model, downward-sloping demand curves for each firm lead to output with average cost above minimum average cost. The difference between the resulting output and the output at minimum long-run average cost is defined as excess capacity. In this chapter, we saw that overcapacity could be used to deter new entry; that is, investments in capacity expansion could convince potential competitors that entry would be unprofitable. (Note that although threats of capacity expansion may deter entry, these threats must be *credible*.)

3. Two computer firms, A and B, are planning to market network systems for office information management. Each firm can develop either a fast, high-quality system (H), or a slower, low-quality system (L). Market research indicates that the resulting profits to each firm for the alternative strategies are given by the following payoff matrix:

Firm B

		H	L
Firm A	H	30, 30	50, 35
	L	40, 60	20, 20

a. If both firms make their decisions at the same time and follow *maximin* (low-risk) strategies, what will the outcome be?

With a maximin strategy, a firm determines the worst outcome for each option, then chooses the option that maximizes the payoff among the worst outcomes. If Firm A chooses *H*, the worst payoff would occur if Firm B chooses *H*: A's payoff would be 30. If Firm A chooses *L*, the worst payoff would occur if Firm B chooses *L*: A's payoff would be 20. With a maximin strategy, A therefore chooses *H*. If Firm B chooses *L*, the worst payoff would occur if Firm A chooses *L*: the payoff would be 20. If Firm B chooses *H*, the worst payoff, 30, would occur if Firm A chooses *L*. With a maximin strategy, B therefore chooses *H*. So under maximin, both A and B produce a high-quality system.

b. Suppose both firms try to maximize profits, but Firm A has a head start in planning, and can commit first. Now what will the outcome be? What will the outcome be if Firm B has a head start in planning and can commit first?

If Firm A can commit first, it will choose *H*, because it knows that Firm B will rationally choose *L*, since *L* gives a higher payoff to B (35 vs. 30). This gives Firm A a payoff of 50. If Firm B can commit first, it will choose *H*, because it knows that Firm A will rationally choose *L*, since *L* gives a higher payoff to A (40 vs. 30). This gives Firm B a payoff of 60.

c. Getting a head start costs money (you have to gear up a large engineering team). Now consider the *two-stage* game in which *first*, each firm decides how much money to spend to speed up its planning, and *second*, it announces which product (H or L) it will produce.

Which firm will spend more to speed up its planning? How much will it spend? Should the other firm spend *anything* to speed up its planning? Explain.

In this game, there is an advantage to being the first mover. If A moves first, its profit is 50. If it moves second, its profit is 40, a difference of 10. Thus, it would be willing to spend up to 10 for the option of announcing first. On the other hand, if B moves first, its profit is 60. If it moves second, its profit is 35, a difference of 25, and thus would be willing to spend up to 25 for the option of announcing first. Once Firm A realizes that Firm B is willing to spend more on the option of announcing first, then the value of the option decreases for Firm A, because if both firms were to invest both firms would choose to produce the high-quality system. Therefore, Firm A should not spend money to speed up the introduction of its product if it believes that Firm B is spending the money. However, if Firm B realizes that Firm A will wait, Firm B should only spend enough money to discourage Firm A from engaging in research and development, which would be an amount slightly more than 10 (the maximum amount A is willing to spend).

4. Two firms are in the chocolate market. Each can choose to go for the high end of the market (high quality) or the low end (low quality). Resulting profits are given by the following payoff matrix:

		Firm 2	
		Low	High
Firm 1	Low	-20, -30	900, 600
	High	100, 800	50, 50

a. **What outcomes, if any, are Nash equilibria?**

A Nash equilibrium exists when neither party has an incentive to alter its strategy, taking the other's strategy as given. If Firm 2 chooses Low and Firm 1 chooses High, neither will have an incentive to change (100 > -20 for Firm 1 and 800 > 50 for Firm 2). If Firm 2 chooses High and Firm 1 chooses Low, neither will have an incentive to change (900 > 50 for Firm 1 and 600 > -30 for Firm 2). Both outcomes are Nash equilibria. Both firms choosing low is not a Nash equilibrium because, for example, if Firm 1 chooses low then firm 2 is better off by switching to high since 600 is greater than -30.

b. **If the manager of each firm is conservative and each follows a maximin strategy, what will be the outcome?**

If Firm 1 chooses Low, its worst payoff, -20, would occur if Firm 2 chooses Low. If Firm 1 chooses High, its worst payoff, 50, would occur if Firm 2 chooses High. Therefore, with a conservative maximin strategy, Firm 1 chooses High. Similarly, if Firm 2 chooses Low, its worst payoff, -30, would occur if Firm 1 chooses Low. If Firm 2 chooses High, its worst payoff, 50, would occur if Firm 1 chooses High. Therefore, with a maximin strategy, Firm 2 chooses High. Thus, both firms choose High, yielding a payoff of 50 for both.

c. **What is the cooperative outcome?**

The cooperative outcome would maximize *joint* payoffs. This would occur if Firm 1 goes for the low end of the market and Firm 2 goes for the high end of the market. The joint payoff is 1,500 (Firm 1 gets 900 and Firm 2 gets 600).

d. **Which firm benefits most from the cooperative outcome? How much would that firm need to offer the other to persuade it to collude?**

Firm 1 benefits most from cooperation. The difference between its best payoff under cooperation and the next best payoff is 900 - 100 = 800. To persuade Firm 2 to choose Firm 1's best option, Firm 1 must offer at least the difference between Firm 2's payoff under cooperation, 600, and its best payoff, 800, i.e., 200. However, Firm 2 realizes that Firm 1 benefits much more from cooperation and should try to extract as much as it can from Firm 1 (up to 800).

5. Two major networks are competing for viewer ratings in the 8:00-9:00 P.M. and 9:00-10:00 P.M. slots on a given weeknight. Each has two shows to fill this time period and is juggling its lineup. Each can choose to put its "bigger" show first or to place it second in the 9:00-10:00 P.M. slot. The combination of decisions leads to the following "ratings points" results:

		Network 2	
		First	**Second**
Network 1	**First**	18, 18	23, 20
	Second	4, 23	16, 16

a.   Find the Nash equilibria for this game, assuming that both networks make their decisions at the same time.

A Nash equilibrium exists when neither party has an incentive to alter its strategy, taking the other's strategy as given. By inspecting each of the four combinations, we find that (First, Second) is the only Nash equilibrium, yielding a payoff of (23, 20). There is no incentive for either party to change from this outcome. If we pick Second for Firm 1 and First for Firm 2, Firm 1 has an incentive to switch to First, in which case Firm 2 is better switching to Second.

b.   If each network is risk averse and uses a maximin strategy, what will be the resulting equilibrium?

This conservative strategy of minimizing the maximum loss focuses on limiting the extent of the worst possible outcome, to the exclusion of possible good outcomes. If Network 1 plays First, the worst payoff is 18. If Network 1 plays Second, the worst payoff is 4. Under maximin, Network 1 plays First. (Here, playing First is a dominant strategy.) If Network 2 plays First, the worst payoff is 18. If Network 2 plays Second, the worst payoff is 16. Under maximin, Network 2 plays First. The maximin equilibrium is (First, First) with a payoff of (18,18).

c.   What will be the equilibrium if Network 1 can makes its selection first? If Network 2 goes first?

If Network 1 plays First, Network 2 will play Second, yielding 23 for Network 1. If Network 1 plays Second, Network 2 will play First, yielding 4 for Network 1. Therefore, if it has the first move, Network 1 will play First, and the resulting equilibrium will be (First, Second). If Network 2 plays First, Network 1 will play First, yielding 18 for Network 2. If Network 2 plays Second, Network 1 will play First, yielding 20 for Network 2. If it has the first move, Network 2 will play Second, and the equilibrium will again be (First, Second).

d.   Suppose the network managers meet to coordinate schedules and Network 1 promises to schedule its big show first. Is this promise credible? What would be the likely outcome?

A move is credible if, once declared, *there is no incentive to change*. Network 1 has a dominant strategy: play the bigger show First. In this case, the promise to schedule the bigger show first is credible. Knowing this, Network 2 will schedule its bigger show Second. The coordinated outcome is likely to be (First, Second).

6. Two competing firms are each planning to introduce a new product. Each will decide whether to produce Product A, Product B, or Product C. They will make their choices at the same time. The resulting payoffs are shown below.

We are given the following payoff matrix, which describes a product introduction game:

		Firm 2		
		A	B	C
Firm 1	A	-10,-10	0,10	10,20
	B	10,0	-20,-20	-5,15
	C	20,10	15,-5	-30,-30

a.   Are there any Nash equilibria in pure strategies? If so, what are they?

There are two Nash equilibria in pure strategies. Each one involves one firm introducing Product A and the other firm introducing Product C. We can write these two strategy pairs as (A, C) and (C, A), where the first strategy is for player 1. The payoff for these two strategies is, respectively, (10,20) and (20,10).

b.   If both firms use *maximin* strategies, what outcome will result?

Recall that maximin strategies maximize the minimum payoff for both players. For each of the players the strategy that maximizes their minimum payoff is A. Thus (A,A) will result, and payoffs will be (-10,-10). Each player is much worse off than at either of the pure strategy Nash equilibrium.

c.   If Firm 1 uses a maximin strategy and Firm 2 knows, what will Firm 2 do?

If Firm 1 plays its maximin strategy of A, and Firm 2 knows this then Firm 2 would get the highest payoff by playing C. Notice that when Firm 1 plays conservatively, the Nash equilibrium that results gives Firm 2 the highest payoff of the two Nash equilibria.

7. We can think of the U.S. and Japanese trade policies as a prisoners' dilemma. The two countries are considering policies to open or close their import markets. Suppose the payoff matrix is:

		Japan	
		Open	Close
U.S.	Open	10, 10	5, 5
	Close	-100, 5	1, 1

a.   Assume that each country knows the payoff matrix and believes that the other country will act in its own interest. Does either country have a dominant strategy? What will be the equilibrium policies if each country acts rationally to maximize its welfare?

Choosing Open is a dominant strategy for both countries. If Japan chooses Open, the U.S. does best by choosing Open. If Japan chooses Close, the U.S. does best by choosing Open. Therefore, the U.S. should choose Open, no matter what Japan does. If the U.S. chooses Open, Japan does best by choosing Open. If the U.S. chooses Close, Japan does best by choosing Open. Therefore, both countries will choose to have Open policies in equilibrium.

b.   Now assume that Japan is not certain that the U.S. will behave rationally. In particular, Japan is concerned that U.S. politicians may want to penalize Japan even if that does not maximize

U.S. welfare. **How might this affect Japan's choice of strategy? How might this change the equilibrium?**

The irrationality of U.S. politicians could change the equilibrium to (Close, Open). If the U.S. wants to penalize Japan they will choose Close, but Japan's strategy will not be affected since choosing Open is still Japan's dominant strategy.

8. You are a duopolist producer of a homogeneous good. Both you and your competitor have *zero* marginal costs. The market demand curve is

$$P = 30 - Q$$

where $Q = Q_1 + Q_2$. Q_1 **is your output and** Q_2 **your competitor's output. Your competitor has also read this book.**

a. **Suppose you will play this game only once. If you and your competitor must announce your output at the same time, how much will you choose to produce? What do you expect your profit to be? Explain.**

These are some of the cells in the payoff matrix:

Firm 2's Output

Firm 1's Output	0	5	10	15	20	25	30
0	0,0	0,125	0,200	0,225	0,200	0,125	0,0
5	125,0	100,100	75,150	50,150	25,100	0,0	0,0
10	200,0	150,75	100,100	50,75	0,0	0,0	0,0
15	225,0	100,50	75,50	0,0	0,0	0,0	0,0
20	200,0	100,25	0,0	0,0	0,0	0,0	0,0
25	125,0	0,0	0,0	0,0	0,0	0,0	0,0
30	0,0	0,0	0,0	0,0	0,0	0,0	0,0

If both firms must announce output at the same time, both firms believe that the other firm is behaving rationally, and each firm treats the output of the other firm as a fixed number, a Cournot equilibrium will result.

For Firm 1, total revenue will be

$$TR_1 = (30 - (Q_1 + Q_2))Q_1, \text{ or } TR_1 = 30Q_1 - Q_1^2 - Q_1Q_2.$$

Marginal revenue for Firm 1 will be the derivative of total revenue with respect to Q_1,

$$\frac{\partial TR}{\partial Q_1} = 30 - 2Q_1 - Q_2.$$

Because the firms share identical demand curves, the solution for Firm 2 will be symmetric to that of Firm 1:

$$\frac{\partial TR}{\partial Q_2} = 30 - 2Q_2 - Q_1.$$

To find the profit-maximizing level of output for both firms, set marginal revenue equal to marginal cost, which is zero:

$$Q_1 = 15 - \frac{Q_2}{2} \text{ and}$$

$$Q_2 = 15 - \frac{Q_1}{2}.$$

With two equations and two unknowns, we may solve for Q_1 and Q_2:

$$Q_1 = 15 - (0.5)\left(15 - \frac{Q_1}{2}\right), \text{ or } Q_1 = 10.$$

By symmetry, $Q_2 = 10$.

Substitute Q_1 and Q_2 into the demand equation to determine price:

$$P = 30 - (10 + 10), \text{ or } P = \$10.$$

Since no costs are given, profits for each firm will be equal to total revenue:

$$\pi_1 = TR_1 = (10)(10) = \$100 \quad \text{and}$$
$$\pi_2 = TR_2 = (10)(10) = \$100.$$

Thus, the equilibrium occurs when both firms produce 10 units of output and both firms earn $100. Looking back at the payoff matrix, note that the outcome (100, 100) is indeed a Nash equilibrium: neither firm will have an incentive to deviate, given the other firm's choice.

b. **Suppose you are told that you must announce your output *before* your competitor does. How much will you produce in this case, and how much do you think your competitor will produce? What do you expect your profit to be? Is announcing first an advantage or disadvantage? Explain briefly. *How much would you pay* to be given the option of announcing either first or second?**

If you must announce first, you would announce an output of 15, knowing that your competitor would announce an output of 7.5. (Note: This is the Stackelberg equilibrium.)

$$TR_1 = \left(30 - (Q_1 + Q_2)\right)Q_1 = 30Q_1 - Q_1^2 - Q_1\left(15 - \frac{Q_1}{2}\right) = 15Q_1 - \frac{Q_1^2}{2}.$$

Therefore, setting $MR = MC = 0$ implies:

$$15 - Q_1 = 0, \text{ or } Q_1 = 15 \quad \text{and}$$
$$Q_2 = 7.5.$$

At that output, your competitor is maximizing profits, given that you are producing 15. At these outputs, price is equal to

$$30 - 15 - 7.5 = \$7.5.$$

Your profit would be

$$(15)(7.5) = \$112.5.$$

Your competitor's profit would be

$$(7.5)(7.5) = \$56.25.$$

Announcing first is an advantage in this game. The difference in profits between announcing first and announcing second is $56.25. You would be willing to pay up to this difference for the option of announcing first.

c. **Suppose instead that you are to play the first round of a *series of 10 rounds* (with the same competitor). In each round, you and your competitor announce your outputs at the same time. You want to maximize the sum of your profits over the 10 rounds. How much will you produce in the *first round*? How much do you expect to produce in the tenth round? In the ninth round? Explain briefly.**

Given that your competitor has also read this book, you can assume that he or she will be acting rationally. You should begin with the Cournot output and continue with the Cournot output in each round, including the ninth and tenth rounds. Any deviation from this output will reduce the sum of your profits over the ten rounds.

d. **Once again you will play a series of 10 rounds. This time, however, in each round your competitor will announce its output before you announce yours. How will your answers to (c) change in this case?**

If your competitor always announces first, it might be more profitable to behave by reacting "irrationally" in a single period. For example, in the first round your competitor will announce an output of 15, as in Exercise (7.b). Rationally, you would respond with an output of 7.5. If you behave this way in every round, your total profits for all ten rounds will be $562.50. Your competitor's profits will be $1,125. However, if you respond with an output of 15 every time your competitor announces an output of 15, profits will be reduced to zero for both of you in that period. If your competitor fears, or learns, that you will respond in this way, he or she will be better off by choosing the Cournot output of 10, and your profits after that point will be $75 per period. Whether this strategy is profitable depends on your opponent's expectations about your behavior, as well as how you value future profits relative to current profits.

(Note: A problem could develop in the last period, however, because your competitor will know that you realize that there are no more long-term gains to be had from behaving strategically. Thus, your competitor will announce an output of 15, knowing that you will respond with an output of 7.5. Furthermore, knowing that you will not respond strategically in the last period, there are also no long-term gains to be made in the ninth period from behaving strategically. Therefore, in the ninth period, your competitor will announce an output of 15, and you should respond rationally with an output of 7.5, and so on.)

9. You play the following bargaining game. Player A moves first and makes Player B an offer for the division of $100. (For example, Player A could suggest that she take $60 and Player B take $40). Player B can accept or reject the offer. If he rejects it, the amount of money available drops to $90, and he then makes an offer for the division of this amount. If Player A rejects this offer, the amount of money drops to $80 and Player A makes an offer for its division. If Player B rejects this offer, the amount of money drops to 0. Both players are rational, fully informed, and want to maximize their payoffs. Which player will do best in this game?

Solve the game by starting at the end and working backwards. If B rejects A's offer at the 3rd round, B gets 0. When A makes an offer at the 3rd round, B will accept even a minimal amount, such as $1. So A should offer $1 at this stage and take $79 for herself. In the 2nd stage, B knows that A will turn down any offer giving her less than $79, so B must offer $80 to A, leaving $10 for B. At the first stage, A knows B will turn down any offer giving him less than $10. So A can offer $11 to B and keep $89 for herself. B will take that offer, since B can never do any better by rejecting and waiting. The following table summarizes this.

Round	Money Available	Offering Party	Amount to A	Amount to B
1	$100	A	$89	$11
2	$ 90	B	$80	$10
3	$ 80	A	$79	$ 1
End	$ 0		$ 0	$ 0

*10. Defendo has decided to introduce a revolutionary video game. As the first firm in the market, it will have a monopoly position for at least some time. In deciding what type of manufacturing plant to build, it has the choice of two technologies. Technology A is publicly available and will result in annual costs of

$$C^A(q) = 10 + 8q.$$

Technology B is a proprietary technology developed in Defendo's research labs. It involves higher fixed cost of production but lower marginal costs:

$$C^B(q) = 60 + 2q.$$

Defendo must decide which technology to adopt. Market demand for the new product is P = 20 - Q, where Q is total industry output.

a.   **Suppose Defendo were certain that it would maintain its monopoly position in the market for the entire product lifespan (about five years) without threat of entry. Which technology would you advise Defendo to adopt? What would be Defendo's profit given this choice?**

Defendo has two choices: Technology A with a marginal cost of 8 and Technology B with a marginal cost of 2. Given the inverse demand curve as $P = 20 - Q$, total revenue, PQ, is equal to $20Q - Q^2$ for both technologies. Marginal revenue is $20 - 2Q$. To determine the profits for each technology, equate marginal revenue and marginal cost:

$$20 - 2Q_A = 8, \text{ or } Q_A = 6, \text{ and}$$
$$20 - 2Q_B = 2, \text{ or } Q_B = 9.$$

Substituting the profit-maximizing quantities into the demand equation to determine the profit-maximizing prices, we find:

$$P_A = 20 - 6 = \$14 \text{ and}$$
$$P_B = 20 - 9 = \$11.$$

To determine the profits for each technology, subtract total cost from total revenue:

$$\pi_A = (14)(6) - (10 + (8)(6)) = \$26 \text{ and}$$
$$\pi_B = (11)(9) - (60 + (2)(9)) = \$21.$$

To maximize profits, Defendo should choose technology A.

b.   **Suppose Defendo expects its archrival, Offendo, to consider entering the market shortly after Defendo introduces its new product. Offendo will have access only to Technology A. If Offendo does enter the market, the two firms will play a Cournot game (in quantities) and arrive at the Cournot-Nash equilibrium.**

i. If Defendo adopts Technology A and Offendo enters the market, what will be the profit of each firm? Would Offendo choose to enter the market given these profits?

If both firms play Cournot, each will choose its best output, taking the other's strategy as given. Letting D = Defendo and O = Offendo, the demand function will be

$$P = 20 - Q_D - Q_O.$$

Profit for Defendo will be

$$\pi_D = (20 - Q_D - Q_O)Q_D - (10 + 8Q_D), \text{ or } \pi_D = 12Q_D - Q_D^2 - Q_D Q_O - 10$$

To determine the profit-maximizing quantity, set the first derivative of profits with respect to Q_D equal to zero and solve for Q_D:

$$\frac{\partial \pi_D}{\partial Q_D} = 12 - 2Q_D - Q_O = 0 \text{ , or } Q_D = 6 - 0.5Q_O.$$

This is Defendo's reaction function. Because both firms have access to the same technology, hence the same cost structure, Offendo's reaction function is analogous:

$$Q_O = 6 - 0.5Q_D.$$

Substituting Offendo's reaction function into Defendo's reaction function and solving for Q_D:

$$Q_D = 6 - (0.5)(6 - 0.5Q_D) = 4.$$

Substituting into Defendo's reaction function and solving for Q_O:

$$Q_O = 6 - (0.5)(4) = 4.$$

Total industry output is therefore equal to 8. To determine price, substitute Q_D and Q_O into the demand function:

$$P = 20 - 4 - 4 = \$12.$$

The profits for each firm are equal to total revenue minus total costs:

$$\pi_D = (4)(12) - (10 + (8)(4)) = \$6 \text{ and}$$
$$\pi_O = (4)(12) - (10 + (8)(4)) = \$6.$$

Therefore, Offendo would enter the market.

ii. If Defendo adopts Technology B and Offendo enters the market, what will be the profit of each firm? Would Offendo choose to enter the market given these profits?

Profit for Defendo will be

$$\pi_D = (20 - Q_D - Q_O)Q_D - (60 + 2Q_D), \text{ or } \pi_D = 18Q_D - Q_D^2 - Q_D Q_O - 60.$$

The change in profit with respect to Q_D is

$$\frac{\partial \pi_D}{\partial Q_D} = 18 - 2Q_D - Q_O.$$

To determine the profit-maximizing quantity, set this derivative to zero and solve for Q_D:

$$18 - 2Q_D - Q_O = 0, \text{ or } Q_D = 9 - 0.5Q_O.$$

This is Defendo's reaction function. Substituting Offendo's reaction function (from part i above) into Defendo's reaction function and solving for Q_D:

$$Q_D = 9 - 0.5(6 - 0.5Q_D), \text{ or } Q_D = 8.$$

Substituting Q_D into Offendo's reaction function yields

$$Q_O = 6 - (0.5)(8), \text{ or } Q_O = 2.$$

To determine the industry price, substitute the profit-maximizing quantities for Defendo and Offendo into the demand function:

$$P = 20 - 8 - 2 = \$10.$$

The profit for each firm is equal to total revenue minus total cost, or:

$$\pi_D = (10)(8) - (60 + (2)(8)) = \$4 \text{ and}$$
$$\pi_O = (10)(2) - (10 + (8)(2)) = -\$6.$$

With negative profit, Offendo *should not* enter the industry.

iii. Which technology would you advise Defendo to adopt given the threat of possible entry? What will be Defendo's profit given this choice? What will be consumer surplus given this choice?

With Technology A and Offendo's entry, Defendo's profit would be 6. With Technology B and no entry by Defendo, Defendo's profit would be 4. I would advise Defendo to stick with Technology A. Under this advice, total output is 8 and price is 12. Consumer surplus is:
$$(0.5)(20 - 12)(8) = \$32.$$

c. **What happens to social welfare (the sum of consumer surplus and producer profit) as a result of the threat of entry in this market? What happens to equilibrium price? What might this imply about the role of *potential* competition in limiting market power?**

From 10.a we know that, under monopoly, $Q = 6$ and profit is 26. Consumer surplus is

$$(0.5)(20 - 14)(6) = \$18.$$

Social welfare is the sum of consumer surplus plus profits, or

$$18 + 26 = \$44.$$

With entry, social welfare is $32 (consumer surplus) plus $12 (industry profit), or $44. Social welfare does not change with entry, but entry shifts surplus from producers to consumers. The equilibrium price falls with entry, and therefore *potential* competition can *limit* market power.

Note that Defendo has one other option: to increase quantity from the monopoly level of 6 to discourage entry by Offendo. If Defendo increases output from 6 to 8 under Technology A, Offendo is unable to earn a positive profit. With an output of 8, Defendo's profit decreases from $26 to

$$(8)(12) - (10 + (8)(8)) = \$22.$$

As before, with an output of 8, consumer surplus is $32; social welfare is $54. In this case, social welfare rises when output is increased to discourage entry.

11. Three contestants, A, B, and C, each have a balloon and a pistol. From fixed positions, they fire at each other's balloon's. When a balloon is hit, its owner is out. When only one balloon remains, its owner is the winner of a $1,000 prize. At the outset, the players decide by lot the order in which they will fire, and each player can choose any remaining balloon as his target. Everyone knows that A is the best shot and always hits the target, that B hits the target with probability .9, and that C hits the target with probability 0.8. Which contestant has the highest probability of winning the $1,000? Explain why.

Intuitively, C has the highest probability of winning, though A has the highest probability of shooting the balloon. Each contestant wants to remove the contestant with the highest probability of success. By following this strategy, each improves his chance of winning the game. A targets B because, by removing B from the game, A's chance of winning becomes much greater. B's probability of success is greater than C's probability of success. C will target A because, if C targets B and hits B, then A will target C and win the game. B will follow a similar strategy, because if B targets C and hits C, then A will target B and will win the game. Therefore, both B and C increase their chance of winning by eliminating A first. Similarly, A increases his chance of winning by eliminating B first. A complete probability tree can be constructed to show that A's chance of winning is 8 percent, B's chance of winning is 32 percent, and C's chance of winning is 60 percent.

12. An antique dealer regularly buys objects at home-town auctions whose bidders are limited to other dealers. Most of her successful bids turn out to be financially worthwhile, because she is able to resell the antiques for a profit. On occasion, however, she travels to a nearby town to bid in an auction that is open to the public. She often finds that on the rare occasions in which she does bid successfully, she is disappointed - the antique cannot be sold at a profit. Can you explain the difference in her success between the two sets of circumstances?

When she bids at the home-town auction which is limited to other dealers, she is bidding against people who are all going to resell the antique if they win the bid. In this case, all of the bidders are limiting their bids to prices that will tend to earn them a profit. A rational dealer will not place a bid which is higher than the price they can expect to resell the antique for. Given that all dealers are rational, the winning bid will tend to be below the expected resale price.

When she bids in the auction that is open to the public she is bidding against the people who are likely to come into her shop. You can assume that local antique lovers will frequent these auctions as well as the local antique shops. In the case where she wins the bid at one of these open auctions, the other participants have decided that the price is too high. In this case, they will not come into her shop and pay any higher price which would earn her a profit. She will only tend to profit in this case if she is able to resell to a customer from out of the area, or who was not at the auction, and who has a sufficiently high reservation price. In any event, the winning bid price will tend to be higher because she was bidding against customers rather than dealers.

13. You are in the market for a new house and have decided to bid for a house at auction. You believe that the value of the house is between $125,000 and $150,000, but you are uncertain as to where in the range it might be. You do know, however, that the seller has reserved the right to withdraw the house from the market if the winning bid is not satisfactory.

a.   Should you bid in this auction? Why or why not?

Yes you should bid if you are confident about your estimate of the value of the house and/or if you allow for the possibility of being wrong. To allow for the possibility of being wrong, you reduce your high bid by an amount equal to the expected error of the winning bidder. If you have experience at auction, you will have information on how likely you are to enter a wrong bid and can then adjust your high bid accordingly.

b.   Suppose you are a building contractor. You plan to improve the house and then to   resell it at a profit. How does this situation affect your answer to (a)? Does it depend on the extent to which your skills are uniquely suitable to improving this   particular house?

You need to be aware of the winner's curse which says that the winner is likely to be the person who most overestimated the value of the house. If there are a range of bids, some below the actual value and some above the actual value, the winner will be the person with the largest overestimate of the value. Again, you need to be very confident in your estimate of the value of the house and/or allow for the possibility of being wrong. If you have made many such bids in the past, you will be able to estimate how often you are wrong and adjust accordingly.

CHAPTER 14
MARKETS FOR FACTOR INPUTS

TEACHING NOTES

The following two chapters examine the markets for labor and capital. Although the discussion in this chapter is general, most of the examples refer to labor as the only variable input to production, with the exception of Example 14.1, which discusses "The Demand for Jet Fuel" by airlines. Labor demand and supply are discussed in the first section, and the competitive factor market equilibrium and economic rent are discussed in the second section. Section 14.3 explores the factor market structure for the case where the buyer has monopsony power, and section 14.4 explores the case of monopoly power on the part of the seller of the factor.

An understanding of this chapter relies on concepts from Chapters 4 through 8 and 10. If you have just covered Chapters 11-13, you might begin by reviewing marginal product, marginal revenue, and cost minimization. You should then discuss marginal revenue product and the profit-maximizing condition MRP_L = w. Explain why we are only interested in the portion of the MP curve below the average product curve (the downward-sloping portion). The derivation of the firm's demand curve for labor is straightforward when labor is the only factor, but becomes more complicated when there are several variable inputs. In particular, you might explain why the MRP_L curve shifts as the firm substitutes one input for another in production in response to a price change by noting that the MRP_L curve is drawn for a fixed level of the other variable input.

When presenting the market labor demand curve, explain that since the input prices change as more inputs are demanded, the market demand curve is not simply the summation of individual demand curves. You can extend the presentation of price elasticity of input demand (see Example 14.1) by discussing the conditions leading to price sensitivity. Elasticity is greater (1) when the elasticity of demand for the product is higher, (2) when it is easy to substitute one input for another, and (3) when the elasticity of supply is higher for other inputs. Elasticity of supply, which was discussed in Chapter 2, is reintroduced in Example 14.2. You should also distinguish between short-run and long-run elasticity (see Figure 14.6).

If you have already covered substitution and income effects, the students will be ready for the derivation of the backward-bending supply curve for labor. Although Figure 14.9 is a straightforward application of these tools, students are often confused by the plotting of income against leisure. Point out that this is just another type of utility maximization problem where the two goods are leisure and income. Income can be thought of as the consumption of goods other than leisure, in that more income buys more goods. You can also implicitly assume that the price of other goods is $1 and the price of leisure is the wage. The supply of labor curve is derived by changing the wage and finding the new level of hours worked. An individual's supply curve of labor is backward bending only when the income effect dominates the substitution effect and leisure is a normal good. Show typical supply curves for each group in Table 14.2. For an experimental study of the labor-leisure trade-off see Battalio, Green, and Kagel, "Income-Leisure Tradeoff of Animal Workers," *American Economic Review* (September 1981).

Section 14.2 brings together labor demand and supply for both competitive and monopolistic product markets. Although economic rent was presented in Chapter 8, it is reintroduced with more detail here. In Section 14.3, carefully explain why the marginal expenditure curve is above the average expenditure curve for a monopsonist (see Figure 14.14). You can discuss how a monopsonist would price discriminate, e.g., pay a different wage rate to each employee. With perfect price discrimination, the marginal revenue expenditure curve would coincide with the average expenditure curve. Although monopsony exists in some markets, the exercise of monopsony power is rare because of factor mobility. However, the employment of athletes by the owners of professional teams provides a good example (see Example 14.4 "Monopsony Power in the Market for Baseball Players"). On this same topic, see Sommers and Quinton, "Pay and Performance in Major League Baseball: The Case of the First Family of Free Agents," *Journal of Human Resources* (Summer 1982). Section 14.4 discusses the case of unions to explore monopoly power on the part of the seller of the input.

REVIEW QUESTIONS

1. Why is a firm's demand- for-labor curve more inelastic when the firm has monopoly power in the output market than when the firm is producing competitively?

The firm's demand curve for labor is determined by the incremental revenue from hiring an additional unit of labor known as the marginal revenue product of labor: $MRP_L = (MP_L)(MR)$, the additional output ("product") that the last worker produced, times the additional revenue earned by selling that output. In a competitive industry, the marginal revenue curve is perfectly elastic and equal to price. For a monopolist, marginal revenue is downward sloping. This implies that the marginal revenue product for the monopolist is more inelastic than for the competitive firm.

2. Why might a labor supply curve be backward bending?

A backward-bending supply curve for labor may occur when the income effect of an increase in the wage rate dominates the substitution effect. Labor supply decisions are made by individuals choosing the most satisfying combination of work and other (leisure) activities. With a larger income, the individual can afford to work fewer hours: the income effect. As the wage rate increases, the value of leisure time (the opportunity cost of leisure) increases, thus inducing the individual to work longer hours: the substitution effect. Because the two effects work in opposite directions, the shape of an individual's labor supply curve depends on the individual's preferences for income, consumption, and leisure.

3. How is a computer company's demand for computer programmers a derived demand?

A computer company's demand for inputs, including programmers, depends on how many computers it sells. The firm's demand for programming labor depends on (is derived from) the demand it faces in its market for computers. As demand for computers shifts, the demand for programmers shifts.

4. Compare the hiring choices of a monopsonistic and a competitive employer of workers. Which will hire more workers, and which will pay the higher wages? Explain.

Since the decision to hire another worker means the monopsonist must pay a higher wage for *all* workers, and not just the last worker hired, its marginal expenditure curve lies above the input supply curve (the average expenditure curve). The monopsonist's profit-maximizing input demand, where the marginal expenditure curve intersects the marginal revenue product curve, will be less than the competitor's profit-maximizing input choice, where the average expenditure curve intersects the demand curve. The monopsonist hires less labor, and the wage paid will be less than in a competitive market.

5. Rock musicians sometimes earn over $1 million per year. Can you explain such large income in terms of economic rent?

Economic rent is the difference between the actual payment to the factor of production and the minimum amount that the factor is willing to accept. In this case, you might assume that there are a limited number of top-quality rock musicians who will continue to play rock music no matter what they are paid. This results in a perfectly inelastic supply curve, or something close to it. Given the high demand for rock music, the wage will be very high and there will be a lot of economic rent. If there was a larger supply of top-quality rock musicians, or a more elastic supply, then the economic rent would be smaller.

6. What happens to the demand for one input when the use of a complementary input increases?

If the demand for the complementary input increases, the demand for the one input will increase as well. When demand for the complementary input increased, there was an effect of the quantity hired and the price paid. Both of these changes will affect the *MRP* of the one input, and hence will affect the quantity hired and the price paid.

7. For a monopsonist, what is the relationship between the supply of an input and the marginal expenditure on it?

> The decision to increase employment means the monopsonist must pay *all* units the higher price, and not just the last unit hired. Therefore, its marginal expenditure curve lies above the input supply curve (the average expenditure curve). Hiring more labor will increase the marginal expenditure which will increase the average expenditure. If the average expenditure is increasing, then the marginal expenditure must be greater than the average expenditure.

8. Currently the National Football League has a system for drafting college players by which each player is picked by only one team. The player must sign with that team or not play in the league. What would happen to the wages of newly drafted and more experienced football players if the draft system were repealed, and all teams could compete for college players?

> The National Football League draft and reserve clause (a primary issue in the 1987-1988 season's strike) creates a monopsonist cartel among the owners of NFL teams. If the draft system were repealed, competition among teams would increase wages of football players to the point where the marginal revenue product of each player would be equal to the player's wage.

9. Why are wages and employment levels indeterminate when the union has monopoly power and the firm has monopsony power?

> When the only seller of an input, a monopolist, faces the only buyer of the input, a monopsonist, the monopolist maximizes profits by setting input supply at a point where marginal revenue is equal to marginal cost, while the monopsonist maximizes profits at the point where marginal expenditure is equal to marginal cost. Thus, the monopolist asks for a price above marginal revenue while the monopsonist offers a price below marginal expenditure. The actual transaction price will be the result of negotiations and will depend on the relative bargaining strengths of the two parties.

EXERCISES

1. Assume that workers whose incomes are less than $10,000 currently pay no federal income taxes. Suppose a new government program guarantees each worker $5,000, whether or not he or she earns any income. For all earned income up to $10,000, the worker must pay a 50-percent tax. Draw the budget line facing the workers under this new program. How is the program likely to affect the labor supply curve of workers?

> The budget line for workers under this program is a straight line at $5,000. This line is shown in the figure and table below. Workers earn $5,000 whether they work or not. If workers work only to earn income, i.e., there are no other benefits such as "getting out of the house" or "gaining experience," there is no incentive to work under the new program. Only wages yielding incomes greater than $10,000 will result in a positive labor supply.

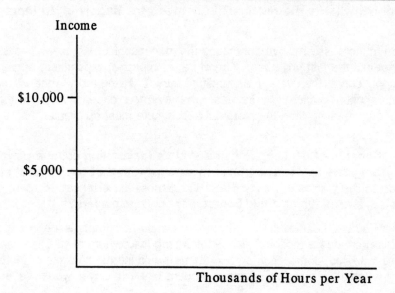

Figure 14.1

Income	After Tax Income	Government Subsidy	Total Income
0	0	5,000	$5,000
$1,000	500	4,500	5,000
2,000	1,000	4,000	5,000
3,000	1,500	3,500	5,000
4,000	2,000	3,000	5,000
5,000	2,500	2,500	5,000
6,000	3,000	2,000	5,000
7,000	3,500	1,500	5,000
8,000	4,000	1,000	5,000
9,000	4,500	500	5,000
10,000	5,000	0	5,000

2. **Using your knowledge of marginal revenue product, explain the following:**

a. **A famous tennis star is paid $100,000 for appearing in a 30-second television commercial. The actor who plays his doubles partner is paid $500.**

Marginal revenue product of labor, MRP_L, is equal to marginal revenue from an incremental unit of output multiplied by the marginal product from an incremental unit of labor. In 2 a, the advertiser is willing to increase expenditures on advertising until an extra dollar on advertising and the extra cost of production are equal to the extra revenue from increased sales. The famous tennis star is able to help increase revenues far more than the actor. In equilibrium, the tennis star helps generate $100,000 in revenue. The wage of the actor is determined by the supply and demand of actors willing to play tennis with tennis stars.

b. **The president of an ailing savings and loan is paid *not* to stay in his job for the last two years of his contract.**

The marginal revenue product of the president of the ailing savings and loan is negative; therefore, the savings and loan is better off by paying the president not to show up.

c. **A jumbo jet carrying 400 passengers is priced higher than a 250-passenger model even though both aircraft cost the same to manufacture.**

The ability of the larger jet to generate more revenue increases its value to the airline, and therefore the airline is willing to pay more for it.

3. The demand for the factors of production listed below have increased. What can you conclude about changes in the demand for the related consumer goods? If demands for the consumer goods remain unchanged, what other explanation is there for an increase in derived demands for these items?

a. **Computer memory chips**

In general, an increase in the demand for a good increases the demand for its factor inputs. The converse is not necessarily true; i.e., an increase in the demand for factor inputs does not necessarily imply an increase in the demand for the final product. The demand for an input may increase due to a change in the use of other inputs in the production process. As the price of another input increases, its demand falls and the demand of substitutable inputs rises. In this case, the increase in the demand for personal computers will increase the demand for memory chips. There are no substitutes for computer memory chips.

b. **Jet fuel for passenger planes**

With an increase in the demand for jet travel, the demand for jet fuel will increase. There are no substitutes for jet fuel.

c. **Paper used for newsprint**

If the circulation of newspapers increases, the demand for newsprint will increase.

d. **Aluminum used for beverage cans**

With an increase in demand for cold drinks in the summer, the seasonal demand for aluminum increases. If glass or plastic have become more expensive then this may affect the demand for aluminum. Changes in the market for recycled aluminum may affect the demand for new aluminum.

4. Suppose there are two groups of workers, unionized and nonunionized. Congress passes a law that requires all workers to join the union. What do you expect to happen to the wage rates of formerly nonunionized workers? of those workers who were originally unionized? What have you assumed about the union's behavior?

In general, we expect that nonunionized workers are earning lower wages than unionized workers. If all workers are forced to join the union, it would be reasonable to expect that the nonunionized workers will now receive higher wages and the unionized workers will receive a wage that could go either way. There are a couple of items to consider. First, the union now has more monopoly power in that there are no nonunion workers to act as substitutes for union workers. This gives more power to the union which means higher wages can in general be negotiated, However, the union now has more members to satisfy. If wages are kept at a high level, there will be fewer jobs, and hence some previously nonunionized workers may end up with no job. The union may wish to trade off some of the wage for a guarantee of more jobs. The average income of all workers will rise if labor demand is inelastic and will fall if labor demand is elastic.

5. Suppose a firm's production function is given by $Q = 12L - L^2$, for L = 0 to 6, where L is labor input per day and Q is output per day. Derive and draw the firm's demand for labor curve if the firm's output sells for $10 in a competitive market. How many workers will the firm hire when the wage rate is $30 per day? $60 per day? (Hint: The marginal product of labor is 12 - 2L.)

The demand for labor is given by the marginal revenue product of labor. This is equal to the product of marginal revenue and the marginal product of labor: $MRP_L = (MR)(MP_L)$. In a competitive market, price is equal to marginal revenue, so $MR = 10$. We are given $MP_L = 12 - 2L$ (the slope of the production function).

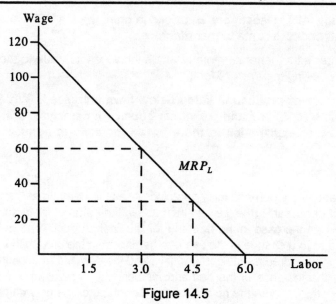

Figure 14.5

Therefore, the MRP_L = (10)(12 - 2L). The firm's profit-maximizing quantity of labor occurs where MRP_L = w. If w = 30, then 30 = 120 - 20L at the optimum. Solving for L yields 4.5 hours per day. Similarly, if w = 60, solving for L yields 3 hours per day.

6. The only legal employer of military soldiers in the United States is the federal government. If the government uses its monopsonistic position, what criteria will it employ when figuring how many soldiers to recruit? What happens if a mandatory draft is implemented?

Acting as a monopsonist in hiring soldiers, the federal government would hire soldiers until the marginal value of the last soldier is equal to his or her pay. There are two implications of the government's monopsony power: fewer soldiers are hired, and they are paid less than their marginal product. When a mandatory draft is implemented, even fewer professional soldiers are hired. Wages for volunteer soldiers fall, pushed down by the fact that wages of the draftees can be very low.

7. The demand for labor by an industry is given by the curve L = 1200 - 10w, where L is the labor demanded per day and w is the wage rate. The supply curve is given by L = 20w. What is the equilibrium wage rate and quantity of labor hired? What is the economic rent earned by workers?

The equilibrium wage rate is determined where quantity of labor supplied is equal to the quantity of labor demanded:

$$20w = 1,200 - 10w, \text{ or } w = \$40.$$

Substituting into either the labor supply or labor demand equations, we find the equilibrium quantity of labor is 800:

$$L_S = (20)(40) = 800,$$

and

$$L_D = 1,200 - (10)(40) = 800.$$

Economic rent is the summation of the difference between the equilibrium wage and the wage given by the labor supply curve. Here, it is the area above the labor supply curve up to L = 800 and below the equilibrium wage. This triangle's area is (0.5)(800)($40) = $16,000.

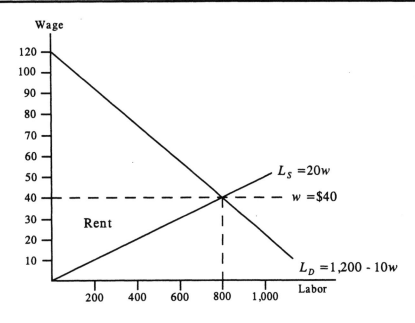

Figure 14.7

8. This exercise is a continuation of Exercise 7. Suppose now that the only labor available is controlled by a monopolistic labor union that wishes to maximize the rent earned by union members. What will be the quantity of labor employed and the wage rate? How does your answer compare with your answer to Exercise 7? Discuss. (*Hint*: The union's marginal revenue curve is given by L = 600 - 5w.)

Recall that the monopolist chooses output by setting marginal revenue equal to the marginal cost of supplying one more unit of output, as opposed to the competitive firm which chooses output by setting price equal to marginal cost, or in other words producing where supply intersects demand. The monopolistic labor union acts in the same way. To maximize rent in this case, the union will choose the number of workers hired so that the marginal revenue to the union (the additional wages earned) is equal to the extra cost of inducing the worker to work. This involves choosing the quantity of labor at the point where the marginal revenue curve crosses the supply curve of labor. Note that the marginal revenue curve has twice the slope of the labor demand curve. Marginal revenue is less than the wage, because when more workers are hired, all workers receive a lower wage.

Setting the marginal revenue curve equal to the supply curve for labor, we find:

$$600 - 5w = 20w, \text{ or } w^* = 24.$$

At w^*, we may determine the number of workers who are willing to work by substituting w^* into the labor supply equation:

$$L^* = (20)(24) = 480.$$

Therefore, if the union wants to maximize the rent that the union members earn, the union should limit employment to 480 members.

To determine the wage the members will earn, substitute L^* into the labor demand equation:
$$480 = 1,200 - 10w, \text{ or } w = 72.$$

The total rent the employed union members will receive is equal to:

$$\text{Rent} = (72 - 24)(480) + (0.5)(24)(480) = \$28,800.$$

This is shown in Figure 14.8.

213

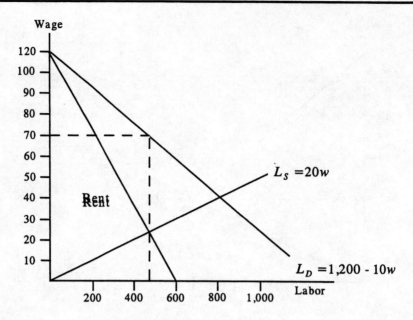

Figure 14.8

Notice that the wage is higher and the number of workers employed is lower than in Exercise (7).

CHAPTER 15
INVESTMENT, TIME, AND CAPITAL MARKETS

TEACHING NOTES

The primary focus of this chapter is on how firms make capital investment decisions, though the chapter also includes some topical applications of the net present value criterion. The key sections to cover are 15.1, 15.2, and 15.4 which cover stocks and flows, present discounted value, and the net present value criterion respectively. You can then pick and choose between the remaining sections depending on your time constraint and interest in the subject. Each of the special topics is briefly described below.

Students will find *NPV* to be one of the most powerful tools of the course. You will notice that this chapter does not derive the rate of time preference; instead, it introduces students to financial decision-making. Students should have no problem comprehending the trade-off between consumption today and consumption tomorrow, but they may still have problems with $(1 + R)$ as the *price* of today's consumption. Emphasize the opportunity cost interpretation of this price. Human capital theory is a topic that bridges Chapters 14 and 15. Interesting issues for discussion include the relationship between wages and education and the return on education. If students understand present value, mastering the *NPV* criterion is easy. However, applying the *NPV* rule is more difficult.

Section 15.3 extends the discussion of present and future values by exploring the connection between the value of a bond and perpetuities. If students understand the effective yield on a bond, you can introduce the internal rate of return, *IRR*, and then discuss why the net present value, *NPV*, is superior to the *IRR* criterion. For a comparison of *IRR* and *NPV*, see Brealey and Myers, *Principles of Corporate Finance* (McGraw-Hill, 1988).

Section 15.5 discusses risk and the risk-free discount rate. You can motivate the discussion of risk by considering the probability of default by different classes of borrowers (this introduces the discussion of the credit market that will take place in Section 17.1). This section introduces students to the Capital Asset Pricing Model. To understand the *CAPM* model, students need to be familiar with Chapter 5, particularly Section 5.4, "The Demand for Risky Assets." The biggest stumbling block is the definition of β. If students have an intuitive feel for β, they may use Equation (15.7) to calculate a firm's discount rate.

Section 15.6, applies the *NPV* criterion to consumer decisions, leading to a wealth of applications. Example 15.4 presents Hausman's analysis of the decision to purchase an air conditioner. Discuss whether the results of this study are reasonable.

Section 15.7 discusses depletable resources and presents Hotelling's model of exhaustible resources. This example is a particularly good topic for class discussion when oil prices are rising. During other periods, you may need to motivate the analysis. For another example, see the problem of cutting timber in Chiang, *Fundamental Methods of Mathematical Economics* (McGraw-Hill, 1984) pp. 300-301. Note that these problems involve calculus but may be solved geometrically.

Section 15.8 examines the market for loanable funds. If you have introduced students to the marginal rate of time preference, you can complete the analysis by introducing the investment-spending frontier, similar to the production-possibilities frontier in Section 7.5 (see Figure 7.10). The investment frontier shows the rate at which consumption today may be transformed into consumption tomorrow. By superimposing indifference curves onto the frontier, you may show the individual's optimal consumption today and tomorrow. This analysis may be extended by discussing borrowing and lending and will serve as an introduction to the analysis of efficiency in Chapter 16.

REVIEW QUESTIONS

1. A firm uses cloth and labor to produce shirts in a factory that it bought for $10 million. Which of its factor inputs are measured as flows and which as stocks? How would your answer change if the firm had leased a factory instead of buying one? Is its output measured as a flow or a stock? What about profit?

Inputs measured in units per time period are flows: how much is used during an hour, day, week, month, or year? Inputs measured in units at points in time are stocks: how much is available during the entire production period? Thus, cloth and labor are measured as service flows, while capital embodied in the factory is measured as a stock. Note that services flow from the capital stock over time. Furthermore, the depreciation on the capital stock is a flow. Leasing the factory implies a flow of payments to the owner of the factory, but the capital stock itself does not change with time. Output flows from the production process. During each period, management sells the shirts and pays for the factors of production. Profit is a residual cash flow.

2. Suppose the interest rate is 10 percent. If $100 is invested at this rate today, how much will it be worth after one year? After two years? After five years? What is the value today of $100 paid one year from now? Paid two years from now? Paid five years from now?

We would like to know the future value, FV, of $100 invested today at an interest rate of 10 percent. One year from now our investment will be equal to

$$FV = \$100 + (\$100)(10\%) = \$110.$$

Two years from now we will earn interest on the $100 ($10) *and* we will earn interest on the interest from the first year, i.e., ($10)(10%) = $1. Thus, our investment will be worth $100 + $10 (from the first year) + $10 (from the second year) + $1 (interest on the first year's interest) = $121.

Algebraically, $FV = PDV(1 + R)^t$, where PDV is the present discounted value of the investment, R is the interest rate, and t is the number of years. After two years,

$$FV = PDV(1 + R)^t = (\$100)(1.1)^2 = (\$100)(1.21) = \$121.00.$$

After five years

$$FV = PDV(1 + R)^t = (\$100)(1.1)^5 = (\$100)(1.61051) = \$161.05.$$

To find the present discounted value of $100 paid one year from now, we ask how much is needed to invest today at 10 percent to have $100 one year from now. Using our formula, we solve for PDV as a function of FV:

$$PDV = (FV)(1 + R)^{-t}.$$

With $t = 1$, $R = 0.10$, and $FV = \$100$,

$$PDV = (100)(1.1)^{-1} = \$90.91.$$

With $t = 2$, $PDV = (1.1)^{-2} = \$82.64$,

With $t = 5$, $PDV = (1.1)^{-5} = \$62.09$.

3. You are offered the choice of two payment streams: (a) $100 paid one year from now and $100 paid two years from now; (b) $80 paid one year from now and $130 paid two years from now. Which payment stream would you prefer if the interest rate is 5 percent? If it is 15 percent?

To compare two income streams, we calculate the present discounted value of each and choose the stream with the highest present discounted value. We use the formula $PDV = FV(1 + R)^{-t}$ for each cash flow. See Exercise (2) above. Stream (a) has two payments:

$$PDV_a = FV_1(1 + R)^{-1} + FV_2(1 + R)^{-2}$$

$$PDV_a = (\$100)(1.05)^{-1} + (\$100)(1.05)^{-2}, \text{ or}$$

$$PDV_a = \$95.24 + 90.70 = \$185.94.$$

Stream (b) has two payments:

$$PDV_b = (\$80)(1.05)^{-1} + (\$130)(1.05)^{-2}, \text{ or}$$

$$PDV_b = \$76.19 + \$117.91 = \$194.10.$$

At an interest rate of 5 percent, you should select (b).

If the interest rate is 15 percent, the present discounted values of the two income streams would be:

$$PDV_a = (\$100)(1.15)^{-1} + (\$100)(1.15)^{-2}, \text{ or}$$

$$PDV_a = \$89.96 + \$75.61 = \$162.57, \text{ and}$$

$$PDV_b = (\$80)(1.15)^{-1} + (\$130)(1.15)^{-2}, \text{ or}$$

$$PDV_b = \$69.57 + \$98.30 = \$167.87.$$

You should still select (b).

4. How do investors calculate the present value of a bond? If the interest rate is 5 percent, what is the present value of a perpetuity that pays $1,000 per year forever?

The present value of a bond is the sum of discounted values of each payment to the bond holder over the life of the bond. This involves the payment of interest in each period and then the repayment of the principal at the end of the bond's life. A perpetuity involves paying the interest in every future period and no repayment of the principal. The present discounted value of a perpetuity is $PDV = \dfrac{A}{R}$, where A is the annual payment and R is the annual interest rate. If $A = \$1,000$ and $R = 0.05$, $PDV = \dfrac{\$1,000}{0.05} = \$20,000$.

5. What is the *effective yield* on a bond? How does one calculate it? Why do some corporate bonds have higher effective yields than others?

The effective yield is the interest rate that equates the present value of a bond's payment stream with the bond's market price. The present discounted value of a payment made in the future is

$$PDV = FV(1 + R)^{-t},$$

where t is the length of time before payment. The bond's selling price is its *PDV*. The payments it makes are the future values, *FV*, paid in time *t*. Thus, we must solve for *R*, which is the bond's effective yield. The effective yield is determined by the interaction of buyers and sellers in the bond market. As the riskiness of the issuing firm increases, buyers must be rewarded with a higher rate of return. Higher rates of return imply a lower present discounted value. If bonds have the same coupon payments, the bonds of the riskiest firms will sell for less than the bonds of the less risky firms.

6. What is the Net Present Value (NPV) criterion for investment decisions? How does one calculate the NPV of an investment project? If all cash flows for a project are certain, what discount rate should be used to calculate NPV?

The Net Present Value criterion for investment decisions is *"invest if the present value of the expected future cash flows from the investment is larger than the cost of the investment"* (Section 15.4). We calculate the *NPV* by (1) determining the present discounted value of all future cash flows and (2) subtracting the discounted value of all costs, present and future. To discount both income and cost, the firm should use a discount rate that reflects its opportunity cost of capital, the next highest return on an alternative investment of similar riskiness. Therefore, the risk-free interest rate should be used if the cash flows are certain.

7. What is the difference between a real discount rate and a nominal discount rate? When should a real discount rate be used in an NPV calculation and when should a nominal rate be used?

The real discount rate is net of inflation, whereas the nominal discount rate includes inflationary expectations. The real discount rate is equal to the nominal discount rate minus the rate of inflation. If cash flows are in real terms, the appropriate discount rate is the nominal rate. For example, in applying the *NPV* criterion to a manufacturing decision, if future prices of inputs and outputs are not adjusted for inflation (which they often are not), a real discount rate should be used to determine whether the *NPV* is positive.

8. How is a risk premium used to account for risk in NPV calculations? What is the difference between diversifiable and nondiversifiable risk? Why should only nondiversifiable risk enter into the risk premium?

To determine the present discounted value of a cash flow, the discount rate should reflect the riskiness of the project generating the cash flow. The risk premium is the difference between a discount rate that reflects the riskiness of the cash flow and a discount rate on a risk-free flow, e.g., the discount rate associated with a short-term government bond. The higher the riskiness of a project, the higher the risk premium.

Diversifiable risk can be eliminated by investing in many projects. Hence, an efficient capital market will not compensate an investor for taking on risk that can be eliminated costlessly. Nondiversifiable risk is that part of a project's risk that cannot be eliminated by investing in a large number of other projects. It is that part of a project's risk which is correlated with the portfolio of all projects available in the market. Since investors can eliminate diversifiable risk, they cannot expect to earn a risk premium on diversifiable risk.

9. What is meant by the "market return" in the Capital Asset Pricing Model (CAPM)? Why is the market return greater than the risk-free interest rate? What does an asset's "beta" measure in the CAPM? Why should high-beta assets have a higher expected return than low-beta assets?

In the Capital Asset Pricing Model (CAPM), the market return is the rate of return on the portfolio of assets held by the market. The market return reflects nondiversifiable risk.

Since the market portfolio has no diversifiable risk, the market return reflects the risk premium associated with holding one unit of nondiversifiable risk. The market rate of return is greater than the risk-free rate of return, because risk-averse investors must be compensated with higher average returns for holding a risky asset.

An asset's beta reflects the sensitivity (covariance) of the asset's return with the return on the market portfolio. An asset with a high beta will have a greater expected return than a low-beta asset, since the high-beta asset has greater nondiversifiable risk than the low-beta asset.

10. Suppose you are deciding whether to invest $100 million in a steel mill. You know the expected cash flows for the project, but they are risky -- steel prices could rise or fall in the future. How would the CAPM help you select a discount rate for an NPV calculation?

To evaluate the net present value of a $100 million investment in a steel mill, you should use the stock market's current evaluation of firms that own steel mills as a guide to selecting the appropriate discount rate. For example, you would (1) identify nondiversified steel firms, those that are primarily involved in steel production, (2) determine the beta associated with stocks issued by those companies (this can be done statistically or by relying on a financial service that publishes stock betas, such as *Value Line*), and (3) take a weighted average of these betas, where the weights are equal to the firm's assets divided by the sum of all diversified steel firms' assets. With an estimate of beta, plus estimates of the expected market and risk-free rates of return, you could infer the discount rate using Equation (15.7) in the text: Discount rate = $r_f + \beta \left(r_m + r_f \right)$.

11. How does a consumer trade off current and future costs when selecting an air conditioner or other major appliance? How could this selection be aided by an NPV calculation?

The *NPV* calculation for a durable good involves discounting to the present all future services from the appliance, as well as any salvage value at the end of the appliance's life, and subtracting its cost and the discounted value of any expenses. Discounting is done at the opportunity cost of money. Of course, this calculation assumes well-defined quantities of future services. If these services are not well defined, the consumer should ask what value of these services would yield an *NPV* of zero. If this value is less than the price that the consumer would be willing to pay in each period, the investment should be made.

12. What is meant by the "user cost" of producing an exhaustible resource? Why does price minus extraction cost rise at the rate of interest in a competitive exhaustible resource market?

In addition to the opportunity cost of extracting the resource and preparing it for sale, there is an additional opportunity cost arising from the depletion of the resource. User cost is the difference between price and the marginal cost of production. User cost rises over time because, as reserves of the resource become depleted, the remaining reserves become more valuable.

Given constant demand over time, the price of the resource minus its marginal cost of extraction, $P - MC$, should rise over time at the rate of interest. If $P - MC$ rises faster than the rate of interest, no extraction should occur in the present period, because holding the resource for another year would earn a higher rate of return than selling the resource now and investing the proceeds for another year. If $P - MC$ rises slower than the rate of interest, current extraction should increase, thus increasing the supply at each price, lowering the equilibrium price, and decreasing the return on producing the resource. In equilibrium, the price of a resource rises at the rate of interest.

13. What determines the supply of loanable funds? The demand for loanable funds? What might cause the supply or demand for loanable funds to shift, and how would that affect interest rates?

The supply of loanable funds is determined by the interest rate offered to savers. A higher interest rate induces households to consume less today (save) in favor of greater consumption in the future. The demand for loanable funds comes from consumers who wish to consume more today than tomorrow or from investors who wish to borrow money. Demand depends on the interest rate at which these two groups can borrow. Several factors can shift the demand and supply of loanable funds. On the one hand, for example, a recession decreases demand at all interest rates, shifting the demand curve inward and causing the equilibrium interest rate to fall. On the other hand, the supply of loanable funds will shift out if the Federal Reserve increases the money supply, again causing the interest rate to fall.

EXERCISES

1. Suppose the interest rate is 10 percent. What is the value of a coupon bond that pays $80 per year for each of the next five years and then makes a principal repayment of $1,000 in the sixth year? Repeat for an interest rate of 15 percent.

We need to determine the present discounted value, *PDV*, of a stream of payments over the next six years. We translate future values, *FV*, into the present with the following formula:

$$PDV = \frac{FV}{(1+R)^t},$$

where R is the interest rate, equal to 10 percent, and t is the number of years in the future. For example, the present value of the first $80 payment one year from now is

$$PDV = \frac{FV}{(1+R)^t} = \frac{80}{(1+0.10)^1} = \frac{80}{1.1} = \$72.73.$$

The value of all coupon payments over five years can be found the same way:

$$PDV = \frac{80}{(1+R)^1} + \frac{80}{(1+R)^2} + \frac{80}{(1+R)^3} + \frac{80}{(1+R)^4} + \frac{80}{(1+R)^5}, \text{or}$$

$$PDV = 80\left(\frac{1}{1.1} + \frac{1}{1.21} + \frac{1}{1.331} + \frac{1}{1.4641} + \frac{1}{1.61051}\right) = \$303.26.$$

Finally, we calculate the present value of the final payment of $1,000 in the sixth year:

$$PDV = \frac{\$1,000}{1.1^6} = \frac{\$1,000}{1.771} = \$564.47.$$

Thus, the present value of the bond is $303.26 + $564.47 = $867.73.

With an interest rate of 15 percent, we calculate the value of the bond in the same way:

PDV = 80(0.870 + 0.756 + 0.658 + 0.572 + 0.497) + (1,000)(0.432), or

PDV = $268.17 + $432.32 = $700.49.

As the interest rate increases, while payments are held constant, the value of the bond decreases.

2. A bond has two years to mature. It makes a coupon payment of $100 after one year and both a coupon payment of $100 and a principal repayment of $1,000 after two years. The bond is selling for $966. What is its effective yield?

We want to know the interest rate that will yield a present value of $966 for an income stream of $100 after one year and $1,100 after two years. Find i such that

$$966 = (100)(1 + i)^{-1} + (1,100)(1 + i)^{-2}.$$

Algebraic manipulation yields

$$966(1 + i)^2 = 100(1 + i) + 1,100, \text{ or}$$

$$966 + 1,932i + 966i^2 - 100 - 100i - 1,100 = 0, \text{ or}$$

$$966i^2 + 1,832i - 234 = 0.$$

Using the quadratic formula to solve for i,

$$i = 0.12 \text{ or } -1.068.$$

Since -1.068 does not make economic sense, the effective yield is 12 percent.

3. Equation (15.5) shows the net present value of an investment in an electric motor factory. Half of the $10 million cost is paid initially and the other half after a year. The factory is expected to lose money during its first two years of operation. If the discount rate is 4 percent, what is the NPV? Is the investment worthwhile?

Redefining terms, Equation 15.5 becomes

$$NPV = -5 - \frac{5}{(1.04)} - \frac{1}{(1.04)^2} - \frac{0.5}{(1.04)^3} + \frac{0.96}{(1.04)^4} + \frac{0.96}{(1.04)^5} + \otimes + \frac{0.96}{(1.04)^{20}} + \frac{1}{(1.04)^{20}}.$$

Calculating the *NPV* we find:

NPV = -5 - -4.81 - 0.92 - 0.44 + 0.82 + 0.79 + 0.70 + 0.67 + 0.62 + 0.60 + 0.58 + 0.55

+0.53 + 0.51 + 0.49 + 0.47 + 0.46 + 0.44 + 0.46 = -0.337734.

The investment loses $337,734 and is not worthwhile.

4. The market interest rate is 10 percent and is expected to stay at that level. Consumers can borrow and lend all they want at this rate. Explain your choice in each of the following situations:

a. Would you prefer a $500 gift today or a $540 gift next year?

The present value of $500 today is $500. The present value of $540 next year is

$$\frac{\$540.00}{1.10} = \$490.91.$$

Therefore, I would prefer the $500 today.

b. Would you prefer a $100 gift now or a $500 loan without interest for four years?

Compare the present value of the interest not paid during four years with $100 today. The present value of the interest is

$$\frac{50}{(1.10)^1} + \frac{50}{(1.10)^2} + \frac{50}{(1.10)^3} + \frac{50}{(1.10)^4} = 45.45 + 41.32 + 37.57 + 34.15 = \$158.49.$$

Therefore, choose the interest-free loan.

c. Would you prefer a $250 rebate on an $8,000 car or one year of financing for the full price of the car at 5 percent interest?

The interest rate is 5 percent, which is 5 percent less than the current market rate. You save $400 = (0.5)($8,000) one year from now. The present value of this $400 is

$$\frac{\$400}{1.10} = \$363.64.$$

This is greater than $250. Therefore, choose the financing.

d. You have just won a million dollar lottery and will receive $50,000 a year for the next 20 years. How much is this worth to you today?

We must find the net present value of $50,000 a year for the next 20 years:

$$NPV = 50,000 + \frac{50,000}{(1.1)^1} + \frac{50,000}{(1.1)^2} + \otimes + \frac{50,000}{(1.1)^{18}} + \frac{50,000}{(1.1)^{19}} = \$425,678.$$

e. You win the "honest million" jackpot. You can have $1 million today or $50,000 per year for eternity (a right that can be passed on to your heirs). Which do you prefer?

The value of the perpetuity is $500,000, which makes it advisable take the million.

f. In the past, adult children had to pay taxes on gifts over $10,000 from their parents, but parents could loan money to their children interest-free. Why did some people call this unfair? To whom were the rules unfair?

Any gift of $N from parent to child could be made without taxation by loaning the child $\frac{\$N(1+r)}{r}$. For example, to avoid taxes on a $50,000 gift, the parent would loan the child $550,000, assuming a 10 percent interest rate. With that money, the child could earn $55,000 in interest after one year and still have $500,000 to pay back to the parent. The present value of $55,000 one year from now is $50,000. People of more moderate incomes would find these rules unfair: they might only be able to afford to give the child $50,000 directly, but it would not be tax free.

221

5. Ralph is trying to decide whether to go to graduate school. If he spends two years in graduate school, paying $10,000 tuition each year, he will get a job that will pay $50,000 per year for the rest of his working life. If he does not go to school, he will go into the work force immediately. He will then make $20,000 per year for the next three years, $30,000 for the following three years, and $50,000 per year every year after that. If the interest rate is 10 percent, is graduate school a good financial investment?

Consider Ralph's income over the next six years, assuming all payments occur at the end of the year. (After the sixth year, Ralph's income will be the same with or without education.) With graduate school, the present value of income for the next six years is $113,631,

$$-\frac{\$10,000}{(1.1)^1} - \frac{\$10,000}{(1.1)^2} + \frac{\$50,000}{(1.1)^3} + \frac{\$50,000}{(1.1)^4} + \frac{\$50,000}{(1.1)^5} + \frac{\$50,000}{(1.1)^6} = \$113,631.$$

Without graduate school, the present value of income for the next six years is

$$\frac{\$20,000}{(1.1)^1} + \frac{\$20,000}{(1.1)^2} + \frac{\$20,000}{(1.1)^3} + \frac{\$30,000}{(1.1)^4} + \frac{\$30,000}{(1.1)^5} + \frac{\$30,000}{(1.1)^6} = \$105,789.$$

The payoff from graduate school is large enough to justify the foregone income and tuition expense while Ralph is in school; he should therefore go to school.

6. Suppose your uncle gave you an oil well like the one described in Section 15.7. (Marginal production cost is constant at $10.) The price of oil is currently $20 but is controlled by a cartel that accounts for a large fraction of total production. Should you produce and sell all your oil now or wait to produce? Explain your answer.

If a cartel accounts for a large fraction of total production, today's price minus marginal cost, $P^t - MC$ will rise at a rate less than the rate of interest. This is because the cartel will choose output such that *marginal revenue* minus *MC* rises at the rate of interest. Since price exceeds marginal revenue, $P^t - MC$ will rise at a rate less than the rate of interest. So, to maximize net present value, all oil should be sold today. The profits should be invested at the rate of interest.

*7. You are planning to invest in fine wine. Each case of wine costs $100, and you know from experience that the value of a case of wine held for t years is (100)t$^{1/2}$. One hundred cases of wine are available for sale, and the interest rate is 10 percent.

a.   How many cases should you buy, how long should you wait to sell them, and how much money will you receive at the time of their sale?

Buying a case is a good investment if the net present value is positive. If we buy a case and sell it after *t* years, we pay $100 now and receive $100t^{0.5}$ when it is sold. The *NPV* of this investment is

$$NPV = -100 + e^{-rt}\left(100t^{0.5}\right) = -100 + e^{-0.1t}\left(100t^{0.5}\right)$$

If we do buy a case, we will choose *t* to maximize the *NPV*. This implies differentiating with respect to *t* to obtain the necessary condition that

$$\frac{dNPV}{dt} = \left(e^{-0.1t}\right)\left(50t^{-0.5}\right) - \left(0.1e^{-0.1t}\right)\left(100t^{0.5}\right) = 0.$$

By multiplying both sides of the first order condition by $e^{0.1t}$, we obtain

$$50t^{-0.5} - 10t^{0.5} = 0 \text{, or } t = 5.$$

If we held the case for 5 years, the *NPV* is

$$-100 + e^{(-0.1)(5)}(100)(5^{0.5}) = 35.67.$$

Therefore, we should buy a case and hold it for five years, where the value at the time of sale is ($100)($5^{0.5}$). Since each case is a good investment, we should buy all 100 cases.

Another way to get the same answer is to compare holding the wine to putting your $100 in the bank. The bank pays interest of 10 percent, while the wine increases in value at the rate of

$$\frac{\frac{d(value)}{dt}}{value} = \frac{50t^{-0.5}}{100t^{0.5}} = \frac{1}{2t}.$$

As long as $t < 5$, the return on wine is greater than or equal to 10 percent. After $t = 5$, the return on wine drops below 10 percent. Therefore, $t = 5$ is the time to switch your wealth from wine to the bank. As for the issue of whether to buy wine at all, if we put $100 in the bank, we will have $100e^{0.5}$ after five years, whereas if we spend $100 on wine, we will have $100t^{-0.5} = (100)(5^{0.5})$, which is greater than $100e^{0.5}$ in five years.

b. **Suppose that at the time of purchase, someone offers you $130 per case immediately. Should you take the offer?**

You just bought the wine and are offered $130 for resale. You should accept the offer if the *NPV* is positive. You get $130 now, but lose the ($100)($5^{0.5}$) you would get for selling in five years. Thus, the *NPV* of the offer is

$$NPV = 130 - (e^{(-0.1)(5)})(100)(5^{0.5}) = -238 < 0.$$

Therefore, you should not sell.

The other approach to solving this problem is to note that the $130 could be put in the bank and would grow to

$$\$214.33 = (\$130)(e^{0.5}),$$

in five years. This is still less than

$$\$223.61 = (\$100)(5^{0.5}),$$

the value of the wine after five years.

c. **How would your answers change if the interest rate were only 5 percent?**

If the interest rate changes from 10 percent to 5 percent, the *NPV* calculation is

$$NPV = -100 + (e^{-0.05t})(100)(t^{0.5}).$$

As before, we maximize this expression:

$$\frac{dNPV}{dt} = (e^{-0.05t})(50t^{-0.5}) - (0.05)(e^{-0.05t})(100t^{0.5}) = 0.$$

By multiplying both sides of the first order condition by $e^{0.05t}$, it becomes

$$50t^{-0.5} - 5t^{0.5} = 0,$$

or $t = 10$. If we hold the case 10 years, *NPV* is

$$-100 + (e^{(-0.05)(10)})(100)(10^{0.5}) = \$91.80.$$

With a lower interest rate, it pays to hold onto the wine longer before selling it, because the value of the wine is increasing at the same rate as before. Again, you should buy all the cases.

8. Reexamine the capital investment decision in the disposable diaper industry (Example 15.3) from the point of view of an incumbent firm. If P&G or Kimberly-Clark were to expand capacity by building three new plants, they would not need to spend $60 million on R&D before start-up. How does this

advantage affect the NPV calculations in Table 15.5? Is the investment profitable at a discount rate of 12 percent?

If the only change in the cash flow for an incumbent firm is the absence of a $60 million expenditure in the present value, then the *NPV* calculations in Table 15.5 simply increase by $60 million for each discount rate:

Discount Rate:	0.05	0.10	0.15
NPV:	140.50	43.50	-15.10

To determine whether the investment is profitable at a discount rate of 12 percent, we must recalculate the expression for *NPV*. At 12 percent,

$$NPV = -60 - \frac{93.4}{(1.12)} - \frac{56.6}{(1.12)^2} + \frac{40}{(1.12)^3} + \frac{40}{(1.12)^4} + \frac{40}{(1.12)^5} + \frac{40}{(1.12)^6} + \frac{40}{(1.12)^7} +$$

$$\frac{40}{(1.12)^8} + \frac{40}{(1.12)^9} + \frac{40}{(1.12)^{10}} + \frac{40}{(1.12)^{11}} + \frac{40}{(1.12)^{12}} + \frac{40}{(1.12)^{13}} + \frac{40}{(1.12)^{14}} + \frac{40}{(1.12)^{15}} =$$

$16.3 million.

Thus, the incumbent would find it profitable to expand capacity.

9. Suppose you can buy a new Toyota Corolla for $15,000 and sell it for $6,000 after six years. Alternatively, you can lease the car for $300 per month for three years and return it at the end of the three years. For simplification, assume that lease payments are made yearly instead of monthly, i.e., are $3,600 per year for each of three years.

a. **If the interest rate, r, is 4 percent, is it better to lease or buy the car?**

To answer this question, you need to compute the NPV of each option. The NPV of buying the car is:

$$-15,000 + \frac{6,000}{1.04^6} = -10,258.11.$$

The NPV of leasing the car is:

$$-3,600 - \frac{3,600}{1.04} - \frac{3,600}{1.04^2} = -10,389.94.$$

In this case, you are better off buying the car because the NPV is higher.

b. **Which is better if the interest rate is 12%?**

To answer this question, you need to compute the NPV of each option. The NPV of buying the car is:

$$-15,000 + \frac{6,000}{1.12^6} = -11,960.21.$$

The NPV of leasing the car is:

$$-3,600 - \frac{3,600}{1.12} - \frac{3,600}{1.12^2} = -9,684.18.$$

In this case, you are better off leasing the car because the NPV is higher.

c. **At what interest rate would you be indifferent between buying and leasing the car?**

You are indifferent between buying and leasing if the two NPV's are equal or:

$$-15,000 + \frac{6,000}{(1+r)^6} = -3,600 - \frac{3,600}{(1+r)} - \frac{3,600}{(1+r)^2}.$$

In this case, you need to solve for r. The easiest way to do this is to use a spreadsheet and calculate the two NPV's for different values of r as is done in the table below. The table shows that at an interest rate of 4.35%, the two NPV's are almost identical.

r	NPV Buy	NPV Lease
0.04	-10258.113	-10389.941
0.042	-10312.461	-10370.532
0.043	-10339.362	-10360.865
0.0435	**-10352.745**	**-10356.04**
0.044	-10366.083	-10351.222
0.045	-10392.626	-10341.604
0.05	-10522.708	-10293.878
0.06	-10770.237	-10200.214
0.07	-11001.947	-10108.865
0.08	-11218.982	-10019.753
0.09	-11422.396	-9932.8003
0.1	-11613.156	-9847.9339
0.12	-11960.213	-9684.1837

10. A consumer faces the following decision: she can buy a computer for $1,000 and pay $10 per month for Internet access for three years, or she can receive a $400 rebate on the computer (so that it costs $600) but agree to pay $25 per month for three years for Internet access. For simplification, assume that the consumer pays the access fees yearly (i.e.,$10 per month = $120 per year).

a. **What should the consumer do if the interest rate is 3 percent?**

To figure out the best option, you need to calculate the NPV in each case. The NPV of the first option is:

$$-1,000 - 120 - \frac{120}{1.03} - \frac{120}{1.03^2} = -1,349.62.$$

The NPV of the second option with the rebate is:

$$-600 - 300 - \frac{300}{1.03} - \frac{300}{1.03^2} = -1,474.04.$$

In this case, the first option gives a higher NPV so the consumer should pay the $1000 now and pay $10 per month for Internet access.

b. **What if the interest rate is 17 percent?**

To figure out the best option, you need to calculate the NPV in each case. The NPV of the first option is:

$$-1,000 - 120 - \frac{120}{1.17} - \frac{120}{1.17^2} = -1,310.23.$$

The NPV of the second option with the rebate is:

$$-600 - 300 - \frac{300}{1.17} - \frac{300}{1.17^2} = -1,375.56.$$

In this case, the first option gives a higher NPV so the consumer should pay the $1000 now and pay $10 per month for Internet access.

c. **At what interest rate is the consumer indifferent between the two options?**

The consumer is indifferent between the two options if the NPV of each option is the same. To find this interest rate set the NPV's equal and solve for r.

$$-1,000 - 120 - \frac{120}{1+r} - \frac{120}{(1+r)^2} = -600 - 300 - \frac{300}{1+r} - \frac{300}{(1+r)^2}$$

$$220 = \frac{180}{1+r} + \frac{180}{(1+r)^2}$$

$$220(1+r)^2 = 180(1+r) + 180$$

$$220r^2 + 260r - 140 = 0.$$

Using the quadratic formula to solve for the interest rate r results in r=40.2% (approximately).

PART IV

INFORMATION, MARKET FAILURE, AND THE ROLE OF GOVERNMENT

CHAPTER 16
GENERAL EQUILIBRIUM AND ECONOMIC EFFICIENCY

TEACHING NOTES

This chapter extends the analysis of many of the earlier chapters in the text. Section 16.1 covers general equilibrium analysis and extends supply/demand analysis to situations where more than one market is involved and there is feedback between the markets. Sections 16.2 and 16.4 use the Edgeworth box to explore efficiency in consumption and production, and in this respect extend the analysis of chapters 4 and 7. Section 16.3 looks at the relationship between equity and efficiency and can be skipped if time is short. Sections 16.5 discusses gains from trade and can also be skipped if time is short. Section 16.6 is a nice summary of Sections 16.2 and 16.4 and the efficiency of competitive markets. Section 16.7 introduces types of market failure.

The distinction between partial and general equilibrium is readily accepted by students, but they might find the graphical analysis of Figure 16.1 intimidating. Although this is not a complete discussion of general equilibrium, students can learn to appreciate the limitations of a partial equilibrium analysis and the need to consider interactions among markets. Stress the importance of using a general equilibrium analysis for economy-wide policies, e.g., raising the minimum wage.

To provide a context for the discussion of exchange economies, you might start by discussing two children trading cookies and potato chips at lunchtime. For a more serious example, see Radford, "The Economic Organization of a POW Camp," *Economica* (November 1945). Students find the definition of Pareto optimality (an allocation is Pareto-efficient if goods cannot be reallocated to make someone better off without making someone else worse off) confusing because of its "double negative" expression (i.e., "cannot" and "without" in the same sentence). Try to express the same idea in other ways, e.g., "An allocation is not Pareto-efficient if goods can be traded so that one person is better off and everyone else is just as well off." Pareto efficiency will be particularly important if you are going to cover externalities. Explain why movements toward the contract curve are Pareto-improving, while movements along the contract curve are not Pareto-improving. Point out that all competitive equilibria are Pareto-efficient but not all Pareto-efficient points are in equilibrium. Emphasize that the competitive equilibrium depends on the initial allocation, which will elucidate the distinction between equity and final allocation in a distribution.

You can use the Edgeworth box to show the distinction between efficiency and equity; e.g., a point on the contract curve near one corner might be less preferred because of equity considerations than a point off the curve but nearer to the middle of the box. This conflict introduces the problem of defining equity and incorporating it into an economic analysis. Table 16.2 presents four definitions of equity. After discussing them, ask the class to vote on which definition is closest to their concept of equity. Then ask the students to defend their choices, which should lead to an interesting discussion.

The analysis in Section 16.4 follows from Section 16.2 by introducing students to production in an Edgeworth box. This analysis leads to the definition of input efficiency and the production contract curve. Apply the definition of Pareto optimality to production. Before discussing the geometry of Figure 16.11, make sure that students know the requirements for output efficiency. Unless you have introduced the investment-possibilities frontier and the accompanying analysis in Chapter 15, the geometry will be new. An alternative approach to Figure 16.10 is to draw the Edgeworth box for exchange inside the *PPF* with one of the vertices at point *C*. Show where the marginal rates of substitution are equal for both individuals and also equal to the marginal rate of transformation. Section 16.5 introduces comparative advantage and applies general equilibrium analysis to the gains from international (two-country) trade. Section 16.7 serves as a bridge between Chapter 16 and the following two chapters.

REVIEW QUESTIONS

1. Why can feedback effects make a general equilibrium analysis substantially different from a partial equilibrium analysis?

A partial equilibrium analysis focuses on the interaction of supply and demand for *one* market. It ignores the influences that shifts in supply and demand in one market might have on markets for complements and substitutes. A general equilibrium analysis attempts to account for the influences on related markets that could, in turn, influence the market of primary concern. Ignoring these feedback effects can lead to inaccurate forecasts of the full influence of changes in either supply or demand. Although analysis should incorporate *all* feedback effects, one task of the economist is to determine the markets that are most closely related to the market of primary concern. Attention is directed toward these markets, thus enabling better forecasts of change in equilibrium prices and quantities.

2. In the Edgeworth box diagram, explain how one point can simultaneously represent the market baskets owned by two consumers.

The Edgeworth box diagram allows us to represent the distribution of two goods between two individuals. The box is formed by inverting the indifference curves of one individual and superimposing these on the indifference curves of another individual. The sides of the box represent the total amounts of the two goods available to consumers. On the vertical axis, we read off the amount to each individual as the difference between the horizontal axis and the point. For one individual, this is the distance from the bottom of the box to the top, and for the other, this is the distance from the top of the box to the bottom. Similarly, the horizontal axis represents amounts of a second good distributed to the two individuals. Each point in the box represents a different allocation of the two goods between the two individuals.

3. In the analysis of exchange using the Edgeworth box diagram, explain why both consumers' marginal rates of substitution are equal at every point on the contract curve.

The contract curve, in the context of an Edgeworth box diagram, is the set of points where the indifference curves of the two individuals are tangent. We know that the marginal rate of substitution is equal to the (negative) slope of the indifference curves. Also, when two curves are tangent at a point, their slopes are equal at that point. Thus, by defining the contract curve as a set of indifference curve tangencies, the marginal rates of substitution between the two goods are equal for the two individuals if we assume convex indifference curves.

4. "Since all points on a contract curve are efficient, they are all equally desirable from a social point of view." Do you agree with this statement? Explain.

If society is only concerned with efficiency and not with equity, then all points on the contract curve are equally desirable. Since it is impossible to make comparisons of utility between individuals, economics focuses on efficiency. But, if we are also concerned with equity (i.e., whether the final allocation is fair), then all points on the contract curve are not equally desirable.

5. How does the utility possibilities frontier relate to the contract curve?

Since each point in an Edgeworth box can be compared to every other point by each individual, individuals can assign a preference ordering to all points. This preference ordering is the utility function. We can graph these preference with levels of satisfaction (utility) for one individual on one axis and levels of satisfaction for a second individual on the other axis. (Of course, more than two individuals can be represented with more axes.) The utility-possibility frontier shows the levels of satisfaction achieved by each of two individuals when they have traded to an efficient outcome on the contract curve. While points that lie between the origin and the utility-possibility frontier are feasible they are not efficient because further trading will leave one individual better off without making the other individual worse off. Points outside the frontier are not feasible unless the individuals are given greater amounts of one or both goods.

6. In the Edgeworth production box diagram, what conditions must hold for an allocation to be on the production-contract curve? Why is a competitive equilibrium on the contract curve?

When constructing an Edgeworth box for the production of two goods with two inputs, each point in the box represents an allocation of the two inputs between the two production processes. With production, each point can be ordered according to the total output. These points lie on isoquants instead of on indifference curves. Since each point simultaneously represents the allocation of inputs to two production processes, it lies on two isoquants, one for each production process. The production contract curve represents all combinations of inputs that are technically efficient. Thus, there would be no way to increase the output of one good without decreasing the output of the other good.

A competitive equilibrium is one point on the production-contract curve. It is the intersection of the production-contract curve and a line passing through the initial allocation with a slope equal to the ratio of prices. (The ratio of prices dictates the rates at which inputs can be traded in the market.) For a competitive equilibrium to hold, each producer must use inputs so that the slopes of the isoquants are equal to one another and also equal to the ratio of the prices of the two inputs. Therefore, the competitive equilibrium is efficient in production. (This equilibrium assumes convex indifference curves.)

7. How is the production-possibilities frontier related to the production contract curve?

We can graph the quantities of each output produced by each allocation (each point in the Edgeworth box) on a two-dimensional graph, where the vertical axis represents the output of one process and the horizontal axis represents the output of the other process. The production-contract curve is represented in this two-dimensional graph as the production possibilities frontier. Points inside this frontier are feasible but inefficient. Points outside the frontier are infeasible and only attainable when more inputs become available or production processes become more efficient.

8. What is the marginal rate of transformation (MRT)? Explain why the MRT of one good for another is equal to the ratio of the marginal costs of producing the two goods.

The marginal rate of transformation, *MRT*, is equal to the absolute value of the slope of the production possibilities frontier. (Since the slope of the frontier is negative, we prefer to work with positive quantities; the magnitude is the absolute value of the slope.) The *MRT* is the rate at which we can trade one output for another (instead of using inputs to produce another unit of one output, we could use them to produce another unit of the other output). Also, we know that the total cost of all inputs is the same at each point because we use the same total amount of each input. In particular, along the production possibilities frontier, the ratio of marginal cost is equal to the ratio of changes in the two inputs (the marginal rate of transformation). Thus, the *MRT* is equal to the ratio of marginal costs of producing the two goods.

9. Explain why goods will not be distributed efficiently among consumers if the MRT is not equal to the consumers' marginal rate of substitution.

If the marginal rate of transformation, *MRT*, is not equal to the marginal rate of substitution, *MRS*, we could reallocate inputs in producing output to leave the consumers better off. Where *MRT* ≠ *MRS*, the ratio of marginal cost will not be equal to the ratio of prices. We could increase the output of one good, sell this output in the market, and use the proceeds to increase the production of the other goods, leaving the consumer better off than in the initial position. Therefore, the initial allocation was not Pareto-efficient. Only when *MRT* = *MRS* will consumers be left worse off with a reallocation of inputs between the production processes.

10. Why can free trade between two countries make consumers of both countries better off?

Free trade between two countries expands each country's effective production possibilities frontier. Assuming each country has a comparative advantage in the production of some good or service, trade allows a country to specialize in the area where it has this advantage. It trades these outputs for those more cheaply produced in another country. Therefore, specialization benefits many consumers in both countries.

11. What are the four major sources of market failure? In each case, explain briefly why the competitive market does not operate efficiently.

The four major sources of market failure are market power, incomplete information, externalities, and public goods. We know from the study of market structures that *market power* leads to situations where price does not equal marginal cost. In these situations, the producer is producing too little. Consumers could be made better off by redirecting inputs into the production of the good produced under a competitive market structure, thereby lowering price until price is equal to marginal cost. *Incomplete information* implies that prices do not reflect either the marginal cost of production or the change in utility from changes in consumption. Either too much or too little (at the extreme, none) is produced and consumed. *Externalities* occur when a consumption or production activity influences other consumption of production activities, and these effects are not reflected in market prices. *Public goods* are goods that can be consumed at prices below marginal cost (at the extreme, freely) because consumers cannot be excluded. In these four cases, prices do not send the proper signals to either producers or consumers to increase or decrease production or consumption. Thus, the market mechanism cannot equate social marginal costs with social marginal benefits.

REVIEW EXERCISES

1. In the analysis of an exchange between two people, suppose both people have identical preferences. Will the contract curve be a straight line? Explain. (Can you think of a counterexample?)

Given that the contract curve intersects the origin for each individual, a straight line contract curve would be a diagonal line running from one origin to the other. The slope of this line is $\frac{Y}{X}$, where Y is the total amount of the good on the vertical axis and X is the total amount of the good on the horizontal axis. (x_1,y_1) are the amounts of the two goods allocated to one individual and $(x_2,y_2)=(X-x_1,Y-y_1)$ are the amounts of the two goods allocated to the other individual; the contract curve may be represented by the equation

$$y_1=\left(\frac{Y}{X}\right)x_1.$$

We need to show that when the marginal rates of substitution for the two individuals are equal ($MRS^1 = MRS^2$), the allocation lies on the contract curve.

For example, consider the utility function $U = x_i^2 y_i$. Then

$$MRS^i = \frac{MU_x^i}{MU_y^i} = \frac{2x_iy_i}{x_i^2} = \frac{2y_i}{x_i}.$$

If MRS^1 equals MRS^2, then

$$\left(\frac{2y_1}{x_1}\right)=\left(\frac{2y_2}{x_2}\right).$$

Is this point on the contract curve? Yes, because

$$x_2 = X - x_1 \text{ and } y_2 = Y - y_1,$$

$$2\left(\frac{y_1}{x_1}\right) = 2\left(\frac{Y - y_1}{X - x_1}\right).$$

This means that

$$\frac{y_1(X - x_1)}{x_1} = Y - y_1, \text{ or } \frac{y_1 X - y_1 x_1}{x_1} = Y - y_1, \text{and}$$

$$\frac{y_1 X}{x_1} - y_1 = Y - y_1, \text{ or } \frac{y_1 X}{x_1} = Y, \text{ or } y_1 = \left(\frac{Y}{X}\right)x_1.$$

With this utility function we find $MRS^1 = MRS^2$, and the contract curve is a straight line. However, if the two traders have identical preferences but different incomes, the contract curve is not a straight line when one good is inferior.

2. Give an example of conditions when the production possibilities frontier might not be concave.

The production possibilities frontier is concave if at least one of the production functions exhibits decreasing returns to scale. If both production functions exhibit constant returns to scale, then the production possibilities frontier is a straight line. If both production functions exhibit increasing returns to scale, then the production function is convex. The following numerical examples can be used to illustrate this concept. Assume that L is the labor input, and X and Y are the two goods. The first example is the decreasing returns to scale case, the second example is the constant returns to scale case, and the third example is the increasing returns to scale case.

Product X		Product Y		PPF	
L	X	L	Y	X	Y
0	0	0	0	0	30
1	10	1	10	10	28
2	18	2	18	18	24
3	24	3	24	24	18
4	28	4	28	28	10
5	30	5	30	30	0

Product X		Product Y		PPF	
L	X	L	Y	X	Y
0	0	0	0	0	50
1	10	1	10	10	40
2	20	2	20	20	30
3	30	3	30	30	20
4	40	4	40	40	10
5	50	5	50	50	0

Product X		Product Y		PPF	
L	X	L	Y	X	Y
0	0	0	0	0	80

1	10	1	10	10	58
2	22	2	22	22	38
3	38	3	38	38	22
4	58	4	58	58	10
5	80	5	80	80	0

Note further that it is not necessary that both products have identical production functions.

3. A monopsonist buys labor for less than the competitive wage. What type of inefficiency will this use of monopsony power cause? How would your answer change if the monopsonist in the labor market were also a monopolist in the output market?

When market power exists, the market will not allocate resources efficiently. If the wage paid by a monopsonist is below the competitive wage, too little labor will be used in the production process. However, output may increase because inputs are generally less costly. If the firm is a monopolist in the output market, output will be such that price is above marginal cost and output will clearly be less. With monopsony, too much may be produced; with monopoly, too little is produced. The incentive to produce too little could be less than, equal to, or greater than the incentive to produce too much. Only in a special configuration of marginal expenditure and marginal revenue would the two incentives be equal.

4. Jane has 8 liters of soft drinks and 2 sandwiches. Bob, on the other hand, has 2 liters of soft drinks and 4 sandwiches. With these endowments, Jane's marginal rate of substitution (MRS) of soft drinks for sandwiches is three and Bob's MRS is equal to one. Draw an Edgeworth box diagram to show whether this allocation of resources is efficient. If it is, explain why. If it is not, what exchanges will make both parties better off?

Given that $MRS_{Bob} \neq MRS_{Jane}$, the current allocation of resources is inefficient. Jane and Bob could trade to make one of them better off without making the other worse off. Although we do not know the exact shape of Jane's and Bob's indifference curves, we do know the slope of both indifference curves *at the current allocation*, because we know that $MRS_{Jane} = 3$ and $MRS_{Bob} = 1$. At the current allocation point, Jane is willing to trade 3 sandwiches for 1 drink, or she will give up 1 drink in exchange for 3 sandwiches. Bob is willing to trade 1 sandwich for 1 drink. Jane will give 3 sandwiches for 1 drink while Bob is willing to accept only 1 sandwich in exchange for 1 drink. If Jane gives Bob 2 sandwiches for 1 drink, she is better off because she was willing to give 3 but only had to give 2. Bob is better off because he was willing to accept one sandwich and actually received 2.

If Jane instead was to trade drinks for sandwiches, she would sell a drink for 3 sandwiches. Bob however would not give her more than one sandwich for a drink. Neither would be willing to enter this trade. Note that this problem results in an unusual solution because according to the information given, Jane will trade away all of her sandwiches in exchange for drinks. Typically, we assume consumers would prefer to have some of either good. Note further that if Jane's MRS at the current allocation was 1/3 instead of 3, she would be willing to trade 1 sandwich for 3 drinks, or she is willing to accept 1/3 of a sandwich in exchange for one drink. Bob however, would give her a whole sandwich for one drink, making Jane better off. This would result in a more balanced final allocation.

5. The Acme Corporation produces *x* and *y* units of goods Alpha and Beta, respectively.

a. Use a production possibility frontier to explain how the willingness to produce more or less Alpha depends on the marginal rate of transformation of Alpha or Beta.

The production-possibilities frontier shows all efficient combinations of Alpha and Beta. The marginal rate of transformation of Alpha for Beta is the slope of the production-possibilities frontier. The slope measures the marginal cost of producing one good relative to the marginal cost of producing the other. To increase *x*, the units of Alpha, Acme must release inputs in the production of Beta and redirect them to producing Alpha. The rate at which it can efficiently substitute away from Beta to Alpha is given by the marginal rate of transformation.

b.   **Consider two cases of production extremes: (i) Acme produces zero units of Alpha initially, or (ii) Acme produces zero units of Beta initially. If Acme always tries to stay on its production-possibility frontier, describe the initial positions of cases (i) and (ii). What happens as the Acme Corporation begins to produce *both* goods?**

The two extremes are corner solutions to the problem of determining efficient output, given market prices. These two solutions are both possible with different price ratios, which could produce tangencies with Acme's end of the frontier. Assuming that the price ratio changes so the firm would find it efficient to produce both goods and, assuming the usual concave shape of the frontier, it is likely that the firm will be able to decrease the production of its primary output by a small amount for a larger gain in the output of the other good. The firm should continue to shift production until the ratio of marginal costs (i.e., the *MRT*) is equal to the ratio of market prices for the two outputs.

6. In the context of our analysis of the Edgeworth production box, suppose a new invention causes a constant-returns-to-scale production process for food to become a sharply-increasing-returns process. How does this change affect the production-contract curve?

In the context of an Edgeworth production box, the production-contract curve is made up of the points of tangency between the isoquants of the two production processes. A change from a constant-returns-to-scale production process to a sharply-increasing-returns-to-scale production process does not necessarily imply a change in the shape of the isoquants. One can simply redefine the quantities associated with each isoquant such that proportional increases in inputs yield greater-than-proportional increases in outputs. Under this assumption, the marginal rate of technical substitution would not change. Thus, there would be no change in the production-contract curve.

If, however, accompanying this change to a sharply-increasing-returns-to-scale technology, there were a change in the trade-off between the two inputs (a change in the shape of the isoquants), then the production-contract curve would change. For example, if the original production function were $Q = LK$ with $MRTS = \dfrac{K}{L}$, the shape of the isoquants would not change if the new production function were $Q = L^2K^2$ with $MRTS = \dfrac{K}{L}$, but the shape would change if the new production function were $Q = L^2K$ with $MRTS = 2\left(\dfrac{K}{L}\right)$. Note that in this case the production possibilities frontier is likely to become convex.

7. Suppose gold (G) and silver (S) are substitutes for each other because both serve as hedges against inflation. Suppose also that the supplies of both are fixed in the short run ($Q_G = 50$, and $Q_S = 200$), and that the demands for gold and silver are given by the following equations:

$$P_G = 850 - Q_G + 0.5P_S \quad \text{and} \quad P_S = 540 - Q_S + 0.2P_G.$$

a.   **What are the equilibrium prices of gold and silver?**

In the short run, the quantity of gold, Q_G, is fixed at 50. Substitute Q_G into the price equation for gold:

$$P_G = 850 - 50 + 0.5P_S.$$

In the short run, the quantity of silver, Q_S, is fixed at 200.

Substituting Q_S into the price equation for silver:

$$P_S = 540 - 200 + 0.2P_G.$$

Since we now have two equations and two unknowns, substitute the price of gold into the price of silver demand function and solve for the price of silver:

$$P_S = 540 - 200 + (0.2)(800 + 0.5P_S) = \$555.56.$$

Then substitute the price of silver into the demand for gold function:

$$P_G = 850 - 50 + (0.5)(555.56) = \$1,077.78.$$

b.   **Suppose a new discovery of gold increases the quantity supplied by 85 units. How will this discovery affect the prices of both gold and silver?**

When the quantity of gold increases by 85 units from 50 to 135, we must resolve our system of equations:

$$P_G = 850 - 135 + 0.5P_S, \text{ or } P_G = 715 + (0.5)(340 + 0.2P_G) = \$983.33.$$

The price of silver is equal to:

$$P_S = 540 - 200 + (0.2)(983.33) = \$536.66.$$

CHAPTER 17
MARKETS WITH ASYMMETRIC INFORMATION

TEACHING NOTES

This chapter explores different situations in which one party knows more than the other, or in other words, what happens when there is asymmetric information. Section 17.1 discusses the case where the seller has more information than the buyer, and section 17.2 discusses market signaling as a mechanism to deal with the problem of asymmetric information. Section 17.3 discusses the moral hazard problem where one party has more information about their behavior than does the other party. Section 17.4 discusses the principal agent problem and section 17.5 extends the analysis to the case of an integrated firm. Both sections address the issue of differing goals between owners and managers. Section 17.6 examines the efficiency wage theory. There are basically four topics that the instructor can pick and choose between depending on time constraints and general interest.

It is best to introduce asymmetric information by reviewing the cases where microeconomics has assumed perfect information. For example, except for Chapter 5 and sections of Chapter 15, we have assumed perfect knowledge of the future (no uncertainty). In models of uncertainty, consumers and producers play "games against nature." In models of asymmetric information, they are playing games with each other.

Many of your students are likely to have bought or sold a used car and will, therefore, find the lemons model interesting. Start your presentation by asking the sellers of used cars how they determined their asking price. Emphasize the intuition of the model before presenting Figure 17.1. If they have understood the model, they should ask a high price to give the impression to buyers that the car they are selling is of high quality. Class discussion could consider whether the government should pass laws requiring warranties in the sale of used cars.

The market for insurance is also one with which most students are familiar. Although car insurance is required in many states, liability limits may vary from policy to policy. Discuss how risk-averse individuals will want to purchase policies with higher limits and how insurance companies determine the riskiness of the insurance. If you have used the example of buying a house in Chapter 15, you may extend it here by considering how bankers determine whether borrowers will default on their home loans.

When discussing market signaling, point out the dual function of education (as training and as a signal of higher productivity). The "Simple Model of Job Market Signaling," which is presented in Section 17.2, might confuse students unfamiliar with discontinuous functions (see Figure 17.2). Explain how educational degrees lead to discontinuities, and stress the relationship between degrees, guarantees, and warranties of educational quality.

Moral hazard is an easy concept to illustrate with examples, but it is important to draw a clear distinction between adverse selection and moral hazard.

The principal-agent problem is presented in the context of the relationship between employer and employee. It can be generalized to the relationship between a regulator and a regulated firm and to the relationship between voters and elected officials. In discussing the problems of monitoring agents, you can reintroduce the concept of transactions costs (from Section 16.2). The most interesting topic of this section is how to design contracts to provide the proper incentives for agents to perform in the interest of the principal. The starred Section 17.5 extends this topic to managerial incentives in an integrated firm. The model can be applied to government contracts, i.e., defense contracts, for a discussion of cost-plus contracting.

The shirking model of efficiency wages is conceptually difficult. After discussing efficiency in Chapter 16, students might wonder what is so efficient about paying workers a wage that is greater than the value of their marginal product. Stress the role of asymmetric information here: firms have imperfect information about individual worker productivity. If you present this model, first read the references in Footnote 17. While Yellen's article is concise, Stiglitz's is more general, discussing shirking on page 20 and the relationship between efficiency wage theory and unemployment on pages 33-37.

REVIEW QUESTIONS

1. Why can asymmetric information between buyers and sellers lead to a market failure when a market is otherwise perfectly competitive?

Asymmetric information leads to market failure because the transaction price does not reflect either the marginal benefit to the buyer or the marginal cost of the seller. The competitive market fails to achieve an output with a price equal to marginal cost. In some extreme cases, if there is no mechanism to reduce the problem of asymmetric information, the market collapses completely.

2. If the used car market is a "lemons" market, how would you expect the repair record of used cars that are sold to compare with the repair record of those not sold?

In the market for used cars, the seller has a better idea of the quality of the used car than does the buyer. The repair record of the used car is one indicator of quality. One would expect that, at the margin, cars with good repair records would be kept while cars with poor repair records would be sold. Thus, one would expect the repair records of used cars that are to be sold to be worse than those of used cars not sold.

3. Explain the difference between adverse selection and moral hazard in insurance markets. Can one exist without the other?

In insurance markets, both adverse selection and moral hazard exist. Adverse selection refers to the self-selection of individuals who purchase insurance policies. In other words, people who are less risky than the insured population will, at the margin, choose not to insure, while people more risky than the population will choose to insure. As a result, the insurance company is left with a riskier pool of policy holders. The problem of moral hazard occurs after the insurance is purchased. Once insurance is purchased, less risky individuals might engage in behavior characteristic of more risky individuals. If policy holders are fully insured, they have little incentive to avoid risky situations.

An insurance firm may reduce adverse selection, without reducing moral hazard, and vice versa. Researching to determine the riskiness of a *potential* customer helps insurance companies reduce adverse selection. Furthermore, insurance companies reevaluate the premium (sometimes canceling the policy) when claims are made against the policy, thereby reducing moral hazard. Copayments also reduce moral hazard by creating a disincentive for policy holders to engage in risky behavior.

4. Describe several ways in which sellers can convince buyers that their products are of high quality. Which methods apply in the following products: Maytag washing machines, Burger King hamburgers, large diamonds?

Some signal the quality of their products to buyers through (1) investment in a good reputation, (2) the standardization of products, (3) certification (i.e., the use of educational degrees in the labor market), (4) guarantees, and (5) warranties. Maytag signals the high quality of its washing machines by offering one of the best warranties in the market. (See *Consumer Reports*, February 1988, p. 82.) Burger King relies on the standardization of its hamburgers, e.g., the Whopper. The sale of a large diamond is accompanied by a certificate that verifies the weight and shape of the stone and discloses any flaws.

5. Why might a seller find it advantageous to signal the quality of a product? How are guarantees and warranties a form of market signaling?

Firms producing high-quality products would like to charge higher prices, but to do this successfully, potential consumers must be made aware of the quality differences among brands. One method of providing product quality information is through guarantees (i.e., the promise to return what has been given in exchange if the product is defective) and warranties (i.e., the promise to repair or replace if defective). Since low-quality producers are unlikely to offer costly signaling devices, consumers can correctly view a guarantee or an extensive warranty as a signal of high quality, thus confirming the effectiveness of these measures as signaling devices.

6. Why might managers be able to achieve objectives other than profit maximization, the goal of the firm's shareholders?

It is difficult and costly for shareholders to constantly monitor the actions of the firm's managers. The firm's owners are in a better position to engage in monitoring, but managers' behaviors still cannot be scrutinized one hundred percent of the time. Therefore, managers have some leeway to pursue their own objectives.

7. How can the principal-agent model be used to explain why public enterprises, such as post offices, might pursue goals other than profit maximization?

Managers of public enterprises can be expected to act in much the same way as managers of private enterprises, in terms of having an interest in power and other perks, in addition to profit maximization. The problem of overseeing a public enterprise is one of asymmetric information. The manager (agent) is more familiar with the cost structure of the enterprise and the benefits to the customers than the principal, an elected or appointed official, who must elicit cost information controlled by the manager. The costs of eliciting and verifying the information, as well as independently gathering information on the benefits provided by the public enterprise, can be more than the difference between the agency's potential net returns ("profits") and realized returns. This difference provides room for slack, which can be distributed to the management as personal benefits, to the agency's workers as greater-than-efficient job security, or to the agency's customers in the form of greater-than-efficient provision of goods or services.

8. Why are bonus and profit-sharing payment schemes likely to resolve principal-agent problems, whereas a fixed-wage payment will not?

With a fixed wage, the agent-employee has no incentive to maximize productivity. If the agent-employee is hired at a fixed wage equal to the marginal revenue product of the average employee, there is no incentive to work harder than the least productive worker. Bonus and profit-sharing schemes involve a lower fixed wage than fixed-wage schemes, but they include a bonus wage. The bonus can be tied to the profitability of the firm to the output of the individual employee, or to that of the group in which the employee works. These schemes provide a greater incentive for agents to maximize the objective function of the principal.

9. What is an efficiency wage? Why is it profitable for the firm to pay it when workers have better information about their productivity than firms do?

An efficiency wage, in the context of the shirking model, is the wage at which no shirking occurs. If employers cannot monitor employees' productivity, then employees may shirk (work less productively), which will affect the firm's output and profits. It therefore pays the firm to offer workers a higher-than-market wage, thus reducing the workers' incentive to shirk, because they know that if they are fired and end up working for another firm, their wage will fall.

EXERCISES

1. **Many consumers view a well-known brand name as a signal of quality and will pay more for a brand-name product (e.g., Bayer aspirin instead of generic aspirin, Birds Eye frozen vegetables instead of the supermarket's own brand). Can a brand name provide a useful signal of quality? Why or why not?**

A brand name can provide a useful signal of quality for several reasons. First, when information asymmetry is a problem, one solution is to create a "brand-name" product. Standardization of the product produces a reputation for a given level of quality that is signaled by the brand name. Second, if the development of a brand-name reputation is costly (i.e., advertising, warranties, etc.), the brand name is a signal of higher quality. Finally, pioneer products, by virtue of their "first-mover" status, enjoy consumer loyalty if the products are of acceptable quality. The uncertainty surrounding newer products inhibits defection from the pioneering brand-name product.

2. Gary is a recent college graduate. After six months at his new job, he has finally saved enough to buy his first car.

a.   Gary knows very little about the differences between makes and models. How could he use market signals, reputation, or standardization to make comparisons?

Gary's problem is one of asymmetric information. As a buyer of a first car, he will be negotiating with sellers who know more about cars than he does. His first choice is to decide between a new or used car. If he buys a used car, he must choose between a professional used-car dealer and an individual seller. Each of these three types of sellers (the new-car dealer, the used-car dealer, and the individual seller) uses different market signals to convey quality information about their products.

The new-car dealer, working with the manufacturer (and relying on the manufacturer's reputation) can offer standard and extended warranties that guarantee the car will perform as advertised. Because few used cars carry a manufacturer's warranty and the used-car dealer is not intimately familiar with the condition of the cars on his or her lot (because of their wide variety and disparate previous usage), it is not in his or her self-interest to offer extensive warranties. The used-car dealer, therefore, must rely on reputation, particularly on a reputation of offering "good values." Since the individual seller neither offers warranties nor relies on reputation, purchasing from such a seller could make it advisable to seek additional information from an independent mechanic or from reading the used-car recommendations in *Consumer Reports*. Given his lack of experience, Gary should gather as much information about these market signals, reputation, and standardization as he can afford.

b.   You are a loan officer in a bank. After selecting a car, Gary comes to you seeking a loan. Because he has only recently graduated, he does not have a long credit history. Nonetheless, the bank has a long history of financing cars for recent college graduates. Is this information useful in Gary's case? If so, how?

The bank's problem in loaning money to Gary is also one of asymmetric information. Gary has a much better idea than the bank does about the quality of the car and his ability to pay back the loan. While the bank can learn about the car through the reputation of the manufacturer (if it is a new car) and through inspection (if it is a used car), the bank has little information on Gary's ability to handle credit. Therefore, the bank must infer information about Gary's credit-worthiness from easily available information, such as his recent graduation from college, how much he might have borrowed while in school, and the similarity of his educational and credit profile to that of college graduates currently holding car loans from the bank. If recent graduates have built a good reputation for paying off their loans, Gary can use this reputation to his advantage, but poor repayment patterns by this group will lessen his chances of obtaining a car loan from this bank.

3. A major university bans the assignment of D or F grades. It defends its action by claiming that students tend to perform above average when they are free from the pressures of flunking out. The university states that it wants all its students to get As and Bs. If the goal is to raise overall grades to the B level or above, is this a good policy? Discuss with respect to the problem of moral hazard.

By eliminating the lowest grades, the innovating university creates a moral hazard problem similar to that which is found in insurance markets. Since they are protected from receiving a below-average grade, some students will have little incentive to work at above-average levels. The policy only addresses the pressures facing below-average students, i.e., those who flunk out. Average and above-average students do not face the pressure of failing. For these students, the destructive pressure of earning good grades (instead of learning a subject well) remains. Their problems are not addressed by this policy. Therefore, the policy creates a moral hazard problem primarily for the below-average students who are its intended beneficiaries.

4. Professor Jones has just been hired by the economics department at a major university. The president of the board of regents has stated that the university is committed to providing top-quality education for undergraduates. Two months into the semester, Jones fails to show up for his classes. It seems he is devoting all his time to economic research rather than to teaching. Jones argues that his research will bring additional prestige to the department and the university. Should he be allowed to continue exclusively with research? Discuss with reference to the principal-agent problem.

In the university context, the board of regents and its president are the principals, while the agents are the members of the faculty hired by the department with the approval of the president and the board. The dual purpose of most universities is teaching students and producing research; thus, most faculty are hired to perform both tasks. The problem is that teaching effort can be easily monitored (particularly if Jones does not show up for class), while the benefits of establishing a prestigious research reputation are uncertain and are realized only over time. While the quantity of research is easy to calculate, determining research quality is more difficult. The university should not simply take Jones' word regarding the benefits of his research and allow him to continue exclusively with his research without altering his payment scheme. One alternative would be to tell Jones that he does not have to teach if he is willing to accept a lower salary. On the other hand, the university could offer Jones a bonus if, due to his research reputation, he is able to bring a lucrative grant or other donations to the university

5. Faced with a reputation for producing automobiles with poor repair records, a number of American companies have offered extensive guarantees to car purchasers (i.e., a seven-year warranty on all parts and labor associated with mechanical problems).

a. In light of your knowledge of the lemons market, why is this a reasonable policy?

In the past, American companies enjoyed a reputation for producing high-quality cars. More recently, faced with competition from Japanese car manufacturers, their products appeared to customers to be of lower quality. As this reputation spread, customers were less willing to pay high prices for American cars. To reverse this trend, American companies invested in quality control, improving the repair records of their products. Consumers, however, still considered American cars to be of lower quality (lemons, in some sense), and would not buy them, American companies were forced to signal the improved quality of their products to their customers. One way of providing this information is through improved warranties that directly address the issue of poor repair records. This was a reasonable reaction to the "lemons" problem that they faced.

b. Is the policy likely to create a moral hazard problem? Explain.

Moral hazard occurs when the insured party (here, the owner of an American automobile with an extensive warranty) can influence the probability of the event that triggers payment (here, the repair of the automobile). The coverage of all parts and labor associated with mechanical problems reduces the incentive to maintain the automobile. Hence, a moral hazard problem is created by the offer of extensive warranties. To avoid this problem, all routine maintenance could be performed as long as the car is under warranty. Note though that manufacturers could stipulate that the warranties will not be honored unless the owner performs and pays for routine maintenance.

6. To promote competition and consumer welfare, the Federal Trade Commission requires firms to advertise truthfully. How does truth in advertising promote competition? Why would a market be less competitive if firms advertised deceptively?

Truth-in-advertising promotes competition by providing the information necessary for consumers to make optimal decisions. "Competitive forces" function properly only if consumers are aware of all prices (and qualities), so comparisons may be made. In the absence of truthful advertising, buyers are unable to make these comparisons because goods priced identically can be of different quality. Hence, there will be a tendency for buyers to "stick" with proven products, reducing competition between existing firms and discouraging entry. Note that monopoly rents may result when consumers stick with proven products.

7. An insurance company is considering issuing three types of fire insurance policies: (i) complete insurance coverage, (ii) complete coverage above and beyond a $10,000 deductible, and (iii) 90 percent coverage of all losses. Which policy is more likely to create moral hazard problems?

Moral hazard problems arise with fire insurance when the insured party can influence the probability of a fire and the magnitude of a loss from a fire. The property owner can engage in behavior that reduces the probability of a fire, for example, by inspecting and replacing faulty wiring. The magnitude of losses can be reduced by the installation of warning systems or the storage of valuables away from areas where fires are likely to start.

After purchasing complete insurance, the insured has little incentive to reduce either the probability or the magnitude of the loss, and the moral hazard problem will be severe. In order to compare a $10,000 deductible and 90 percent coverage, we would need information on the value of the potential loss. Both policies reduce the moral hazard problem of complete coverage. However, if the property is worth less (more) than $100,000, the total loss will be less (more) with 90 percent coverage than with the $10,000 deductible. As the value of the property increases above $100,000, the owner is more likely to engage in fire prevention efforts under the policy that offers 90 percent coverage than under the one that offers the $10,000 deductible.

8. You have seen how asymmetric information can reduce the average quality of products sold in a market as low-quality products drive out the high-quality ones. For those markets in which asymmetric information is prevalent, would you agree or disagree with each of the following? Explain briefly:

a.   The government should subsidize *Consumer Reports*.

Asymmetric information implies an unequal access to information by either buyers or sellers, a problem that leads to inefficient markets or market collapse. Subsidizing the gathering and publishing of information can be advantageous in general because it helps consumers make better decisions and promotes honesty on the part of the firm.

Although *Consumer Reports* provides evaluations for products ranging from hamburgers to washing machines, it refuses to let its name be used as an endorsement of a product. While government support of *Consumer Reports* would be likely to increase the ability of consumers to distinguish between high- and low-quality goods, it is probable that the Consumers Union, publisher of *Consumer Reports,* would reject government subsidization because such subsidization might taint the objectivity of the organization. Note that the government has already provided an indirect subsidy to the publication by granting the Consumers Union nonprofit status.

b.   The government should impose quality standards — e.g., firms should not be allowed to sell low-quality items.

Option *b* involves a cost of monitoring. After imposing quality standards, the government must either administratively monitor the quality of goods or adjudicate disputes between the public and the manufacturers. Note, however, that low-quality goods may be preferred if they are sufficiently cheaper.

c.   The producer of a high-quality good will probably want to offer an extensive warranty.

This option provides the least-cost solution to the problems of asymmetric information. It allows the producer to distinguish its products from low-quality goods because it is more costly for the low-quality producer to offer an extensive warranty than for the high-quality producer to offer one.

d.   The government should require *all* firms to offer extensive warranties.

By requiring *all* firms to offer extensive warranties, the government negates the market signaling value of warranties offered by the producers of high-quality goods.

9. **Two used car dealerships compete side by side on a main road. The first, Harry's Cars, sells high-quality cars that it carefully inspects and, if necessary, services. On average, it costs Harry $8,000 to buy and service each car that it sells. The second dealership, Lew's Motors, sells lower-quality cars. On average, it costs Lew only $5,000 for each car that it sells. If consumers knew the quality of the used cars they were buying, they would gladly pay $10,000 on average for Harry's cars, but only $7,000 on average for Lew's cars.**

Unfortunately, the dealerships are new and have not had time to establish reputations, so consumers don't know the quality of each dealership's cars. Consumers, however, figure that they have a 50-50 chance of ending up with a high-quality car, no matter which dealership they go to, and are thus willing to pay $8,500 on average for a car.

Harry's has an idea. It will offer a bumper-to-bumper warranty for all cars it sells. He knows that a warranty lasting Y years will cost $500Y on average, and it also knows that if Lew's tries to offer the same warranty, it will cost Lew's $1000Y on average.

(a) **Suppose Harry's offers a one-year warranty on all cars it sells. Will this generate a credible signal of quality? Will Lew's match the offer, or will it fail to match it so that consumers can correctly assume that because of the warranty, Harry's cars are high quality and so worth $10,000 on average?**

If Harry were to offer a one-year warranty, the average cost to him of each car will rise from $8,000 to $8,500. By offering the warranty, Harry will communicate the high quality of his cars and will be able to sell them for $10,000, which means that Harry's profit per car will increase from $500 (8500-8000) to $1,500 (10,000-8500).

Lew will match Harry's warranty. Without offering the warranty, Lew is able to make $2,000 per car (7000-5000). If he were to offer the warranty, each car will now cost Lew $6,000, but as consumers will not be able to determine the quality of the cars Lew will make $2,500 per car (8500-6000).

(b) **What if Harry offers a two-year warranty? Will this generate a credible signal of quality? What about a three-year warranty?**

If Harry offers a two-year warranty each car will cost him $9,000. He will earn $1,000 per car as consumers will recognize the higher quality of his cars.

With a three-year warranty Harry would be making $500 per car, the same that he would have made had he not signaled the higher quality of his cars with a warranty. Therefore, Harry would not offer a three-year warranty.

(c) **If you were advising Harry, how long a warranty would you urge him to offer? Explain why.**

Harry will need to offer a warranty of sufficient length such that Lew will not find it profitable to match the warranty. Let t denote the number of years of the warranty, then Lew will offer a warranty according to the following inequality:

$$(8,500 - 5,000 - 1,000t) \leq 7,000 - 5000, \text{ or } 1.5 \leq t.$$

Therefore, I would advise Harry to offer a 1.5 year warranty on his cars as Lew will not find it profitable to match the warranty.

10. **A firm's short-run revenue is given by $R = 10e - e^2$, where e is the level of effort by a typical worker (all workers are assumed to be identical). A worker chooses his level of effort to maximize his wage net of effort w - e (the per-unit cost of effort is assumed to be 1). Determine the level of effort and the level of profit (revenue less wage paid) for each of the following wage arrangements. Explain why these differing principal-agent relationships generate different outcomes.**

a. **w = 2 for e ≥ 1; otherwise w = 0.**

There is no incentive for the worker to provide an effort which exceeds 1, as the wage received by the worker will be 2 if the worker provides one unit of effort but will not increase if the worker provides more effort.

The profit for the firm will be revenue minus the wages paid to the worker:

$$\pi = (10)(1) - 1^2 - 2 = \$7.$$

In this principal-agent relationship there is no incentive for the worker to increase his or her effort as the wage is not related to the revenues of the firm.

b.   **w = R/2.**

The worker will attempt to maximize the wage net of the effort required to obtain that wage; that is, the worker will attempt to maximize:

$$w - e = \frac{10e - e^2}{2} - e, \text{ or } 4e - 0.5e^2.$$

To find the maximum effort that the worker is willing to put forth, take the first derivative with respect to effort, set it equal to zero, and solve for effort.

$$\frac{d\left(4e - 0.5e^2\right)}{de} = 4 - e = 0, \text{ or } e = 4.$$

The wage the worker will receive will be

$$w = \frac{R}{2} = \frac{10(4) - 4^2}{2} = 12.$$

The profits for the firm will be

$$\pi = ((10)(4) - 4^2) - 12 = \$12.$$

With this principal-agent relationship, the wage that the individual worker receives is related to the revenue of the firm. Therefore, we see greater effort on the part of the worker and, as a result, greater profits for the firm.

c.   **w = R - 12.5.**

Again, the worker will attempt to maximize the wage net of the effort required to obtain that wage; that is, the worker will attempt to maximize:

$$w - e = \left(10e - e^2\right) - 12.50 - e, \text{ or } 9e - e^2 - 12.50.$$

To find the maximum effort that the worker is willing to put forth, take the first derivative with respect to effort, set it equal to zero, and solve for effort:

$$\frac{d\left(9e - e^2 - 12.5\right)}{de} = 9 - 2e = 0, \text{ or } e = 4.5.$$

The wage the worker will receive will be

$$w = R - 12.50 = \left((10)(4.5) - 4.5^2\right) - 12.5 = 12.25.$$

The profits for the firm will be

$$\pi = ((10)(4.5) - 4.5^2) - 12.25 = \$12.50.$$

With this principal-agent relationship, we find that the wage of the worker is more directly related to the performance of the firm than in either *a* or *b*. We find that the worker is willing to supply even more effort resulting in even higher profits for the firm.

CHAPTER 18
EXTERNALITIES AND PUBLIC GOODS

TEACHING NOTES

This chapter discusses the remaining types of market failure which were introduced at the end of Chapter 16, and which were not covered in Chapter 17. Section 18.1 defines the concept of externalities, both positive and negative. Section 18.2 discusses methods of correcting for the market failure that arises in the presence of externalities. These two sections give a good self-contained overview of externalities as a type of market failure. The next two sections, 18.3 and 18.4, explore the relationship between the existence of externalities and property rights. Section 18.5 discusses public goods and section 18.6 offers a brief discussion of determining the optimal level of the public good to provide. Overall the chapter provides a good solid overview of some very interesting problems. Any instructor who had the time and desire to expand upon the presentation in the chapter could find a wealth of information by consulting an environmental or resource economics textbook. There are an abundance of examples related to pollution or natural resource issues that you could choose to talk about. Check your local newspaper for ideas.

The consumption of many goods involves the creation of externalities. Stress the divergence between social and private costs, and the difference between the private (industry competitive) equilibrium and the socially optimal (efficient) equilibrium. You can use the students knowledge of consumer and producer surplus to explore the welfare gain of moving to the efficient equilibrium. Exercise (5) presents the classic beekeeper/apple-orchard problem, originally popularized in Meade, "External Economies and Diseconomies in a Competitive Situation," *Economic Journal* (March 1952). Empirical research on this example has shown that beekeepers and orchard owners have solved many of their problems: see Cheung, "The Fable of the Bees: An Economic Investigation," *Journal of Law and Economics* (April 1973).

One of the main themes of the law and economics literature since 1969 is the application of Coase's insight on the assignment of property rights. The original article is clear and can be understood by students. Stress the problems posed by transactions costs. For a lively debate, ask students whether non-smokers should be granted the right to smokeless air in public places (see Exercise (4)). For an extended discussion of the Coase Theorem at the undergraduate level, see Polinsky, Chapters 3-6, *An Introduction to Law & Economics* (Little, Brown & Co., 1983).

The last two sections focus on public goods and private choice. Point out the similarities and differences between public goods and other activities with externalities. Since students confuse nonrival and nonexclusive goods, create a table similar to the following and give examples to fill in the cells:

	Exclusive	Nonexclusive
Rival	Most Goods	Air and Water
Nonrival	Congestion	Public Goods

The next stumbling block for students is achieving an understanding of why we add individual demand curves vertically rather than horizontally. Stress that by summing horizontally you are asking the total quantity supplied/demanded at any given price. By summing vertically you are asking the total willingness to pay for a given quantity.

The presentation of public choice is a limited introduction to the subject, but you can easily expand on this material. A logical extension of this chapter is an introduction to cost-benefit analysis. For applications of this analysis, see Part III, "Empirical Analysis of Policies and Programs," in Haveman and Margolis (eds.), *Public Expenditure and Policy Analysis* (Houghton Mifflin, 1983).

REVIEW QUESTIONS

1. Which of the following describes an externality and which does not? Explain the difference.

a.   A policy of restricted coffee exports in Brazil causes the U.S. price of coffee to rise, which in turn also causes the price of tea to rise.

Externalities cause market inefficiencies because the price of the good does not reflect the true social value of the good. A policy of restricting coffee exports in Brazil causes the U.S. price of coffee to rise, because supply is reduced. As the price of coffee rises, consumers switch to tea, thereby increasing the demand for tea, and hence, increasing the price of tea. These are market effects, not externalities.

b.   An advertising blimp distracts a motorist who then hits a telephone pole.

An advertising blimp is producing information by announcing the availability of some good or service. However, its method of supplying this information can be distracting for some consumers, especially those consumers who happen to be driving near telephone poles. The blimp is creating a negative externality that influences the drivers' safety. Since the price charged by the advertising firm does not incorporate the externality of distracting drivers, too much of this type of advertising is produced from the point of view of society as a whole.

2. Compare and contrast the following three mechanisms for treating pollution externalities when the costs and benefits of abatement are uncertain: (a) an emissions fee, (b) an emissions standard, and (c) a system of transferable emissions permits.

Since pollution is not reflected in the marginal cost of production, its emission creates an externality. Three policy tools can be used to reduce pollution: an emissions fee, an emissions standard, and a system of transferable permits. The choice between a fee and a standard will depend on the marginal cost and marginal benefit of reducing pollution. If small changes in abatement yield large benefits while adding little to cost, the cost of not reducing emissions is high. Thus, standards should be used. However, if small changes in abatement yield little benefit while adding greatly to cost, the cost of reducing emissions is high. Thus, fees should be used.

A system of transferable emissions permits combines the features of fees and standards to reduce pollution. Under this system, a standard is set and fees are used to transfer permits to the firm that values them the most (i.e., a firm with high abatement costs). However, the total number of permits can be incorrectly chosen. Too few permits will create excess demand, increasing price and inefficiently diverting resources to owners of the permits. Typically, pollution control agencies implement one of three mechanisms, measure the results, reassess the success of their choice, then reset new levels of fees or standards or select a new policy tool.

3. When do externalities require government intervention? When is such intervention unlikely to be necessary?

Economic efficiency can be achieved without government intervention when the externality affects a small number of people and when property rights are well specified. When the number of parties is small, the cost of negotiating an agreement among the parties is small. Further, the amount of required information (i.e., the costs of and benefits to each party) is small. When property rights are not well specified, uncertainty regarding costs and benefits increases and efficient choices might not be made. The costs of coming to an agreement, including the cost of delaying such an agreement, could be greater than the cost of government intervention, including the expected cost of choosing the wrong policy instrument.

4. An emissions fee is paid to the government, whereas an injurer who is sued and held liable pays damages directly to the party harmed by an externality. What differences in the behavior of victims might you expect to arise under these two arrangements?

When victims can receive the damages directly, they are more likely to file a claim, initiate a suit, and try to overstate their damages. When victims are not able to receive the damages directly, they are less likely to report violations and are less likely to overstate their damages. In theory, emissions fees paid to the government require the polluting firm to pay compensation for any damage inflicted and hence to move towards the socially optimal level of production. An individual who is injured by a firm's polluting behavior is again less likely to file a complaint if they do not feel they can directly receive the compensation.

5. Why does free access to a common property resource generate an inefficient outcome?

Free access to a resource means that the marginal cost to the user is less than the social cost. The use of a common property resource by a person or firm excludes others from using it. For example, the use of water by one consumer restricts its use by another. Because private marginal cost is below social marginal cost, too much of the resource is consumed by the individual user, creating an inefficient outcome.

6. Public goods are both nonrival and nonexclusive. Explain each of these terms and show clearly how they differ from each other.

A good is *nonrival* if, for any level of production, the marginal cost of providing the good to an additional *consumer* is zero (although the production cost of an additional *unit* could be greater than zero). A good is *nonexclusive* if it is impossible or very expensive to exclude individuals from consuming it. Public goods are *nonrival* and *nonexclusive*. Commodities can be (1) exclusive and rival, (2) exclusive and nonrival, (3) nonexclusive and rival, or (4) nonexclusive and nonrival. Most of the commodities discussed in the text to this point have been of the first type. In this chapter, we focus on commodities of the last type.

Nonrival refers to the *production* of a good or service for one more customer. It usually involves a production process with high fixed costs, such as the cost of building a highway or lighthouse. (Remember that fixed cost depends on the period under consideration: the cost of lighting the lamp at the lighthouse can vary over time, but does not vary with the number of consumers.) Nonexclusive refers to *exchange*, where the cost of charging consumers is prohibitive. Incurring the cost of identifying consumers and collecting from them would result in losses. Some economists focus on the nonexclusion property of public goods because it is this characteristic that poses the most significant problems for efficient provision.

7. Public television is funded in part by private donations, even though anyone with a television set can watch for free. Can you explain this phenomenon in light of the free rider problem?

The free-rider problem refers to the difficulty of excluding persons from consuming a nonexclusive commodity. Non-paying consumers can "free-ride" on commodities provided by paying customers. Public television is funded in part by contributions. Some viewers contribute, but most watch without paying, hoping that someone else will pay so they will not. To combat this problem these stations (1) ask consumers to assess their true willingness to pay, then (2) ask consumers to contribute up to this amount, and (3) attempt to make everyone else feel guilty for free-riding.

8. Explain why the median voter outcome need not be efficient when majority rule voting determines the level of public spending.

The median voter is the citizen with the middle preference: half the voting population is more strongly in favor of the issue and half is more strongly opposed to the issue. Under majority-rule voting, where each citizen's vote is weighted equally, the preferred spending level on public-goods provision of the *median voter* will win an election against any other alternative.

However, majority rule is not necessarily efficient, because it weights each citizen's preferences equally. For an efficient outcome, we would need a system that measures and aggregates the willingness to pay of those citizens consuming the public good. Majority rule is not this system. However, as we have seen in previous chapters, majority rule is equitable in the sense that all citizens are treated equally. Thus, we again find a trade-off between equity and efficiency.

EXERCISES

1. A number of firms located in the western portion of a town after single-family residences took up the eastern portion. Each firm produces the same product and, in the process, emits noxious fumes that adversely affect the residents of the community.

a. Why is there an externality created by the firms?

Noxious fumes created by firms enter the utility function of residents, and the residents have no control over the quantity of the fumes. We can assume that the fumes decrease the utility of the residents (i.e., they are a negative externality) and lower property values.

b. Do you think that private bargaining can resolve the problem? Explain.

If the residents anticipated the location of the firms, housing prices should reflect the disutility of the fumes; the externality would have been internalized by the housing market in housing prices. If the noxious fumes were not anticipated, private bargaining could resolve the problem of the externality only if there are a relatively small number of parties (both firms and families) and property rights are well specified. Private bargaining would rely on each family's willingness to pay for air quality, but truthful revelation might not be possible. All this will be complicated by the adaptability of the production technology known to the firms and the employment relations between the firms and families. It is unlikely that private bargaining will resolve the problem.

c. How might the community determine the efficient level of air quality?

The community could determine the economically efficient level of air quality by aggregating the families' willingness to pay and equating it with the marginal cost of pollution reduction. Both steps involve the acquisition of truthful information.

2. A computer programmer lobbies against copyrighting software. He argues that everyone should benefit from innovative programs written for personal computers and that exposure to a wide variety of computer programs will inspire young programmers to create even more innovative programs. Considering the marginal social benefits possibly gained by his proposal, do you agree with his position?

Computer software as information is a classic example of a public good. Since it can be costlessly copied, the marginal cost of providing software to an additional user is near zero. Therefore, software is nonrival. (The fixed costs of creating software are high, but the variable costs are low.) Furthermore, it is expensive to exclude consumers from copying and using software because copy protection schemes are available only at high cost or high inconvenience to users. Therefore, software is also nonexclusive. As both nonrival and nonexclusive, computer software suffers the problems of public goods provision: the presence of free-riders makes it difficult or impossible for markets to provide the efficient level of software. Rather than regulating this market directly, the legal system guarantees property rights to the creators of software. If copyright protection were not enforced, it is likely that the software market would collapse, or that there would be a significant decrease in the quantity of software developed and supplied, which would reduce the marginal social benefits. Therefore, we do not agree with the computer programmer.

3. Assume that scientific studies provide you with the following information concerning the benefits and costs of sulfur dioxide emissions:

Benefits of abating (reducing) emissions:	**MB=400-10A**
Costs of abating emissions:	**MC=100+20A**

where A is the quantity abated in millions of tons and the benefits and costs are given in dollars per ton.

a.   What is the socially efficient level of emissions abatement?

To find the socially efficient level of emissions abatement, set marginal benefit equal to marginal cost and solve for A:

$$400-10A=100+20A$$

$$A=10.$$

b.   What are the marginal benefit and marginal cost of abatement at the socially   efficient   level of abatement?

Plug A=10 into the marginal benefit and marginal cost functions to find the benefit and cost:

$$MB=400-10(10)=300$$

$$MC=100+20(10)=300.$$

c.   What happens to net social benefits (benefits minus costs) if you abate 1 million   more tons than the efficient level? 1 million fewer?

Net social benefits are the area under the marginal benefit curve minus the area under the marginal cost curve.   At the socially efficient level of abatement this is equal to area a+b+c+d in Figure 18.3.c or

$$0.5(400-100)(10)=1500 \text{ million dollars.}$$

If you abate 1 million more tons then the net social benefit is area a+b+c+d-e or

$$1500-0.5(320-290)(1)=1500-15=1485 \text{ million dollars.}$$

If you abate 1 million less tons then the net social benefit is area a+c or

$$0.5(400-310)(9)+(310-280)(9)+0.5(280-100)(9)=1485 \text{ million dollars.}$$

d.   Why is it socially efficient to set marginal benefits equal to marginal costs rather   than abating until total benefits equal total costs?

It is socially efficient to set marginal benefit equal to marginal cost rather than total benefit equal to total cost because we want to maximize net benefits which are total benefit minus total cost. Maximizing total benefit minus total cost means that at the margin, the last unit abated will have an equal cost and benefit. Choosing the point where total benefit is equal to total cost will result in too much abatement, and would be analogous to choosing to produce where total revenue was equal to total cost. If total revenue was always equal to total cost by choice, then there would never be any profit. In the case of abatement, the more we abate, the costlier it is. Given that funds will tend to be scarce, dollars should be allocated to abatement only so long as the benefit of the last unit of abatement is greater than or equal to the cost of the last unit of abatement.

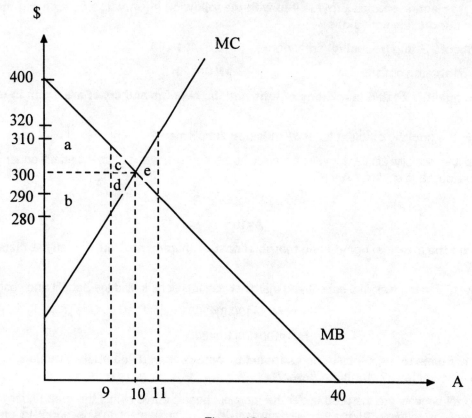

Figure 18.3.c

4. Four firms located at different points on a river dump various quantities of effluent into it. The effluent adversely affects the quality of swimming for homeowners who live downstream. These people can build swimming pools to avoid swimming in the river, and firms can purchase filters that eliminate harmful chemicals in the material dumped in the river. As a policy advisor for a regional planning organization, how would you compare and contrast the following options for dealing with the harmful effect of the effluent:

a.   An equal-rate effluent fee on firms located on the river.

First, one needs to know the value to homeowners of swimming in the river. This information can be difficult to obtain, because homeowners will have an incentive to overstate this value. As an upper boundary, if there are no considerations other than swimming, one could use the cost of building swimming pools, either a pool for each homeowner or a public pool for all homeowners. Next, one needs to know the marginal cost of abatement. If the abatement technology is well understood, this information should be readily obtainable. If the abatement technology is not understood, an estimate based on the firms' knowledge must be used.

The choice of a policy tool will depend on the marginal benefits and costs of abatement. If firms are charged an equal-rate effluent fee, the firms will reduce effluents to the point where the marginal cost of abatement is equal to the fee. If this reduction is not high enough to permit swimming, the fee could be increased. Alternatively, revenue from the fees could be used to provide swimming facilities, reducing the need for effluent reduction.

b.   An equal standard per firm on the level of effluent that each can dump.

Standards will be efficient only if the policy maker has complete information regarding the marginal costs and benefits of abatement, so that the efficient level of the standard can be determined. Moreover, the standard will not encourage firms to reduce effluents further when new filtering technologies become available.

c. **A transferable effluent permit system in which the aggregate level of effluent is fixed and all firms receive identical permits.**

A transferable effluent permit system requires the policy maker to determine the efficient effluent standard. Once the permits are distributed and a market develops, firms with a higher cost of abatement will purchase permits from firms with lower abatement costs. However, unless permits are sold initially, rather than merely distributed, no revenue will be generated for the regional organization.

5. Medical research has shown the negative health effects of "secondhand" smoke. Recent social trends point to growing intolerance of smoking in public areas. If you are a smoker and you wish to continue smoking despite tougher anti smoking laws, describe the effect of the following legislative proposals on your behavior. As a result of these programs, do you, the individual smoker, benefit? Does society benefit as a whole?

Since smoking in public areas is similar to polluting the air, the programs proposed here are similar to those examined for air pollution. A bill to lower tar and nicotine levels is similar to an emissions standard, and a tax on cigarettes is similar to an emissions fee. Requiring a smoking permit is similar to a system of emissions permits, assuming that the permits would not be transferable. The individual smoker in all of these programs is being forced to internalize the externality of "second-hand" smoke and will be worse off. Society will be better off if the benefits of a particular proposal outweigh the cost of implementing that proposal. Unfortunately, the benefits of reducing second-hand smoke are uncertain, and assessing those benefits is costly.

a. **A bill is proposed that would lower tar and nicotine levels in all cigarettes.**

The smoker will most likely try to maintain a constant level of consumption of nicotine, and will increase his or her consumption of cigarettes. Society may not benefit from this plan if the total amount of tar and nicotine released into the air is the same.

b. **A tax is levied on each pack of cigarettes sold.**

Smokers might turn to cigars, pipes, or might start rolling their own cigarettes. The extent of the effect of a tax on cigarette consumption depends on the elasticity of demand for cigarettes. Again, it is questionable whether society will benefit.

c. **Smokers would be required to carry government issued smoking permits at all times.**

Smoking permits would effectively transfer property rights to clean air from smokers to non-smokers. The main obstacle to society benefiting from such a proposal would be the high cost of enforcing a smoking permits system. In addition, the cost of the permit raises the effective price of the cigarettes and the resulting affect on quantity smoked will depend on the elasticity of demand.

6. A beekeeper lives adjacent to an apple orchard. The orchard owner benefits from the bees because each hive pollinates about one acre of apple trees. The orchard owner pays nothing for this service, however, because the bees come to the orchard without his having to do anything. Because there are not enough bees to pollinate the entire orchard, the orchard owner must complete the pollination by artificial means, at a cost of $10 per acre of trees.

Beekeeping has a marginal cost of MC = 10 + 2Q, where Q is the number of beehives. Each hive yields $20 worth of honey.

a. **How many beehives will the beekeeper maintain?**

The beekeeper maintains the number of hives that maximizes profits, when marginal revenue is equal to marginal cost. With a constant marginal revenue of $20 (there is no information that would lead us to believe that the beekeeper has any market power) and a marginal cost of $10 + 2Q$:

$$20 = 10 + 2Q, \text{ or } Q = 5.$$

b. **Is this the economically efficient number of hives?**

If there are too few bees to pollinate the orchard, the farmer must pay $10 per acre for artificial pollination. Thus, the farmer would be willing to pay up to $10 to the beekeeper to maintain each additional hive. So, the marginal social benefit, *MSB*, of each additional hive is $30, which is greater than the marginal private benefit of $20. Assuming that the private marginal cost is equal to the social marginal cost, we set *MSB* = *MC* to determine the efficient number of hives:

$$30 = 10 + 2Q, \text{ or } Q = 10.$$

Therefore, the beekeeper's private choice of $Q = 5$ is not the socially efficient number of hives.

c. **What changes would lead to the more efficient operation?**

The most radical change that would lead to more efficient operations would be the merger of the farmer's business with the beekeeper's business. This merger would internalize the positive externality of bee pollination. Short of a merger, the farmer and beekeeper should enter into a contract for pollination services.

7. There are three groups in a community. Their demand curves for public television in hours of programming, T, are given respectively by

$$W_1 = \$150 - T, \qquad W_2 = \$200 - 2T, \qquad W_3 = \$250 - T.$$

Suppose public television is a pure public good that can be produced at a constant marginal cost of $200 per hour.

a. **What is the efficient number of hours of public television?**

The efficient number of hours is the amount such that the sum of the marginal benefits is equal to marginal cost. Given the demand curves representing the marginal benefits to each individual, we sum these demand curves vertically to determine the sum of all marginal benefits. Figure 18.6.a shows each demand curve and the summation.
Therefore, from Figure 18.7.a or the table below, one can see that *MSB* = *MC* at $T = 100$ hours of programming.

	Willingness to Pay			
Time	Group 1	Group 2	Group 3	Vertical Sum
0	150	200	250	600
50	100	100	200	400
100	50	0	150	200
150	0	0	100	100
200	0	0	50	50
250	0	0	0	0

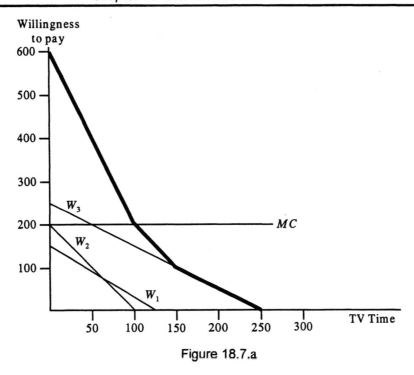

Figure 18.7.a

b. **How much public television would a competitive private market provide?**

To find the number of hours that the private market would provide, we add the individual demand curves horizontally. The efficient number of hours is such that the private marginal cost is equal to the private marginal benefit. The demand curves for groups 1 and 3 lie below $MC = \$200$ for all $T > 0$. With marginal cost equal to $200, only group 3 would be willing to pay $200. At that price, 50 hours of programming would be provided on a subscription.

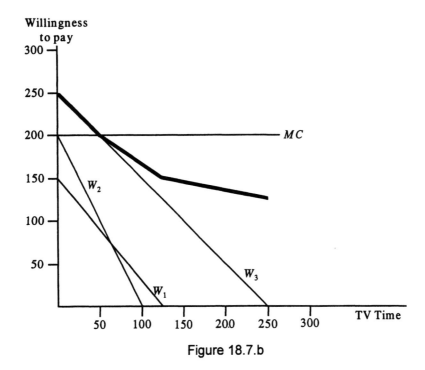

Figure 18.7.b

Quantity Demanded

Price	Group 1	Group 2	Group 3	Horizontal Sum
250	0	0	0	0
200	0	0	50	50
150	0	25	100	125
100	50	50	150	250
50	100	75	200	375
0	150	100	250	500

8. Reconsider the common resource problem as given by Example 18.5. Suppose that crawfish popularity continues to increase, and that the demand curve shifts from C = 0.401 - 0.0064F to C = 0.50 - 0.0064F. How does this shift in demand affect the actual crawfish catch, the efficient catch, and the social cost of common access? (*Hint*: Use the marginal social cost and private cost curves given in the example.)

The relevant information is now the following:

Demand: $C = 0.50 - 0.0064F$

MSC: $C = -5.645 + 0.6509F$.

With an increase in demand, the demand curve for crawfish shifts upward, intersecting the price axis at $0.50. The private cost curve has a positive slope, so additional effort must be made to increase the catch. Since the social cost curve has a positive slope, the socially efficient catch also increases. We may determine the socially efficient catch by solving the following two equations simultaneously:

$$0.50 - 0.0064F = -5.645 + 0.6509F, \text{ or } F^* = 9.35.$$

To determine the price that consumers are willing to pay for this quantity, substitute F^* into the equation for *marginal social cost* and solve for C:

$$C = -5.645 + (0.6509)(9.35), \text{ or } C = \$0.44.$$

Next, find the actual level of production by solving these equations simultaneously:

Demand: $C = 0.50 - 0.0064F$

MPC: $C = -0.357 + 0.0573F$

$$0.50 - 0.0064F = -0.357 + 0.0573F, \text{ or } F^{**} = 13.45.$$

To determine the price that consumers are willing to pay for this quantity, substitute F^{**} into the equation for *marginal private cost* and solve for C:

$$C = -0.357 + (0.0573)(13.45), \text{ or } C = \$0.41.$$

Notice that the marginal social cost of producing 13.45 units is

$$MSC = -5.645 + (0.6509)(13.45) = \$3.11.$$

With the increase in demand, the social cost is the area of a triangle with a base of 4.1 million pounds (13.45 - 9.35) and a height of $2.70 ($3.11 - 0.41), or $5,535,000 more than the social cost of the original demand.

9. The Georges Bank, a highly productive fishing area off New England, can be divided into two zones in terms of fish population. Zone 1 has the higher population per square mile but is subject to severe diminishing returns to fishing effort. The daily fish catch (in tons) in Zone 1 is

$$F_1 = 200(X_1) - 2(X_1)^2$$

where X_1 is the number of boats fishing there. Zone 2 has fewer fish per mile but is larger, and diminishing returns are less of a problem. Its daily fish catch is

$$F_2 = 100(X_2) - (X_2)^2$$

where X_2 is the number of boats fishing in Zone 2. The marginal fish catch MFC in each zone can be represented as

$$MFC_1 = 200 - 4(X_1) \qquad\qquad MFC_2 = 100 - 2(X_2).$$

There are 100 boats now licensed by the U.S. government to fish in these two zones. The fish are sold at $100 per ton. Total cost (capital and operating) per boat is constant at $1,000 per day. Answer the following questions about this situation:

a.   If the boats are allowed to fish where they want, with no government restriction, how many will fish in each zone? What will be the gross value of the catch?

Without restrictions, the boats will divide themselves so that the average catch (AF_1 and AF_2) for each boat is equal in each zone. (If the average catch in one zone is greater than in the other, boats will leave the zone with the lower catch for the zone with the higher catch.) We solve the following set of equations:

$$AF_1 = AF_2 \text{ and } X_1 + X_2 = 100 \text{ where}$$

$$AF_1 = \frac{200X_1 - 2X_1^2}{X_1} = 200 - 2X_1 \quad \text{and}$$

$$AF_2 = \frac{100X_2 - X_2^2}{X_2} = 100 - X_2.$$

Therefore, $AF_1 = AF_2$ implies

$$200 - 2X_1 = 100 - X_2,$$

$$200 - 2(100 - X_2) = 100 - X_2, \text{ or } X_2 = \frac{100}{3} \quad \text{and}$$

$$X_1 = 100 - \left(\frac{100}{3}\right) = \frac{200}{3}.$$

Find the gross catch by substituting the value of X_1 and X_2 into the catch equations:

$$F_1 = (200)\left(\frac{200}{3}\right) - (2)\left(\frac{200}{3}\right)^2 = 13,333 - 8,889 = 4,444, \quad \text{and}$$

$$F_2 = (100)\left(\frac{100}{3}\right) - \left(\frac{100}{3}\right)^2 = 3,333 - 1,111 = 2,222.$$

The total catch is $F_1 + F_2 = 6,666$. At the price of $100 per ton, the value of the catch is $666,600. The average catch for each of the 100 boats in the fishing fleet is 66.66 tons.

To determine the profit per boat, subtract total cost from total revenue:

$$\pi = (100)(66.66) - 1,000, \text{ or } \pi = \$5,666.$$

Total profit for the fleet is $566,600.

b.   If the U.S. government can restrict the boats, how many should be allocated to each zone? What will be the gross value of the catch? Assume the total number of boats remains at 100.

Assume that the government wishes to maximize the net social value of the fish catch, i.e., the difference between the total social benefit and the total social cost. The government equates the marginal fish catch in both zones, subject to the restriction that the number of boats equals 100:

$$MFC_1 = MFC_2 \text{ and } X_1 + X_2 = 100,$$

$$MFC_1 = 200 - 4X_1 \text{ and } MFC_2 = 100 - 2X_2.$$

Setting $MFC_1 = MFC_2$ implies:

$$200 - 4X_1 = 100 - 2X_2, \text{ or } 200 - 4(100 - X_2) = 100 - 2X_2, \text{ or } X_2 = 50 \text{ and}$$
$$X_1 = 100 - 50 = 50.$$

Find the gross catch by substituting X_1 and X_2 into the catch equations:

$$F_1 = (200)(50) - (2)(50^2) = 10,000 - 5,000 = 5,000 \quad \text{and}$$
$$F_2 = (100)(50) - 50^2 = 5,000 - 2,500 = 2,500.$$

The total catch is equal to $F_1 + F_2 = 7,500$. At the market price of $100 per ton, the value of the catch is $750,000. Total profit is $650,000. Notice that the profits are not evenly divided between boats in the two zones. The average catch in Zone A is 100 tons per boat, while the average catch in Zone B is 50 tons per boat. Therefore, fishing in Zone A yields a higher profit for the individual owner of the boat.

c. **If additional fishermen want to buy boats and join the fishing fleet, should a government wishing to maximize the net value of the catch grant them licenses? Why or why not?**

To answer this question, first determine the profit-maximizing number of boats in each zone. Profits in Zone A are

$$\pi_A = (100)\left(200X_1 - 2X_1^2\right) - 1,000X, \text{ or } \pi_A = 19,000X_1 - 200X_1^2.$$

To determine the change in profit with a change in X_1 take the first derivative of the profit function with respect to X_1:

$$\frac{d\pi_A}{dX_1} = 19,000 - 400X_1.$$

To determine the profit-maximizing level of output, set $\dfrac{d\pi_A}{dX_1}$ equal to zero and solve for X_1:

$$19,000 - 400X_1 = 0, \text{ or } X_1 = 47.5.$$

Substituting X_1 into the profit equation for Zone A gives:

$$\pi_A = (100)\left((200)(47.5) - (2)\left(47.5^2\right)\right) - (1,000)(47.5) = \$451,250.$$

For Zone B follow a similar procedure. Profits in Zone B are

$$\pi_B = (100)\left(100X_2 - X_2^2\right) - 1,000X_2, \text{ or } \pi_B = 9,000X_2 - 100X_2^2.$$

Taking the derivative of the profit function with respect to X_2 gives

$$\frac{d\pi_B}{dX_2} = 9,000 - 200X_2.$$

Setting $\dfrac{d\pi_B}{dX_2}$ equal to zero to find the profit-maximizing level of output gives

$$9,000 - 200X_2 = 0, \text{ or } X_2 = 45.$$

Substituting X_2 into the profit equation for Zone B gives:

$$\pi_B = (100)((100)(45) - 45^2) - (1,000)(45) = \$202,500.$$

Total profit from both zones is $653,750, with 47.5 boats in Zone A and 45 boats in Zone B. Because each additional boat above 92.5 decreases total profit, the government should not grant any more licenses.